Illuminate
Publishing

CW01095764

WJEC/Eduqas
Sociology
for AS & Year 1

Janis Griffiths

John McIntosh

Published in 2015 by Illuminate Publishing Ltd, P.O Box 1160, Cheltenham, Gloucestershire GL50 9RW

Orders: Please visit www.illuminatepublishing.com
or email sales@illuminatepublishing.com

British Library Cataloguing in Publication Data

A catalogue record for this book is available from the British Library

ISBN 978-1-908682-74-1

Printed by Severn, Gloucester

05.21

The publisher's policy is to use papers that are natural, renewable and recyclable products made from wood grown in sustainable forests. The logging and manufacturing processes are expected to conform to the environmental regulations of the country of origin.

Every effort has been made to contact copyright holders of material reproduced in this book. If notified, the publishers will be pleased to rectify any errors or omissions at the earliest opportunity.

This material has been endorsed by WJEC and offers high quality support for the delivery of WJEC qualifications. While this material has been through a WJEC quality assurance process, all responsibility for the content remains with the publisher.

Editor: Geoff Tuttle

Design and layout: John Dickinson

Acknowledgements:

Cover: ssguy/Shutterstock

Intro: p8/9 Aleks.k/Shutterstock

Socialisation: p10 AF Archive/Alamy, Twin Design/Shutterstock; p12 pcruciatti/Shutterstock, Christopher Meder/Shutterstock; p14 Stuart Miles/Shutterstock, Peter Baxter/Shutterstock; p16 Monkey Business Images/Shutterstock; p17 IPG GutenburgUKLtd/istockphoto.com; p18 oliveromg/Shutterstock; p20 Cartoonresource/Shutterstock; p22 Monkey Business Images/istockphoto.com; p24 American Spirit/Shutterstock; p25 Air Images/Shutterstock, Christian Bertrand/Shutterstock; p26 Peter Hermes Furian/Shutterstock, Walter Galloway/istockphoto.com; p27 Rawpixel/Shutterstock, Featureflash/Shutterstock; p28 jane/istockphoto.com, Pavel L Photo and Video/Shutterstock; p29 Pressmaster/Shutterstock, rnl/Shutterstock; p30 John Dickinson, Marcokenya/Shutterstock; p31 James Davies/Alamy

Theory: p32 Curioso/Shutterstock, Halfpoint/Shutterstock; p34 Stephen Parker/Alamy; p36 1000 Words/Shutterstock, Prometheus72/Shutterstock; p38 Steve Mann/Shutterstock, patpitchaya/Shutterstock; p39 Cartoonresource/Fotolia; p41 Durantelallera/Shutterstock; p42 Kzenon/Shutterstock, cesc_assawin/Shutterstock; p44 Complot/Shutterstock, Landmark Media/Shutterstock; p45 Elnur/Shutterstock; p46 Antoniodiaz/Shutterstock, Serg-dibrova/Shutterstock; p48 Radharani/Shutterstock; p49 Nomad-soul/Shutterstock; p50 Brian S/Shutterstock, Anna Maltseva/Shutterstock, Helga Esteb/Shutterstock; p51 Heritage Image Partnership Ltd/Alamy; p52 Photographee.eu/Shutterstock; p53 Allstar Picture Library/Alamy; p54 Mark William Richardson/Shutterstock, Brendan Howard/Shutterstock; p56 Michaelpuche/Shutterstock, Simon Laprida/Shutterstock; p57 Aleutie/Shutterstock

Research: p.58 donskarpo/Shutterstock; p59 Pictorial Press Ltd/Alamy; p60 William Casey/Shutterstock; p61 Office for National Statistics; p62 Oliveromg/Shutterstock; p63 Tattywelshie/istockphoto; p64 Feng Yu/Shutterstock; p65 Zimmtws/Shutterstock; p66 Ambrophoto/Shutterstock; p68 mindscanner/Shutterstock; p70 Alexander Raths/Shutterstock, NetPhotos/Alamy; p71 AF Archive/Alamy; p72 Cultura Creative/Alamy; p74 gpointstudio/Shutterstock, onebluelight/istockphoto.com, Wavebreakmedia/Shutterstock; p75 Africa Studio/Shutterstock, Minerva Studio/Shutterstock, iodrakon/Shutterstock; p76 Office for National Statistics; p77 Everett Collection/Shutterstock; p78 buttet/Shutterstock, Photographee.eu/Shutterstock; p79 chrisdorney/Shutterstock; p80 Netphotos/Alamy; p81 mini.fini/Shutterstock; p82 Avesun/Shutterstock; p83 g-stockstudio/Shutterstock; p84 mama_mia/Shutterstock; p86 Vectomart/Shutterstock, salejean/Shutterstock; p87 ra2studio/Shutterstock; p88 SpeedKingz / Shutterstock, Cathy Topping/Alamy, Monkey

Business Images/istockphoto.com; p90 Mr Pics/Shutterstock, Ivelin Radkov/Shutterstock; p91 Kentoh/Shutterstock, Cunaplus/Shutterstock; p92 Alphaspirit/Shutterstock; p93 Andrii Kondiuk/Shutterstock

Family: p94 Kobby Dagan/Shutterstock, Elizbieta Sekowska/Shutterstock, martindoucet/istockphoto.com; p96 Pressmaster/Shutterstock; p97 Pavel L Photo and Video/Shutterstock; p99 Photographee.eu/Shutterstock, Iakov Filimonov/Shutterstock, Kentoh/Shutterstock; p100 KUCO/Shutterstock, Rob Hainer/Shutterstock; p102 Catchlight Visual Services/Alamy; p104 Susan Law Cain/Shutterstock, Lev Radin/Shutterstock; p105 John James/Alamy, video1/istockphoto.com; p106 Lena Pan/Shutterstock, Kurhan/Shutterstock; p107 Inga Marchuk/Shutterstock; p109 ChameleonsEye/Shutterstock; p114 Zurijeta/Shutterstock, Pressmaster/Shutterstock; p116 wavebreakmedia/Shutterstock; p.117 Monkey Business Images/Shutterstock; p118 Robert Kneschke/Shutterstock; p119 Monkey Business Images/Shutterstock; p122 Monkey Business Images/Shutterstock; p123 Goodluz/Shutterstock, Lucky Business/Shutterstock; p124 http://www.allposters.co.uk, David Fowler/Shutterstock; p126 Elena Efimova/Shutterstock, Casper1774 Studio/Shutterstock, Jurgita/Shutterstock; p127 bbevren/Shutterstock; p128 Ollyy/Shutterstock, Aleutie/Shutterstock; p129 Monkey Business Images/Shutterstock; p130 Brian A Jackson/Shutterstock; p131 Almagami/Shutterstock, Dubrova/Shutterstock; p132 Everett Historical/Shutterstock; p133 Image Point Fr/Shutterstock; p134 Aleph Studio/Shutterstock; p135 & p136 (twice) Trinity Mirror/Mirrorpix/Alamy; p137 leungchopan/Shutterstock

Youth Cultures: p138 Photofusion Picture Library/Alamy; p140 David Fowler/Shutterstock; p142 Eugenio Marongiu/Shutterstock; p144 360b/Shutterstock; p146 Bahadir Yeniceri/Shutterstock; p148 Lucky Business/Shutterstock, Dudarev Mikhail/Shutterstock; p149 David J. Green – Lifestyle/Alamy; p150 Lena Lir/Shutterstock; p152 michaeljung/Shutterstock, Diane Diederich/iStock; p153 Edyta Pawlowska/Shutterstock; p154 O Driscoll Imaging; p156 Warren Goldswain/Shutterstock; p157 Daleen Loest/Shutterstock; p158 Everett Collection/Shutterstock, Matt Cheveralls/Shutterstock; p160 Ian Sinclair/Shutterstock; p162 Monkey Business Images/Shutterstock, Nejron Photo/Shutterstock; p163 Neftali/Shutterstock; p164 Vector1st/Shutterstock; p165 Jaguar/Shutterstock; p166 Maria Bobrova/Shutterstock, Evgeniya Karpova/Shutterstock; p167 Neftali/Shutterstock, dpaint/Shutterstock, enciktat/Shutterstock; p169 Odua Images/Shutterstock; p170 IgorGolovniov/Shutterstock, nevodka/Shutterstock, Everett Historical/Shutterstock; p171 ostill/Shutterstock; p172 Semmick Photo/Shutterstock, STILLFX/Shutterstock, Christian Bertrand/Shutterstock; p173 Rosli Othman/Shutterstock; p174 CREATISTA/Shutterstock, Stephane Bidouze/Shutterstock; p175 Marcel Jancovic/Shutterstock; p176 dnaveh/Shutterstock, Picsfive/Shutterstock, bikeriderlondon/Shutterstock; p178 Yuriy Rudyy/Shutterstock; p179 meunierd/Shutterstock; p182 Ilia Torlin/Shutterstock; p183 Franz Pfluegl/Shutterstock; p184 AC Rider/Shutterstock, ChameleonsEye/Shutterstock; p186 Everett Collection/Shutterstock; p187 Marco Aprile/Shutterstock; p188 veroxdale/Shutterstock; p190 CREATISTA/Shutterstock; p191 Johann Knox/Shutterstock; p192 s_bukley/Shutterstock, Featureflash/Shutterstock; p193 Stokkete/Shutterstock; p194 Anna Demjanenko/Shutterstock; p195 Lisa-Lisa/Shutterstock; p196 Harmony Gerber/Shutterstock; p197 Monkey Business Images/Shutterstock; p198 Sascha Burkard/Shutterstock; p200 Rido/Shutterstock

Education: p202 Cathleen A Clapper/Shutterstock, JStone/Shutterstock; p203 Becky Stares/Shutterstock; p204 stocker1970/Shutterstock; p206 Hannamariah/Shutterstock, Stuart Jenner/Shutterstock, Andreas G Karelias/Shutterstock; p207 michaeljung/Shutterstock; p210 Everett Collection/Shutterstock, Shaun Wilkinson/Shutterstock; p211 Frederic Legrand – COMEO/Shutterstock; p212 BasPhoto/Shuttterstock; p215 Monkey Business Images/Shutterstock; p216 Michaelpuche/Shutterstock; p217 Pres Panayatov/Shutterstock; p219 kotoffei/Shutterstock; p220 Nick_Thompson/istockphoto.com; p222 Chris Loneragan/Shutterstock; p224 robinimages2013/Shutterstock; p226 wavebreakmedia/Shutterstock; p227 thinglass/shutterstock; p229 Twin Design/Shutterstock; p230 criben/Shutterstock, BasPhoto/Shutterstock; p231 Monkey Business Images/Shutterstock; p234 father/Shutterstock; p.235 Atelier/Shutterstock; p237 Tilil/Shutterstock; p240 Elnur/Shutterstock, moneymaker11/Shutterstock; p241 AF Archive/Alamy, creative soul/fotolia; p244 Luisa Fernandez Gonzalez/Shutterstock; p245 michaeljung/Shutterstock; p247 photobac/Shutterstock, Slava Samusevich/Shutterstock; p248 Robert Kneschke/Shutterstock; p250 Anton Bielousov/Shutterstock, Serhiy Kobyakov/Shutterstock; p252 Photostock10/Shutterstock; p253 Wallenrock/Shutterstock; p256 Irina Mosina/Shutterstock, Alexander Chaikin/Shutterstock; p257 Greir/Shutterstock; p258 Krasimira Nevenova/Shutterstock; p260 Andrey_Popov/Shutterstock, Suzanne Tucker/Shutterstock; p261 Cynthia Farmer/Shutterstock

Exam questions: p265 YanLev/Shutterstock; p267 Fuzzbones/Shutterstock; p275 wavebreakmedia/Shutterstock

Contents

3

How to use this book

The contents of this textbook are designed to guide you through to success in either the WJEC or Eduqas Sociology AS level examination. It also supports Component 1 and 2 of the full Eduqas A level. It has been written by experienced teachers and examiners in order to help you to do well in your course.

The book is organised in a similar way to the examination, so the topics will match the sections on the examination paper. Theory is very important in sociology, so we have written an introductory section to introduce you to the important points of each theory. In the topics, there will be development of those key theory ideas. If you need to remind yourself of anything then you can always turn back to this section.

The optional topics we have covered are the most popular topics in the full examination.

The contents we have covered are as follows:

- Socialisation, culture and identity (compulsory content that gently introduces you to key debates in sociology)
- Sociological theory (additional brief introduction to ideas used throughout the content of the options)
- Families and households
- Youth cultures
- Education
- Methods of sociological enquiry (Research methods)
- Examination guidance: (this offers an explanation of what we believe is required for success in the Eduqas/WJEC examinations)
- An important feature of this book is the Sample Questions that appear towards the end of each topic. These are designed to give you practice in using and applying your knowledge. They are not drawn from the specification or the Sample Assessment Material that WJEC/Eduqas have produced; rather they are based on our interpretation of that material.

This book and AS qualifications

The book is intended to support you in AS level study for both Eduqas and WJEC. It will support Eduqas candidates in the first year of study for A level but not the second year of study.

Which qualification are you studying for?

You may be studying for either Eduqas qualifications or WJEC qualifications. This book covers examination requirements for both. Most of the content is very similar in all of the specifications, and the questions and markschemes only differ slightly. For more information, look at the examination guidance section of this book and the examination papers and markschemes of the qualification for which you are studying and discuss these with your teacher.

Eduqas AS/ A level examination content
England

In England, most candidates will be studying for the Eduqas AS or A level. See the full specification at **www.eduqas.co.uk.**

The Eduqas AS level is half of the content of the full A level but is of an equal challenge to the full A level.
- For a full Eduqas A level, there will be three components, or examinations. Note that only the first two components are covered in this textbook.
- For a full Eduqas AS level, there will be two components and this textbook includes enough topics to help you prepare for the exams.

	Component 1	Component 2
Eduqas AS level	Introductory Core Families and households or Youth cultures Education	Methods of sociological enquiry (Research methods)
	120 marks available (70% of qualification)	50 marks available (30% of qualification)
	2 hours and 30 minutes	1 hour and 15 minutes
Eduqas A level	Introductory Core Families and households or Youth cultures Education	Methods of sociological enquiry (Research methods)
	120 marks available (40% of qualification)	60 marks available (20% of qualification)
	2 hours and 30 minutes	1 hour and 45 minutes

WJEC AS examination content

Wales

In Wales, most candidates will be studying for the WJEC AS and A level. For the full WJEC specification content go to www.wjec.co.uk

⊙ The AS is less challenging and worth 40% of the full A level qualification.

⊙ The AS is a stepping stone to the full A level qualification, so ideas introduced at AS level will be developed on the full A level paper.

	Unit 1	Unit 2
WJEC AS level	Introductory Core Families and households or Youth cultures	Research Methods (Methods of sociological enquiry) Education
	60 marks available (15% of full A level qualification)	90 marks available (25% of full A level qualification)
	1 hours and 15 minutes	2 hours

The information and topics in the book will reflect the questions that *could* appear in the examinations. However, it isn't enough just to learn the facts for sociology examinations; you also need to start thinking and developing skills of analysis and evaluation.

Alongside the key information for each topic, there is a variety of features that will help you to think sociologically and to prepare you for the examination:

⊙ Interesting facts
⊙ Discussion questions
⊙ Information about famous people and famous studies
⊙ Quotations to get you thinking
⊙ Ideas for further study including websites, YouTube and the wider media.

All these will make your study of sociology more interesting and boost your chances of success. There are few simple answers in sociology, so we have tried to challenge you to think for yourself and to provide you with activities that will develop your understanding.

Key terms

Initially, sociology can feel like learning a whole new language. If you are to get into the top mark bands, you need to use the language of sociology, so the glossary is an important feature. Many of the short open response questions will be based around explaining the meaning of a term, or describing a concept. Your extended response essays should always start with an explanation of the key term in the question. The rest of your answer should focus on ideas and debates related to that key term.

Being a good student

A good sociologist is one who is interested in the social world and who wants to understand how it is organised and what effect it has on people. This means that good candidates will be taking a serious interest in what is happening around them. They should be watching how people behave and trying to understand what it is that affects how people act. They should be talking to people around them to see how the world has changed and looking for new and interesting viewpoints.

Good students need to be able to see things from other people's points of view and have an interest in how other people see the world. They need to have opinions that they can back up with evidence and the willingness to share and discuss their ideas.

You will do better in sociology if you read widely. We have suggested books, websites and studies that you might find useful to get you thinking like a sociologist.

Reading newspapers and looking at news websites will help you to get a bigger picture of the world. This has two effects:

⊙ You will be able to read and write more quickly in the examination, and your language skills will improve.
⊙ You will develop background knowledge and examples that you can refer to when you want to display your understanding of the world.

Good luck with your course!

Assessment in Eduqas and WJEC Sociology

Assessment is covered in more detail in the examination section at the end of this book. However, before you start to study, it will help you if you understand the key skills that you are being tested on. These consist of:

- **Assessment Objective 1 (AO1)** – describing what you know
- **AO2** – applying your knowledge
- **AO3** – analysing/evaluating this knowledge.

All mark schemes offer marks for the different skills and markers are trained to look for them and to recognise them.

Assessment objective 1

(AO1 Knowledge and understanding) assesses your ability to write about sociological theories, concepts and evidence to demonstrate your understanding of this knowledge. Use the detail in the book to answer the possible questions, and you can develop your understanding with the extension activities.

Assessment objective 2

(AO2 Application of knowledge) assesses your ability to apply your sociological knowledge. This AO is asking you to demonstrate that you can choose appropriate evidence to back up your ideas and that you can apply them to contemporary society. When you are presented with ideas in the book, think about how you can apply them to the real world around you.

Assessment objective 3

(AO3 Analysing and evaluating) assesses your ability to make judgements on the concepts and studies you have learned about. Identify the strengths and weaknesses of an idea or an argument and consider whether it is useful or not. Thus, you should look at the results of research and theories and decide if you think they are useful to help you understand the contemporary world.

What is an 'assessment objective'?

This is what the examiners who read your answers will be looking for. They look for proof on your paper that you can do these things at speed! Exam questions do not just assess how much sociology you know – they are tests of skills related to this knowledge.

Look at how you might find these three assessment objectives met in a single paragraph:

Sociology is the systematic study of contemporary society. Sociologists therefore are concerned with collecting evidence about what is happening in the social world and commenting on it. In order to do this, they look at what other writers have written and they also collect evidence through using research processes that are clearly understood by other people. Thus, they will gather evidence in a variety of clearly understood ways. This is a strength of sociology because people can make judgements as to the quality of the evidence.

Writing skills

Sociological skills are assessed through your ability to write extended answers to questions. You will therefore need to practise writing well and at speed. Look for tips throughout the book.

Features in the book

Aims – a clear objective for the topic based on the exam specification, together with a very small written summary of why the objective is so important to success in sociology.

Aims
⊙ **To explain what is meant by**

Getting you thinking – a distinctive stimulus or source that opens each topic, providing an immediate reference or starting point from which to get you thinking.

Getting you thinking

Glossary – important words, terms, concepts all highlighted on the page and defined in a glossary at the back of the book.

Glossary

Access
Before any information can be collected, the researcher needs access to those under study,

> *Don't these schools do enough damage making all these kids think alike, now they have to make them look alike too?*
> George Carlin

Quotations – a range of quotes from different theorists, commentators and key individuals supporting the text.

Tip – helpful advice from the authors about points to bear in mind for the exam to help you get the best grade you can.

Tip
This perspective may be called social action theory,

Extended writing
Describe changes to family structure in modern England and Wales.

Extended writing – a feature provided at the end of each topic that is similar to the sort of exam question you might come across on topics, together with some guidance on how you can best answer it and the sorts of points to bear in mind.

Sample questions – provided for each topic to show you the type of questions that might appear in an exam, how they are presented and structured and that often they include a visual, written or data source on which to comment.

Sample questions

Check your own learning – a simple self-test at the end of each topic to help you make sure you've got the main points understood.

Check your own learning

Famous names – short biographies of the key names within sociology.

Famous names
A H Halsey (1923–2014)

Discussion point
• What would happen to British society if all welfare benefits were stopped tomorrow?

Discussion point – thoughts and ideas for debate and discussion prompted by key points within topics and sub-topics.

Research idea – suggestions for research activities linked to each topic.

Research idea
Find one normal daily

Thinking skills
Construct a short questionnaire (no more than five questions)

Thinking skills – questions that encourage further discussion where you apply your own critical thinking to a topic.

Developing understanding – a short follow-on feature linked to parts of topics but providing a greater level of detail and increased understanding.

Developing understanding

INTERESTING FACT

Interesting fact – clarification or amplification of key points mentioned in the text, but given greater detail or explanation in the margin.

Stretch and challenge – extension activities and tasks designed to get you thinking at a higher level.

Activity – practical on-the-spot questions to reinforce your understanding.

Activity

Policy points
▶ The system of government in the United Kingdom is complex,

Policy points – these demonstrate how sociological thinking or theory actually translates into government policy or actions, giving a real-world application to some of the sociology you study.

Ideas that are used throughout all sociology

To succeed in sociology, you will need to use certain key ideas that form part of all sociological study. We have put these important ideas at the start of this text so that we can avoid repeating the most important ideas throughout the book. If you understand these terms, it will make all your study of sociology much easier. Look at the marginal features where you will see how some of these ideas can be applied in order to help us understand contemporary life.

Don't expect to understand these ideas immediately but if you try and apply them to all of your learning in sociology they will become much clearer. When you revise you should return to these concepts. There are good reasons for putting these ideas at the front of the book:

- As you come to understand these concepts, the debates will be easier to understand.
- Key concepts may form the basis of many short response questions.
- You should use these terms in extended response essays in order to demonstrate that you have met the assessment objective AO1.

Social order

Early sociologists were interested in social order because they wanted to understand how society holds itself together; they were interested in the way that individuals who each have personal needs act cooperatively to achieve and create a society. Modern sociologists tend to be more interested in how people interact with each other.

Social structure

This refers to the social institutions that help people live together, things such as families or religions.

Social control

It is about the written and unwritten rules that we all follow in order to make our society run smoothly. For example, there are written laws regarding the way we drive that make our roads safer. However, many women feel under social pressure to control their eating because magazines constantly emphasise the message that thin is beautiful.

Social values

These are the basic beliefs that we all share in order to work together as social groups. They form the standards for good behaviour in a society and so are an important part of social control.

Social actions

These are behaviours that have a motive; for example, anything we do that has a thought or a reason behind it. Sociologists are interested in social actions because they want to understand the reasons that people have for their actions.

Culture

Many of our actions only make sense in terms of the way of life of the group of people to whom we belong. Culture consists of a set of ideas, beliefs and socially expected behaviours that belong to a social group.

Socialisation

We learn to belong to a culture from the moment of birth. This process of learning the rules of our culture is known as socialisation. Socialisation is a continuous process that carries on throughout our lives as we learn new rules and ways of behaving.

Social identity

This idea suggests that we learn who we are, our expected behaviours and how we think of ourselves from the people around us. Females develop a social identity as women because others expect females to act and think in a certain way.

Social power

Society is a complex organisation and some people in a society have more ability than others to influence how people think and act. This ability to influence other people's behaviours is known as social power.

Social differentiation

This is when whole social groups such as males and females, older people or the disabled are treated differently on the basis of their social identity. They may have less or more power to influence society.

Social stratification

This is an extreme form of differentiation. It is claimed that we actually value some social groups more than others. People who belong to the valued groups are seen as being at the top of society whereas others are seen as somehow lesser. Those in the top layers of society have better lives and more opportunity than those at the bottom.

Consensus

Some sociologists, such as functionalists, think that society holds together because we all agree on the rules and organisations of the society to which we belong. It is claimed that we share social values.

Conflict

Other sociologists such as Marxists and feminists say that society is highly differentiated and that different groups of people are in competition with each other for social power. This leads to conflict because people at the top of society are able to control those who have less social power because they set the rules for everyone else to follow.

Social change

Societies do not remain the same over time. There are many reasons why they change and so identifying change and the reasons for change is an important part of the work of sociologists. Many people view social change as positive or a normal condition of society, but others see change as negative.

Social policy

People often wish to control social change, often to improve society. They do this on the basis of their beliefs about what a good society should be. Therefore, their values will influence their thinking. When political parties have power then they will have guidelines or principles that they will apply to the changes they make to society. These guidelines become social policies.

Aims

⊙ **To explain what is meant by culture**

Whenever humans come together in groups, they create a culture. This takes the form of a shared set of rules, understanding and expected behaviours. The study of culture is basic to sociology.

For some people their mobile phone means more to them than just a form of communication.

Topic 1: What is culture?

Getting you thinking

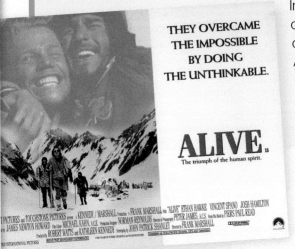

THEY OVERCAME THE IMPOSSIBLE BY DOING THE UNTHINKABLE.

ALIVE is
The triumph of the human spirit.

In 1972 a plane carrying members of a rugby team from Uruguay crashed high in the Argentinian Andes mountains. The survivors quickly ran out of food and realised that any rescue could take many days, if not weeks. It became apparent that the only source of food they had was the flesh of their friends who had died in the crash. After prolonged discussion, most of the survivors made the difficult decision to eat the human flesh. Those who would not, died.

You can read about this event in the book *Alive* by Piers Paul Read, or look for the film that was made.

Why was it a difficult decision to eat the human flesh?

What would you have done in those circumstances?

Defining culture

Culture is a term used to describe the way of life of a group of people. It refers to how they are expected to behave, what they tend to believe, and how they think. All individuals are part of a culture; they may even belong to more than one culture. For example, Asian heritage people born in Britain will be part of British culture, but may also have traditions, religions and beliefs that belong to their Asian background.

Culture differs from society. Culture refers to the beliefs, traditions and ideas that people share. The people who share those ideas form a society. Thus culture is a broader term than society. Modern sociologists tend to be more interested in culture than society, because they feel that it is culture that creates society.

Material culture

Material culture refers to the physical things that people create and attach emotional meaning to. For example, clothing, houses, cars and food may mean a lot to people; these items are not just objects but symbols of something important. The wearing of certain items of clothing to a football match means more to some fans than protecting the body from cold, for example.

Non-material culture

This refers to ideas that people share, for example their rules, traditions, languages and history. Non-material culture is important because it helps people to understand their social world and gives them guidelines for how to behave.

The social construction of culture

A social construction is any idea that is created and given special meaning by people. For example, motherhood means a lot more than the ability to give birth and raise a child; there is a distinct set of social rules for being a good mother in Western culture, which may vary from other cultures. Korean mothers are expected to be self-sacrificing to an extraordinary degree, whereas British mothers may also want private and personal lives. Motherhood, therefore, is a social construction. Culture is a social construction because it varies from social group to social group. It exists, but only in our minds, and cultures can vary quite significantly in what they see as normal and what they believe to be the correct way to act.

Collectivist cultures

These are cultures which tend to emphasise belonging to the group as more important than personal freedom. China and Japan typically are seen as collectivist cultures.

Individualist cultures

These are cultures which tend to emphasise individual freedom and personal gain, sometimes at the expense of others. European and North American cultures tend to be individualistic.

People learn their culture from others around them. Children are deliberately taught how to behave, and adults have to learn what to do in each new situation they find themselves in.

Aspects of culture

Anything created by people, including ideas and beliefs, is part of culture. It includes a range of things such as food traditions, clothing, government, education, language, religion and beliefs, art, music, shared history and laws.

Cultures can be very diverse, meaning that they differ a great deal. Things that seem normal in one culture would be unacceptable in another. For example, many Muslims refuse to drink alcohol or eat pork; the consumption of alcohol is illegal in some Islamic countries. Many non-Muslim British people enjoy alcohol and pork. This idea is known as cultural diversity.

Not everyone in a culture will follow all of the cultural rules. If people break rules individually, they will be known as deviant. However, when entire social groups behave differently from most people, they are known as a subculture. Examples might include some youth groups such as Goths, or perhaps drug users and criminals may form subcultures.

Culture and social control – what are the rules?

One of the most important roles of a culture is social control of the members of that culture. Rules are created and followed by most people who belong to that culture. People who do not follow the social rules of their culture can expect to be seen as not fully members of their culture. They will experience punishment in some way and this punishment is known as a sanction. Equally, those who follow the rules will be admired.

Activity

Find out more from the Internet about other cultures, for example, American educational sites have a lot of material you can read about the culture of Japan, which is seen as a collectivist culture.

> *Culture makes people understand each other better. And if they understand each other better in their soul, it is easier to overcome the economic and political barriers. But first they have to understand that their neighbour is, in the end, just like them, with the same problems, the same questions.*
>
> **Paulo Coelho**

Tip

Remember that crime and deviance are not the same; deviance is when a social rule is broken, crime is the breaking of a written law.

There are generally two accepted forms/types of control:

- *Formal control* – is where institutions in society exist to force people to behave, so it is linked to the concept of power. In British culture, these institutions consist of the legal system and the police, though other institutions also control people. Think of the way people may be controlled by schools, or the army if they join the Armed Forces. These institutions have the power to punish people severely if their rules are broken.

The police are an agency of formal control because we are expected to obey them. What would British society be like if we had no police officers?

- *Informal control* – is slightly more complicated. The most effective way of controlling people is through the internalisation of moral codes. If people are taught what their culture believes is correct when they are children, they may not challenge those beliefs. The rules act as a conscience and people will not break them even if it may result in their own death. People who break moral codes are known as deviants.

Culture and social control – unwritten rules

The processes of informal control are of particular interest to sociologists. Travis Hirschi, a functionalist writer, pointed out that breaking rules can give people considerable advantage in life. Despite this, most people do not commit serious crime. He believed that criminals and deviants lacked proper **socialisation**.

There are a number of unwritten rules and codes that control behaviour:

- *Norms* – are the expected behaviours for a culture. A **norm** in one culture may not be normal in another; for example, in UK we do not choose to eat insects, whereas some cultures value insect protein, for example the Maori culture of New Zealand.
- *Mores* – are ways of behaving that are seen as good, or moral. For example, most people would agree that stealing from old people is wrong, thus those who cheat old people have broken a moral taboo.
- *Values* – are linked to the concept of non-material culture. They are the basic rules shared by most people in a culture. They reflect what people feel should happen in society. For example, people feel that they should have the right to say what they feel about a government, thus freedom of speech is a **value**.
- *Beliefs* – many of us take our system of values and morals from our personal beliefs about society. These are generally individual to the person, but they may influence how we act. Often people take their beliefs from their culture or religion.

Kangaroo meat is an excellent source of protein and is very low in fat. Could you eat kangaroo meat? Give reasons for your answer.

- *Roles* – are the expected behaviours for any situation that we may find ourselves in. They can be very influential in controlling our behaviour, because we do not question roles much of the time. For example, teachers are expected to tell children how to behave, and so, most of the time children will do as they are told.
- *Status* – is a person's standing or position in society. It is based on respect. For example, people tend to respect doctors and they have a high status. We allow doctors freedom to do things that we would not allow other people to do, for example to inject us or give us drugs.

Cultures and social change

Few cultures stay the same over time. Any differences in the way that people generally think or act can been seen as social change. One of the most significant social changes in British culture over the last 50 years has been in terms of the roles and expected behaviours for men and women. Women have been seen to gain status and now take a more active part in society. This has had an effect on men, who also now take on a wider range of social roles. Some sociologists, such as functionalists, view social change as a problem while others, such as Marxists, believe it to be a normal state of affairs for society.

Cultural diversity

Cultural diversity is a term used to describe the differences in behaviour between cultures. This is more complex than simply comparing cultures, though anthropologists have done this and shown how infinitely complex and different human cultures are. Human cultures vary over time as well, so life in Britain in the 1970s was significantly different from life today.

Sample questions

Morris dancing is an ancient cultural **tradition** which is still practised in England and in some parts of Wales. Dancers traditionally wear white and have ribbons, bells, sticks, swords and handkerchiefs as part of their costume. In Wales, the Isca Morris team wear Welsh colours of red and green and dancers wear a traditional knitted cap. Some Morris dancers blacken their faces as a disguise. Dancing teams will have their own musicians. Usually dancers dance outside in summer, but they may dance in pubs.

With reference to the item and sociological knowledge

- **a)** Explain the meaning of the term **tradition**.
- **b)** Using the item and sociological knowledge, explain **two** aspects of culture.

Check your own learning
Match the words to their meanings.

Start	End
a) Culture	the ideas that people share
b) Material culture	emphasise the importance of living as a group
c) Non-material culture	the way of life of a group of people
d) Social construction	moral codes become part of everyday thinking
e) Collectivist cultures	people are forced to behave
f) Individualistic cultures	this is any idea that is created and given meaning by people
g) Formal social control	the physical things that people create
h) Informal social control	emphasise personal freedom and choice

Tip

The changes that take place in society may form an important part of the questioning for the examination. This will be a very important issue when you come to apply your sociological knowledge to topics that form the options.

Extended writing

Using sociological knowledge, explain what is meant by 'cultural diversity'.

Guidance: Such a question is likely to be linked to some stimulus material (known as 'the item'). You need to be able to define the term accurately and illustrate the definition with suitable examples. Your examples can include reference to differences in beliefs, behaviour or other aspects of culture. As the question requires an explanation, it is not enough to describe cultural differences; why cultures vary needs to be discussed also.

Write about 200 words.

Aims

⊚ **To explain the significance of the nature–nurture debate**

There is a long-standing debate in the social sciences regarding the question of whether people are more influenced by genetics or by their upbringing. Biologists and psychologists tend to suggest that genetics is a major factor in behaviour. Sociologists acknowledge genetics but argue that social factors over-ride biology.

INTERESTING FACT

Cyril Burt (1883–1971)
This psychologist studied twins who had been bought up separately to investigate the impact of inheritance (nature) and family environment (nurture) on intelligence. He concluded that inheritance was the most important factor. His work influenced social policy and was used to justify selection in education. Since he died, his work and findings have come under close scrutiny and it appears that some of his data was falsified.

According to legend, Romulus and Remus, the mythical founders of Rome, were raised by wolves. Research real feral children, such as Oxana Malaya, on the Internet and then consider how likely this story is to be true.

Topic 2: What is the nature–nurture debate?

Getting you thinking

Which is more important in the development of your personality, looks and beliefs? The way you were born or the way you were brought up?

Nativism

Many of our physical characteristics are inherited. In addition, certain personality traits appear to be linked to genetics, so people with specific genetic conditions may have an associated personality type. For example, William's syndrome is associated with very high levels of sociability. Many Downs people are exceptionally loving. This has led many scientists to argue that people are 'hard-wired' to behave in certain ways.

Nativists take an extreme position with regard to genetics. They argue that the social characteristics of people have arisen through evolution. Logically this leads to highly challenging political positions such as the belief that women are hard-wired to domestic labour and child-rearing while men are sexually aggressive. Such arguments have been used to justify both the oppression of women and extreme racist opinions.

Nature theories

These theories are less extreme than nativism, but the view that human behaviour is prompted by biology rather than society is still significant. Such ideas appear in daily life through common expressions such as 'boys will be boys'. The academic argument originates alongside theories of evolution, and the position is that people are governed by instincts, which are fixed patterns of behaviour that are inherited and influence human actions. There is evidence drawn from psychologists which seems to suggest that certain characteristics such as intelligence are highly inheritable from parents to children. However, the evidence is not so strong when one considers that intelligent parents may also have brought up their children in a way that reflects their intelligence.

Biological imperatives

All animals have certain biological imperatives. These are the things they do to survive and reproduce. Examples of such imperatives for humans include eating and sleeping. Nature theories suggest that humans are ruled by biological imperatives and therefore do not have free will, meaning they have no choice in their actions.

Nurture theory

Nurture theory is the view that society and culture override human genetics and instincts. It is argued that social expectations lead to humans controlling their actions. We all eat; however, where and how we do this vary considerably from culture to culture. For example, historically South Koreans and Hawaiian peoples bred dogs for human consumption. Thus, whilst science might help explain some aspects of human behaviour and support the case for nativist and nature theories, it does not entirely answer the question of why humans act as they do.

Sociologists tend to argue that cultural imperatives over-ride biology and that humans must learn their culture from others, through the process known as socialisation. Thus, sociology tends to support nurture theory.

Feral children

One of the strongest arguments in favour of nurture theory comes from the study of children who have not received correct socialisation. They are known as feral children. There are occasional cases of children who have been deprived of human society for some or all of their childhood years. Nature theories suggest that they should act in a human fashion because behaviour is instinctive. The reality is that many of these children are seriously damaged; for example, they do not acquire speech and rarely behave according to the cultural norms for their society.

Sample questions

Cultural differences within and between societies are used as evidence by those who favour **nurture** explanations of human behaviour. Gender roles cannot be the result of biology, they argue, if they vary from society to society or change over time. Margaret Mead (1901–1978) is best known for her studies of different societies in the Pacific and south Asia. She showed that gender roles and expectations about sexual behaviour varied in these societies and they were also different from the expectations in the USA.

   a) With reference to the item and sociological knowledge, explain what is meant by the term **nurture**.

   b) Using the item and sociological knowledge, explain **two** ways in which the study of gender supports nurture explanations of human behaviour.

Extended writing

Explain what the study of feral children may tell us about the importance of socialisation.

Guidance: This question is an opportunity to outline the nature–nurture debate. You will need to define the term feral children. Some examples of feral children need to be provided and used to outline a clear understanding of the socialisation process. You should explain how the lack of suitable nurturing has an impact on the cultural awareness of the individuals concerned.

Write 300 words

Research idea

Find one normal daily situation, such as eating a meal or going out. With a study partner, ask a range of people what they think are the rules for normal behaviour in that situation. How much agreement is there between what each of your respondents says?

Discussion points

- If intelligence was found to be inherited, what impact would that have on the way education is organised?
- Assume criminality was a genetic feature of some people's personality. How would this influence the treatment of criminals?

Real-life example

GENIE WILEY was discovered in the 1970s when she was 13 years old. Her father kept her isolated from others for her whole life. He often tied her up to prevent her moving about. As well as being malnourished when child protection officers found her, she had failed to develop the language and social skills expected of a teenager, providing evidence of the importance of nurture. You can find out more on this and other cases on the Internet.

Check your own learning

True or false?

   a) Sociologists favour nature theories.

   b) Cultures are very similar throughout the world.

   c) Feral children are well integrated into society.

   d) Class and gender affect what we learn.

   e) British culture has changed a great deal since the 1970s.

   f) Nativists believe that human behaviour is completely the result of genetics.

Aims

◉ **To explain the process of socialisation**

Sociologists believe that humans learn to behave in a way that is appropriate to their cultures through a process known as socialisation. Socialisation begins from the moment of birth and extends to the point of death. Through a variety of processes, we are taught how to behave in the way that is expected of us by others of our culture.

Thinking skills

Can you think of any situation where people are likely to ignore or break rules? What justifications or excuses might they offer?

Topic 3: How do we learn to be social?

Getting you thinking

Whenever we move to a new school, start a new job or join a new club, we have to learn how to fit in. At school and college there will probably be an induction programme, introducing the new organisation and your place in it: a tour of the building, timetables, what equipment you need to have with you, who can help you, getting ID cards. We have to learn the new rules for the social group that we are joining.

Discuss with a study partner what you might need to learn to fit in with life in a new school or new job. Develop your thinking by discussing what you would need to know in a new country.

Talcott Parsons and socialisation

One of the most influential early sociologists was Talcott Parsons, an American writer, who claimed that socialisation is the process by which humans learn and internalise their culture's norms and values. He claimed that people learn specific beliefs and forms of behaviour appropriate to their cultures, and so their society becomes internalised and part of their personality development.

He claimed that there are three stages to socialisation:

1. *Primary socialisation* – the child learns from the immediate family in the home. It adopts the beliefs and values of the family and learns the expectations that the parents have of the child.
2. *Secondary socialisation* – this is where the child learns what wider society expects of its members, and it generally takes place outside the home. Secondary socialisation is acquired from agencies of socialisation such as friendship groups, education, the mass media and religious organisations.
3. *Tertiary socialisation* – this is adult socialisation and takes place when people need to adapt to new situations such as becoming a parent, changing jobs, coping with illness or disability or retirement.

Then there are two elements to socialisation:

1. *Formal socialisation* – these are processes where people are deliberately and consciously manipulated to ensure they learn to follow certain rules. This can happen through educational processes in particular where children may be taught to obey those in authority.
2. *Informal socialisation* – this is a more haphazard process where people learn to fit into their culture by watching and learning from others around them. People learn what is seen as acceptable behaviour and their own place in their society.

Parsons believed that if people behaved in a way that was unusual or strange, then this was evidence of poor socialisation within the family. He did not consider the possibility that people may know the rules, but deliberately choose not to follow them for logical reasons of their own.

Agents of socialisation

Any social group or organisation that passes on cultural norms and values to others can be described as an agency of socialisation. It is through these agents that we learn the expected rules for our society. Examples of agencies of socialisation include the family, education, the mass media, peer groups, religion and work.

The aims of family socialisation

Much family socialisation is deliberate. Parents consciously teach children how to become functioning members of their society. They aim to pass on a variety of social skills to their children:

⊙ The ability to do certain things, such as read and swim.
⊙ The desire to achieve ambitions, such as gain a job or do well in school.
⊙ The ability to survive in the outside world and avoid danger, by teaching them to recognise and deal with threats.
⊙ To learn social roles to support them in adulthood, such as parenting skills or gendered behaviours.
⊙ The ability to think about the social roles of others and how people interact with each other – what people think of as 'good manners'.

Family and habitus

Pierre Bourdieu, a French Marxist sociologist, claimed that because members of families tend to belong to the same social backgrounds and ethnic groups, children learn a set of behaviours and perceptions that mark them out from others with different backgrounds. For example, we will have a similar accent, set of manners and patterns of thinking to our family members. He called this set of similarities, a habitus. Our habitus is therefore the social situation in which we feel comfortable and at home.

The family as an agent of primary socialisation

The family teaches the basic social attitudes, norms and values of the culture to the child. Much work on primary socialisation processes has been undertaken by feminists and it has focussed on the way that children acquire their sense of identity from their family, in particular, the way that they learn gender roles:

Religion is part of socialisation.

Developing understanding

Highlighting the practical effect of habitus are stories involving those who unexpectedly find themselves in a new social situation. Role switching is often used as a device in the media for film plots such as *All screwed up* (2009) and TV reality shows such as *The World's Strictest Parents*, or *Wifeswap*. Choose a pair of people who could swap lives and think what each would have to learn to survive as the other.

Imitation – children learn social skills by watching and copying their parents. Thus, they will learn when and what to eat, how to control their bodily functions and what it is appropriate to say and do.

What might these children be learning from playing with adults around them?

Tip

If a question asks you to refer to the item, then you must mention the item in your answer or you cannot reach the top mark bands.

Role models – the people that children will copy become their **role models**. Children are often encouraged to act like the same sex-parent, thus girls may be given domestic toys and learn to act like their own mothers.

Sanctions – children may be punished for incorrect behaviour and praised for acceptable behaviour. A boy who is seen as unacceptably feminine may be pushed into more typically male behaviour in British culture and teased or rejected if he acts in a non-masculine manner.

Expectations – boys may develop better spatial skills than girls because parents may expect them to be better at sport and spend more time playing physical games with boys.

Agencies of secondary socialisation

Once children move out of the family, they begin to encounter the wider social world and must learn a new set of appropriate behaviours in order to fit into larger society. Secondary socialisation is not usually very personal. Talcott Parsons believed that secondary socialisation helped the individual develop a separate identity in order to deal with strangers. The agencies which pass on secondary socialisation include the mass media, education, friendship and peer groups, and working environments. School, in particular, was a bridge between the family and the wider society.

Sample questions

Being a parent can be one of the most rewarding and fulfilling experiences of your life, but that doesn't mean it's easy. No matter what age your child/children is/are, your work is never done because you are teaching social **norms** and values to your child. To be a good parent, you need to know how to make your children feel valued and loved, while teaching them the difference between right and wrong. At the end of the day, the most important thing is to create a nurturing environment where your children feel like they can thrive and develop into confident, independent, and caring adults.

Adapted from http://www.wikihow.com/Be-a-Good-Parent

a) With reference to the item and sociological knowledge, explain the meaning of the term **norms**.

b) Using the item and sociological knowledge, explain how families pass on culture to children.

Check your own learning

Match the words to their meanings.

Concepts	Meanings
a) Socialisation	People are deliberately and consciously manipulated to ensure they follow social rules
b) Primary socialisation	Children learn and copy from their parents and others
c) Formal socialisation	The process by which humans learn and internalise their culture's norms and values
d) Agent of socialisation	A social situation in which we feel comfortable and at home
e) Habitus	The child learns from the immediate family in the home
f) Imitation	Any social group or organisation that passes on cultural norms and values to others

Extended writing

Outline the ways in which the family contributes to socialisation.

Guidance: This is an opportunity to demonstrate your knowledge by making use of relevant vocabulary and showing your understanding by introducing appropriate examples. You should emphasise the role of the family in primary socialisation and contrast informal and formal socialisation. The impact of social expectations, reflected through role models, imitation and the use of sanctions can be linked to different aspects of social behaviour, including gender roles.

Write about 250-300 words.

INTERESTING FACT

The toy maker, Lego, came in for a great deal of criticism when its Lego Friends range, aimed primarily at girls, seemed to reinforce traditional gender stereotypes. Following widespread negative publicity, in 2014 the Lego Research Institute was launched, featuring three female scientists. How might toys be part of the socialisation process for children?

STRETCH and CHALLENGE

The idea that women are 'naturally' good at caring and men are 'naturally' better at parking the car or putting up shelves is increasingly under challenge from researchers. Use the Internet to explore the debate, start by searching for something like 'Male and female ability differences down to socialisation, not genetics'.

Aims

- The socialisation process is complex and involves a number of different agencies

Some are more important than others but all help us learn the culture of our society and how we are expected to behave. You need to know at least two ways in which any agency of socialisation passes on culture.

Getting you thinking

"We only have a few rules around here, but we really enforce them."

What do you need to learn to ensure that you fit in and behave appropriately at work? What will be the consequences if you do not fit in quickly?

The key agencies of socialisation on the specification are:

Family
Education
Media
Peer groups and
    youth cultures
Religion
Work

Social control

Social control refers to the idea that people's behaviour and thoughts are regulated by society. Agencies of socialisation are therefore also agents of social control because they are concerned with training people to fit into their cultures.

- *Formal control* – this is the deliberate training of people to follow rules. Many social organisations and even society itself have strict rules. These are generally codified (written down) so that everyone is aware of them. If those rules are broken, then people can expect punishment (formal sanctions). For example, a murderer may expect to go to prison.
- *Informal control* – this form of control is not so obvious, but is just as important. It consists of people following unwritten rules such as norms, morals and values. Breaking an unwritten rule is just as dangerous for an individual, but the informal sanctions may be less obvious. For example, someone who fails to wash has not broken a written rule, but can expect to be ignored and rejected by others.

The family and children

The family is arguably the most important agency of socialisation. It is from our families that we learn the basic rules of our culture. For many people, the family remains the most important agency of socialisation throughout their lives; for others, agencies of secondary socialisation become dominant. Thus, the family is seen as the agent of primary socialisation because it is the first and most important agency to which we are exposed.

There are differences in cultural traditions in child-rearing. For example, many cultures disapprove of violence directed at children. In Scandinavian countries, physical punishment of children is illegal, whereas in Britain, some parents believe smacking to be an acceptable part of child discipline. However, although techniques of child-rearing vary from culture to culture, the basic processes remain similar.

Parenting is a complex procedure. Parents will pass on cultural rules and norms through actions such as:

1. Protection of the child from harm including the possibility of social disapproval, so children may be taught appropriate manners. This will begin very early, with children being taught to maintain bodily hygiene or to greet people properly.
2. Guided and deliberate teaching of the traditions and rules of a culture, so children are taught family history or cultural traditions such as Christmas or Bonfire Night. Children may speak a different language in the home from that used in wider society.
3. Social control occurs when children are sanctioned through praise or punishment. Thus children may be grounded for infringements of family rules, or rewarded for success in school or sport.
4. Children will copy the behaviour of family members in a process known as imitation. Family members become role models, and are copied by children who then learn their social roles from the adults around them.

Family socialisation is not necessarily a one-way process with adults controlling children. There may also be complex social interactions between parent and child, where the child may influence the adult. Pester power has been identified as a powerful agent of control. Advertisers deliberately target children, particularly at Christmas, and the children then may demand toys or treats from parents who find it difficult to refuse.

The family and the socialisation of adults

Talcott Parsons believed that marriage performed a vital function for society and the individual. He claimed that one of the most important functions of the family was the stabilisation of the adult personality. He believed that parents have separate roles within the family. The male has an instrumental role, so his task is to earn money from the family. However, in contrast, the female has an expressive role, so her task is to look after the emotional well-being of the family and take care of children. Family socialisation is therefore a continuing process with adults passing on their expectations to their partners and encouraging them to fit into socially expected patterns of behaviour.

This is a very controversial theory and it has been heavily criticised, particularly by feminists. Nevertheless, the idea that adults need to adapt to changing life situations is an area that is becoming of more interest to contemporary sociologists. Life course research shows how socialisation is a lifelong process as individuals' behaviour changes over time as they move into new roles with different expectations.

Agencies of secondary socialisation

Peer groups

For sociologists the peer group is made up of people who are the same age and status as oneself. Often the term is used to imply friends and friendship, but this is not necessarily so. The people in your class are your peer group, but it is possible that whilst you like some people, others are very unpleasant or even bullies. Your peer group are probably the first people that you encounter as you develop independence from your family, so they can be very influential, particularly in your teenage years.

Early friendships – young children are very responsive to other children and begin to form friendships when they are about three or four years of age. Children develop group norms and behaviours which may differ from those of the families from which they come. Iona and Peter Opie demonstrated in their work that children often had a

STRETCH and CHALLENGE

Consumer research in 2013 concluded that the total cost of 'pester power' in the UK was £2 billion a year. Parents spent an average of £460 a year giving in to demands from children for things they didn't need. Top of the list were sweets, snacks and junk foods. Researchers said that children were repeating the messages of commercials they had seen. Use the information and your own sociological knowledge to explain why so many people are concerned about the impact of advertising on children.

Thinking skills

Pressure to fit in with peers can be felt at any stage of life. In the workplace it is often your immediate colleagues who are most important to you. The downside of this is that it can be difficult to highlight problems or challenge inappropriate behaviour. Recent examples include hospitals and other care settings where employees have covered up poor care by colleagues. List the good and the bad effects of peer pressure on people's behaviour.

street culture from which adults were excluded and that this developed through play.

Peer pressure – adolescent peer groups, in particular, can be very supportive of each other, so young people gain a sense of independence from their families by belonging to friendship groups. Peer pressure is the process whereby people modify their behaviour in order to fit in with the group. It can be a powerful force, particularly for young people, but anyone of any age can experience it. Research has shown that people are very fearful of social rejection, so groups can exert a powerful pressure on individuals who fail to conform to group norms.

Education

Education is a very powerful agency of socialisation and a number of processes have been identified through which children acquire culture both formally (deliberately) and informally (without necessarily being aware that it is happening). All sociologists agree that schools socialise children and prepare them for the world of work. However, functionalists see this as generally a good thing but Marxists are very critical of what may be being taught to children.

What are these children learning about the social world in their lessons?

The formal curriculum – schools deliver knowledge of culture to children. The formal curriculum is what is taught in timetabled lessons. It can be influential as 'facts' may be given to children who are not in a position to query what they are being told. Althusser, a French Marxist, said that education exists to teach children that an unfair society is perfectly acceptable. He argued that children are taught that if they fail, it is their own fault and not the failing of an unjust society. In addition, there are cases where the formal school curriculum is used to pass on deliberately false 'facts' to children.

The hidden curriculum – there are a number of different definitions of the hidden curriculum and it is a 'contested concept'. This means that it is the subject of debate. The general opinion is that it is the set of assumptions and beliefs that are taught unintentionally by schools. It includes the values and beliefs that are implicit in textbooks, rules, uniforms and the daily life of the school. Feminists in the 1970s and 1980s, for example, pointed out that many school textbooks of the time either ignored the presence of women or placed them in domestic roles. As a result, traditional gender roles for girls were reinforced.

Religion

Religion can be a powerful force for socialisation even for those who do not belong to a religious group or practise traditional religious beliefs. British society and family law is based on Christian traditions such as monogamy (the practice of maintaining marriage to one person at a time), though many British people are not only not Christian, but may come from traditions where multiple marriage is acceptable or a norm.

Collective conscience – Emile Durkheim, one of the founders of sociology, claimed that it was impossible to have any form of social life without a set of socially accepted and shared values and norms. He called those shared beliefs the **collective conscience**. He argued that religion embodied the collective conscience because it established the principles and beliefs that make society both stable and well-ordered.

Parental faith – in religious families children will be very profoundly affected by the beliefs of their parents. Erikson pointed out that children have little or no choice but to take on the beliefs of their parents who will train their children in the community aspects of religious belief. For example, children will pass through various traditions such as Christmas, Passover or Ramadan with their families. There may be rites of passage such as communion or bar mitzvah. They may wear items associated with their religion. They will attend ceremonies such as weddings, be educated at faith schools and view religious practice and belief as a normal part of life.

Media

There has been a long history of concern with the effects of the media among sociologists and psychologists who believe it to be a very powerful agency of socialisation. There is claimed to be a link between youth violence and the media. As early as the 1960s, a psychologist, Albert Bandura, claimed that there was a direct link between exposure to watching violence and violent play among children. Despite some criticism of his experiment, it is still seen by many as powerful evidence that the media have a major impact on children, and this impact can be negative.

Copycat behaviour – Bandura's claim is that children model their behaviour on the behaviour of the role models they see on television. There have been a number of cases of murderers who claim to have modelled their behaviour on films. Increasing numbers of films and video games appear to glamorise mass murder and killing sprees. The level of concern is such that in some countries, the laws governing children's television and gaming are very strict indeed.

Hypodermic syringe model – early Marxist theories of the media suggested that the media act as a drug directly injected into people's minds and affecting their beliefs. As people cannot escape from the media because it is everywhere, they accept the messages that are passed on to them without question. Children are seen as particularly vulnerable because they are less able to tell the difference between reality and fiction. Moreover, in children's television, violence is often shown as heroic, with people solving problems through fights rather than sitting down and discussing issues as adults should do.

Discussion point

- How does religion affect the lives of the non-religious? Think of laws and moral beliefs to start with.

Research idea

How would you design a research project to investigate the effects of the media on children? What problems might you experience?

INTERESTING FACT

The impact of the media is sometimes surprising. In 2013 the film star Angelina Jolie revealed that she had had a mastectomy as genetic tests showed she was at a very high risk of developing breast cancer. In the months following the news coverage of this story NHS referrals for the genetic screening more than doubled. What does this tell us about the power of the media?

Activity

Work is an important part of social identity. Suggest ways in which your job could affect your social life.

⭐ INTERESTING FACT

Education is not always value free. For example in 2008, 20 Korean men each chopped off one of their own fingers in protest at the Japanese school history textbook which failed to mention war crimes committed by Japanese troops against the Koreans in World War 2.

http://www.tes.co.uk/article.aspx?storycode=350656

Tip

In questions where you are asked to focus on 'explaining ways', you are being asked to talk about a social process. If you were to write about the hidden curriculum, for example, say how it works.

Work

Work is a very important agent of adult socialisation. People have to adapt to the demands of their work position. This can be done through formal training: doctors take many years to learn the knowledge to become a medical professional, but they also have to learn how to behave as doctors should. This process is often more informal, but they need to learn the social skills that we call 'bedside manner' if they are to be good at their jobs.

Canteen culture – this is a term often associated with the police force, but canteen culture exists in all workplaces. Workers need to understand the practices of other employees, their beliefs, how to deal with certain problems and the attitudes that they will need to survive. They will be expected to be punctual and work hard. They may even be expected to learn how to survive a full day at work through tricks and tactics that mean that they do not work too hard and place too high a physical burden on themselves.

McDonaldisation of work – Ritzer (1993) described how workers in certain industries, such as fast food restaurants, were trained not to show initiative. People expect that if they go to a chain restaurant anywhere in the world, the food and behaviour of staff will be predictable. This is achieved through insisting that staff wear uniforms, the menus remain standard and workers behave in exactly the same way in every single restaurant. Thus, interactions are scripted with phrases such as 'Have a nice day!'. Work becomes repetitive, boring and routine. Imagination and talent are not necessary for such jobs.

Sample questions

How to Survive the First Day of School

Your first day of school is the chance to make your first impression on your **peer group**. Dress nicely. The outfit you choose will tell others what type of person you are. Relax. Find good and true friends. Follow the rules, but don't be a Goody-Two-Shoes! Study at home, no need for the nickname 'Nerd' going around. If you have weird habits like chewing pencils or picking your nose in public then hide those habits, as they can be embarrassing. Set a good impression.

Adapted from http://www.wikihow.com/Survive-the-First-Day-of-High-School

a) With reference to the item and sociological knowledge, explain the meaning of the term **peer group**.

b) Using the item and sociological knowledge, explain any **two** ways in which children may be socialised in schools.

Extended writing

Using sociological evidence and examples, explain the meaning of the term hidden curriculum in education.

Guidance: In your option choice, you will be expected to consider key terms and to write a little about them. You will need to explore the idea of the hidden curriculum in some detail, perhaps mentioning that Marxists link it to social control of children, whereas functionalists believe that it is the way that they learn social norms. Feminists see the hidden curriculum as one way in which children are taught gender roles in schools.

Write about 300 words.

Check your own learning

Match the start and ends of the following sentences:

Start	End
a) Peer pressure is the process	the assumptions and beliefs that are taught unintentionally in schools
b) Hidden curriculum refers to	collective conscience as a set of socially accepted and shared norms and values
c) Durkheim referred to the	media and it is claimed people model their actions on what they see on the television
d) Copycat behaviour is associated with the	and is where workers understand the work practices and attitudes of other employees
e) Canteen culture is associated with the police force	whereby people modify their behaviour in order to fit in with a group

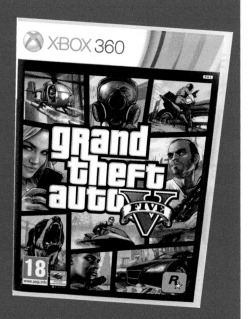

★ INTERESTING FACT

In 2008, six teenagers went on an all night rampage, terrorising the town of Nassau in New York State. Their evening began with a mugging outside a supermarket, before parading along the high street carrying baseball bats and a crow bar, robbing one motorist and smashing a passing vehicle with a bat. A local police officer Det. Sgt Anthony Repalone told the press 'It was determined that they were emulating the character in that Grand Theft Auto game, going on a crime spree' using weapons and tactics inspired by the controversial video game.

Adapted from http://kotaku.com/5019960/teen-crime-spree-inspired-by-grand-theft-auto

Research ideas

Talk to teachers. Do they think that different furniture layouts in schoolrooms affect the way that children behave and learn?

What might this child learn about his culture from watching television with his father? What other things do children learn from their parents?

STRETCH and CHALLENGE

Search Google Books for McDonaldization. You can read most of Ritzer's book online.

Aims

⊙ **To explain how we learn our identity from agencies of socialisation**

Each person has a sense of identity. This is our sense of who we are, our relationships to other people and our place in the social world. This sense of self may include elements of gender, religion, ethnicity, age and position. We learn this identity from out interactions with others, thus it is gained through the process of socialisation. You will understand how we develop our sense of identity from agencies of socialisation.

Topic 5: What is the link between socialisation and identity?

Getting you thinking

Write down ten different words to summarise who you think you are. Ask others around you to do the same. How many of those words are social categories (girl, British) and how many are personality characteristics (clever, hardworking)? What does this tell us about the importance of society in telling us who we are?

Identity, self and others

Many early sociologists were interested in culture. However, even before World War 1, Max Weber in Germany and George Herbert Mead in the USA were developing ideas about the way that people develop a sense of meaning for their lives. G H Mead, for example, suggested that people do not act on logic or rationality, but on their sense of understandings and meanings. For example, a pet dog or cat may have no financial value and has a short life span, but many people will pay hundreds of pounds on vet's bills because for them, their pet has meaning as part of their family.

This understanding has triggered sociological and psychological research into how we develop our sense of meaning and identity and this approach to sociology is generally known as interactionism. Identity can be variable, depending on our social situations. This is because it reflects the views of others. We may not feel particularly Welsh till we go to England. Males may not feel particularly male, until they are placed in an all-female environment.

Sociologists have identified two elements to identity:

1. *Primary identity* is our sense of self.
2. *Secondary identity* consists of the roles we play in society.

We develop a sense of the meaning of who we are, our identity, in a number of ways:

1. We are told who we are by others. For example, a pupil will not be accepted in the school staff room because teachers will say, 'You are a pupil, get out of here'. Sometimes these identities can be seen as positive: manager, professional footballer, doctor. Frequently identities can be seen as negative, so, for example, disabled or gay people often have to face difficult and unpleasant interactions with, and reactions from, others.
2. We may choose different identities depending on where we are. In school or college, a student identity is acceptable and people will behave and dress accordingly, but

they will dress and behave differently if they expect to be allowed into a club. Identity is therefore linked to an expected social role.

3. Identity may give us meaning. For example, people will wear obvious signs of their religious and ethnic background as a signal to others. Women who wear a burka in public are making a clear statement of identity as religious Islamic people.

4. Some identities may be imposed on us; these are known as ascribed statuses. For example, daughter or sister are statuses that are automatically given. In the Hindu religion you are born into a caste and remain in that group for life.

5. Some identities may be chosen; these identities are achieved statuses. For most people their job is an example of an achieved status – they have had to do something to get into that position or role.

Sullivan, a psychiatrist, developed the concept of the 'significant other'. In sociology, the term is used to describe a person, or a group of people who have a major influence on a person's sense of self-identity. Thus many agencies of socialisation can be seen as significant others, for example, for religious people, those who preach will be significant others.

The term 'other' may also be used in terms of the development of self-identity. In this case, the other is the person we are not. Thus, men may define themselves as masculine by rejecting any behaviours that they feel are female or feminine.

Learning gender identity through socialisation

One of the most important identities we may have is that of gender. Our biological sex will carry with it a set of cultural expectations. These cultural expectations are our gender roles. From even before birth, a child may be treated differently according to its biological sex. Many parents choose to know what sex they are expecting so they can decorate a nursery, buy gender-appropriate clothes and toys and choose a gender-appropriate name despite there being very little difference in the appearance and behaviour of babies on the basis of sex.

Gender identities
Farley (1990) pointed out that in Western cultures, expected male identities include:

- Leadership
- Control of social situations
- Decision making
- Active, unemotional and aggressive behaviours.

Expected feminine identity behaviours include:

- Physical dependency and weakness
- Emotionalism
- Lack of control
- Passive, caring and family orientated.

Family
Ann Oakley described processes of gender socialisation and claimed that children learned the expected behaviour for their gender through the following primary socialisation processes:

Topic 5: What is the link between socialisation and identity?

Thinking skills

The boxer, Amir Khan, is a British (Bolton in the north-west of England) born Muslim, with parents from Pakistan. He supports Bolton Wanderers and is very active with charity work. He has ties to many different social groups, all of which influence his identity and behaviour. Think about the social groups you belong to and summarise your identities in a sentence. Describe how your behaviour reflects the membership of these different groups.

Famous names

Ann Oakley

Born in 1944, Ann Oakley is a feminist sociologist who has written extensively on the roles of women in modern society. Her earliest research concentrated on the family, collecting qualitative data about women's attitudes to housework.

What does this choice of toy tell the boy about his gender identity?

Activity

What social class are you? Try this quiz:

http://www.bbc.co.uk/news/ magazine-22000973

Are you surprised by what you have learned?

Why do you think that is?

STRETCH and CHALLENGE

Search BBC news website for social class. There are a variety of useful articles to read.

- *Manipulation* – parents encourage behaviour that is normal for the gender and discourage what they may see as inappropriate gender behaviour. For example, phrases such as 'boys don't cry'.
- *Canalisation* – boys and girls are channelled into appropriate activities, so boys are given 'male' toys that encourage physical activity and girls are offered dolls to encourage caring.
- *Verbal appellations* – girls will be called 'angel' and 'princess' whereas boys are often 'little monster' or other more aggressive names.
- *Different activities* – girls are taken to dance classes or kept at home to help, whereas boys are sent out to play, or taken to football training.

This idea was developed and criticised by Statham in 1986 who said that even if parents avoid purposeful gender socialisation, cultural and social expectations were so powerful that children still behave in gendered ways because of the powerful influence of secondary socialisation.

Media

Judith Butler (1990) points out that the media stereotyping of gender roles is so powerful it is difficult to avoid gender socialisation and gendered behaviour. There is a large amount of literature on body image in the media, with unnatural or unusual body types being presented as both the ideal and the norm for both men and women. There is a pressure on people to conform. Naomi Wolf (1990) complained that the idea of a perfect body image was a means to control and exploit women. Celebrities such as Kate Winslett and Brad Pitt have actively complained about the way that their images are manipulated through Photoshop to present unnaturally perfect images. They argue that it contributes to eating disorders and emotional problems among the vulnerable young.

Learning class identity through socialisation

Social class is an important concept in sociology. It is used to describe entire groups of people of similar education, income and occupational background. Traditionally in Britain we talk of people being upper, middle and lower (or working) class, but in reality the class groupings are more complex than that. Those who are in the upper class are the extremely wealthy and powerful, they often own land and property. There are few of them, but they have access to political and **social power**. In practical terms for much discussion, most sociologists refer to two basic class groupings:

- The middle classes who are generally employed in professional work and have good incomes and high levels of education.
- The working class, who include those who have never worked or had jobs. This is the majority of the population and these people tend to be those who have fewer educational qualifications and who work in jobs where they are paid wages.

Education

Many sociologists argue that middle-class and working-class culture in Britain are different. People may take pride in their social class background and position.

Savage (1992) argued that the lifestyles of people in the middle class differ from those of the working class. They have more disposable income and are able to spend it on living comfortably lifestyles in pleasant houses, with nice cars, holidays and leisure

Items are often sold to people as either for males or for females. List examples such as watches, clothing, etc.

activities. Their children can expect to attend good schools, go to university and gain high-paying jobs. Pierre Bourdieu, a French sociologist, talked in terms of cultural capital. He claimed that people with middle-class backgrounds have been socialised into the culture of the dominant ruling class and teachers. They are more likely to succeed in school than working-class children. Education therefore is an important agency of socialisation into class identity.

Work

In 2005, Savage wrote that one of the typical features of working-class people was their view of themselves as 'ordinary' people as opposed to those in the higher professions. In 1999, Charlesworth explored working-class life in Rotherham and claimed that people had always gained class identity from work. He claimed that in recent years, working-class people could not rely on gaining the kind of working-class jobs that had traditionally given them pride. They therefore experienced lives of negativity, lack of culture and over-exposure to the media. Because they have no jobs, they have limited money and find it difficult to participate in the more active social lives of the wealthy. Now it is lack of work and poor working conditions that teach people their class.

Learning ethnic identity through socialisation

In the past, people were divided into social groups based on supposed biological differences and these groups were known as races. Thus, sociologists will use the term racism to describe hatred or fear of people on the basis of socially significant physical features. Recent genetic research shows that previous theories of race overstate differences between peoples, and sociologists now use the term ethnicity to describe people who share cultures. An ethnic group will tend to have similar ancestry, sense of history, traditions, beliefs and language. These are socialised differences, thus they must be learned, often in childhood.

Family

The first place people learn their ethnicity is within the family, often through the language spoken in the home. For example, many British families use a domestic language other than English. There are groups of Welsh, Polish, Somali and other

How does race differ from ethnicity? Why should sociologists reject notions of race?

language speakers who choose to use their own culture at home, though they are perfectly fluent in English outside the home. Tariq Modood (2005) suggested that in addition to language, there may be food, dress and family traditions which teach ethnicity. Miri Song said that Chinese families reward children who support family businesses or show family loyalty, seeing them as 'more Chinese'.

Religion

For many families, ethnic identity is passed on through religious practice. Ghuman (1999) found religious training to be very important in encouraging Asian cultural values of obedience, loyalty and respect among the children of Asian migrants into the UK. Butler (1995) said that religion was central to the way that Muslim girls created an identity for themselves and that Islam provided a real moral guide to young women. Veiling was seen by many as a positive statement of cultural identity and pride. The concept of 'izzat' or family honour was very important. Pryce suggested that religious belief could even provide an identity that rejected mainstream culture, so Rastafarianism offered West Indians pride in rejecting the racism of wider British culture.

Learning national identity through socialisation

National identity is somewhat different from cultural identity even though the ideas of culture and nation overlap. Nationhood is linked to a specific geographical region. Thus, whilst all people born in the UK have legal rights as citizens of the United Kingdom, there are those who feel themselves to have a particular loyalty to Wales, Cornwall, Northern Ireland or Scotland.

Extreme nationalism – this is often distrusted because it can give rise to extreme forms of behaviour, for example early 20th-century German nationalism was a key factor in the rise of Nazism. One of its key features is intolerance of others.

Civic nationalism – this is often seen as more positive because it can unite different groups of people together so they feel pride in their country. Governments often encourage it, so for example, in the USA, children salute the national flag each morning in school.

How is this man expressing his sense of Welsh national identity?

Sport

One of the ways in which people are socialised into nationality is through major sporting events such as the World Cup tournaments in athletics, rugby, football and other sports. Athletes will parade in national colours and costumes, anthems are played, countries are placed in league tables. Individuals become national heroes and are supported by huge fan bases. Most importantly of all, many of these competitions become the focus of massive media attention so images of athletes with national flags are almost unavoidable. Poulton and Maguire (2012) described the media coverage of 'Team GB' in the lead up to the London Olympics as being linked to fears of the breakup of the UK through the Scottish Independence movement.

Cultural traditions and shared history

Many relatively new nations, such as Australia, which officially became a separate nation in 1900, or New Zealand, which was founded by the Treaty of Waitangi in 1840, celebrate National Days. This is a way of uniting people, many of whom will have different ethnicities, into a sense of belonging to their new nation. Within the UK, there is a marked sense of nationality for the people of Wales, Northern Ireland and Scotland, often born out of a sense of having been dominated by English culture. For example, in Wales, historically, the use of the Welsh language was discouraged but now in schools, the use of the language is encouraged and Welsh children are expected to study the Cwricwlwm Cymreig (Welsh Curriculum) through which students would learn the 'culture, environment, economy and history of Wales, and the influences which have shaped the country of today'.

Sample questions

In 2006 the Scottish tennis player, Andy Murray, provoked upset when his answer to the question, 'Who will you be supporting in the World Cup?' was 'Anybody but England!'. Intended, he said, as a joke, the episode illustrated the importance of different **national identities** within Britain. The option to be British during the Olympics but Welsh/English/Scottish/Northern Irish during the Commonwealth Games or the football World Cup underlines the point that we have multiple, overlapping identities.

   a) With reference to the item and sociological knowledge, explain the meaning of the term **national identities**.

   b) Using the item and sociological knowledge, explain any **two** ways in which we gain a sense of our national identity.

Check your own learning

True or false?

   a) G H Mead said that people act purely on logic.

   b) Identity can depend on the social situation we are in.

   c) Our sense of self is known as a secondary identity.

   d) Ascribed status is what we are born with and is difficult to change.

   e) Achieved status is a chosen identity.

   f) Some actors and actresses have complained about being Photoshopped to make them look perfect.

   g) People can feel pride in extreme nationalism because it encourages tolerance of others.

In 2013 the new owner of Cardiff City caused controversy when he changed the club colours from blue to red, the club colours are an important part of their traditions and identity said the fans.

Extended writing

Describe the key features of national identity.

Guidance: If you are asked to describe, this means that all you need to do is give a good range of facts in some sort of order that makes sense. Identity is a complex idea and needs to be explored in a sentence or two, before you begin to look at national identity and how people gain a sense of what their national identity is. You should separate out ethnic identity, which is cultural, from national identity, which is linked to a particular place and is geographical.

Write about 300 words.

Topic 1: What is theory?

Aims

- To explain the importance of theory and evidence to sociology

Sociology is a theoretical subject. This means that it does more than describe society, it tries to provide reasons for why things are as they are. If you are going to understand society, then it is important that you know what others have said.

Research idea

Tattoos have become very fashionable since the 1990s. Create a theory by suggesting reasons why this may be so. How might you set about researching evidence to support your theory?

Getting you thinking

Feminism is a theory which suggests that the male gender dominate women in society. Feminists support their theory with evidence including the fact that women tend to be lower paid, experience sexual harassment and violence and there are far fewer female MPs than males in Parliament.

What kind of evidence would you look for if you wanted to support a theory that said society was absolutely perfect exactly as it is?

What is a theory?

In sociology, a social **theory** is a set of ideas that are used to explain our society. It offers an overview to explain how things are. People often use the word 'perspective' to describe a theory, because a perspective is also a viewpoint or a way of looking at things.

What is a concept?

A **concept** is an idea. Sociological concepts are the ideas that go together to make an overall theory. Each theory will have a number of underlying concepts that are used to explain different parts of society.

What is the importance of evidence?

Anything you say in support of a theory is known as evidence. Some evidence can be weak; for example, if all you can offer is an opinion (I think that ...) then that does not back up a theory very well. Strong evidence that supports a theory would come from previous research or facts. If you are going to write about a theory, you will need to use evidence to support your views. This is why you need to be able to talk about theories, concepts and research in sociology.

Why do we have complex language in sociology?

Many words have a lot of different possible meanings. In sociology it is important that we use the key sociological terms to show that we know the subject. These terms should be defined so that there can be no misunderstanding. You will find that each of the major theories uses a slightly different kind of language, so sometimes you will recognise theories by the language and concepts.

A brief history of sociological theory

The word sociology was popularised by Auguste Comte (1798–1857) who believed that the study of society should be scientific. This is still a powerful idea, although many of Comte's other ideas are now disregarded.

Early sociologists such as Marx (1818–1883), Weber (1864–1920) and Durkheim (1858–1917) were living in a time when social changes were occurring rapidly and they were interested in explaining those changes, each in their different ways. Each of those early sociologists was working in a different country and attempting to understand a different set of social problems. Each wrote a number of influential books based on their own interests and training, and as a result, sociological theory has its origins in a number of different disciplines: history, philosophy, educational theory, economics and psychology.

Each of those early writers has been the source of a number of theories about society, so there is debate amongst the major theories. Each has its strengths and weaknesses in terms of how well it explains society. New theories have also been developed as a response to social change; so, for example, the rise in the influence of women in society is linked to a social theory known as feminism.

However, it is not as simple as that. There may be debate amongst the major theories but there is also serious debate within theories as well. Not everyone who agrees with a particular sociological theory, in general, will also accept all of the detail, so debates develop, with people using different evidence to back up ideas. Thus sociology is a subject where there are debates, but sometimes no definitive possible answers.

Sociology and social policy

The ideas of sociologists have been very influential. This can be on a massive scale. Marxist ideas have been very influential in 20th-century history giving rise to revolutions and wars. They have also affected daily life in our own country in various ways because they have influenced government and law makers.

A social policy is a plan or an action which lawmakers and government agencies put into place in order to improve or change society. Many sociologists argue that their theories should be used to influence government thinking. Anthony Giddens, a famous British sociologist, argued that the point of sociology was to:

- Understand how society works.
- Understand different cultures.
- Help people to understand themselves and their own thinking.
- Assess whether governments are successful or not.

Theories and public policy

A belief about society is known as an ideology. Each theoretical perspective in society is linked to an ideology which influences the way that sociologists advise governments.

- *Functionalists* – tend to claim that they provide scientific and factual evidence. However, they are generally linked to conservative politics because they claim that society is effective as it is. Thus, they will support traditional family structures and argue against lone parenthood.
- *Marxists* – are critical of society and claim that political structures favour the rich. They are linked to policies that support working people and poor people.
- *Feminists* – believe that politics work to support male control of society, so feminists will argue that laws should be made to support the interests of women.

Theoretical thinking

Sociological thinking can affect social policy in two ways:

Facts – sociology can provide evidence and facts about what is happening in society so we can describe social change.

Theory – social theory can help us to explain what is happening and predict the results of changes in law or society.

Whenever a theory appears to you as the only possible one, take this as a sign that you have neither understood the theory nor the problem which it was intended to solve.

Karl Popper

What does this quotation tell us about the nature of theories and sociological debates?

Research idea

Look at the websites of political parties and see which social theories influence their policies.

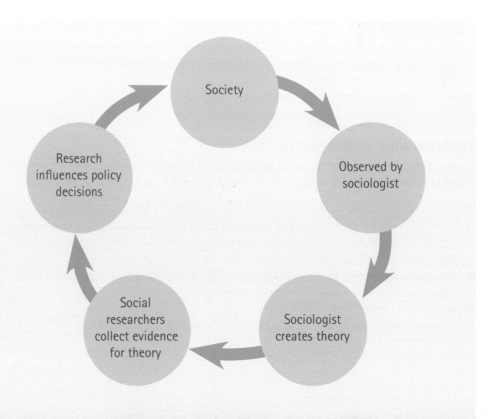

New Right thinking in action: Commercially run care homes replace state-provided old age care.

Tip

Sociology is expected to be scientific, which means that you are dealing with facts and evidence. It is seen as bad style if you refer to yourself in answers by using phrases such as 'In my opinion...' or 'I think that...'

The link between social theory and social policy is a complex one.

⊚ *The New Right* – claim that sociologists should deliberately influence governments and believe that the correct way to run society is to remove power from government. They want to allow commercial interests and companies to run society instead. They believe that competition between organisations such as schools and hospitals will improve services.

Using theory in examinations

You will be expected to use and refer to theory in your examination answers for the following reasons:

⊚ Theories tend to try to explain facts and issues about society with just a few basic ideas that are then developed and debated.
⊚ Theories can help us to predict future events.
⊚ Theories help us to understand and interpret social relationships.
⊚ Theories can give us a way of summarising social structures and patterns that we can observe in society.
⊚ Theories provide a framework for ideas.

Society

Observed by sociologist

Sociologist creates theory

Social researchers collect evidence for theory

Research influences policy decisions

- Understanding and referring to theories helps the examiner to see that you have been reading around the subject.
- Criticising theories is a way of displaying evaluative and analytical skills (AO3).
- The alternative to a theory is common sense, and that cannot be trusted because it can be inconsistent and based on opinions and not factual evidence.

Sample questions

The French sociologist, Emile Durkheim described his **theory** of sociology as being the 'science of social facts'. He said a social fact is any social invention such as a belief, culture or a religion that is shared by a number of people and that affects their behaviour. He set out to prove that the action of committing suicide is a social fact and he did it by collecting evidence in the form of official statistics from a number of different geographical areas. He was able to show that in the north of Europe, suicide was more common than in the south, for example.

a) With reference to the item and sociological knowledge, explain the meaning of the term **theory**.

b) Using the item and sociological knowledge, explain **two** reasons why sociologists use evidence to support theories about society.

Check your own learning
Match the following words and concepts to their meanings:

a)	A set of ideas that are used to explain how or why things are as they are	Concept
b)	This is an idea, together concepts are used to create theory	Sociology
c)	Facts or opinions that can be used to support or contradict a theory	Social policy
d)	The systematic study of society	Theory
e)	Arguments that take place between major theories or within them	Evidence
f)	A plan or an action that governments put into place to change or improve society	Debates

Extended writing

Discuss reasons why sociologists use theory in order to study society.

Guidance: If you are asked to discuss something in an essay, it means that you should talk about it in some detail taking into account different ideas and evidence. In this case you need to consider a range of reasons why sociologists need theory, perhaps referring to more than one to show how they offer insights. You will therefore find it helpful to look at all of the material on the pages, not just the main body of writing. The extension activities are designed to increase your understanding.

Write about 250 words.

Developing understanding
A theory is a general prediction about society which is based on previous research and ideas. A hypothesis is a term used in sciences and refers to a specific prediction which will then be tested.

STRETCH and CHALLENGE

- Organised violence in the form of war has been practised by most European cultures over the centuries. What different theories could you suggest to explain war and military adventures?
- If you were in government, what policies might you put in place to prevent war? Use each of your theories to explain why warfare occurs.

Aims

◉ To understand the principles of functionalist theories of society

Functionalism is a view of society that is concerned with understanding social order and social organisation. It is based on the view that society can only exist if people share values and culture; this is called a **consensus** view of society. People and social institutions such as the family, education and politics all contribute to the smooth running of society because values are shared. Anything that disrupts the smooth running of society is seen as a problem affecting how well our social systems work. When functionalists study any aspect of society they always want to know: how does it contribute to the social order and stability?

Discussion point

● Suggest ten things that families or education do that could possibly be very bad for individuals and society as a whole.

Research methods

How might you set up a research project in a school or college to investigate the idea that there is a link between intelligence and the ability to pass examinations.? What problems might you experience with this research?

Topic 2: Functionalism

Getting you thinking

Two very different images, one society. Do jobless people and the businessman Richard Branson, of Virgin, share the same norms and values? How would their experiences in life differ? Discuss the extent to which people in modern Britain can be said to have shared values.

The organic analogy and functionalism

Functionalist theory is based on the view that society works in a similar way to a human body, the **organic analogy**. Various organs do different jobs and without some key organs, the body would die. In the same way, social institutions have different roles, and if some do not work, the society cannot survive. So the family reproduces the members of society, both physically and culturally (though socialisation). The education system produces an educated workforce. In this way, the functionalist approach tends to be conservative, because it is assumed that ordered societies work well. Functionalist thinkers are associated with the **positivist** (scientific) approach to research so they gather quantitative data, often basing their work on government statistics.

Criticising functionalism

This view of society was very popular in the 1940s and 1950s in the USA, but by the 1970s, was being challenged by other theories on the basis that:

◉ It suggests we already live in the best possible world.
◉ It does not explain why and how societies change.
◉ It overlooks the effects of major social inequalities such as sexism and class division.
◉ It tends to view individuals as being governed by social rules and overlooks the extent to which people choose how to act and think.
◉ Marxists have criticised functionalism because they think it supports capitalism and overlooks alternative ways of organising society.
◉ Despite it claiming to be scientific, there is not much research evidence to support functionalism.

Despite the fact that it is less popular than it once was in sociology, functionalism provides a starting point for the theories of the New Right and so has had some influence on government, especially in the areas of welfare and family policies.

Strengths of functionalism

◉ It suggests how people are socialised into the values of their culture.
◉ It is apparent that people do appear to share values and ideas much of the time.
◉ It provides a starting point for other theories to develop from.
◉ It explains the roles of important social institutions.

Recognising functional thinking

It is possible to recognise theories by the language that is used to analyse society. Functionalist writers tend to talk in terms of values, organisations and institutions.

They look at society as a whole, and so they do not look at individuals. This approach is known as **macro-sociology** because it is a big picture of how things work. Thus functionalists tend to argue that some forms of family are 'better' for society than others, or considering education they claim that the system works to get the 'best' people into the important jobs for society. These institutions exist in order to train new citizens through the process of socialisation. Inequality is good for society as it encourages the most able to take on responsibilities.

Functionalists see society as made up of different but interdependent parts, all of which rely on each other to work effectively for the good of the whole of society.

Important functionalist thinkers

Emile Durkheim (1858–1917)

Durkheim is best known for creating the earliest rules for studying society in a scientific fashion, by looking at government statistics. His main interest was in exploring the ways that society held itself together and what joined people together. He identified religion in traditional societies and education in modern societies as key institutions.

Talcott Parsons (1902–1979)

At one stage, Parsons was probably the most influential sociologist in the USA. He wrote extensively and also translated the work of other sociologists. He claimed that social systems develop as they do because they are functional or beneficial for society.

Robert Merton (1910–2003)

Robert Merton claimed that we learn our goals and the rules of behaviour from our society. Thus society governs our actions and we share our views of appropriate behaviour with others. Crime is caused when people cannot attain social goals through the culturally accepted rules of behaviour.

Sample questions

Davis and Moore (1967) studied education from a functionalist perspective, and they suggested that education exists to select the most talented and intelligent people to take on the most important and significant jobs in society. They called this idea, **role allocation**. They said that the higher pay that these jobs offer encourages healthy competition, which only the cleverest will be able to achieve. Thus, they claim that education sorts people on the basis of their ability. Only the cleverest will pass examinations.

   a) Using material from the item and sociological knowledge, explain the meaning of the term **role allocation**.
   b) Explain **two** weaknesses of this functionalist view of the education system.

Check your own learning

Match the following words and concepts to their meanings:

a)	The process of learning the expected norms and values of society	Consensus
b)	The idea that society works in the same way as a human body	Positivism
c)	Shared agreement in society about how things should be	Functionalism
d)	Looks at how the whole of society works and is not interested in interactions between individual people	Organic analogy
e)	A view of society that requires the sociologist to consider how social institutions work for the benefit of society	Macro sociology
f)	A scientific view of society based on the idea of looking at how people behave	Socialisation

Extended writing

Discuss functionalist theories of society.

Guidance: You will need to explain the functionalist view of society, using the key terms of functionalist writing. You could then write about the history of functionalism as an idea but this may be complicated if you do not really understand the differences between the various functionalist writers. A better method is to then talk about the strengths and weaknesses of functionalism, referring to writers, other theories and evidence. Whilst functionalism is no longer popular, it is still enormously useful as it explains why society holds itself together. This could be a useful conclusion.

Write about 500-750 words.

Aims

⊙ To understand the principles of Marxist theories of society

Marxism is a view of society that is concerned with economics and social control. It is based on a view that there are two social classes and that capitalist society is based on the oppression and exploitation of the poor by the rich. This is a conflict view of society. In many ways, Marxism is similar to functionalism because it is concerned with social order and social structure, but whereas a functionalist sees this as good for society as a whole, a Marxist sees it as benefitting just the rich and powerful. A Marxist will tend to study social organisations to see how they operate to control the actions and thinking of poorer people.

Topic 3: Marxism

Getting you thinking

Billionaire Richard Branson has been backing a project for sub-space tourism, so that anyone who can afford something in the region of £150,000 can take a minutes-long trip into space. This will consume valuable fossil fuels and arguably contribute to global warming in order that a few hugely wealthy individuals can see Earth from space. The same sum of money could be used by Oxfam to drill 18,000 wells. This would provide clean water in developing countries and limit death from typhus, cholera and water-borne disease such as diarrhoea, which kill millions of people each year.

Do you find the space project to be exciting or worrying? Is it acceptable that a billionaire can spend so much on a luxury item when other people are dying from lack of very basic facilities?

What do you think is most important to capitalism? People, the planet or profit?

Marxism

Marx believed that in all but the most primitive societies, some people were more powerful than all of the rest. These people were able to maintain their position of power because they controlled the resources, the government systems and most importantly, the ideas of society. Modern society is organised in an economic system known as capitalism. In capitalism, the entire economic system is organised for the production of profit and the wealth creation is entirely owned by private individuals for their own benefit. Karl Marx believed this to be fundamentally morally wrong, whereas functionalists believe it to be efficient and acceptable. Thus, Marxism is a conflict view of society because Marxists believe social groups have different needs and wants but some people can satisfy every want, whereas other people cannot have even their basic needs met. Conflict will therefore arise between the rich and the poorest people.

"Put up a big splashy banner that says,
'Thanks for another great year, peasants.'"

Research idea

Look up countries that have had Marxist revolutions, for example Russia, Cuba and China. How far can they be described as good for workers?

Criticising Marxism

Karl Marx has had an enormous influence on world history. People used his ideas as a justification for overthrowing governments in many countries and establishing alternative societies. These have often been unpleasant dictatorships. That fact may not mean that his analysis of capitalism is incorrect. However, there are criticisms of his view of society that you should be aware of:

◉ Marx only looks at economic relationships and overlooks the fact that people have a range of reasons for their actions: culture, tradition, gender.

◉ Marxism is focussed on class inequality and thus overlooks other inequalities such as gender, age, disability, sexual orientation and ethnicity.

◉ Marx tended to view class in terms of conflict between the wealthy (bourgeoisie) and the poor (proletarians). He did not foresee that a middle class would develop.

◉ Marxists argue that poor people do not understand that they are oppressed; so, if you agree with Marx, you understand society. However, if you disagree with Marxism, you are seen as not understanding society and having 'false consciousness'. This is fairly insulting to people who do not accept Marxist analyses.

Despite the fact that Marxism is popular in sociology, it has been less influential in affecting government policy in the contemporary UK. Plausibly, this is because governments tend to be composed of people from rich backgrounds.

Strengths of Marxism

It is easy to criticise Marxist thinking for being over-pessimistic about society, but its influence on sociology and social thinking has been enormous:

◉ Much global and national inequality can be explained using Marxist analyses.

◉ Marxism tends to assume that change is normal for society, so this can be used to explain why societies develop through history.

◉ Marx illustrates the significance of social class in terms of people's access to wealth and power.

Discussion point

● Suggest what would happen to society if everyone was really equal in terms of wealth, access to power and ability to influence other people's ideas.

Policy point

▶ Marxism has been traditionally associated with the 'far left' in politics and trades unionism.

Recognising Marxist thinking

Marxists are concerned with social class and capitalism above all. Marxist writers tend to talk in terms of social control, power and **ideology**. Ideology refers to belief systems and Marxists argue that the powerful control people through their control of ideas and knowledge about the world. Marxists tend to look at the media, family and education in terms of how they affect people's thinking. Marxists also consider how people are controlled through politics and legal systems, so that people who challenge authority are oppressed. Not all Marxists are in full agreement with Marx's writings, more recent writers are known as neo-Marxists.

Important Marxist thinkers

Karl Marx (1818–1883)

Karl Marx was a philosopher and economist; he was also a political activist who developed a theory of how capitalist society worked. He argued that capitalists and their workers were in a constant state of conflict. Employers need to keep wages low to maximise profit and workers want rights such as better wages and working conditions.

Louis Althusser (1918–1990)

Althusser is a neo-Marxist because he developed Marxist theory. He claimed that some institutions in society, such as the police and military, were designed to control through oppression of workers. These he called **repressive state apparatus**. However, **ideological state apparatus** controlled through ideology. Institutions such as family and education give us ideas about the world.

Sample questions

More than a quarter of a million workers in Wales are paid less than the living wage, according to a major new report. Research published by KPMG shows that 261,000 people – nearly one in four (24%) workers – receives less than the amount considered necessary to meet basic living costs. The highest share of people earning less than the living wage was found in Conwy and Powys (both 32%) and Monmouthshire (30%).

Across the UK, 5.28 million people – 22% of the workforce – are paid below this rate.

The findings come as the Living Wage Foundation has set a new rate of £7.85 per hour.

Commenting on the report, Wales TUC National Officer Julie Cook said: 'People deserve a fair day's pay for an honest day's work'. But low pay is blighting the lives of hundreds of thousands of families in Wales. And it's adding to the deficit because it means more is spent on tax credits and less collected in tax.

http://www.walesonline.co.uk/news/wales-news/nearly-one-four-workers-wales-8037037

a) Summarise the item on the low wage economy in Wales.
b) Explain **two** reasons why employers may wish to keep wages low for many workers in England and Wales.

Research methods

How might you set up a research project in a workplace to investigate the idea that employers force employees to work for low wages and long hours. What problems might you experience with this research?

STRETCH and CHALLENGE

How might the following agencies of socialisation (functionalism) actually be agencies of social control (Marxism)?

Religion, family, police and law courts, media, education, peer groups

Check your own learning

Match the start and ends of the following sentences:

Start	End
a) Karl Marx was an economist	to belief systems that people have about how society should be run.
b) Capitalism is a social system	policy because many politicians come from wealthy backgrounds.
c) Ideology refers	based on the maximisation of profit for the owners.
d) Marxists assume that	are said to have 'false consciousness'.
e) People who do not agree with Marxist analysis	and believed that all social relationships could be explained in terms of who controlled wealth.
f) Marxists have not been very influential in government	change is natural to society.

Extended writing

Discuss Marxist theories of society.

Guidance: To gain marks you should show understanding of Marxism, but also how other writers have applied Marxist ideas and developed them. Avoid criticising Marxism as a political system; most societies that were organised on Marxist lines, such as the former USSR, happened long after Marx had died. Focus on the description of social relationships and how capitalists are able to maintain their positions of wealth and power through the control of laws and through the control of ideas.

Write about 500-750 words.

Developing understanding

Do additional reading on functionalism and Marxism in textbooks and on the Internet. Create a list of ways in which the two perspectives are very similar, and then identify the differences between the theories.

STRETCH and CHALLENGE

You can read the *Communist Manifesto* by Marx and Engels online. It is a little challenging but it will give you an overview of Marxist thinking.

What does this image suggest to you about the Marxist view of society?

41

Topic 4: Feminism

Aims

- To understand the principles of feminist theories of society

There is plenty of evidence to support the view that men and women do not have equal wealth, power and status in society. Women are under-represented in important areas of life such as the legal system, business and politics. There are different theories to explain these gender differences in society. Biological theories have been used in the past, usually by men: women's roles are determined by their child-bearing role. Feminists offer an explanation based on culture, pointing to **patriarchy** as the reason for gender inequality.

Getting you thinking

In 2013, the Fawcett Society found that women are more likely to be in low-paid work than men, earning 15% less on average, and are more likely to experience poverty in old age. The Fawcett Society argues that this economic inequality prevents women from gaining political power and public influence.

What reasons can you suggest for this inequality? What could the government do to reduce the gap between men and women at work?

Feminism

There are many different feminist theories but they share some concerns. One important theme is that the contribution women have made to society in the past has often gone unrecognised. They agree that gender inequality can be seen in the home and family, at work and in the way women are treated in the media. **Feminism** can be seen as a conflict theory, focussing as it does on differences between males and females. It is also structural as it looks at society as a whole.

Gender difference

Gender differences are highlighted in the way female bodies are treated as objects in advertising and the media; women are used, often in a sexualised way, to promote products and activities such as sport. In this way women are marginalised and seen as different by men who gain masculinity by emphasising that they are 'other' and different from women. Women are often seen as the 'property' of their men and are denied opportunities to express themselves as fully human.

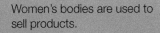
Women's bodies are used to sell products.

Gender inequalities

Gender inequality is difficult to challenge and change. Men dominate the key institutions of society and are reluctant to lose their dominance. Furthermore violence, or the fear of violence, controls women, especially those who challenge male supremacy. There is much evidence that many women are exploited and abused by men.

Social inequalities

One area of life where inequality is most obvious is work. Women are discriminated against in the workplace, concentrated in low-paid, low-status work. This limits their economic power and can mean dependence on men. These limited choices and lack of control over their personal lives add to their oppression.

Criticising feminism

In the media, feminism is often presented negatively, as aggressive anti-male opinion; however, this is misleading. As a result of this negative portrayal many women who have feminist beliefs are reluctant to identify themselves as feminists. Other more significant criticisms are that:

- Feminists tend to overlook other forms of inequality like race, age and disability or perhaps where males are victims.
- Women are not one shared social group; differences between women are as significant as differences between men and women; women vary along class and ethnic lines.
- Class inequality is overlooked; some well-paid middle-class women are only able to pursue their careers by employing domestic labour at very low wages.
- Campaigns by women have resulted in significant legal and social changes; this suggests that male attitudes and behaviours are changing.
- The gender system can be damaging to both males and females in our society, so women may feel oppressed but males are forced into an aggressive role.

Strengths of feminism

Feminism is correct in highlighting social and economic gender inequality. Women and men are socialised differently and have different opportunities.

- Sexism does exist. Women experience it in the media, the workplace and the home. It ranges from degrading sexual comments, discrimination in employment to threats of violence.
- Women have always been important to society, but this has been overlooked. History has been enriched as feminists have uncovered the contribution women have made.
- Feminists have demonstrated that the sexualisation of women's bodies in the media and the idealising of certain body shapes is damaging to women's self-esteem.
- The evidence of inequality is easily demonstrated by analysing the statistics: women on average earn less than men and are under-represented at the top of organisations.

Recognising feminist thinking

As a conflict theory, feminism shares some of the ideas and language used by Marxists. Patriarchy rather than class is used to explain inequalities; ideology is a common theme. Feminist sociologists have focussed on family and the workplace. They are also interested in sexuality and body image issues.

Discussion point

- In 2014, Salma Hayek, an actress, said 'I am not a feminist. If men were going through the things women are going through today, I would be fighting for them with just as much passion. I believe in equality.' Why do you think some women reject the label 'feminist'?

Research methods

How might you set up a research project to investigate whether boys and girls are treated equally in a school? What problems might you experience?

Activity

Google the term 'Everyday Sexism Project'. What do you learn about the position of women in modern society?

To what extent does this image reflect the modern view of feminism? How accurate is it in your view?

Germaine Greer (shown) claimed that men hate women. Is this true?

Invent one single law that would improve gender equality in modern Britain.

Important feminist thinkers

Sue Sharpe

Sharpe studied the attitudes of working class girls in London and compared two different samples. In 1970, she found them to be concerned with marriage, love and attracting a husband. By the 1990s, similar girls were concerned with financial independence and did not want their mothers' life experiences.

Germaine Greer (1939–)

Greer is an Australian feminist whose best known work is *The Female Eunuch* (1970). This book outlined her argument that women had been 'castrated' (turned into eunuchs) by a patriarchal society that demeaned and hated women. She argues that girls are socialised into a traditional idea of femininity that limits their options and creates powerlessness. She argued for 'women's liberation', with women identifying their own values and priorities, rather than accepting those defined by a patriarchal society.

Sample questions

Gender inequality in Wales continues to be a problem.

Areas which need urgent attention include domestic violence: over 150,000 women in Wales suffering from some form of gender-based violence every year; pay: in 2013 ONS showed the gap in average hourly earnings between all male and female workers in Wales was 16.5%, with men earning £11.70 per hour and women £9.77. Governments need to ensure that equality exists in all areas of life; for example, there is no women's prison in Wales, meaning that mothers locked away in far off locations struggle to see families. A 2011 survey of 50 top Welsh companies found only two women were in the senior position. In early 2012, there was only one female council leader, and only 25% of Welsh councillors were women.

http://www.wcia.org.uk/una/welshminister.html http://www.walesonline.co.uk/news/gender-pay-gap-wales--6415287

a) Summarise the information in the item about gender inequality in Wales.
b) Explain **two** reasons why feminists wish to challenge social inequalities affecting males and females.

Check your own learning

Match the following words and concepts to their meanings:

Meaning		Word
a)	The control of society by men	Gender
b)	A movement that aims for political, social and economic equality for women	Sexism
c)	The process of defining yourself as what you are not, so men have an identity as 'not feminine'	Patriarchy
d)	Social differences between men and women	Sex
e)	Biological differences between men and women	Feminism
f)	An action or belief that discriminates against a person on the grounds of their sex	Other

Extended writing

Discuss feminist theories of society.

Guidance: Feminism is not one theory, but a view of society that supposes that females are not valued in the same way as men. Feminism is more properly a movement or way of thought rather than a sociological perspective. You will need to show you understand this point before considering feminist approaches to sociology. There is a variety of feminist concerns such as family, education and work. Importantly, although women appear to have many of the same rights and opportunities as men, an evaluative essay would also question the extent to which women have really become the equal partners of men in modern Britain.

Write about 500 words.

Discussion point

- Why is the idea of men dressing in female clothing often seen as humorous, whereas women may wear male clothing with fewer comments being made? What does this tell you about the relative status of men and of women?

Research idea

Find out more about feminism by looking at the website of the Fawcett Society, www.fawcettsociety.org.uk

Aims

⊙ **To understand the principles of interactionism in sociology**

Interactionists start with people rather than social structures. According to interactionism, how we see the world influences how we behave, or interpret social situations and then decide how to act. It is associated with **qualitative** research methods such as **ethnography**, based on observations and interviews. If we want to understand why people behave in the way they do, we need to understand their view of the social world.

Topic 5: Interactionism

Getting you thinking

I wish I knew what she is thinking when she looks at me and smiles

I wish I knew what he is thinking when he looks at me and smiles

Look at the image. Why do the people each need to know what the other is thinking? How would that knowledge affect their behaviour towards each other?

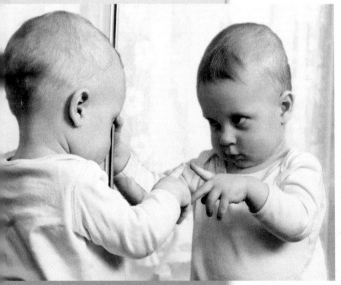

Cooley suggested that we develop a sense of self through our interactions with others. We gain an impression of who we are through an understanding of how others behave towards us. He called this the looking-glass self.

Interactionism

This approach focusses on what goes on within (rather than between) social institutions, it is seen as a **micro-sociological** theory. In particular it looks at interaction between people, for example between teachers and students, and students and students. This is in contrast to the structural theories that ask how the education system fits into society.

Interactionists see people as social actors who have a choice about how they play their roles in society. Most of the time behaviour is predictable but this is not an automatic response; according to this theory, we choose or decide how to act or behave. Our behaviour is based on interpretation; it is not simply a reflex. Interpretation means we have to think about what is going on and decide what it means and what our response to it should be.

Interpreting meanings is something we do all the time: for example, learning to drive involves learning the meanings of the various road signs; we do not automatically respond to a red light by stopping, we have to recognise the meaning of the red light.

Interactionism is based on the work of Weber and Mead who both argued that people's actions and beliefs are based on how they understand and interpret the social world.

Shared understanding, beliefs and views are learned through socialisation. These shared views Mead called social constructions. These constructions then influence behaviour. Stereotypes demonstrate this; entire groups of people may be viewed in a particular, usually over-simplified, way; for example, 'nurses are angels'. Others then act as though this stereotype is reality and are surprised when nurses show themselves to be much like the rest of us.

Criticising interactionism

Interactionism has been influential in sociology, but it is criticised for not taking into account the importance of large-scale social structures such as education or family in people's lives. Other criticisms include:

◉ It cannot explain social inequality and overlooks material and social differences between groups of people.
◉ It does not explain how or why societies change.
◉ It cannot explain why some people have more power than others to affect society and impose their meanings.
◉ It can sometimes be seen as trivial because it focusses on relatively small-scale aspects of social life.

Strengths of interactionism

Interactionism helps us to understand small-scale interactions that cannot be explained by structural theories such as feminism or functionalism.

◉ It explains how people develop a sense of self-identity.
◉ It draws attention to areas of life that are overlooked by other theories.
◉ It offers understanding of social processes.
◉ It gives rise to quantitative methods of research which offer insight and depth. These are known as ethnographic methods.
◉ It has influenced research conducted by feminists and Marxists.

Recognising interactionist thinking

Interactionists tend to look at social processes so they use concepts such as the labelling theory to explain the idea of identity. The idea is that powerful people apply a label to others, such as, 'clever', 'criminal' or 'insane' and then act as though the label were true. They look at meanings, beliefs and understanding of social phenomena. When interactionists study family, they look at how people negotiate tasks, and in education, they consider processes within schools and the impact they have on children's self-concepts.

> *The belief that one's own view of reality is the only reality is the most dangerous of all delusions.*
>
> **Paul Watzlawick**

Discussion point

• What behaviour is appropriate for a student in college or daily life? How many of the things you do would you be comfortable with your parents or teachers knowing about? What does this tell you about social rules?

Tip

This perspective may be called social action theory, interpretivism or symbolic interactionism depending on the resources you use.

Important interactionist thinkers

William Thomas (1863–1947)

Thomas studied the biographies of Polish people, who had migrated to America, to understand their culture. He later studied crime, taking the viewpoint that crime made sense to the criminal. His main contribution to sociology was that people generally think before they act and thus, their definitions of the situation affected their decision making.

Erving Goffman (1922–1982)

Goffman claimed that each person was like an actor in the drama of his or her own life. People play out roles and behave in the way that is expected for them in that situation, so a person may be a mother in one interaction, but a daughter or a friend in others. In each situation, a different way of behaving would be appropriate.

Principles of Interactionism

```
                    Humans can think
                    for themselves

People form groups                          Thinking is affected
on the basis of                             by other people
shared groups and
understanding

    People may modify                    People learn the
    or change the                        meanings that are
    meanings to suit                     shared by others
    themselves
```

> If men define situations as real, they are real in their consequences.
>
> **William Thomas**

Hollywood films often show people as evil through stereotypes such as scars or smoking. How might this effect our behaviour in real life when we see people with scars or disability?

Activity

Ask people to draw a scientist. How many draw pictures of men despite the fact that many scientists are female?

Sample questions

In 2004, the Welsh Assembly government funded a study of twenty-one teenagers and nine adults (teachers, youth workers and librarians) into Internet usage and the meaning that technology has in the lives of Welsh children. **Ethnographic** research was used in order to provide real-life accounts of everyday use of social media. It found that the mobile phone was central to the lives of all the teenagers involved. They used technology to communicate and to keep in contact with friends, continuing conversations started elsewhere. Technology overlapped with rather than replaced face-to-face contact.

Adapted from http://www.wisekids.org.uk/conferences.htm

a) Using material from the item and sociological knowledge, explain the meaning of the term **ethnographic**.

b) Using material from the item and sociological knowledge, explain **two** reasons why ethnographic research techniques were suitable for this topic of research.

How would you explain this man's appearance? Do others in your group explain it the same way? What does this tell you about how we interpret behaviour?

Check your own learning

Match the words with their meanings.

Meaning	Word
a) A research method based on exploring cultures from the point of view of the subject of the study	Social role
b) The study of small scale social interactions	Ethnography
c) Communication between two or more people	Labelling theory
d) An idea created by society and not objective fact	Micro-sociology
e) Research designed to obtain data about meaning and understanding	Social interaction
f) The expected and normal behaviours for people in any given social situation	Social construction
g) When people attach an idea to a person and then act as though the label was true	Qualitative research

Thinking skills

Using the ideas of interactionism, consider how you decide what to wear when:
- Going to school or college.
- Meeting your friends.
- Preparing for a job interview.

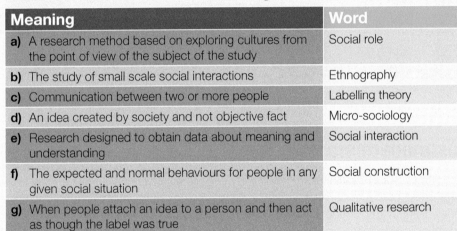

Extended writing

Assess the contribution of interactionist theory to our understanding of society today.

Guidance: Interactionism has given rise to a variety of different approaches to the study and analysis of society. All are concerned with the idea that we create social meaning. Mead, for example, says we develop a sense of self where we see ourselves from the perspective of others in society. Goffman says we 'act' out our place in the world. Becker says people are labelled by others and this influences the way that they see themselves. However, the question demands more than a simple explanation of the basic interactionist theories. You will need to point out the strengths and weaknesses of this perspective for our understanding of modern society, so that requires you to note that it is useful for small-scale analysis but does not explain the structure of society.

Write about 500 words.

Activity

You can read Erving Goffman's famous 1956 study *The Presentation of Self in Everyday Life* online. This is where he explains his theory.

Aims

⊙ **To understand the principles of postmodernism in sociology**

Postmodernism is based on a view of society and its development through different stages: traditional, modern and postmodern. It is the most recent of the sociological perspectives, developing as a reaction to traditional sociology which has tended to see social change as progress, usually towards a single, 'best' form of society. Postmodernism challenges this, arguing that contemporary society is characterised by diversity and choice.

Topic 6: Postmodernism

Getting you thinking

The first image shows a Maori warrior from New Zealand. His facial tattoos tell other Maori about his tribe, history and family. They are an indication of his social status and prestige. They are also religious in meaning and extremely painful to create. What do the tattoos on the young woman tell you about her?

Lady Gaga in her meat dress is postmodern. She is challenging traditional ideas of dress and of food.

Postmodernists

In traditional societies magic or religion were used to provide explanations for the social world. These beliefs were known as meta-narratives (or big stories) that offered people guidance and hope. In modern societies, science and rational thought became the meta-narrative. Sociological theories such as Marxism and functionalism suggested that they had the answers to make the world a better and safer place. Sociologists from each perspective believed that life would be improved in the following ways:

⊙ Functionalism claimed society needed shared values between people.
⊙ Marxists believe that class differences need to be disposed of.
⊙ Feminists believe that men and women should be equal and society free of patriarchy.

However, according to postmodernists, this sort of certainty is inappropriate, there is no absolute truth; knowledge and beliefs are relative. Relativism says there are several versions of reality, not just one. Trust in single explanations has been replaced by questioning and doubts and people can now make their own choices as to what to believe and how to behave.

Modernism and postmodernism

Modernist beliefs	Postmodernism
Society creates order out of chaos; the purpose of sociology is to learn how society works and improve it	People create society as they go along. It is not possible to 'know' society; or how society works as it is not a 'thing'
Knowledge produced by science is the truth	Truth is just another opinion
People follow social rules because it makes good sense to do so	There are no rules, so people choose to do what pleases them
Gender is fixed at birth and based on sex	Gender and sexuality are a matter of personal choice
Theories can offer the answers to the problems of society	Theories are pointless because they all have weaknesses
People tend to belong to one particular belief system such as Marxism or Christianity	People choose what to believe in a 'pick and mix' of different ideas
People gain satisfaction and value from making things	People gain satisfaction from buying things which give them an identity, this is consumerism
Society is constantly improving itself and the world can only get better	Society only changes, things do not improve
People belong to known social groups such as genders or classes	Social groups are fragmented, so people choose their gender or class

Ceci n'est pas une pipe.

Rene Magritte created this image to challenge people's perception of reality. The phrase is 'This is not a pipe', meaning that the picture is not real, but an image. Michel Foucault used this image to discuss the way that reality and image are blurred in contemporary society.

Criticising postmodernism

The most obvious criticism of postmodernism is clear: if knowledge is relative, then postmodernism is no more valid than the theories it criticises. Other problems include:

- The work of postmodernists tends to be descriptive as it cannot be used as the basis of sociological research. Identifying social diversity does not explain it.
- The theory states that there is no theory. This is a contradiction in itself.

Strengths of postmodernism

Postmodernism offers a number of insights into contemporary society:

- It shows that social attitudes are changing as older belief systems have less influence.
- People responding to choices helps explain social change.
- It highlights the impact of the media and consumerism on modern culture.

Recognising postmodernist thinking

Postmodernists tend to think in terms of choice and uncertainty. They emphasise that change is natural to society and that no particular way of life is correct. They discuss the way that people are individualistic, concerned with image and with consumption of products, especially technology and the media. They agree with interactionists that people interpret the world and then develop that idea to say that people construct the reality that suits their needs.

> There are no hard distinctions between what is real and what is unreal, nor between what is true and what is false. A thing is not necessarily either true or false; it can be both true and false.
>
> **Harold Pinter**

Important postmodernist thinkers

Jean Francois Lyotard (1924–1998)

Lyotard claimed that there are no useful meta-narratives in modern society because all of them are too simplistic. Knowledge is no longer a way in which we can be controlled by the powerful because modern technology means we all can access it. Ideas can now be judged on how useful they are, not on their 'truth'.

Jean Baudrillard (1929–2007)

Baudrillard was interested in the media. He said that we are swamped by media images and messages so that all we do is consume. We do not buy products because we like them, we buy them because they give us an identity of some kind. In our society, appearance and image are all we care about because there is no reality to life.

Characteristics of postmodern societies

- People do not have rigid beliefs about morals
- People form groups on the basis of shared understanding
- People have more choices over their lives
- People learn the meanings that are shared by others
- **Postmodernism**
- Consumerism: people buy into an identity
- People are more influenced by the media and technology
- People are more individualistic. They want to be 'different'
- Globalisation means that people are more aware of other cultures

Make a list of different brand names for sportswear, drinks, consumer goods, cars, cosmetics and perfumes, cafes and restaurants, supermarkets and shoes. Go through the brand names and discuss with a study partner what that brand means to you, so for example, what kind of people eat at Wetherspoon's or McDonalds? What products would you need to use to appear rich and successful?

Discussion point

- Is it true that ideas such as right and wrong have no meaning in contemporary society?

Postmodernists believe that there are no rules, so people choose to do what pleases them. What would be the effect on society if people simply did what they felt like doing?

Sample questions

The Valleys was a television show based in Cardiff, broadcast between 2012 and 2014. It followed young people from the South Wales valleys as they moved to Cardiff. According to **postmodernists**, such television shows illustrate how shallow postmodern society is. The characters are presented as real people but in actual fact, they were playing a part because they were on television. They would have quickly been dropped from the show if they had not behaved in a way that made for good television. Participants in shows like this (or *TOWIE, Made in Chelsea*) are treated as stars. When the show ends, they will return to their former lives. Thus, there is very little that is real about reality television.

a) Using material from the item and sociological knowledge, explain the meaning of the term **postmodernist**.

b) Using material from the item and sociological knowledge, explain **two** reasons why some sociologists say that contemporary society is postmodern.

Check your own learning

Match the start and ends of the following sentences:

Start	End
a) Postmodernism is a recent perspective	because people value consumption and image over reality.
b) Consumer society has developed in postmodern society	claim to offer the truth as they say everything is relative.
c) The media are important to postmodern writers as	are leading meaningless lives because all they care about is image.
d) Postmodernists are critical of all theories that	it emerged in France in the 1980s.
e) Baudrillard suggests that people	because they reject the idea that there is anything with meaning.
f) Postmodernists are difficult to understand and to read	they claim contemporary society is swamped with media ideas.

Extended writing

Outline the key features of the postmodernist approach to sociology.

Guidance: Questions referring to theories are usually linked to one of the other topics in the specification. Before you can apply any sociological theory you need to be able to accurately and concisely present its key features. An overview of postmodernism will contrast it with modernist approaches and emphasise increased choice and diversity.

The key features of each theory can be used as a framework for discussing issues connected to that topic, for example the family and how/why it has changed.

Write about 250 words.

Activity

There are a number of video clips explaining postmodernism on YouTube. Watch some in order to develop your understanding.

Aims

- ◉ **To understand the principles of New Right thinking**

The New Right are not generally thought of as being a sociological perspective, though a few sociologists do agree with some of the thinking. It is significant because it is a political viewpoint that has had a massive effect on British politics and social policy since the early 1980s. It builds on functionalist thinking, and argues that taxation is bad for society and that competition and commercial thinking provides choice and efficiency. It is particularly critical of the welfare state and this has implications for almost everyone at one time or another because we all rely on health provision, education, pensions and benefits.

> *Trickle-down theory is the principle that the poor, who must subsist on table scraps dropped by the rich, can best be served by giving the rich bigger meals.*
>
> **William Blum**

The NHS; is it based on collectivist or individualist principles?

Topic 7: The New Right

Getting you thinking

There are areas of poverty and deprivation throughout modern Britain. To what extent do you think that people who live in poor conditions have brought it on themselves by being lazy?

The New Right

This is a conservative and traditional view of society which assumes that capitalism is the best of all possible economic systems. According to the New Right, capitalism is efficient and fair because it is based on competition between people for scarce resources. Only efficient companies, providing goods and services that people want, will thrive and make a profit. Competition and profit make sense because they encourage efficiency. Those who are the best will gain success. Those who fail have failed through some fault of their own.

New Right social policies are particularly associated with the Conservative Party. In 1979, Margaret Thatcher became Prime Minister and prompted massive changes in political thinking that still influence our society. There was a shift away from state support for people (**collectivism**) towards competition and the introduction of competition into the welfare state (**individualism**) such as schools and the NHS. Trickle-down theory suggests that if rich people are allowed to keep more of their earnings, they will spend more and invest in businesses. This makes everyone wealthier because the economy improves and poorer people can go and get jobs. Taxation was reduced so that people who were rich could retain more of their income and spend it as they chose.

All the main parties have been influenced by these ideas: private sector firms built and own many NHS hospitals built under the Labour government of 1997–2010 which also introduced the system that makes claimants for sickness benefits go for health assessments; since 2010 the Conservative/Liberal Democrat Government has cut some child and other benefits, and contracted out public services like probation. Pension ages have been increased. The public mood is critical of those who take benefits.

Criticising the New Right

Some of the ideas of the New Right are contradictory; for example, the basic belief that the state should not interfere in people's lives is contradicted by their insistence on rejecting certain types of family (gay and single parents).

- The New Right tend to blame the victims of inequality for their own problems.
- The New Right believe that people have equal access to the rewards of society. This clearly overlooks the fact that entire social groups may be disadvantaged for reasons beyond their control.
- There is little to suggest that trickle-down theory is correct. Most evidence says it is not.
- The theory has been used to justify media stories that demonise the poor and disadvantaged so there are many stories about welfare cheats but tax dodging by the wealthy is not seen as a problem.

Strengths of the New Right

- This has been enormously influential on government policy.
- This seems to appeal to popular thinking about society.

Recognising New Right thinking

The New Right value ideas such as freedom to choose, competition, market forces and personal responsibility. They will refer to the underclass and lone parent families in critical terms. They see benefits and low wages as an issue and refer to 'problem families'.

Important New Right thinkers

Charles Murray (1943–)

Murray claims that welfare benefits are too generous and create a culture where poor people become dependent on the state. There is an entire underclass of people who are too lazy to work. These people are generally single parent families. He claims that families without fathers lead to a breakdown of public morality and an increase in crime.

Discussion point

- What would happen to British society if all welfare benefits were stopped tomorrow?

Research idea

Find out more about the policies of Margaret Thatcher, Prime Minister 1979–1990.

Activity

Starting at birth and working to eventual old age and death, consider the various ways in which people are being supported by the welfare state.

Can society really be seen as a race where everyone has an equal chance to succeed?

Activity

Look at the website of the New Policy Institute to read research into poverty and society.

www.npi.org.uk

This will be good preparation for your full A level examination.

Activity

Do you think poor people are responsible for their poverty? Make points for and against.

Important New Right thinkers

David Marsland (1939–)

Marsland does not believe that poverty is a problem in Britain. He suggests that universal benefits such as health care and education stop people from being reliant on themselves. People are on low incomes because of their unwillingness to work. Marsland says that sociology is biased against capitalism and ignores the value of work to individuals, overlooking the way that people gain self-esteem from their jobs.

Marsland's starting point is that individuals should take responsibility for themselves and the welfare state should be as small as possible, only supporting those who cannot help themselves.

According to Marsland, the growth of the welfare state in the second half of the 20th century has fostered a 'culture of dependency' which encourages people to seek help and welfare from the state. Most claimants, he says, could rely on their own efforts to support themselves and their families. The welfare state has undermined the value of work to individuals. He believes that services such as education and health care could be more efficiently provided by private sector or voluntary organisations, replacing the taxation funded public sector. By reducing the size of the state, less taxation would be needed; this would leave individuals with more choice and freedom over how to spend their money.

Some forms of taxation in Britain

INCOME TAX

BETTING TAX

VAT

CUSTOM DUTIES ON IMPORTS

CAPITAL GAINS TAX

Sample questions

According to research by the New Policy Institute, nearly a quarter of the population of Wales in 2013 lives in **poverty**. Of those 700,000 people, at least half are from working families. The key issues appear to be that there is low pay and underemployment, where people work fewer hours than is needed to make a good income for their families; 30% of families where one member is in part-time work live in poverty. Only 7% of full-time workers are poor. If people earn less than the living wage of £7.45 an hour, they are likely to be poor.

   a) Summarise the item on **poverty** in Wales.
   b) Using material from the item and sociological knowledge, explain **two** reasons why some sociologists criticise New Right theories.

Check your own learning
Match the word with its meaning.

a)	Allowing the wealthy to keep more of their money means that everyone in a society becomes richer	Conservative Party
b)	A political party that supports traditional values and believes in limited government control over people	Capitalism
c)	A political philosophy that believes in the rights of individuals over the good of society and in low taxation	Welfare state
d)	An economic system based on making profits	Trickle-down theory
e)	The system where the government looks after health and well-being of its citizens	Taxation
f)	Payments made to the government through a variety of methods in order to support its spending on welfare and other priorities	New Right

Extended writing

Outline the key features of the New Right approach to society.

Guidance: An answer to this question should note that the New Right is a political theory rather than a sociological one, though acknowledging the influence it has had on sociology, research and social policy. The emphasis on individualism rather than collectivism can be a useful starting point which can be linked to social policies on education and the family.
Write about 250 words.

Student loans and fees: are these based on individualist or collectivist principles? See page 11 to remind yourself of the terms.

Aims

- To understand that sociologists can use a range of methods to collect information and to recognise the factors that influence their choices

Sociologists are not content to have unsupported opinions; they require evidence to support and justify the claims they make. Collecting evidence involves a wide range of research methods. You need to be aware of the different methods sociologists use to collect evidence, what influences their choice of methods, the advantages and disadvantages of different methods and how sociologists select who to study. There is no such thing as a good or bad research method. The issue is, 'which method is appropriate for this research?'. This question is answered by considering some key concepts that are identified below.

Topic 1: Approaches to social research

Getting you thinking

Helsinki is the world's most honest city say researchers.

A study of honesty in major world cities concluded that the residents of Helsinki are the most honest, with those in Lisbon being the least honest. They conducted a simple social experiment, deliberately 'losing' wallets with plenty of contact details inside. Overall just less than half were returned; the highest proportion were reunited with their owners in Helsinki. The wallets lost in Lisbon were the most likely to stay with the finders.

http://www.rd.com/slideshows/most-honest-cities-lost-wallet-test/

Research findings like this are often the basis of news stories. What do you need to know about the research before deciding how useful it is?

Key concepts

- **Validity:** Data is said to be valid if it is genuine, an accurate reflection of what is being studied. Does the data measure what it claims to measure? **Demographic** data is usually seen as valid; the number of births and deaths officially counted each year in England and Wales is close to the actual figure; few births or deaths go unreported or unrecorded. On the other hand, crime statistics collected by the police represent only some of the crimes committed, many crimes go unreported for a number of reasons; for this reason these figures are not regarded as valid.
- **Reliability:** If a research study is repeated and similar findings recorded, then the data and the method are seen as reliable. Some methods are easier to use in a standardised way than others, with the person collecting the data having less impact on the process. Collecting information using a **questionnaire** is more consistent than if an interview is used, for example; in much the same way that a thermometer measures temperature and it does not matter who is using it.

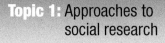

- **Representativeness**: Research is carried out on a small section (or sample) of society; only the Census studies the whole population. When considering the value of the findings of a study, it is important to ask how representative those studied are of the rest of society. If the group is untypical then the findings may be of little value. One criticism that feminists made of research carried out in the 1950s and 1960s was that it often focussed on men, ignoring women and so was unrepresentative of society as a whole.
- **Generalisability**: This is where data obtained from a small group of people can be applied to a whole population. If the data is not representative then it cannot be generalised. Studies of educational attainment that are based solely on boys cannot be generalised to the education system as a whole because they do not include girls.
- **Objectivity**: Although sociologists will investigate issues that they are interested in, the research must be conducted in an impartial and unbiased way. To remain objective means that your personal values and beliefs should not affect how the issue is approached or how the data collected is interpreted.
- **Ethics**: Ethics are issues of right and wrong. In research it is wrong to harm anyone and so steps should be taken to protect people. Sometimes the ethical issues are complex and can affect what research is possible or how the research is carried out. There are professional guidelines to help sociologists.

Research idea

Investigate the highly unethical Tuskeegee study to understand why ethics are important to research.

Approaches to research

Broadly speaking there are two major approaches to research in sociology:

- Those sociologists, who adopt a scientific approach, collecting quantitative data, are known as positivists.
- Interpretivists, who prefer qualitative data, are looking for meanings and emotions in human behaviour.

However, the realist approach suggests that there are strengths and weaknesses to both positivism and interpretivism. Consequently, in practice, sociologists have to be flexible and adopt the approach that works best in the circumstances or a combination of methods.

Famous names

Durkheim

Emile Durkheim developed the positivist approach and showed how scientific method could be applied to the study of social behaviour. He illustrated this with a study of suicide. He used government data to show that that the type of society influenced the amount of suicide that took place.

Positivism

Positivism involves collecting information about social facts, which are aspects of behaviour that can be counted and measured. Examples include the age at which people get married or how many students have enrolled at university. As data is collected, trends and patterns can be identified in these statistics. It may be possible to detect correlations between two sets of information; as more people go to university, what happens to the average age of marriage? Is the relationship consistent? Is there a causal relationship between the social facts or do they just coincide? This mimics the scientific approach and the desire to find laws which explain behaviour in the natural world.

There is a link between cannabis use and schizophrenia, but is this a causal or a non-causal relationship?

This topic has a large vocabulary; you need to be familiar with the relevant terms, many of which can form the basis of an examination question. Answers will be considerably improved if you can make accurate use of the relevant concepts.

Causal and non-causal relationships

A causal relationship is where one specific thing can be said to make another thing happen. For example:

However, not everyone who smokes gets lung cancer and some people who do not smoke also get lung cancer. Thus, a non-causal relationship may look like this:

Interpretivism

This approach prefers to collect detailed accounts in words. This enables the researcher to find out what people's feelings, attitudes and experiences are. Thus, it is qualitative data. Rather than counting how many people go to university, interpretivists would want to know why people go to university, what was university life like. They do not look for causal relationships because they see human behaviour as different from the behaviour of things in the natural world: humans consider what things mean and then decide to act.

Realism

Positivists are sometimes criticised because social research cannot exactly mimic the approach of natural sciences, for example social experiments cannot be set up in the controlled way that laboratory experiments can be. It is clear that humans are **reflexive**; things have meaning for us and we respond to our emotions. However, it is also clear that there are trends and patterns in social behaviour, these can be observed and measured. Realists argue that the best way to proceed is to recognise that both interpretivism and positivism are useful. They select methods that are the most suitable for the issue that is being studied.

Selecting research methods

Sociologists have to decide how they will collect data for their research. The decisions they make will depend on a range of factors including:

- What they wish to find out.
- The topic or issue being studied.
- What information is already available.
- Their preference for quantitative or qualitative data.
- How much time and money they have.

Some of these factors might be connected; for example, a study of crime rates will require quantitative data and the government collects this already, so a starting point will be a **secondary source**. A study of the effects of crime on victims is more likely to require qualitative data; this may be available from earlier studies but it is likely that a researcher would collect their own **primary data**.

Primary data and secondary sources

Sociologists can collect their own information or make use of data collected by others.

◉ Primary data (or primary sources) has been collected by those who are using it; for example, Jan Pahl used interviews to investigate how families made decisions.
◉ Secondary data (or secondary sources) is information collected by others; a common source is statistics collected by the government such as the Census or the British Household Panel survey. Other sources that can be referred to include media content and contemporary letters and diaries.

Quantitative data

Positivists tend to favour quantitative data, counting and measuring aspects of social behaviour. Such data is needed if the researcher is testing a hypothesis which suggests that there is a causal or non-causal relationship between two social variables.

Qualitative data

Interpretivists prefer qualitative data. The key feature of this type of data is the absence of numbers. Rather than measuring and counting, qualitative data attempts to capture how people experience social events and what they mean to them. Answers from interviews or summaries of what has taken place and been said in a group provide descriptive accounts.

Box 1 Quantitative data

In 2013, 49% of 20–24 year olds in the UK lived with their parents, up from 42% in 2008

Young people aged 20–24 living with their parents, UK, 1996–2013

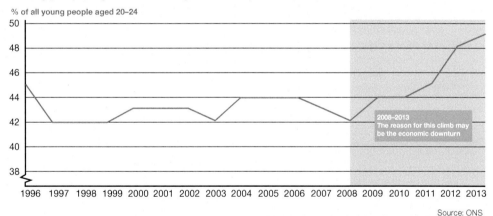

% of all young people aged 20–24

2008–2013
The reason for this climb may be the economic downturn

Source: ONS

Outline the trends shown in the graph.

Box 2 Qualitative data

Understanding the attitudes and experiences of smokers is important if the difficulties that those trying to quit smoking have experienced are to be understood and if effective support is to be given. For this reason a doctor in Canada conducted in-depth interviews with some of his patients, asking them to describe in their own words why they wanted to give up smoking, what attempts they had made and what had helped or hindered them.

http://tobaccocontrol.bmj.com/content/14/6/425.abstract

Can you think of any problems with a study involving a doctor interviewing his own patients about their smoking?

Thinking skills

Triangulation

Breeze (2013) investigated the attitudes of employees and managers about their firm's charity fundraising activities. She collected information from observations of formal staff meetings and informal settings such as coffee breaks. She also conducted interviews with senior staff, who provided the 'official view' of the firm's philanthropic activities as well as acting as gatekeepers to the workforce. Why did she use a variety of methods? How might the information she collected in formal settings differ from what she heard informally?

Triangulation

Frequently, researchers make use of more than one method to collect their data; this often involves using quantitative and qualitative methods for the same study. In this way, different types of data, revealing different things about the research topic, can be compared. For example, observation often reveals what people really do in a social situation; questionnaire or interview answers tell us what people say they do. Each method has its own advantages and disadvantages; reliability is seen as a strength of questionnaire data, whilst observation data can be more valid.

Another advantage of triangulation is that the information found through one method can assist in deciding how to use another. For example, the material collected by a qualitative approach can be used to develop hypotheses for testing against quantitative data. A small-scale study of students using unstructured interviews to investigate their views about tuition fees for higher education can be developed into a questionnaire-based study, using a much larger sample, allowing the findings to be generalised, if the hypothesis is supported.

Sample questions

Parental complaints and OFSTED

During spring 2007 OFSTED (the English school inspectors) undertook a consultation exercise about its plans to respond to parental complaints, under new powers contained in the Education and Inspections Act 2006. Ofsted conducted an online survey, face-to-face meetings with national organisations and commissioned **qualitative research** to gather the views of parents whose circumstances made them harder to reach than others, through group and individual interviews.

http://www.ofsted.gov.uk/resources/parental-complaints-report-consultation-responses

a) With reference to the item and sociological knowledge explain the meaning of the term **qualitative research**.

b) With reference to the item and sociological knowledge explain **two** reasons why some researchers use qualitative methods to collect their data.

Guidance

Your response to part a) should include an accurate definition (AO1) and be supported by relevant examples, one of which should be based on the item (AO2).

Your response to part b) requires two reasons so there is no point in adding a third to your answer, it will not gain you extra marks. Identifying the reasons demonstrates your knowledge (AO1). The reasons you discuss should be supported by relevant examples and it is essential to refer to the item (AO2).

Quantitative researchers would ask about how many people marry and at what age. Qualitative researchers would want to know why people marry and what meaning marriage has in modern society.

Check your own learning

Match the beginnings and ends of the sentences.

a)	Quantitative data	are concerned with what is right or wrong.
b)	Validity	is based on many factors.
c)	The choice of research method	follow scientific methods.
d)	Interpretivists	is favoured by positivists.
e)	Positivists	refers to the accuracy of data.
f)	Ethics	consists of words.
g)	Qualitative data	place an emphasis on meanings.

Extended writing

Discuss the factors that sociologists consider when deciding what research methods to use.

Guidance: In this essay, you should identify the key factors, building on the information above by including examples of real-life research. You will need to show that some of the factors are practical (time, access) and others are more theoretical (positivism, interpretivism). You may also need to refer to realism and the combination of methods in order to increase both reliability and validity.

Write about 500-750 words.

Famous example

Occam's Razor

The principle of Occam's Razor underlies scientific study. It states that 'When you have two competing theories that make exactly the same predictions, the simple one is better'. This then leads scientific sociologists to undertake quantitative research, and reject qualitative.

Research and policy

▶ The UK Census

The Census is a headcount of the entire population of the UK on one night every 10 years. Statistics from the UK Censuses provide a detailed snapshot of the population and its characteristics, and underpin funding allocation to provide public services.

Adapted from http://www.ons.gov.uk/ons/guide-method/census/2011/uk-census/index.html

Census data puts people into categories or groups. How can data from the census be used to plan:

◉ Educational provision?

◉ Health care?

Person 1 - continued

32 Answer the remaining questions for your main job or, if not working, your last main job.
⤷ Your main job is the job in which you usually work (worked) the most hours

33 In your main job, are (were) you
an employee?

39 If you had a job l
If you didn't hav

40 In your main jol
workplace?
⤷ if you work

Aims

⊚ To outline how questionnaires and interviews are used by sociologists to collect primary data

⊚ To consider the advantages and disadvantages associated with them

There are a number of different methods that sociologists can use to collect their primary data. These include:

- Surveys
- Questionnaires
- Interviews
- Focus groups
- Observation.

Many surveys are carried out online: what are advantages and disadvantages of this?

Topic 2: Primary research methods: surveys, questionnaires and interviews

Getting you thinking

Children 'satisfied, yet fear of bullying remains'

Analysis of research into childhood in the UK paints a mixed picture of high satisfaction on the one hand, and fears of bullying and crime on the other. Data compiled by the Office of National Statistics (ONS) finds over three-quarters (77 per cent) of children aged 10–15 are satisfied with their lives. Yet 12 per cent of those aged 10–15 reported being a victim of crime, and 12 per cent said they were frequently bullied.

The ONS used data from the Household Longitudinal Survey and Understanding Society.

http://www.socialscienceforschools.org.uk/the-scoop/2014/The_Scoop_Oct14.aspx

Is this an example of qualitative or quantitative data? Is it primary or secondary data?

Surveys

Strictly speaking a survey isn't a method of collecting data but refers to the study as a whole. The term usually refers to a large-scale quantitative study rather than smaller-scale qualitative research. Data is usually collected by means of questionnaires or structured interviews. Well-known examples in Britain include the British Social Attitudes Survey and the Crime Survey for England and Wales (formerly the British Crime Survey). Each year 3000 people are asked questions about their attitudes to a wide range of social issues; 50,000 people in England and Wales are questioned about their experiences of crime in the previous 12 months.

Questionnaires

A questionnaire is a list of questions, either on paper or, increasingly, online. Paper questionnaires can be distributed in person or through the post. The person completing the questionnaire – the respondent – reads and answers the questions on their own; there is no need for a researcher to be present. In this way a large number of people can be involved relatively quickly and cheaply. Because all respondents answer exactly the same questions, this method is seen as producing reliable data: if the study was repeated by another researcher then similar results could be expected.

Advantages of questionnaires

Most questionnaires require either very short answers or the selection of an answer from a number of options. This makes it is easy to quantify answers and identify any trends or patterns. The method is best suited for collecting information for 'how many' type investigations, that is, those that require quantitative data. It is less useful for studies interested in why people do things as there is limited opportunity for respondents to explain themselves. For positivists the quantitative data collected is useful as it can be used to test hypotheses.

Other advantages of questionnaires:

- They are a relatively quick and cheap way of collecting data.
- Answers to closed questions can usually be quickly and easily quantified.
- Because the researcher doesn't have to be present, a large sample can be studied in a short time.
- Because they are standardised, the reliability of the data is not affected by using different people to administer the questionnaire.
- Because they are usually anonymous, respondents might be more honest.
- With the development of the Internet, researchers are not limited to small geographic areas.
- Revisiting the same sample (longitudinal studies) allows for the identification of change over time.

INTERESTING FACT

Famous longitudinal studies include:

1958 Child Develeopment Study

1970 British Cohort Study

2000 Millenium Cohort Study

See www.cls.ice.ac.uk

Closed questions:

- How many people live in your household?
- What is the highest level of qualification you have? (please circle)

  none / GCSE / A level / degree / higher degree
- How would you rate the food here? (please circle)

  unacceptable / poor / satisfactory / good / excellent

Open questions:

- What do you like about your job?
- What do you think about giving the vote to 16–18 year olds?
- If you could change one thing about this school, what would it be?

Many closed questions offer a choice of answers.

Disadvantages of questionnaires

Most questionnaires rely on closed questions in which the choice of answer has been limited to those selected by the researcher. This could mean that the respondent has to choose an answer that doesn't exactly reflect their thoughts or behaviour. So they pick the least inaccurate option. Certainly they are not answering in their own words. Although questionnaires are seen as a reliable method, this may be at the cost of validity. Of course whether data is valid or not depends to a very large extent on what it aims to measure, so in many circumstances a questionnaire is appropriate.

Other disadvantages of questionnaires:

- Respondents might not understand the questions.
- They do not allow the respondent to explain their answers.
- What the researcher has decided is important may not be important to the respondent.
- Postal questionnaires have a very poor response rate, and this affects the quality of the sample and the ability to generalise from the findings. Similarly, if questionnaires are left for respondents to complete at their leisure, many go unreturned.
- We can't be sure that everyone interprets questions and the options with closed questions in the same way; for example, one person's 'satisfactory' might be another respondent's 'poor'.
- Creating a good quality questionnaire is difficult. Often researchers will use a **pilot study** to check that the questions are understood by respondents and help collect relevant information.
- Respondents may not tell the truth, especially if it is a sensitive topic.

Interviews

Interviews can be structured, semi-structured or unstructured (this last is also known as 'in-depth'). A **structured interview** is basically a questionnaire with the questions read out and the answers recorded by the interviewer. **Unstructured interviews** are more like a conversation, with the questions and answers not following any fixed, pre-determined path. Semi-structured interviews are somewhere between the questionnaire and conversation extremes.

One advantage of interviews is their flexibility, not only are there different types of interview, it is easier to include a mixture of closed and **open-ended questions** allowing both quantitative and qualitative data to be collected.

Structured interviews

This involves the interviewer asking all of the respondents exactly the same questions in the same way. This type of interview is chiefly used to collect quantitative data.

Advantages:

- One obvious advantage of structured interviews over questionnaires is that if the respondent is unsure about something, perhaps the language in a question, the interviewer can explain things.
- The standardised approach helps make the data reliable.
- Data can be collected more quickly this way than using other interview methods.
- The presence of the researcher can improve response rates.

Disadvantages:

- It is more time consuming than a questionnaire.
- The presence of the interviewer might result in **interviewer bias**, and respondents may give socially accepted answers rather telling the truth.
- A rigid interview schedule can limit the opportunity for the respondent to explain or discuss their answers.

Unstructured interviews

Also known as 'in depth' interviews, this type has very little structure at all. The interview is more like a conversation, concentrating on a limited number of topics or questions. As the interview proceeds, questions can be asked to follow up earlier responses. Unstructured interviews are used when the researcher requires qualitative data.

Advantages:

⊙ The absence of a tightly defined schedule allows a discussion to develop and this can allow the interview to explore issues in great detail.
⊙ The more 'natural' setting can encourage more openness and honesty, resulting in more valid data.
⊙ The respondent is able to answer in their own words.
⊙ Because of their face-to-face nature, the interviewer might be able to notice if the respondent is telling the truth or not. The body language of the respondent can be observed.
⊙ As the answers are not restricted to a sheet of paper, interviews are more likely to use open-ended questions and allow respondents to elaborate their views and feelings.

Disadvantages:

⊙ Unstructured interviews are very time consuming to conduct and so smaller samples are usually studied.
⊙ The interviewer has to be highly skilled.
⊙ Analysing the information collected is more complicated and subjective.
⊙ As each interview will be different, the data can be less reliable.
⊙ Interviewer bias: the answers that respondents give can be influenced by the interviewer. Respondents may want to please the interviewer and so they give what they think is the 'correct', socially acceptable answer, rather than say what they really think or do.
⊙ A related problem is the way that the ethnicity, age, or sex of the respondent and interviewer can affect the relationship and thus the answers that are given.

> ### Examples of qualitative data from unstructured interviews:
>
> Interviewer: 'So you pack your suitcase on the day of your 18th birthday and you're off?'
>
> Nicola: 'Yeah. That's very simply what it is'
> (20-year-old woman, Liverpool)
>
> David described his feelings at the suddenness of his move out of care:
>
> 'It's like they tricked me. They didn't even tell me where I was going. They just put my stuff in a case and took me there.'
> (David, 19 year old, London)
>
> http://www.barnardos.org.uk/someone_to_care_final_feb2014.pdf

Semi-structured interviews

These have less flexibility than unstructured interviews and less rigidity than structured interviews. Semi-structured interviews usually consist of a series of open-ended questions linked to the issues the researcher wants to cover and are sometimes also called focussed interviews. This type of interview shares some of the advantages and disadvantages of the other methods.

Advantages:

⊙ Falling between the structured and unstructured interviews, they avoid some of the disadvantages associated with them.

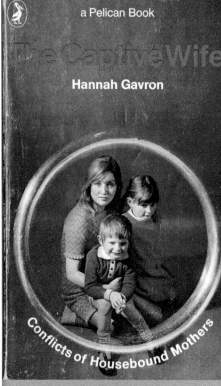

a Pelican Book

The Captive Wife

Hannah Gavron

Conflicts of Housebound Mothers

Gavron's research was based on interviews with young mothers and it was an influential study when published. Along with work by other writers such as Oakley, it helped establish feminism as an important part of sociology.

Discussion point

● The Hawthorne Effect (see page 73) is when people's behaviour is affected by the fact they are being studied. How might this influence the results of interviews?

- The use of open-ended questions gives opportunities for the interviewer and respondent to discuss topics in detail, qualitative data can be obtained.
- The researcher is able to prompt or encourage the respondent to give fuller answers.
- The interviewer can follow up issues that are mentioned by the respondent, so research is not confined to what the researcher thought in advance would be important.

Disadvantages:

- Falling between the structured and unstructured interviews, they don't have all the advantages associated with them.
- The interviews are not standardised so the data may be less reliable.
- Interviewer bias might be a problem.
- Can be expensive and time-consuming.

Focus groups

Focus groups can be seen as a development of the interview approach which has been adopted by sociologists from the field of consumer research. A group of people will be encouraged to discuss an issue, with a researcher acting as a moderator or facilitator helping to keep the discussion on topic and to encourage all members of the group to participate. The discussion is usually recorded so the distraction of note-taking is avoided. The conversational setting is seen as more naturalistic than a one-to-one interview and responses can be more wide-ranging. This approach collects qualitative data.

Advantages:

- The views and opinions of group members can be explored in some detail.
- A group discussion can be more informative and revealing.
- A focus group is useful when it is a group and their views that are being studied.
- It collects information from several respondents more quickly and therefore more cheaply than using interviews.
- The group members can influence the discussion, perhaps introducing ideas that the researcher had not considered.

Disadvantages:

- The group moderator needs to be highly skilled to keep the discussion focussed and to prevent it being dominated by forceful participants.

- Some participants may not feel able to share their views in a group setting.
- As small numbers are studied, the results are unlikely to be representative.
- As each focus group is unique, the results are unlikely to be reliable.
- A dominant group member might influence the contributions of others, reducing the validity of the data.
- As with other qualitative methods, it can be difficult to analyse the data that is collected.

New technologies and research

Many companies and research organisations gather quantitative data online; one of the largest such organisations is SurveyMonkey https://www.surveymonkey.com and some groups will actually pay participants for filling in surveys for marketing purposes.

There are many sources of data and research available in the UK. The largest is possibly the ONS or government website www.ons.gov.uk. However, a range of other websites exists such as the UK Data Archive http://data-archive.ac.uk/home, the Economic and Social Research Council www.esrc.ac.uk and the UK Data Service http://ukdataservice.ac.uk You might want to think about the effect of new technologies on how research data can be gathered and stored.

Sample questions

In late 2013, Barnardo's carried out qualitative research to understand more about the most vulnerable care leavers and the support provided to offer them the best help with making the transition to adulthood.

The research was based on **in-depth interviews** and **focus groups** with 62 young people, plus the workers supporting them in 15 services, and investigated the challenges faced by care leavers as they make the transition to adult life.

http://www.barnardos.org.uk/what_we_do/policy_research_unit/research_and_
publications/on-my-own

a) With reference to the item and sociological knowledge explain what is meant by **focus groups**.
b) With reference to the item and sociological knowledge assess the usefulness of **in-depth interviews** as a research method.

Check your own learning

Fill in the missing words:

a) Those who answer questions asked in an interview are termed _ _ _ _ _ _ _ _ _ _ .

b) If the study can be repeated and similar results collected,
it is said to be _ _ _ _ _ _ _ _ .

c) The impact of the person asking the questions is known as _ _ _ _ _ _ _ _ _ _ _
_ _ _ _ .

d) Questionnaires can use _ _ _ _ and _ _ _ _ _ _ questions.

e) _ _ _ _ _   _ _ _ _ is said to be truthful.

f) Unstructured and structured are two types of _ _ _ _ _ _ _ _ _ _ .

reliable   valid data   respondents   open

interviewer bias   interview   closed

Extended writing

To investigate what factors influenced examination success, the Scottish government researchers used a questionnaire to collect information from students. One of the questions was 'how much time do you spend doing homework in a normal week: less than 1 hour / 1 or 2 hours / 3 or 4 hours / 5 or more hours?'

http://www.scotland.gov.uk/
publications/2006/06/
29141936/13

With reference to the item and sociological knowledge assess the strengths and weaknesses of questionnaires as a research method.

Guidance: An otherwise excellent answer that does not refer to the item will not gain full marks. The discussion of the strengths and weaknesses should make use of the key concepts such as reliability, validity and so on. In this way you can demonstrate your knowledge (A01); relating this to the item and to other examples from your studies shows your ability to apply knowledge (A02) and assess the strengths and weaknesses involves evaluation (A03).

Write about 500-750 words.

Aims

- To explain why researchers make use of observational methods to collect their data

- To consider the advantages and disadvantages of the different techniques that can be used

Key terms

Covert research – is when the study group does not know they are being studied.

Overt research – is open and known about.

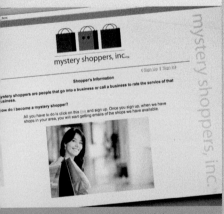

A commercial application of the covert participant observation method.

Topic 3: Primary research methods: observations

Getting you thinking

Anja Declercq (2000) spent several months as an observer, investigating how different nursing homes develop their care for residents suffering from dementia. Although she had permission from the management of the homes to conduct the research, some of the staff had suspicions about the purpose of her presence and this may have affected what information she was given. At times she found the dementia upsetting and this too may have affected the data collected.

Why might the staff have been suspicious about the presence of an observer? What impact could the presence of an observer have on the behaviour of the staff? How could the researcher's emotional reaction affect the data collected?

Observation

A problem common to all the methods that involve asking questions is that respondents may not always tell the truth – they may give the answers they feel are expected of them. To know how people actually behave it may be more useful to watch them, hence the use of observation to collect data.

Observation involves the researcher watching a group's behaviour in their usual setting. There are two types of **observation** used in social research, **participant** and **non-participant**. In addition, each can also be used openly (**overtly**) or secretly (**covertly**). The methods that involve a researcher immersing him or herself into a group and its culture are sometimes termed **ethnography**. Ethnographic studies are often rich in descriptive detail whilst lacking quantitative data. Observation is typically used by interpretivists, who seek to understand how people experience and make sense of the world around them.

Non-participant observation

Non-participant observation involves the researcher being with a group, but not being a part of it. If quantitative data is required then non-participant observation will be preferred over participant observation. This enables the researcher to observe and count instances of the behaviour they are interested in.

Participant observation

Sociologists using participant observation become, as far as possible, a member of the group being studied. This method is an example of ethnography, the collection of detailed accounts of a group's usual behaviour. The researcher joins in the activities of the group and, by sharing their experiences, is able to understand the social world from their point of view. For example, a number of studies of schools have been based on the sociologist joining the school as a teacher. The researcher has to decide whether or not to reveal their presence to the group. By remaining a covert observer then the Hawthorne Effect can be avoided (see p73).

Advantages of covert participant observation:

- One advantage of using covert participant observation is that it enables sociologists to study otherwise hard to reach groups, those who might not co-operate with overt research. Detailed qualitative data can be obtained revealing more about why people behave the way they do and what it means to them.
- If the group behaves normally then the resulting data will be valid.
- Observation often involves sitting back and letting things take their usual course and can be very effective. In one of the most influential participant observation studies, *Street Corner Society*, Whyte stated, 'As I sat and listened I learnt the answers to the questions that I would not have had the sense to ask.'
- The data records what actually happens as the method does not rely on the respondents answering questions honestly.

Problems of covert participant observation:

- A practical problem for researchers using participant observation is that the researcher has to rely on their memory of events and who said what. This is likely to be influenced by what they think is important; when the point of research is to understand things from the point of view of those being studied, there is an inevitable tension, if not contradiction. If there is a delay before notes can be written up, how can we be sure that the recollection is accurate?
- With hard to reach groups there is the practical problem of gaining access to the group: how can an outsider get into the group without revealing their purpose? One approach is gain the trust and 'sponsorship' of a key individual, a gatekeeper. The gatekeeper then is aware of the researcher. However, the gatekeeper might find it difficult to behave normally.
- Once established within a group, the researcher has to be careful not to draw too much attention to him or herself or to interfere with the normal behaviour of the group. This is all part of the process of gaining trust and it can be a lengthy process.
- Covert research raises significant ethical issues, especially those of consent and deception. The researcher may have to decide what to do if the group is behaving illegally or immorally.
- If the group being studied is unaware of the research, there is an issue of safety of the researcher, especially if the group concerned is involved in illegal behaviour.
- There is a danger of 'going native', i.e. losing objectivity and starting to identify with the group under study.

A GLASGOW GANG OBSERVED
JAMES PATRICK

Developing understanding

For a view of life in an asylum based on Ken Kesey's experience of working in a mental hospital, watch the film *One Flew over the Cuckoo's Nest* or read Ken Kesey's book of the same name.

Thinking skills

Goffman's study of a mental health hospital, *Asylums* (1961) was based on covert participant observation. Most of the staff and all of the patients knew Goffman as a PE assistant. He wanted to know what was really going on and how the patients responded to their 'mentally ill' label. What ethical issues are raised here? Could he have used another method for his research?

Advantages of overt participant observation:

⦿ The ethical issues of deception and obtaining consent are resolved.
⦿ The researcher can ask questions openly without the fear of 'giving the game away'.
⦿ Record making and note-taking is easier, making the data more accurate.

Disadvantages of overt participant observation

⦿ The Hawthorne Effect is more likely to occur if the group is aware of the presence and purpose of the researcher.
⦿ The question of how far the researcher should become involved, especially in deviant activity, remains.

Advantages of overt non-participant observation:

⦿ It is easier to make a record of what is happening, especially if the group knows they are being observed.
⦿ The ethical issues of deception and obtaining consent are resolved.
⦿ The researcher can ask questions openly without the fear of 'giving the game away'.
⦿ This method allows the collection of quantitative data as well as qualitative data.
⦿ The researcher is not likely to be involved in behaving illegally.

Problems with overt non-participant observation:

⦿ In everyday life we do not expect those we are with to be taking notes or recording events. This affects the usefulness of overt research, as the Hawthorne Effect has an impact.
⦿ By remaining on the edge of a group, not joining in, then the researcher is not fully experiencing their life. This might undermine the aim of the research.

INTERESTING FACT

Barker's (1984) study of the Unification Church, or Moonies, took several years. It involved a number of methods so is an example of triangulation. In addition to questionnaires and interviews she attended many Moonie events as a non-participant observer.

One-way glass at the back of the room, or remote monitored cameras, allows observation to be unobtrusive. What are the advantages and disadvantages of this as a method? Remember that ethics may be an important issue.

Thinking skills

List the practical problems a participant observer would face when studying one of the following:
⦿ A nursery class.
⦿ Staff in a large department store.
⦿ Life in a travelling circus.

Problems of observation in general:

⊙ Observational studies are very dependent on the researcher and as such each study is unique and so difficult to replicate. The advantage of validity is accompanied by questions about the reliability of the data.

⊙ It can be difficult for the observer to remain detached and objective; their own feelings can affect how they interpret what they see.

⊙ The information might be rich and detailed but how far can the findings be generalised to the rest of society? Are the findings representative?

Sample questions

James Patrick's study of a Glasgow gang was conducted using covert participant observation. He was introduced to the gang by a key member but the rest of the gang did not know that Patrick was studying them, raising important **ethical issues**, as he was expected to take part in illegal activities and did not let the gang know he was a researcher. He hid his true identity so that the gang would not know who he was and then track him down.

   a) With reference to the item and sociological knowledge explain the meaning of the term **ethical issues**.

   b) Using material from the item and sociological knowledge, explain **two** possible reasons why the researcher chose to use covert participant observation.

   c) Explain **two** weaknesses of participant observation as a research method.

   d) With reference to sociological studies, discuss the strengths and weaknesses of qualitative methods in sociological research.

Extended writing

Declercq conducted observation in nursing homes, investigating the care of elderly people. She highlighted the problem of remaining objective: 'Obviously, I liked some staff members better than others. And some of them liked me better than others. I preferred the way some nurses or nursing assistants interact with the residents to the way others do. But I had to keep silent and not show that I was annoyed so as not to have an impact on the way the people I observed, behaved. Nevertheless, my observations are bound to be influenced by what I felt. I might have seen and heard things differently because of positive or negative feelings.'

    Anja Declercq '(Participant) Observation in Nursing Home Wards for People Suffering from Dementia: The Problems of Trust and Emotional Involvement'

With reference to the item and sociological knowledge, discuss the advantages and disadvantages of participant observation as a research method.

Guidance: An otherwise excellent answer that does not refer to the item will not gain full marks. The discussion of the strengths and weaknesses should make use of the key concepts such as objectivity, generalisability, validity and ethics. In this way you can demonstrate your knowledge (AO1); relating this to the item and to other examples from your studies shows your ability to apply knowledge (AO2) and assessing the advantages and disadvantages involves evaluation (AO3).

Write about 500-750 words.

The Hawthorne Effect

The Hawthorne Effect is when people behave differently if they know that they are being studied. Think about what happens in school if there are inspectors visiting. This affects the validity of the data collected. Some researchers argue that if a study lasts long enough a relationship of trust is created and over time everyone behaves more or less 'naturally'. In some circumstances, though, sociologists decide to hide the fact that they are doing research. This raises **ethical issues**.

Check your own learning

Complete the following:

1. The Hawthorne Effect means

_____

_____

2. Covert observation means

_____

_____

3. Participant observers

_____

_____

4. The best type of observation for quantitative data is

_____

_____

5. Access to a group can be obtained through a

_____

_____

Summarise the advantages and disadvantages associated with each primary research method on small cards. For AS, you generally require at least **two** strengths and **two** weaknesses, which you should be able to develop and explain with examples and using the key terminology of Topic 1 in this section.

Aims

◉ **To explain why sociologists make use of secondary sources and to outline the advantages and disadvantages of doing so**

Sociological research often starts with a review of existing information; some research may be based entirely on material that has been collected by others. Such information is known as secondary data. Secondary data can be broadly classed under three headings; existing sociological research, **official statistics** and finally personal documents and media accounts. Most research begins with a review of existing research findings about a topic and some studies rely on secondary data alone as evidence.

An important part of any research is the literature review.

Topic 4: Secondary sources

Getting you thinking

Guy Lansley analysed the answers to 'What is your main language?', one of the questions on the 2011 Census. The data showed almost 100 verbally spoken languages with 4.1m people reporting a main language other than English or Welsh. In London alone more than 80 languages are spoken. Other findings included:

◉ 1.7m recorded a language other than English as their main language in London.
◉ Just over 690,000 people used a European language which wasn't one of British origin as their main language.
◉ Polish speakers numbered almost 150,000.
◉ More than half a million identified a south Asian language as their main language; 100,000 identified an East Asian language.
◉ Over 130,000 people identified their main language as one native to Africa.

http://www.theguardian.com/news/datablog/2013/oct/18/census-2011-england-wales-diversity-languages-map

Why would the researcher have used the census for this investigation, instead of collecting his own primary data?

What are secondary sources?

Secondary sources is the name given to any research used by a study that was not created for the study and which came from the work of another researcher. Thus, the original author creates primary data, but other people who use the same information are using secondary sources and should credit the original writer in their work.

Why use secondary sources?

There are practical reasons for using secondary sources.

◉ Before collecting their own, new data, it makes sense for researchers to be aware of what information already exists. A **literature review** will indicate what sorts of questions have already been asked about a topic and any aspects that have been controversial or influential on the subject of debate.

- Time and money can be saved if the information needed already exists, and in the case of official statistics there may be more information available than a sociologist could collect.
- If a study is concerned with social change, and comparing contemporary society with the past, then it is inevitable that existing sources have to be explored.

Problems with secondary sources

Secondary sources are not without their problems, though. It is unlikely that the data was collected with sociological research in mind and there can be issues of validity, reliability and representativeness.

Existing sociological research

An important part of research is the literature review. This is an appraisal of existing research into a topic; it includes a summary of what is already known, as well as highlighting areas of debate or gaps in knowledge. As part of this review, the relationship between different sociological theories and the evidence that has been collected can be examined. The methods used in the initial research can be assessed and the quality of evidence considered in terms of its reliability and validity. An important question is how up-to-date the information is, older material may not be relevant. This then sets the context for new research, as the new research will comment on what is already known.

Official statistics

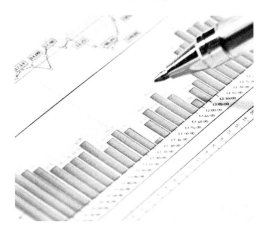

Official statistics are probably the most widely used secondary source in sociological research. They are most likely to be used by positivists; the approach to research that prefers quantitative data. The advantages of using official statistics include:

- Availability. Governments and other public bodies collect and publish vast amounts of freely available data about the population and events within society. The Census in the UK is the single biggest example; every 10 years there is a survey that goes beyond a head count to collect information about family and household structure, housing quality, education and health. So much information is collected that the official publication of it takes several years. Other important official statistics are produced more frequently about births and deaths, crime, work and unemployment, health and social care.
- Identification of trends and patterns. Because official statistics have been collected for many years then it is possible for sociologists and others to identify change in society. For example, the Census helps sociologists understand more about family and household structures and how they have changed over time. Marriage and divorce statistics can be examined in the light of legal changes.
- The capacity to make international comparisons. Sociologists often look beyond and across national boundaries: are changes in the UK reflected elsewhere in the world? Does the employment status of women vary from country to country? Official statistics are the obvious starting point for such comparative studies. Famously, Durkheim's study of suicide started with official statistics from across Europe.

Thinking skills

Researchers usually conduct a literature review before conducting research. Explain two possible reasons why they would need to do this.

Research idea

How could you use the personal advertisements in newspapers to research gender or dating behaviour in modern society? Discuss ideas with your study partners.

Problems with official statistics

However, official statistics do have some limitations:

- The data has not been collected with sociological research in mind. This could lead to practical problems in using data. The categories used in the official statistics may not correspond with those the sociologist is interested in.
- The way that the statistics are collected changes over time. The categories used and their definitions can be modified. For example, the way that the Registrar General places different occupations into different social classes has altered a number of times. This makes it very difficult to compare contemporary statistics with the past.
- Those responsible for compiling the statistics may not work in a uniform way; this affects the reliability and validity of the data. For example, what is counted as an 'unauthorised absence' may vary from school to school. We know that many crimes that are reported to the police are not recorded.
- Although some official statistics might be both reliable and valid (most demographic data for example), they do not tell us why something happened, they only record how many. For example, we know from official statistics how many divorces there have been, but we do not know why the marriages have ended.

Thinking skills

Many crimes are not reported to the police. What reasons can you suggest for this? What does this mean for sociological explanations of crime that are based on the official crime statistics?

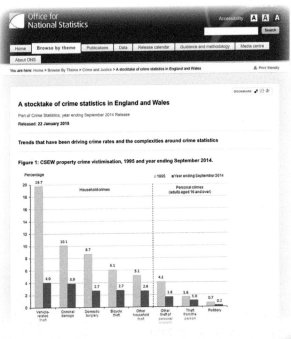

Personal documents

Some personal documents have been used by sociologists to gain insights into everyday life. They analyse documents such as diaries and letters to try and understand the meanings and motives of people. This type of material is qualitative and often richly detailed, showing how events and changes in society were perceived by those experiencing them. The advantage of this is the availability of the material, especially if the research is investigating events that took place several years ago. There are difficulties in asking someone during an interview or in a questionnaire about their feelings 40 or 50 years ago; if you have access to diaries or letters contemporary to the events then the information is more likely to be valid. However, such data is inevitably unrepresentative of the population as a whole. Not everybody writes or keeps letters or diaries; the nature of what is written can be also be affected by the intended audience, if any. Would letters to parents contain the same accounts of events as letters sent to friends?

A more systematic approach to personal documents is that of mass observation. This began in the 1930s when a panel of volunteer writers was enrolled to record their observations of everyday life. This continued through the Second World War and into the 1950s. The Mass Observation Project (MOP) was re-established in 1981 and each year volunteers contribute responses to a list of open-ended questions sent out by the project covering both personal and social issues. The MOP archive is now a major resource for social investigators.

The mass media

The mass media are a secondary source but some studies using the mass media produce primary data, for example content analysis comparing the coverage of men's and women's sport. This would be an example of quantitative data. Such an approach is fairly straightforward, and the data produced is reliable, but simply measuring how much airtime or how many column inches are devoted to a subject does not tell us much about the nature of the content. More complicated are studies of the mass media and their content that are more qualitative in approach, what does the content mean or signify? This requires more interpretation by the researcher and conclusions may be more subjective.

The content of newspapers, especially the 'letters' page, might give insights to public opinion, identifying what issues were arousing feelings and the range of views on those topics. However, not everyone writes to newspapers; the letter writers may not be a representative sample of the public. There is also a process of editorial selection taking place.

Sample questions

Selwyn and Nandy used **secondary data** from the 2011 Census to examine informal care within families, especially the extent to which the extended family provided care to relatives. This was possible as the Census included a question on the relationships of household members. Their analysis showed some regional differences and differences between ethnic groups in the extent to which children lived with relatives other than their parents.

a) With reference to the item and sociological knowledge explain the meaning of the term **secondary data**.
b) Using material from the item and sociological knowledge, explain **two** possible reasons why the researchers decided to use secondary data in their research.
c) Explain **two** weaknesses of using official statistics.
d) With reference to sociological studies, discuss the advantages and disadvantages of using secondary sources in sociological research.

Check your own learning

a) List three types of secondary sources that sociologists might use.
b) Define 'literature review'.
c) List the advantages and disadvantages of using official statistics in sociological research.

Extended writing

Police fix crime statistics to meet targets, MPs told
The pressure to meet targets is affecting the way that police forces record crime, a committee of MPs was told. An officer from the Metropolitan Police claimed that rape and sexual offences were being under-reported by as much as a quarter. Burglaries were recorded as the less serious offence of criminal damage. His evidence was similar to that given by a former West Midlands Chief Inspector describing practices such as recording thefts as 'lost property'.
Adapted from http://www.bbc.co.uk/news/uk-25002927

With reference to the item and to sociological studies discuss the value of official statistics as a source of information.
Guidance: Your answer to this question should demonstrate that you understand the debate in sociology about the reliability and validity of official statistics. You need to offer relevant examples and correctly use sociological terminology. A range of advantages and disadvantages should be identified and discussed, including practical and theoretical issues.
Write about 500-750 words.

Research idea

The Mass Observation Archive specialises in material about everyday life in Britain. It contains papers generated by the original Mass Observation social research organisation (1937 to early 1950s), and newer material collected continuously since 1981. Find out more by looking at their website:

http://www.massobs.org.uk/index.htm

STRETCH and CHALLENGE

Look at the online editions of newspapers and the readers' comments that accompany some stories. How useful are the comments as an indicator of public opinion? Will sociologists of the future make use of this source?

Aims

- To identify and outline the key features of the sampling methods that sociologists can make use of

- To understand the differences between the various methods and be able to explain why a particular method has been used by sociologists

- To be able to identify which methods are likely to result in data that can be generalised to the target population

It is very rarely the case that researchers are able to make contact with all members of the target population (the social group that they are interested in); consequently only some members of the population are studied, this is known as the sample. When choosing a sample, the aim is to select a representative sample, that is, a sample with the same characteristics as the population as a whole. If your sample is representative then it is reasonable to generalise your results. This is exactly the same assumption that is made when a small blood sample is used to diagnose infections or when manufacturers sample items from the production line.

Topic 5: Sampling and sampling methods

Getting you thinking

If researchers investigating young people's participation in sport issued questionnaires to pupils at a number of fee paying schools, what impact would this have on the value of the data collected?

Discuss this with a study partner. If you were to repeat the study, how would you do it differently?

What sampling methods are available?

There are a number of sampling methods (or techniques) that sociologists can use, some are more likely to provide a representative sample than others.

Representative samples:

- Random sample
- Stratified sample
- Quota sample
- Systematic sample.

Non-representative samples:

- Snowball sample
- Volunteer/self-selecting sample
- Purposive and opportunity sample.

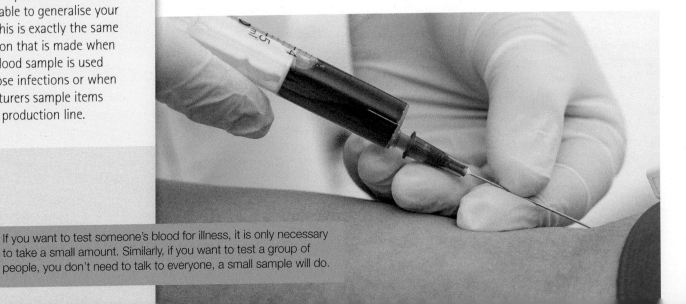

If you want to test someone's blood for illness, it is only necessary to take a small amount. Similarly, if you want to test a group of people, you don't need to talk to everyone, a small sample will do.

Sample frame

The representative sampling methods usually start off with a **sampling frame**; this is a list of all the members of the target population. This might be the register in a school, the details of club members or the electoral register. From this list the participants are picked, they are identified by name.

Random sample

This method is also known as a simple random sample. If this method is being used then each member of the target population has exactly the same chance of being picked; this resembles the numbers being picked in a lottery. A simple method would be to take names from a hat, more sophisticated ways involve computer generated random numbers. Despite the apparent fairness of this method there is the possibility that the sample may not be

representative, for example if taking a random sample inside a school this method could produce a sample that is disproportionately male or female.

Stratified sample

This way of selecting a sample avoids the problem above. Instead of having one sample from the target population as a whole, the population is divided up and then each section is sampled. Thus it can be ensured that the correct proportions of, say males and females, are selected. A sample frame is still used, but it needs to be one that includes the relevant information about the population's characteristics.

Quota sample

This is similar to stratified sampling but it does not require a sample frame. Instead of named individuals being identified for the sample, the researcher calculates how many people from each group are required. The researcher approaches people who match the characteristics, e.g. 20 males aged under 40, until the 'quota' is filled. This is the method used by market researchers who collect data in public places like shopping centres.

Systematic sampling

Systematic sampling, or systematic random sampling, involves having a systematic approach to selecting participants; for example every 10th name on a list or every 5th house in the street. This is clearly not random as not everyone has an equal chance of being selected, but it is seen as a fair way of proceeding.

Snowball sampling

For some research topics there will not be an easily available sample frame which leads to respondents. In these cases a researcher may rely on a gatekeeper to gain access to a group. This gatekeeper then introduces the researcher to another person and from there

Random samples resemble a raffle or a lottery in that everyone has an equal chance of taking part, or winning.

Remember that sampling is not a method. It is part of the process of research design.

Thinking skills

You have been asked to collect information about how staff and students travel to your school or college. Outline how you would collect:

- ⊙ A random sample
- ⊙ A quota sample
- ⊙ A stratified sample.

the snowball starts to roll and get bigger. Hard to reach groups or those who wish to avoid attention might be approached in this way. This method is not random and the sample is unlikely to be representative.

Volunteer sample

In the absence of a sample frame another approach is to invite people to volunteer for the research. Such self-selecting samples are very unlikely to be representative of the target population, only those with a strong interest are likely to come forward to take part. With the development of online research and software that is widely available, more studies, especially those undertaken by students, make use of volunteer samples. This can be seen as an example of opportunity or purposive sampling.

Purposive sampling

When a researcher has limited time and/or there is no sampling frame available, they might simply set out to find people with characteristics that are relevant to the purpose of the study. This saves time in approaching those who are unsuitable but it will not be a representative sample.

Opportunity sampling

The method is also known as convenience sampling. The sample is made up of those who are readily available, willing to take part and suitable for the aim of the research. It is the method most likely to be used by students who lack the time and resources available to professional researchers.

Extended writing

This message was posted on the mumsnet website.

Questionnaire for uni work on working mothers and housework

Hi,

I am doing a research project on the 'double shift' theory. Where its believed that the woman does two shifts in regard her paid job and then maintenance of home and children.

I am looking for married mums and co-habiting mums that work who are able to get this questionnaire back to me quickly. Doesn't matter how many hours you work just as long as you work and live with a partner/husband.

http://www.netmums.com/coffeehouse/working-childcare-692/working-689/560234-questionnaire-uni-work-working-mothers-housework.html

With reference to the item and sociological studies explain the importance of sampling methods in sociological research.

Guidance: This question requires you to show understanding of one of the key stages in planning and carrying out research. The size and nature of the sample can have important implications for the quality and value of the data collected. Representative studies are generally regarded as being more useful than those based on **non-representative sampling**. Your answer should include relevant examples and make accurate use of appropriate terminology.

Write about 500-750 words.

Check your own learning
Match the word with its meaning.

a)	This is a list of all the people in in the target population	Opportunity sample
b)	This sample is one which shares the same characteristics of the population under study	Quota sample
c)	The researcher studies whoever is willing and available to take part in the study	Representative sample
d)	A sampling frame can be sub-divided and then a sample is taken from each sub-group	Random sample
e)	This is used when there is no sampling frame available	Sampling frame
f)	This sample is where every member of the target population has the same chance of being selected	Stratified samples

Sample questions

Pupils' approaches to subject option choices

The study of subject choices was conducted in two stages. Initially a questionnaire was used to collect data from pupils at 12 schools. The second stage was based on interviews with a **stratified sample** of 144 pupils from four of the schools in the initial survey.

Adapted from http://www.esrc.ac.uk/my-esrc/grants/R000221661/read

a) With reference to the item and sociological knowledge explain what is meant by a **stratified sample**.

b) With reference to the item and sociological knowledge, explain **two** possible reasons why the researchers decided to use a stratified sample in their research.

Activity

You are researching lifestyles for the local health centre. Identify the sampling methods outlined below:

1. Choosing every 10th name on the doctor's list.

2. Numbering every patient and selecting 100 names.

3. Interview every patient who visits the health centre on the first Monday of the month.

4. Put a poster up in the health centre asking for volunteers.

5. Divide the patient list up into groups of males and females of different age groups; then sample from each group.

The purpose of representative sampling is to create representative and generalisable data for analysis. Why is this a strength of quantitative research?

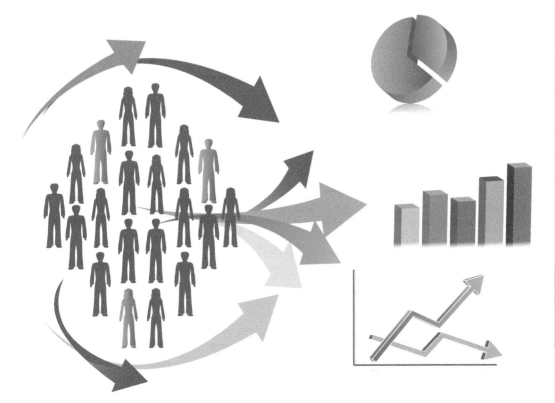

Aims

⦿ **To identify and explain the ethical issues considered when conducting sociological research**

Until 1947, there were no guidelines governing research on people. However, as a result of a variety of cases where people have been injured or harmed by medical research, there are now strict rules governing all research which could possibly harm participants. These rules vary slightly from country to country and also according to disciplines, but they are designed to protect people from researchers. The rules are strict, and if they are broken then people may lose their right to do research. No research should be undertaken without reference to an ethics committee whose job it is to look at possible dangers.

Topic 6: Ethics in sociological research

Getting you thinking

At some point in new drug development researchers have to test the effects of the drug on humans. Around 100 clinical trials take place in the UK each year and they are carefully managed to minimise the possibility of harm to those who volunteer to take part. On occasions, though, things can go wrong. In 2006, six men had to be treated in intensive care for organ failure shortly after being treated with a new treatment (TGN1412). One man had to have toes and fingers amputated and all are likely to suffer long term ill-effects.

Would you be willing to take part in clinical trials of new drugs?

What information and safeguards would you require?

Would being paid make it more attractive?

What are 'ethics'?

Ethics are concerned with the right and wrong way of behaving. Here we are concerned with the right way of behaving when conducting sociological research. The British Sociological Association has produced a detailed statement, outlining the principles that sociologists should consider; the issues include the responsibilities towards those being studied, legal issues and the relationship between those funding the research and those actually doing the research.

The key issues include:

⦿ Safeguard the interests of those involved.
⦿ Research should be worthwhile.
⦿ The techniques used should be appropriate.

All of these are connected. The main focus is on safeguarding the subjects of research. In practice this involves considerations of:

- Consent
- Avoiding deception
- Confidentiality and anonymity
- Sensitivity
- Avoiding causing harm.

Consent

Before taking part in research it is usually accepted that the subjects know that research is taking place and that they agree to take part. This consent should be 'informed', that is, they should know aims of the research and any potential risks. In medical research the risks are to the health of the participants. In sociological research they are more likely to be connected to the relationships the subjects have if information can be linked to particular individuals. It is also accepted that consent can be withdrawn at any time. For research involving young or vulnerable people, the consent might be given by parents or carers.

Deception

If the subjects of the research are unaware or misled about its aims, then they have been deceived. Covert research is thus in breach of the general rule about consent and so its use is controversial; the BSA guidelines say covert research should only be undertaken when essential information cannot be collected in any other way.

Consent form

If you would like to take part, please read this form carefully, tick the boxes that apply and sign your name.

We would like to talk to you about your experiences of going to Children's Hearings, about whether or not you felt you could join in, and about people who might have helped you do this. Would you like to talk to us?

Yes ☐

No ☐

We would like to tape what you say so that we don't forget it. We will not let anyone else listen to it, and we will not tell anyone your name or what you said.

Are you OK with this?

Yes ☐

No ☐

You can stop whenever you like. We will not mind.

If you have read the leaflet and are happy to take part, please sign below.

Signed ....

Name ....

Age .... years   Date ....

Famous example

Laud Humphreys' *Tea Room Trade* 1970 was an ethnographic study of anonymous male–male sexual encounters in public toilets in the USA. At the time, gay sex was illegal. Toilets were known as tea rooms in the slang of the USA gay community. The study has been criticised for the way it was undertaken: Humphrey collected his data without gaining consent, instead he pretended to be a voyeur with a sexual interest in watching men have sex. He followed up his observation with interviews, tracking down men through their car number plates; he told them the interviews were part of a public health study. His work helped people understand more about male homosexual behaviour, but did the benefits outweigh the danger he placed people in?

Humphries interviewed people in their own homes after observing their behaviour in toilets.

Thinking skills

Suggest three situations when it might be acceptable to deceive the subjects of research.

83

Famous names

Ken Pryce was famous for an ethnographic study of black communities in Bristol, *Endless Pressure*. Pryce's work also illustrates the potential dangers that researchers face: he was studying criminal gangs in Jamaica and disappeared. His body was later found washed up on a beach in 1987.

Thinking skills

What topics might affect the emotional well-being of a researcher? In what circumstances might a researcher be physically at risk?

Anonymity

It is very unusual for participants in research to be identified. The names of people, organisations and places are not usually provided. This should encourage participants to be open and honest, secure that whatever they say cannot be directly linked back to them.

Confidentiality

If anonymity is linked to the subjects of research, confidentiality refers to protecting the information that is collected. Ensuring that there are robust systems in place to prevent unauthorised and unnecessary access is important. This can also include avoiding collecting information that can be used to link data to individuals. This issue might also have legal implications, as the Data Protection Act might be relevant in some cases.

Sensitivity

Many of the issues that sociologists are interested in are sensitive, they touch on aspects of personal life and things that people might prefer not to discuss. Topics such as aspects of family life, criminal or deviant behaviour, the effects of discrimination, all require careful handling. This includes how the subject matter is handled, for instance avoiding placing a respondent under emotional pressure, and taking care with the data once it has been collected, ensuring that it is not used in a way that leads to problems for the subjects.

Avoiding harm

Those who agree to take part in sociological research should not be disadvantaged as a result. Protecting the identity of the participants and ensuring that answers to questionnaires or interviews remain confidential are thus essential. Protecting the researcher from harm is also important. It would be unethical for research to proceed without also considering the interests of the researcher. As we saw with participant observation, at times the researcher can be exposed to danger. As doing research is part of the job of a sociologist, all the health and safety at work guidelines are relevant. Protecting the physical and emotional well-being of the research team is part of the planning and management of a research project.

Sample questions

Equality and ethical research statement

Research conducted by the Social Care Workforce Research Unit is a valuable activity and contributes to the well-being of society. Unit members have a responsibility to ensure that the physical, social and psychological well-being of research participants is not adversely affected by the research. We strive to protect the rights of those we study, their interests, sensitivities and privacy, while recognising the difficulty of balancing potentially conflicting interests. Research should show awareness of **ethics**.

Extract from Social Care Workforce Research Unit, King's College, London

a) With reference to the item and sociological knowledge explain the meaning of the term **ethics**.

b) Using material from the item and sociological knowledge, explain **two** possible reasons why the Social Care Workforce Research Unit has a code of ethics.

c) With reference to the item and sociological knowledge, explain **two** potential ethical issues regarding research into people with learning disability.

Check your own learning

Complete the paragraph, using the words provided:

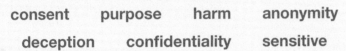

consent   purpose   harm   anonymity

deception   confidentiality   sensitive

Ethics are an important part of sociological research. Researchers must ensure that participants come to no .... Those taking part must give their .... and be informed about the .... of the research. .... is generally to be avoided. .... topics need particularly careful handling. Avoiding revealing personal details protects the .... of respondents. The Data Protection Act also protects the .... of participants.

Extended writing

In the 1980s, an American student, Mario Brajuha was conducting a participant research project into waiting on tables in a restaurant in Long Island. He was working as a waiter and making notes on his observations. The restaurant was destroyed in a fire. The police suspected that the fire was started deliberately and demanded to see Brajuha's notes. He refused to hand them over because ethically, he said that he should protect his sample of people. He was threatened with a court order and imprisonment. Later, the defendants in the case also demanded his notes but he still refused on ethical grounds. The suspects died and the case was dropped.

http://catalog.flatworldknowledge.com/bookhub/1806?e=barkan-ch02_s04

With reference to sociological studies, discuss the importance of ethics to sociological research.

Guidance: Answers to this question require knowledge of the main ethical issues, and examples of how they have been dealt with by sociologists when conducting their research. For example, the research study referred to in the item illustrates the principle of confidentiality. As part of your revision you could match each of the issues to different examples. The best answers will recognise that ethical concerns may affect decisions about what is studied and about how data is collected.

Write about 500-750 words.

Tip

Although the two terms are very different 'ethics' and 'ethnic' are often confused in examinations. Avoid this basic error by ensuring that you read the question paper carefully, the examination is not a place for skim reading. You also need to check what you are writing; to move from ethics to ethnic completely changes your answer.

INTERESTING FACT

You can find the British Sociological Association's Statement of Ethical Practice on www.britsoc.co.uk.

Aims

Before any research project can be started a number of practical issues have to be addressed. These influence how the research is conducted and may affect the findings of the research. The first question to be answered is: what to investigate? Answers to the other questions tend to follow on from this.

There are a number of practical issues, which are inter-related not only with each other but with theoretical and ethical issues discussed elsewhere. The key practical issues are:

- Choosing a research topic
- Funding the research
- Operationalising concepts
- Identifying the target population
- Negotiating access
- Timescales.

Topic 7: Practical issues

Getting you thinking

How can sociologists study relationships? It is easy to find out how many marriages there are each year, and the number of divorces is also recorded. What is more difficult to investigate is the quality and nature of relationships. Could you study 'love'? How would you define and measure it?

How does a sociologist decide what topic to research?

The choice of research topic is affected by a range of factors; personal influences can be important. What interests a sociologist will reflect their life and experiences. John Williams, for instance, was a lifelong football fan and this is reflected in his investigations into football hooligan culture.

Events and trends in society can also be relevant; the concern with equality of opportunity in education in the post-war years influenced the work of Halsey and others. The developing feminist movement of the 1960s influenced the work of many sociologists such as Ann Oakley and Hannah Gavron, in turn their work contributed to the development of feminism.

Sociologists will also be influenced by the type of theory they prefer. Interactionists tend to study what goes on inside organisations and institutions; structuralists explore the relationship between institutions and wider society.

Finance and funding the research

An important factor is the availability of funding. Money for research comes from a variety of sources. Government departments may directly commission and pay for research into issues they regard as important. Businesses are also interested in knowing more about society, using the knowledge to develop new goods and services and target marketing campaigns. Sociologists might respond to government or business invitations to conduct research that they are keen to have done. Alternatively, sociologists could have their own agenda and seek funding to conduct their work.

Famous names

John Williams

John Williams used participant observation to investigate football hooligans. His choice of research topic reflected his own interest in football and a current concern with bad behaviour at and around matches. This meant that money was available to fund research into this social problem.

What practical problems might he have faced when conducting his research?

Famous names

A H Halsey (1923–2014)

The work of Halsey has focussed on social inequality in modern Britain, especially in the education system, and on the extent of social mobility within society. His work links sociological research with social policy as he was an advisor to Labour politicians; the evidence that he and his colleagues collected in the 1950s and 1960s contributed to the decision to develop comprehensive schools and move away from selection at the age of 11.

Some money is made available through the Economic and Social Research Council; in 2014/15 its budget was £213 million. The ESRC supports research which contributes 'to the economic competitiveness of the UK, the effectiveness of public services and policy, and the quality of life'.

Ultimately, unless funding is available for a project, it will not happen.

Operationalising concepts

Very often what sociologists wish to know about are concepts: social inequality, power or gender, for example. Before these concepts can be investigated, they must first be defined. Without a definition to guide the research, there would be no clear idea of what precisely was under study. Educational achievement, for example, is too general a notion to form the basis of research. Examination results, though, are clearly defined; how many people have reached a particular level in the National Curriculum or how many have achieved 5 A*–Cs in their GCSEs are specific and measurable outcomes.

Moving from a concept to something defined and measurable is known as operationalising the concept.

Having defined educational success in a way that can be measured, data can be collected to test hypotheses. It has been suggested that the introduction of coursework into the examination system has benefitted girls, and their examination results have improved more rapidly than have those of boys.

Other examples of 'operationalising the concept' include:

- Social class is usually studied by arranging different types of jobs into groups.
- Marital breakdown is measured by the number of separations and divorces recorded.
- Attendance at religious services is one way in which secularisation is studied.

Social policy and the family

▶ In 2014 North Somerset council began a research project to investigate the benefits of helping more teenagers stay with their families and out of the care system. The focus of the research is the suitability of the government's 'social impact bond' policy as a way of helping children who are 'at the edge of care'.

Thinking skills

How might accepting government or business funding influence what is researched and what use the findings are put to?

Thinking skills

Look again at the ESRC's criteria for funding research. Suggest three possible research projects that you think should be funded. Their website is at www.esrc.ac.uk

87

Students celebrating their examination results. Gender differences in education can be studied by comparing girls' and boys' results.

Thinking skills

Suggest how the following concepts could be operationalised:
- Gender inequality
- Health
- Poverty
- Deviance.

Tip

The decisions researchers have to make can be organised under the heading PET: Practical, Ethical and Theoretical.

Devise revision cards for each of these headings with a summary of the important points.

Identifying the target population

A key stage in any research project is identifying the target population; who is it that the researcher wants to be able to draw a conclusion about, once the study is completed? It is from the target population that the sample to be studied is drawn. Any conclusions drawn from data collected about the sample can only be generalised to the population the sample came from.

For example, researchers exploring gender differences in education at 16-plus may identify their target population as students making their A level choices. If the conclusions are to be generalised to this population then the sample should be representative and include males and females, those at single-sex and co-educational schools, sixth-form and further education colleges and so on.

Negotiating access

Once the target population has been identified and the sampling method decided upon the researcher has to make contact with the potential research participants. Initially this can involve access to an organisation, for example a school or a workplace. Access here is in the hands of the organisation's management, they are the gatekeepers; before they give permission for research to take place, they will need to be assured that the research is worthwhile and that their interests will not be damaged.

With informal groups, the gatekeeper is likely to be a key member of the group, someone who is respected by others and who can 'sponsor' the researcher.

This practical concern is closely linked to the ethical issue of 'consent': those taking part in research should agree to take part and have the opportunity to withdraw. This is true of organisations as well as individuals.

Time and money

The amount of time and money available to any research project will be limited. These resource limits affect the size of the research team that can be involved and more importantly the research methods that are used and the size of the sample studied. With more money a larger sample can be used. A bigger sample, if carefully chosen, is more likely to be representative and therefore your data will be more generalisable. Interviews can be used as well as or instead of questionnaires; this would provide more detailed information.

Likewise, with more time available, time-consuming methods like participant observation become an option: Whyte's *Street Corner Society* was based on 5 years of research. With more time a longitudinal study becomes possible, enabling the investigation of social changes over time.

Sample questions

In 2014 a **longitudinal study** costing over £4million investigating dementia was started. Over a two-year period 1500 people with early-stage dementia will be interviewed three times in their homes. Wherever possible the participants' carers will be present. The interviews will collect information about the challenges posed by dementia and how people adjust to their condition.

http://www.esrc.ac.uk/my-esrc/grants/ES.L001853.1/read

a) With reference to the item and sociological knowledge, explain what is meant by a **longitudinal study**.

b) With reference to the item and sociological knowledge explain the impact of practical issues on research.

Check your own learning

Match the beginnings and ends of the sentences.

Start	End
a) Practical considerations for researchers include	personal experiences, events in society and political priorities.
b) The target population	operationalise a concept.
c) The choice of research topic can be influenced by	operationalisation, time, money, and access.
d) Funding for research can come from	access to target populations and samples.
e) Gatekeepers control	refers to the group that the researcher wishes to generalise her findings to.
f) Defining in measurable form is to	government, business or research councils.

Topic 7: Practical issues

Thinking skills

You are investigating bullying at school.

⦿ Write a letter to a head teacher asking for permission to conduct research in their school.

⦿ What practical issues do you need to think about?

⦿ What research method would be suitable? Why?

Extended writing

As an A level Sociology student you have been asked to design a research project to collect data about the impact of part-time work on educational achievement.

Describe the key elements of your project design, identifying and explaining the factors influencing your decisions.

Guidance: This is an opportunity to bring together and apply your knowledge and understanding of the research process. You should have a clear plan for your answer: the PET acronym provides a framework. It is very important that your answer is related to the scenario stated in the question. Generalised discussions of research methods, sampling or the other important issues will not be highly rewarded. For example, you should explain how 'part-time work' and 'educational achievement' are to be operationalised; what practical problems of access would you encounter? Are there any ethical issues related to this particular scenario?

Write about 500-750 words.

Aims

- ⦿ Understand that the choice of research topic and the methods used to collect data is influenced by a number of factors: practical, ethical (considered in Topics 6 and 7) and now, theory

- ⦿ Realise that just as there are different sociological perspectives (functionalism, Marxism, interactionism and so on) to the study of society, so there also different theories about how to collect evidence and what type of evidence to collect

Topic 8: Theories of research

Getting you thinking

Looking for evidence: sociologists use a variety of different research methods to collect evidence. Depending on their theoretical approach, they are also interested in different types of evidence. Who prefers to rely on quantitative data? Who emphasises the value of qualitative data?

Theories

There are three theories to discuss:

- ⦿ Positivist
- ⦿ Interpretivist
- ⦿ Realist.

Positivism

This approach is associated with the work of Comte and Durkheim who wanted to create a 'science of society'. The other theories have developed in reaction to positivism. Positivism is based on the assumption that there are 'social facts' waiting to be identified and studied; this requires quantitative data. Social facts are aspects of behaviour that can be seen, counted and measured. Whether or not they are being studied, these social facts exist and they influence the behaviour of people in society.

For example, the age at which people get married might appear to be based on individuals and couples making their own decision. Positivists argue that analysis of the evidence shows that there is an identifiable pattern to age at marriage that most people conform to; there are social expectations about marriage, part of society's culture, that influence decisions.

As data is collected, trends and patterns can be identified in these statistics; positivists seek to explain these trends by reference to other trends and developments in society. The average age of marriage has increased in the last 150 years or so. At the same time other changes have taken place: life expectancy has increased, education lasts much longer for most people and there are more women are in the workforce. Are any (or all?) of these connected to the change in marriage behaviour? Are there correlations between these sets of information? Do all the trends move in the same direction?

Thinking skills

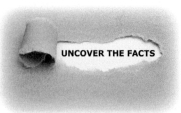

UNCOVER THE FACTS

Positivists assume that there are social facts to be identified and measured. Is this true?

More importantly, is there a causal relationship between these social facts, i.e. is one change bringing about another? Questioning the data in this way mimics the scientific approach and the desire to find laws which explain behaviour in the natural world.

Interpretivism

This approach prefers to collect detailed accounts in words, that is qualitative data. This enables the researcher to find out about people's feelings, attitudes and experiences. Rather than counting how many people get married or at what age, interpretivists would want to know why people get married, what marriage means and how this meaning has changed. As women's roles have changed, does this affect how marriage is seen; do people have different expectations of marriage in the 21st century compared to previous generations? They do not look for causal relationships because they see human behaviour as different from the behaviour of things in the natural world: humans consider what things mean and then decide to act.

Realism

Positivists are sometimes criticised because social research cannot exactly mimic the approach of natural sciences, for example social experiments cannot be set up in the controlled way that laboratory experiments can be. As the interpretivists point out, it is clear that humans are reflexive: social institutions and the behaviour of others have meaning for

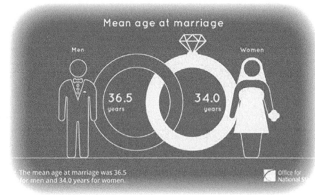

Image: Office for National Statistics

In 1981 the average age at marriage for men was 29.6 years, for women 26.9 years. By 2012 it had increased as shown above.
What other social facts might be linked to this change?

Interpretivists study what marriage means in society. Positivists would look at how many people marry or divorce.

us and we interpret social situations before acting. However, it is also clear that there are trends and patterns in social behaviour, these can be observed and measured. Realists argue that the best way to proceed is to recognise that both interpretivism and positivism are useful and use the methods that are the most suitable for the issue that is being studied.

If the research is investigating trends in the numbers of marriages, then it makes sense to refer to official statistics. If the aim is to find out more about the experience and expectations of marriage and how they have changed, then it is more appropriate to use interviews. Often sociologists will combine approaches as they are interested not only in the *what* or *how many* questions, they also want to know about the meanings and significance that people give to their behaviour.

Thinking skills

Same-sex marriages: what do they tell us about the social meaning of marriage in the 21st century? How have social definitions of marriage changed?

STRETCH and CHALLENGE

You can find examples of recent research on socresonline.org.uk and esrc.ac.uk. Use the sites to investigate what sociologists have been finding out about the family, youth cultures or education. The language may be challenging, but your understanding and vocabulary will benefit.

Realists suggest that the best approach to research is to recognise that both positivism and interpretivism can be useful when studying society.

Tip

Remember to refer to real-life examples of research in your responses to questions about research methods. Try to use up-to-date examples. See page 271 for more advice.

The influence of the realist approach can be seen in research which makes use of **methodological pluralism** and triangulation. Methodological pluralism recognises that no single approach has all the answers to questions about society and understanding behaviour. Likewise, triangulation in research recognises that all the research methods available to sociologists have both strengths and weaknesses. To fully appreciate what is going on in society and to know how and why people behave as they do, it is necessary to adopt a range of techniques.

Much modern research uses a mix of methods to balance the need for both validity (which comes from qualitative methods) and reliability (which is more typical of quantitative methods). Qualitative methods can add depth of understanding, but quantitative methods offer depth. In a study of Polish migrants to Cardiff, for example, Knight used secondary statistical data to build a picture of the 'typical' Polish migrant, and qualitative data gathered from semi-structured interviews to challenge that image. She was able to present a picture of Polish migration that showed a slightly different social background from the traditional view, but that many Polish migrants had been successful in the British job market because of social skills and a willingness to learn English.

Money inevitable **population**
shelter insufficient condition
loss
low
care
poverty inability
issue
survival
lack
denial
capacity
society
severe
family
health care needs individuals
inequality restricted corruption
million people help

Famous names

Peter Townsend (1928–2009)

Townsend is best known for his studies of poverty and the ideas of 'absolute poverty' and 'relative poverty'. He saw that poverty was not only about how much money or how many possessions people had. Poverty was also about how people's living standards compared to those around them. This recognises that what counts as poverty is socially constructed.

Sample questions

Almost half of all adults in England say they experience feelings of loneliness, according to a BBC poll. **Quantitative data** shows that one in five people say they are lonelier now than they were 10 years ago, with London said to be the loneliest place with a figure of 52% compared to 45% in the south west of England.

a) With reference to the item and sociological knowledge explain what is meant by **quantitative data**.

b) With reference to the item and sociological knowledge assess the strengths and weaknesses of the positivist approach to research.

Thinking skills

What would positivists want to know about poverty? How would they collect their evidence?

What aspects of poverty would interest interpretivists? What research methods would they use?

Extended writing

With reference to sociological studies discuss the theoretical issues that influence sociological research.

Guidance: In answering this question you will be able to demonstrate your understanding of the positivist, interpretivist and realist approaches to research. You should briefly outline the key assumptions that underlie the approaches and show how criticism of one approach can lead to the development of alternatives. Referring to relevant research studies, drawn from any area of your studies, you should discuss the advantages and disadvantages of each approach.

Write about 500-750 words.

Check your own learning

Answer the following questions:

a) The scientific approach is associated with which theory?

b) Meanings and understandings are the focus of which theory?

c) Positivists usually collect what type of data?

d) Interpretivists usually collect what type of data?

e) Which approach suggests that a combination of methods is often useful?

Tip

This may be a good time to revise the advantages and disadvantages of the different approaches to research methods.

Family

Topic 1: What is family?

Aims

- To understand that most people live in some form of family, and that views about what a family is, or should be, vary

Some sociologists refer to the family as a specific arrangement of a group of people who are linked by legal or blood relationships. Family was usually defined in terms of nuclear family. These are heterosexual parents and their children who were linked by blood, adoption or law. Increasingly, this view of family is changing and some sociologists now view family in terms of the emotional relationships that people choose to have with each other. Families tend to be composed of groups of people who share close interactions. Modern definitions of family therefore tend to consider the emotional links between family members.

Getting you thinking

With a study partner, suggest as many different reasons as you can why gay families have become more socially acceptable in modern Britain since 1967.

Traditional sociological view of family

In the 1930s, functionalist sociologists suggested that families are essential for the survival of society. They outlined the functions of families, seeing them as being good for individuals and society as a whole. Later functionalists suggested that the ideal family consisted of a heterosexual couple and their children. This idea has influenced family policy in the UK and many politicians have stated that families following this structure are superior to any other family form.

Changing sociological views of family

Even in the late 1900s, there were powerful arguments to suggest that traditional families oppressed people, especially women. This idea really took hold in the 1970s with the rapid growth of feminism and the social changes that took place in the lives of women. Family patterns have changed rapidly. Weston (1991) suggested that many people now live in families of choice to emphasise the way that many people no longer choose traditional family forms and that any definition of family should focus on emotional connection.

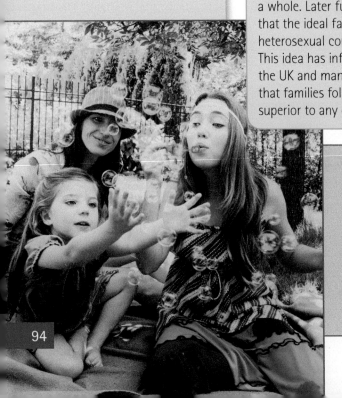

Ethnography and family sociology

One of the most influential studies of family life in Britain took place in the 1950s in the London district of Bethnal Green. Michael Young and Peter Willmott wrote about *Family and Kinship in East London* (1957) using ethnographic approaches to describe social attitudes and relationships in families. Little statistical data was gathered, most of the writing described people's lives. This work challenged many of the assumptions of functional sociology because it discovered that working-class people in London lived in extended families, close to their parents. Women, in particular, offered each other support in terms of caring, washing and shopping.

Similar work was carried out in Swansea in the early 2000s by Charles, Davies and Harris, and it found that families were focussed on female relationships. It found that nuclear families were only a short part of people's lives. It also suggested that while many people do not have partners or children, there are those for whom marriage and remarriage mean that large numbers of people have a series of highly complex family arrangments to which they belong at the same time.

Defining families, households and kinship

Defining family – in the past, family was usually defined in terms of nuclear family. These are heterosexual parents and their children who were linked by blood, adoption or law. Nowadays this definition no longer fits well, because families tend to be composed of groups of people who share close interactions. Modern definitions of family tend therefore to consider the emotional links between family members.

Kinship – this is a slightly more complex notion. Kinship refers to the patterns of relationship and the sense of duty that people feel towards those they see as family. These can vary from culture to culture, with different kinship relationships being recognised and valued.

Household – refers to the people who share a house and its facilities. These people may or may not be related. For example, a servant may be a member of your household, but is not considered family.

Extended family – this refers to people who surround the parents and children: grandparents, aunts and uncles, cousins. In traditional working-class areas, and in some Asian heritage families, extended families may share a home or live very close together.

The functionalist view of family

In the 1950s, Talcott Parsons took the view that families develop patterns and structures that are appropriate to the culture to which they belong. This was the dominant sociological position probably until the 1970s. Parsons claimed that in modern society, the best form of family was a nuclear family (heterosexual parents and their children). He was supported in this view by George Murdock (1949) who undertook a review of families in around 250 cultures. This led him to the view that families in all societies have the same four key functions: sexual, reproductive, economic and educational.

Parsons's theory was that nuclear families:

- Do not require the support of wider family as much as in the past.
- Women choose an expressive (emotional role) in families, but men are instrumental (they earn the family money).
- Are a form of comfort for men, who work outside the home but can relax within it (this is known as the warm bath theory).
- Are also biologically natural and have developed through evolution to fit the different biological roles of men and women.
- Provide the best environment in which to bring up healthy and well-socialised children.

Activity

There were a number of readable books about family life in the 1950s in the East End of London, known as the Bethnal Green studies. These were by Michael Young and Peter Willmott and can be read online.

Research idea

How many different types of family are you aware of among your friends and family? How could you research different family styles?

Activity

Discuss how children might benefit from being part of a large extended family.

Activity

Discuss the advantages and disadvantages of nuclear families.

Criticisms of the functionalist view of the family

There are obvious direct criticisms of the functional view of family, the most obvious being that it is ideological. It promotes a view of family that was popular at that time and says that because it exists, therefore it is the best family form. Marxists and feminists have made many criticisms, however:

- Many nuclear families are not safe places for women and children; the evidence that is used is the high rate of domestic abuse in many Western countries. Mirrlees-Black (1999) described the prevalence of such abuse as part of a larger study, the British Crime Survey.
- It overlooks alternative sexualities such as LGBT, forcing those who are not heterosexual into family roles that do not allow them to express themselves.
- Women are expected to take on a lesser role and have limited power because the family money is seen as belonging to the male who earned it. Thus it is not an equal partnership (Player, 2013).
- Parsons is seen as having an over-optimistic view of family life.
- Parsons focusses on family structure and therefore does not recognise that family is more complex in terms of relationships and emotions.
- Parsons overlooks the fact that even at the time he was writing, many different family forms existed.

This view of society and nuclear families does not explain why nuclear families have arisen in the first place.

Because nuclear families exist they must be functional for society

If we look at society, we should be looking for nuclear families and why they exist

Nuclear families do exist and so therefore they are the best kind of family

Thus, other forms of family are not good for society

- Functionalism is often described as forming a circular argument that runs along these lines: 'because something exists, it must therefore be useful to society, so therefore it exists'.

Are traditional views of family still relevant today?

There are two lines of argument in answer to this question:

1. Family structure debates

These argue that there is increasing variety in family and household type and far more tolerance of people who do not fit into traditional patterns of nuclear family. More variation in family types is being identified and described. For example, same-sex families are not uncommon, and shared parenting between people who may have a child together but not live with each other is also accepted. Population change and social change mean that defining a family by structure is no longer particularly useful. It could be argued that those who define family in terms of structures and relationships are ignoring the complicated emotional reality of most people's family lives.

2. Theoretical debates

These viewpoints look at family in terms of emotions and organisation. They are not so interested in what a family looks like, but are concerned to discuss the role of family life in individual lives. There are a number of strands to consider:

- *Marxism* views family as a source of social inequality and a tool of an unequal social system. The inequality between the genders, and the adults and children in a family socialises people into accepting that some people have more access to power and wealth than others. Marxists argue that children are trained into the values and behaviours of their parents. Families feel that they must work hard to earn the money to buy goods some of which are not essential for life, but expensive and highly desirable (computer games, fancy computers and televisions, mobile telephones and new cars).

- *Feminism* views family as oppressing women who effectively work to support the family without either pay or recognition. Wallace (1990), for example, says that women are expected to do the emotional work of the family, work outside the home and do housework in the home. She calls this the triple shift. Oakley points to the way that families socialise children into traditional gender patterns which perpetuate gender inequality.

- *Interactionism* views the family in terms of roles and behaviours. It looks at family life in terms of what it means for people in terms of emotional bonding and the way that we develop a sense of identity from our families. Interactionists would want to know, for example, who people see as being family, and this can be complicated.

Do families oppress women?

STRETCH and CHALLENGE

Using sociological evidence and examples, explain the meaning of the term family.

Family and policy

▶ In August 2014, the current Conservative Prime Minister gave a family policy speech that you can read on

www.gov.uk/government/speeches/
david-cameron-on-families

What view of family is he promoting – family structure or family relationships? How far do you agree or disagree with his ideas?

Activity

Fill in the missing words

Functionalist sociologists view the _ _ _ _ _ _ as being a specific arrangement of a group of people who are linked by blood or _ _ _ _ _ ties. They tend to claim that the _ _ _ _ form of family is a _ _ _ _ _ _ _ _ family consisting of _ _ _ _ _ _ _ _ _ _ _ _ parents and their children. More recent theories of family suggest that the actual _ _ _ _ _ _ _ _ _ of the family is unimportant, what is important is the _ _ _ _ _ _ _ of the relationships and the _ _ _ _ _ _ _ _ _ in families. They say that many people no longer choose _ _ _ _ _ _ _ _ _ _ family forms because they view emotional _ _ _ _ _ _ _ _ _ _ as more important.

They will look at how families often have special languages and rituals which form part of the negotiation of relationships – birthday parties, meals together, gifts and family discussion.

◉ *Postmodernists* refer to families of choice, where friendships may be more significant than blood relations. Pahl (2000) describes the way that people have become socially and geographically mobile so the supportive role once taken by family members is now often filled by friends.

Sample questions

Lone parents with dependent children, 2001 to 2011

a) Summarise the content of the bar chart showing the numbers of lone parents with dependent children between 2001 and 2011.

b) With reference to the item and sociological knowledge explain **two** reasons for the increase in the number of lone parents with dependent children in the contemporary UK.

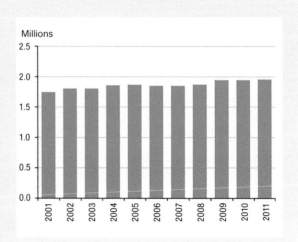

Check your own learning

Link the theoretical perspective to the view point.

a)	Nuclear families are the best family structures for society.	Feminism
b)	Families operate for the benefit of men and oppress women and children.	Marxism
c)	People live in families of choice and sometimes their friends are more important than blood relatives.	Functionalism
d)	Families should be studied in terms of relationships, rituals and meanings that bind them together	Post-modernism
e)	Traditional families support capitalism by oppressing women and mirroring the inequalities of wider society.	Interactionism

Extended writing

Assess the view that the nuclear family is the best family type for society.

Guidance: You will need to identify which perspective believes that nuclear families are best for society. This is functionalism. After that, you have two possible routes to a conclusion. One is to focus on functionalism, offering reasons why functionalists hold this belief, and then criticising functionalism itself. The other is to explain functionalism, and then referring to other theories, criticise functionalism. This is possibly the easier route; ensure that you use the other theories to assess functionalism in every paragraph. Examiners will be looking very carefully for the use of the term, and if you check the mark schemes, you will see the terms context or relevance being used in every column.

Write about 500 words.

In what ways can a family be said to be like a warm bath? Which, if either of these images is a realistic view of modern family life?

Research methods revision

A 2014 survey has found women devote well over the equivalent of a working day each week to household chores – double the amount undertaken by men.

The poll for BBC Radio 4's *Woman's Hour* suggests that women estimate that they spend an average of 11-and-a-half hours doing housework, while men say they do just six.

http://www.huffingtonpost.co.uk/2014/10/06/women-housework-compared-men-poll_n_5937536.html

Questions

a) How valid do you think the findings in this study are?

b) How might the sample chosen have affected the results?

Many women claim that the nuclear family is a breeding ground for domestic violence.

What is your view?

Family

Aims

◉ **To recognise some of the changes that are taking place in family structure and then to outline some reasons for those changes**

Sociologists are concerned with two tasks when it comes to family change. The first is to describe how families are changing. A number of new family structures appear to be emerging and becoming quite normal. The question for sociologists is to accurately identify patterns and trends of change. Newspaper accounts, for example, can be surprisingly inaccurate and make changes seem more dramatic than they are. The second task is to outline why those changes have occurred, and to look at how social change elsewhere in society is affecting family structures.

Tip

You may be asked to describe and to explain family change in British society. For revision purposes, it might be sensible to have two revision lists, one describing new family forms and the other giving a list of reasons why families have changed.

What is the link between family change and the economy?

Topic 2: Describing family change

Getting you thinking

Families then and now

Families have fewer children now than in the past. What sociological reasons can you suggest for this?

Family change

The traditional nuclear male breadwinner and female housewife family structure is declining. Despite it being viewed as an ideal family type by Parsons and other sociologists, most people agree that it is now probably a thing of the past. There are very many possible reasons: one is that there is less well-paid male work in the economy and another is that women have become more significant in the paid workforce and expect satisfying careers of their own. This illustrates the complexity of the link between family and society. Changes in the workforce have influenced family life, but changes in men's and women's expectations of family life have had an influence on society.

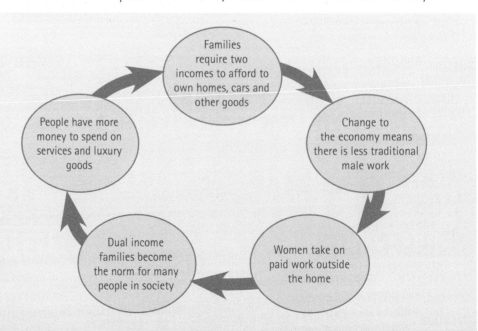

Families require two incomes to afford to own homes, cars and other goods

Change to the economy means there is less traditional male work

Women take on paid work outside the home

Dual income families become the norm for many people in society

People have more money to spend on services and luxury goods

Demography

Demography is the study of population and population change. Demographers are interested in patterns of social structure, which describe what is actually happening at the moment. They are also interested in predicting trends, which means that they look at the past and see how things are changing so they can make predictions about future population structures.

The demography of the UK is changing quite dramatically and much of that change is linked to birth and death rates, though other changes are taking place, too:

- People are living for longer, not only that, but they remain healthy for longer, too. There are increasing numbers of older people who have been widowed, or never married, who live alone.
- Women are generally choosing to have fewer children. The average number of children per family is below two. The average age of the mother when a first child is born tends to be much older; in 2013 the average age of new mothers was 30 according to government figures. Many couples make a deliberate choice to remain child-free. Approximately 20% of women will not have a child.
- There are higher rates of divorce since the 1950s, but marriage remains the most common form of partnership between adults in our society. Many people live together or form families without marriage, often delaying a wedding or choosing not to marry. This is cohabitation.
- Many children still live in a traditional family unit in one household, with two parents, though one of those parents may not be a biological relation. There are increasing numbers of children who have spent part of their childhood in a single parent household. Many people delay or choose not to marry, even if they have children together.
- People can openly participate in single-sex families in the UK and many other countries, so people do not need to hide their sexuality if they are gay.
- People may be in long-term relationships or not, as they please, but prefer to live on their own whatever their relationship status, this is known as elective singlehood. It is estimated that approximately 20% of adults live alone, though many may be elderly widowed.
- Adult children may remain in the family home for much longer than would have been common in the past as a result of rising house prices, tuition fees at university and lack of work for younger people. Some adult children may move out and return, perhaps on relationship breakdown and they are known as boomerang children, others never leave.
- Migration is changing family patterns, so traditional nuclear and extended family patterns may be more typical of Asian heritage British than of longer established populations.

New family forms

Beanpole family – in the past, families often had many children, so a structure diagram would have shown a triangular shape. Modern family trees are longer and thinner. There are fewer people in each generation, but they live longer. Rising divorce rates may also add to the effect, as some children will be part of more than one family.

Sandwich generation – people live longer and have children later. Children tend to leave home later in life. This leaves an estimated 2.4 million people in the UK (YouGov 2013) who are responsible for both their own dependent children and their elderly parents at the same time. It is argued that this puts emotional and financial strain on people, usually women in mid to later life.

INTERESTING FACT

Men now make up nearly 10 per cent of those who care for children while their partner goes out to work, official employment statistics have shown. There were 227,000 men staying at home to look after family between September and November 2012, a rise of 19,000 compared to the same period in 2011 and the highest increase since figures began in 1993. The change may be due to men losing their jobs in the recession and either failing to find new employment or deciding that it did not make financial sense for them to return to work if their partner was a high earner.

http://www.telegraph.co.uk/women/9822271/Rise-in-stay-at-home-fathers-fuelled-by-growing-numbers-of-female-breadwinners.html

Research methods

How can secondary sources be used to investigate family life in the past?

Academic texts prefer to use the term 'verticalised family' to describe the beanpole family. Remember that examiners will be looking for evidence of key language and wider reading, so using an alternative academic term will emphasise your AO1 skills.

How can the changes in the family be seen as reflecting the impact of feminism on society?

Single parents by choice – it has now become perfectly acceptable for adults to choose to have a child without taking on a long-term adult partner. This can be a direct choice, perhaps as an adoption, or as a result of a relationship break up before the birth of a child. Smart and Neale (1999) suggest that the existence of divorce causes many people to hold the view that parent–child relationships are more satisfying than adult partnerships.

Single parenthood through relationship breakdown – Berrington (2014) suggests that it is difficult to generalise because of the variety of new family types preceding lone parenthood. However, despite popular myth, most single parents are people, generally women in their thirties, who have experienced marriage or relationship breakdown. Many remain single parents only until they find a new partner. Numerous government reports have linked lone-parenthood through relationship breakdown with poverty and deprivation.

Blended or reconstituted family (see left) – in the past, these were known as step-families and usually were the result of the death of a parent; however, it is estimated that in the UK 10% of families have two adult parents but children from more than one relationship. It is possible that the actual number may be higher as blended families are often cohabiting rather than married.

Unmarried couples with children – not all children born to unmarried mothers are the product of lone-mother relationships. Many are born into established relationships. There are slight legal differences in the relationship of the child to the father, but emotionally there seems to be little difference. There is some evidence that non-married couples are more vulnerable to break up than married couples, but whether that is due to a wedding certificate or other social factors is not clear.

Gay family – there is little that is new about gay families. Historically, couples have always chosen to live in same-sex relationships. Recent changes to the law mean that same-sex couples have the same legal rights as heterosexual couples. Heaphy (2013) points out that what is new is that this is now publicly acknowledged and need not be hidden.

Living apart together (LAT) – this is a new family form identified by Levin in 2004. Couples have a household each, although they maintain a close partnership. This family form is found in Scandinavia, but Levin argues it can follow cohabitation, when people become financially secure and choose to live in separate homes.

Co-parenting (parenting partnerships) – this is a parenting situation where there are two (or more) people parenting a child, but they have never been in a romantic relationship, married or cohabiting. Gay people have possibly always done this discreetly, but can be open about this pattern now.

Discussion point

- Centenarians (people over 100 years of age) in England and Wales
  - 1982 – 2,560
  - 1992 – 4,460
  - 2002 – 7,090
  - 2012 – 12,320
  - *Source: ONS estimates*

What does this tell us about changes to population and life expectancy in modern England and Wales?

The sociological debate: Intimacy versus social breakdown

Gillies (2003) and Jamieson (1998) have said that statistical analysis of family forms and household structures all point to an increased diversity in the ways that people choose to live together. Many social commentators and politicians view this change in family life as threatening and negative, implying a breakdown in social relationships. The alternative view is that families are becoming more democratic and based on choices. There is a further view, Crow (2002), which suggests that the amount of change is over-stated, and that there has always been a variety of family types, but people were more discrete about things because in the past, alternative families were seen in a negative and critical light.

Sample questions

Households with dependent children, by family type (2006)

	Thousands	**Percent of all households with children**
Married couple	8,585	66
Cohabiting couple	1,412	11
Lone mother	2,829	22
Lone father	254	2

http://webarchive.nationalarchives.gov.uk/20130401151715/http://www.education.gov.uk/publications/eOrderingDownload/Appendix-G_SIRC-report.pdf

a) Summarise the content of the table.

b) What evidence does it offer to support the view that the nuclear family is no longer important in contemporary Britain?

Check your own learning

Match the family type to the description.

a)	Adults choose to have a child without taking on a long-term adult partner.	Beanpole family
b)	Two adult parents but children from more than one relationship.	Sandwich generation
c)	People in England and Wales who are responsible for both their own dependent children and their elderly parents at the same time.	Co-parenting (parenting partnerships)
d)	Modern family trees are longer and thinner. There are fewer people in each generation.	Blended or reconstituted family
e)	The parents are in a relationship, but have not married.	Gay family
f)	Same-sex couples with children.	Living apart together (LAT)
g)	Childlessness is an active choice with partners focussing on each other.	Unmarried couples with children
h)	Couples have a household each, although they maintain a close partnership.	Single parents by choice
i)	This is a parenting situation where there are two (or more) people parenting a child, but they have never been in a romantic relationship.	Child freedom

Extended writing

Describe changes to family structure in modern England and Wales.

Guidance: In this style of question, you will simply be asked for facts. You do not need to give reasons for family change, simply write about the different types of family structure. Comment on examples from the media so, for example, the rock star Elton John and his civil partner, David Furnish, have now had two children with a surrogate mother and are an example of a gay family. You will gain marks for each type of family structure that you can accurately name and offer a definition and an example for.

Write about 300 words.

Discussion point

- New Right theorists have argued that liberal views on the family have led to a range of social problems including crime, unemployment and AIDS. Charles Murray suggested that government policies should reinforce traditional nuclear families and aim to prevent alternative family forms developing. With a study partner, make points for and against the policy of reinforcing nuclear families.

103

Aims

Aims

⦿ **To understand that the reasons for family and social change are many and varied**

The family is a very important institution in society so changes to the family will affect society. However, social change itself also has had a huge impact on family life. Sociologists are interested in the relationships between family and society as a whole; it would probably be impossible to identify all of the reasons for social and family change but there are a few key issues that can be identified and investigated. These issues are inter-related, as you will have seen in the last chapter and it can sometimes be difficult to sort out specific causes and effects of social changes.

Topic 3: Explaining family change

Getting you thinking

The little girl in the picture is probably at retirement age now, or even a pensioner and entering old age.

⦿ What changes have taken place in the world since she was a small child? Suggest some things she might have experienced in her life time.

⦿ What different family types might she have experienced throughout her life?

Changing norms and values

There have been some quite considerable changes in social norms and values, particularly with regard to morality and sexuality over the past 50 years or so. For example, sex outside marriage would once have been seen as a huge issue of shame for a family if discovered, so men and women would generally marry very quickly if a pregnancy occurred. Women who had children outside marriage could expect a very difficult time, and often had their children forcibly removed for adoption. However, the Office for National Statistics reported in 2013 that the percentage of children born to unmarried and never-married mothers in England and Wales was 47.5%, although many were in long-term partnerships with the father. It is expected by 2016, the number of children born to unmarried women will be larger than the number of children born to married parents. The figure in 1938 was below 5% of children. As the shame of birth outside marriage has receded, the number of single parents and cohabiting parents has increased.

Are gay families a cause or a result of family change?

Legal changes and the family

An enormous amount of legislation affecting family life has been passed over the last 50 years or more. Recent examples include the introduction of civil partnerships in 2004 and then same-sex marriage in 2014. As a result, there has been an increased awareness of LGBT relationships, and public figures are now openly in same-sex relationships. Barely a year has passed over the last 50 years without some legislative change affecting family life, from changes in taxation, to benefits rules or laws relating to marriage and divorce. However, it remains an issue of debate among sociologists as to whether changes in the law have led to changing family values, or whether the law is simply following public opinion.

Courts can also have a surprisingly direct influence and effect on family life. They can impose decisions on parents to protect children. In 2013, a family court ordered two sisters to be given MMR injections against their and their mother's wishes because their father felt the jab 'was in their best interests'. Recently, parents have been sent to prison and fined for allowing children to take time off school.

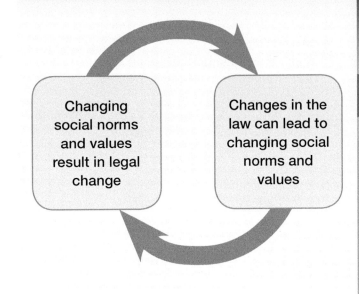

Debates on whether and when women should be allowed legal abortion suggest that attitudinal shifts can be swift and affect public policy and laws. Abortion became legally available in England, Scotland and Wales in 1968 after a long campaign for women's rights. This was possibly because of unacceptably high death rates among women due to attempted and illegal abortions (assessed at approximately 15% of deaths of women of child-bearing age). However, by 1974, there were attempts to make abortion illegal again, by 1990 there were specific lowered time limits placed on legal abortion. There is still public controversy around the issue.

Economics and family change

There have been major changes to the UK economy over the long term that have had dramatic effects on family life.

- The loss of the single male breadwinner in a family has been caused by a fundamental shift in the nature of employment. Macionis and Plummer estimate that in 1911, 45% of British workers were employed in manufacturing. These would mostly have been men. Now, the major employer is the **service sector**, such as call centres, IT, retail and entertainment. The new jobs can be done by men or women as service sector work relies on people skills, not physical strength. So as the jobs market for men has declined, fewer families are headed by a man who earns enough in a single job to be able to support a non-working wife and their children.
- Lewis (2012) has pointed out that there have been government and EU policies aimed at encouraging women, especially those with children, into the workforce. The increase in female employment has changed family life as women can have more control over decisions about spending and do not need to remain in unsatisfactory relationships. However, women are delaying childbearing and having fewer children. Many of these children are reared by grandparents (see right) or through commercial child-minding. Thus, parent–child relationships have been affected.
- Flour and Buchanan (2001) pointed out that as marriage is no longer economically necessary for women, fewer people are choosing to marry. The average age of marriage is increasing steadily. Drew (1998) suggested that as marriage is now a matter of choice, people who marry have higher expectations of happiness and if those expectations are not met, they can start again. This means that there has been a loss of shame in divorce. Divorce is far easier to obtain as a result of legal changes. Thus, if people no longer feel shame in divorce, and divorce is easier to obtain, people (women in particular) may be more likely to hold on to employment as an insurance against relationship breakdown (Ermisch, 1996).

Causes and effects of social change are not easily separated.

Tip

There is a huge variety of causes for family change that you could discuss and this topic only mentions a few. Bear in mind, that however many you know and whatever the question, you will still only have a limited amount of time to write in the examination whatever the focus of the question. You will need to use the skill of selection (AO3) in order to decide what you think is important and back it up with examples (AO1).

The HP Sauce factory in Aston, West Midlands was closed in 2007 – just one example of manufacturing industry decline.

Are grandparents taking on more childcare?

Black Friday: consumer advertising to encourage near 'panic' buying.

- Marxists claim that families are increasingly a unit of consumption and this is a pressure for social change in families. Capitalists target advertising at families; items such as groceries, food, holidays and cars. Families are taught to believe that they need these things, so parents are under pressure, often from their children, to buy items such as fashion goods, phones and technology. Children can exert pester power because they believe that they need to spend money in order to fit in with and impress their friends. This benefits the capitalists who encourage people both to buy products and generate profits, but who work very hard in order to purchase more items.

Changing technology

This is a vast area of social change and has had a huge impact on society and family life. Often, it is easy to assume that technology refers simply to computers. The effect of computers and entertainment technology on daily life has been enormous, but the term could include medical, transport, buildings or work technology. For example, IVF is a form of medical technology that enables previously childless people to have children. The microwave oven, despite being first developed in the 1940s, became a common household item in the 1980s due to social changes that meant working women had less time for cooking.

Silva (2009) has suggested that technology has changed but not damaged family life. She argues that technological change is often a response to social need. For example, as people have migrated around the world, the development of the mobile phone and social networking means that family connections can be maintained over huge distances. However, others such as Gergen (1991) have taken a more negative view and argue that families have become more fragmented as a result of technology. People no longer sit in one place together as they once might have done, as houses are better heated and more comfortable and there may be a source of entertainment in each room. He described the saturated family, talking in terms of family confrontation caused by people who no longer share time, values or opinions. Postmodernists, however, see this as simply a form of family diversity, we are no longer bound by the same social rules or views of what family life should be.

Theoretical thinking

Robert Chester, from a functionalist viewpoint, has suggested that the amount of family diversity is exaggerated and says that the nuclear family is still the most common family type. For example, people may not marry, but they still live as couples.

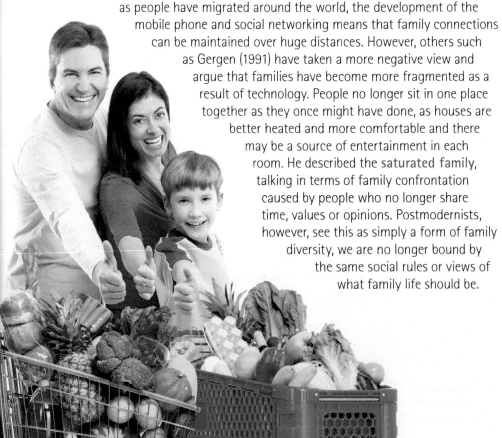

To what extent are modern families a unit of consumption?

Sample questions

In 2002, 1,000 households were surveyed in the Swansea area in an attempt to **replicate**, or to repeat, an **ethnographic** study undertaken in 1960 in the same area. This study used interviews conducted over a five-month period of time.

Whilst there was a large amount of demographic change in families with fewer children and more working mothers, the researchers discovered that the most important social links were between women in families and that this was similar to 1960.

Adapted from Social Change and the Family (2005) Harris et al.

a) Summarise the item on family change in the Swansea area.
b) Explain **two** reasons why there has been family change in the Swansea area since the 1960s.
c) Using material from the item and sociological knowledge, explain the meaning of the term, **replicate**.
d) Using material from the item and sociological knowledge, explain the meaning of the term, **ethnographic**.

Check your own learning

Complete the table.

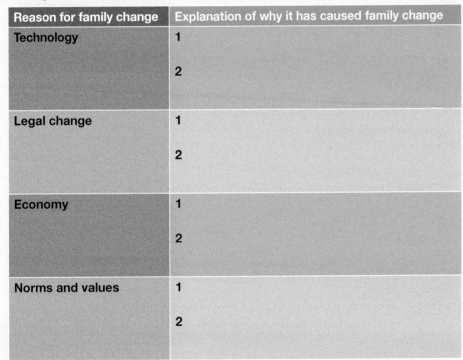

Reason for family change	Explanation of why it has caused family change
Technology	1
	2
Legal change	1
	2
Economy	1
	2
Norms and values	1
	2

Extended writing

Discuss sociological reasons for increasing family diversity.

Guidance: This question is asking you to explain reasons why there is a wider variety of different family types in England and Wales now than in the past. You can offer a range of possible reasons, but notice that you are asked for 'sociological reasons'. This means that you must present evidence, facts, theories and use the important terminology. You should describe various changes in the family and then look at possible reasons, such as the changing role of women, changes in norms and values. You should refer to studies wherever possible.

Write about 500-750 words.

Discussion point

- How would your family life change if you had no televisions, computers or phones? Perhaps ask older relatives about their childhood experiences without such items. How were their experiences of childhood different from yours?

Do I have a baby or not? Do I marry the father of the baby? Do I have a baby and go to work? Do I delay motherhood? Shall I freeze my partner's sperm till I am ready for pregnancy? Do I want to marry another woman? Do I even want a child?

Modern women have choices regarding childbearing that would not have been possible for their mothers because of the effects of social pressure and social change.

Topic 4: Demography and social change

Whilst there is some disagreement among sociologists about which are the most significant social changes, most commentators agree that changes in the marriage and divorce rates, the rise of cohabitation, longer life expectancy, declining fertility and the growth in singlehood are very significant. Each of these demographic changes requires careful discussion for one of two reasons. The first is that they could form the basis of examination questions, but the second is because they illustrate wider issues of change in the family.

Getting you thinking

Attitudes towards single parents have changed. Until quite late in the 20th century unmarried mothers were often sent to have their baby away from their local community and were encouraged to give up their children for adoption. This reflected the **stigma** attached to pregnancy outside of marriage. In some cases the young woman was labelled as mentally ill or defective, with a lengthy stay in a mental health hospital resulting from the pregnancy. Now almost half of babies are born to women who are not married, though many will be cohabiting or in other long-term relationships.

Discussion point: What would be the consequences for modern society if lone parenthood were banned?

Marriage

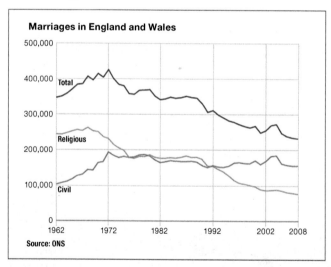

The line graph shows that the total number of marriages has dropped by about a third between 1962 and 2008. The highest number of marriages was in 1972, and although the decline has not been annual, the trend shows that the number of marriages is falling. There have been slight rises in marriage; for example, between 2002 and 2008 there was a clear rise, but the overall trend has been for marriage rates to fall. Interestingly, in the 1970s and 1980s, while marriage rates were relatively high, the number of religious ceremonies fell.

New Right thinkers tend to believe that government policy has not supported marriage and that the **welfare system** encourages people not to marry. Right-wing thinker, Sheila Lawlor, in 2012, claimed that paid maternity leave should be scrapped because it encouraged women to go back to work part-time and they then claimed in-work tax credits because they earned low pay. She argued that young women depend on the state to pay for their children. Charles Murray (1990) links welfare payment to unmarried women, illegitimate births, crime and refusal of young men to get jobs because they no longer need to be responsible for the children they father.

There is evidence that formal traditional religious belief in England and Wales is being replaced by personal and individual beliefs. This process is known as **secularisation**. The

Christian church believes very strongly in the religious nature of a marriage vow. Not only that, but the belief is that sex should only take place within a married relationship. As fewer people are involved in organised religion, this means that people feel less pressure to marry in order to either have sex or children.

Divorce

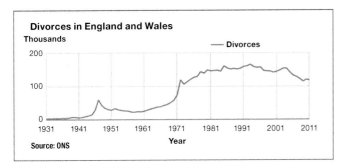

Question: Summarise the content of the graph showing divorce statistics since 1931.

For most people divorce was almost impossible for legal, cost and social reasons until the 1940s and very difficult until the 1970s. The figures in the table reflect legal changes as much as anything. The recent fall in divorce numbers is almost entirely due to the fall in marriage rates and the increase in cohabitation. In 1949, Legal Aid for divorce and the availability of divorce courts in cities other than London meant more people could afford divorce. In 1971, the Divorce Reform Act made it easier to obtain a divorce and more changes in 1984 and in 1996 continued that trend. The New Right argue that it is too easy divorce and this results in casual attitudes to marriage. However, given that fewer people are choosing to marry, the probability is that few people marry in the assumption that they can or will divorce if marriage does not work.

Social attitudes towards divorce have changed. It was a matter of deep shame for a family until the 1960s. This can be linked to secularisation; Wilson (1966) argues that as the influence of formal religion declined, the belief of the Church that people should stay married became irrelevant. Fletcher (1966) claimed that people expected more of marriage than in the past. Probably the most significant social change is the social status of women who no longer need to be married because they have economic independence. One significant contributory factor to this social change has been the rise of feminism. Women have come to expect more from life than marriage and domestic work.

What social factors contribute to divorce?

Cohabitation

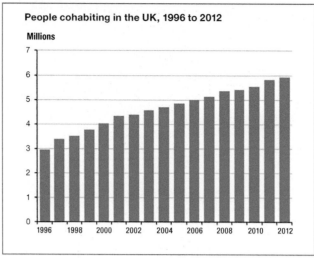

People cohabiting in the UK, 1996 to 2012

Source: ONS

Question: Summarise the content of the graph showing cohabitation since 1996.

> Love and marriage go together like a horse and carriage.
>
> **Sammy Cahn**

Social attitudes towards sex outside marriage have changed, but cohabitation has shown the most change. Fewer people are accepting of extra-marital sex or same-sex relationships than are accepting of cohabitation. Coast (2009) used the British Panel Survey to look at cohabitation, which she defined in terms of a sexual but non-married partnership. She claimed that evidence suggests that cohabitation is normal for couples. Because more people have experienced cohabitation, more people accept it as a valid living arrangement. In the past, cohabitation was seen as a form of 'trial' marriage. Recent studies have suggested that teenagers now expect a period of cohabitation, even when marriage or a long-term partnership is not the goal of the relationship. Morgan (2012), a New Right commentator, suggests that people choose cohabitation because they are scared of divorce.

A second reason for cohabitation could be economic. There is pressure on couples to have expensive 'dream' weddings and so some couples wait until they are more financially secure and established in careers and home before taking the step of formalising their relationship. A survey of 450 people conducted in 2013 by a law firm, Seddons, and reported in the Daily Mail, found that 16% do not want to marry until they have bought a house and 40% felt they could not afford a wedding. Only 25% felt marriage was not necessary.

Singlehood

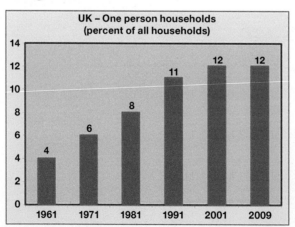

UK – One person households (percent of all households)

Source: http://ukhousebubble.blogspot.co.uk/2011/02/one-is-lonely-number.html

Question: Summarise the content of the graph showing singlehood since 1961.

The graph shows a steady rise in single person households over the period 1961 to 2009. The single most significant rise was in the ten-year period 1981–1991 when single person households rose by 3%.

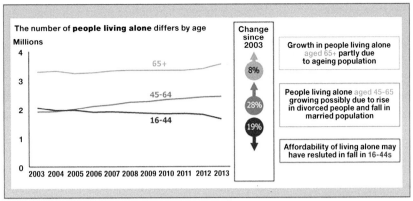

Source: ONS

People most likely to live alone are those who are older, particularly women over 75 who have been widowed (on average women live longer than men), but there is a steady increase in slightly younger people who have divorced and now choose singlehood. Many of these are males who have left a family home. The fastest growth is among this social group. The Census shows that men who lived alone in 1981 were still alone in later life. Smith et al. (2005) and Chandler et al. (2004) suggest that most older people who live alone will not live with other people again.

One of the reasons identified for the increase in singlehood has been what Durkheim called the cult of the individual. He claimed that as traditional farming lifestyles broke down, people began to put themselves before community. Today, people are required to be true to themselves, and so, for example, as Klinenburg (2012) pointed out, living alone is seen as a mark of success among younger people. Community pressure would once have held unsatisfactory marriages together, now people are pressured to leave unhappy relationships. Research has suggested that people who have never married are as happy as those who do, and much happier than the widowed and divorced.

Life expectancy

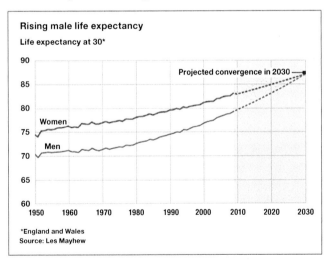

Question: Summarise the content of the graph showing life expectancy since 1960.

Life expectancy refers to how long people can expect to live, on average. Many factors have contributed to longer life expectancy, including improved living standards, better health care and effective sanitation. Women generally live longer than men, though the gap is reducing as lifestyles change and the traditional dangerous male industries have declined. There is also reduced death associated with frequent childbirth and illegal abortion for women.

One other obvious cause of increased life expectancy is technological. Improved medical technology means that we can now expect to survive illnesses that might have killed us in the past, and we are vaccinated against diseases that might kill us when we are children. Homes are safer and cleaner. Poor hygiene was a major killer in the earlier part

Discussion point

- For some people there is forced singlehood as a result of the end of a relationship. Others have chosen to live alone: elective singlehood. How might this affect the way that singlehood is experienced?

Activity

Go to www.NHS.UK and search life expectancy to see recent research on how life expectancy is changing in modern Britain.

Activity

Use the term living alone in a search engine and look at the sites that turn up. What do they tell you about modern attitudes to living alone? List the advantages and disadvantages of living alone.

99% of all statistics only tell 49% of the story.

Ron DeLegge II, Gents with No Cents

of the last century so public health priorities such as baths in homes and fresh clean water help us to live longer.

Fertility

Question: Summarise the content of the bar graphs showing children per family since 1996.

Fewer women are having children than in the past. Those who have children, have fewer. There are many reasons for these changes in fertility. The most obvious is the technology of contraception. Until the 1960s, finished family size was largely a choice that men made. By the 1960s, contraception had become more reliable, and the availability of the contraceptive pill meant that women could choose whether or not to have children. The impact of this change was far wider than controlling family size. It separated sex from marriage and gave women far greater independence to control their lives. They could work, freed from the need to provide childcare. The health of women and children improved. It became apparent that, when given the choice, women often chose not to have large families.

The ability of women to control their own reproduction led to a massive change in women's attitudes. Feminism meant that they began to demand other rights, such as the right to abortion on demand. Once women could control their bodies, they began to enjoy rights, such as the right to equal pay, the right to abortion and the choice of higher education and fulfilling work. These all had an impact on fertility: women now start their families later, and have smaller families. Small families are now seen as desirable for social and economic reasons; women expect more from their lives than domestic work and childbirth.

> *Politicians use statistics in the same way that a drunk uses lamp-posts – for support rather than illumination.*
>
> **Andrew Lang**

Source: Labour Force Survey Datasets

1. Dependent children as those living with their parent(s) and either (a) aged under 16, or (b) aged 16 to 18 in full-time education, excluding children aged 16 to 18 who have a spouse, partner or child living in the household.

Sample questions

Marital and civil partnership status of the resident adult population in England and Wales, 2001 and 2011

Source: ONS

a) Summarise the content of the bar chart showing the relationship status of the adult population of England and Wales.

b) Explain **two** sociological reasons for the growth in the number of single people.

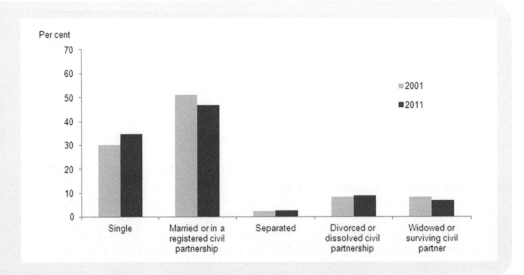

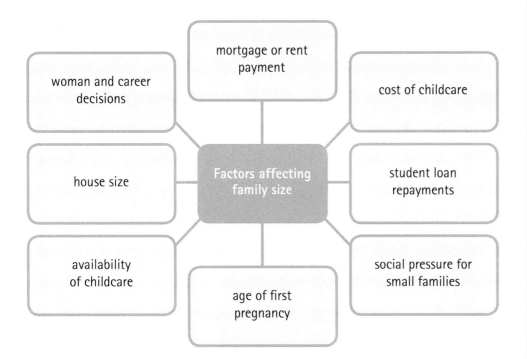

For each of the demographic changes to the family that are discussed, make a list of reasons that are not mentioned in the topic. Develop further ideas for factors that could have contributed to the changes described.

Check your own learning

Complete the following table. Select reasons for living alone and put them where they make most sense:

Money to be able to live alone   Good health   Relationship breakdown

Partner dies   Leaving parents' home   Job reasons

Removed from parental home   Individuality   No one to share home with

Good social networks   Children leave home

Reasons for singlehood and living alone	Choice factors	Situational factors
Younger people		
Older people		

Extended writing

Discuss sociological reasons for increased family diversity in the contemporary England and Wales.

Guidance: There is a vast array of reasons why family diversity is increasing. In order to make sense of the question and to organise your answer in a clear and comprehensible way, it would be sensible to pick out four or five reasons. Choose ones such as legal change, medical technology, the changing status of women, demographic change and normative change. Explain each with reference to some form of family type and reference to a study or theory that you might have covered in class.

Write about 500-750 words.

Aims

◉ **The experience of childhood varies from generation to generation, and as society changes, so does the relationship between children and adults**

It is difficult to generalise about people's experiences of childhood. These would be different according to geography, gender, ethnicity and social class. Relying on memory is not valid, because memories are selective and can be inaccurate. However, there are arguments to say that childhood is a recent social idea, mostly found in Western countries where children are valued and protected. However, there are also fears that children's experiences of childhood mean that childhood is now disappearing again, or is actually bad for children and society.

Topic 5: Describing family relationships: children

Getting you thinking

In 2014, the Conservative/ Liberal Democrat coalition government proposed that emotional abuse of children should become a criminal offence. With your study partner, discuss arguments for and against this policy.

Childhood

- laws controlling children (e.g. alcohol)
- fewer children in families
- children are a market for consumer goods
- changes in family structure (e.g. divorce)
- Reasons for changes in childhood
- children are no longer expected to work
- laws protecting children (age of consent)
- children are legally entitled to education

In the 1950s Parsons merely viewed children in terms of requiring socialisation into adulthood. Children were not often studied as a separate sociological issue, which reflects social attitudes to children and childhood. Many of the early researchers such as Aries (1960) were arguing from a historical background and looking at social change. They argued that childhood was a social construction and that the idea of children as separate and special had only developed over the last 150 years in the West. Indeed, in many developing countries, children are still seen as a source of income for families and are expected to work and contribute to the family economy.

It was not till the 1980s that there was much interest in childhood from sociologists. For example, feminists did not direct attention to the sexual abuse of children in families until 1988. At the same time, there was government interest in children, and international agreement in 1989 to the UN Convention on the Rights of the Child. In the UK, the Children Act (1989) gave a number of agencies a duty to protect the welfare of children and encouraged support for family and parents.

The social construction of childhood

James and Prout (1997) emphasised the socially constructed nature of childhood. They said that the fact that children are immature is a biological fact, but the meanings societies attach to that make childhood a separate area of study. They said that children's relationships with adults and other children are worthy of study, as children are not passive, but active participants in creating childhood. They suggested that ethnography is a useful way of studying childhood.

Mayall (1994, 2002) argues that children should be studied because they have an expressive and instrumental role in families. They may support their parents, they make relationships and they often take care of younger siblings or older people. Hey (1997), in a study of girl's friendships, points out that girls can be supportive and sharing, but they also bitch, fall out and exclude others from their social networks. Frosh (2002) studied boys and how they constructed masculinity, finding that being 'manly' prevented boys from discussing or managing emotions.

Pilcher (1995) said that a key feature of modern childhood is that it is seen as separate and special. It is even argued that British society has become child-centred. As parents have fewer children, most of whom they can expect to reach adulthood, they invest more time and energy in their children. Children have consumer goods and government services. Laws protect them; doctors look after their emotional and physical well-being. Parents become pressurised to buy things in order to satisfy their children.

Much sociological and political debate centres on the view that children and childhood are threatened. In 1994, Neil Postman said that childhood is disappearing and used as evidence:

⊙ Children have rights.
⊙ Children can access the adult world through television.
⊙ Children imitate adult behaviour in dress, and in criminal activity.

Research methods

What are the difficulties involved in studying children? Think of practical and ethical issues.

Discussion point

● What difficulties might you experience if you wanted to test the idea that emotional climate affects the quality of parenting?

Perhaps now more than ever it is hard to be a child and tough to be a parent. Children are told that they are unhappy, stressed or damaged and parents are told that they are selfish, irresponsible and failing.

Equality and diversity forum

115

By the age of seven, a child born today will have spent the equivalent of a full year watching television. A hundred years ago television did not exist. What impact might this have on experiences of childhood?

STRETCH and CHALLENGE

Find out more about Parenting Orders which were set up as a result of the Crime and Disorder Act 1998.

http://www.familylives.org.uk/advice/teenagers/behaviour/what-is-a-parenting-order/

https://www.gov.uk/if-my-child-gets-in-trouble-with-police

Discussion point

- In 2006, a senior politician, David Cameron, said 'some relationship experts describe the moment of childbirth as the "Magic Moment" ... Making sure that both parents are really engaged at the moment of birth is therefore important'. Not everyone would agree with David Cameron. In 2010, the former footballer, John Barnes missed the birth of his child, opting to commentate on a premiership football match. Who do you think is right?

By 2006, Sue Palmer had described modern **childhood** as being **toxic** (poisonous) because working parents mean that children have less adult time, they are vulnerable to damage through technological change, junk food, and television. This, she claimed, leads to obesity, self-harm, drug abuse, early sex and parenthood and binge drinking. It has now become a media issue with many stories of bad parenting, and television programmes showing people how to parent. Furedi (2008) suggests that parenting is now seen as a complex skill which people must learn in order to fulfil their duties as parents. Gillies has pointed out that this is a class and gender issue for mothers, because the New Right have identified poverty as being linked to poor parenting; but what of the affluent parent who subcontracts childcare to nannies, nurseries and boarding school?

In evaluation, however, the case for the end of childhood is not so clear cut because childhood has been extended. More and more adult children rely on parental help because they cannot afford to leave the family home. In addition, education is now being extended to people up to the age of 18.

Public policy and family

Since the 1990s, there have been many attempts by government to intervene in specific elements of family life and relationships. There have been 'family friendly' policies in work, and parents are encouraged to participate in the life of schools. In the *Every Child Matters* framework (2003) teachers and officials are expected to identify children at risk of harm, for example concerns about childhood obesity have led to monitoring of food given in packed lunches.

Sample questions

Though there have been many changes in family life, the **traditional nuclear family** remains with us. Changes have occurred as the role women play has changed: more women work outside as well as inside the home, and there are fewer children. The family has also been affected by the development of the welfare state, technology and changing social attitudes.

a) Describe the features of a **traditional nuclear family**.
b) Explain **two** reasons why there have been changes in childhood in the contemporary England and Wales.

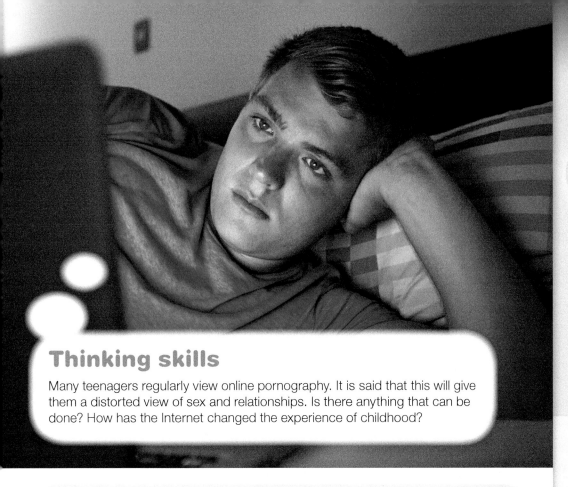

Discussion point

- Why do you think some childcare and child rearing practices are regarded as better than others by politicians? What would postmodernists say about this judgemental approach?

Thinking skills

Many teenagers regularly view online pornography. It is said that this will give them a distorted view of sex and relationships. Is there anything that can be done? How has the Internet changed the experience of childhood?

Research idea

Find out more about childhood and parenting in the Chinese community by using Google to research Amy Chua who writes about 'tiger mothers'.

Check your own learning

Match the family type to the description.

a)	This is an idea or concept that people share and believe to be reality.	Child-centred
b)	Taking care of people's emotions.	Emotional climate
c)	Parents focus their attention on their children rather than other aspects of their lives.	Disappearing childhood
d)	Items that can be bought: computers, toys, clothing.	Toxic childhood
e)	Children do not have a special time to be children but are miniature adults.	Social construction
f)	The atmosphere and quality of family relationships within a household.	Consumer goods
g)	The modern experience of childhood is poisonous and harmful to children.	Expressive role

INTERESTING FACT

A team of researchers from the University of Sussex studied 173 families with at least two children aged between 4 and 8 years. They found that better educated parents were less harsh with discipline and more constructive. Families who were more emotional and angry tended to have poorer relationships, particularly between children and mothers. The research suggested that mothers influence the family emotional climate more than fathers do.

Extended writing

Discuss the view that modern childhood is toxic to children.

Guidance: This essay asks you to look at one particular theory, so you will need to describe and explain that theory. However, you will also need to define childhood, so you may need to think about the question of whether childhood is just one part of life or whether it is qualitatively different from other stages of life. What are the risks to modern children? How realistic is it to view modern childhood as toxic? There are arguments both for and against that view.

Write about 500 words.

Aims

- ⦿ As family structures and forms have changed, so have relationships within couples, and the aim of this topic is to look at some of those changes

One of the many influences of interpretivism and of feminism on sociology since the 1970s has been the increased importance of social connections and social meanings as a topic of study. Functionalist accounts of family relationships tended to present the nuclear family as positive and centred on the female/mother role. By the 1970s, however, sociologists were hugely critical of this perspective. Feminists said that women were denied social roles outside the home because of the expectation that they would devote their lives to their family. The feminist critique developed within the context of increasing divorce, singlehood and single-parenthood all affecting family relationships at the same time as women's involvement in the labour market was changing.

Inequality between the genders in relationships may exist in more than one dimension.

Topic 6: Describing family relationships: conjugal relationships

Getting you thinking

Who in your family is responsible for decisions regarding money, taking on the work of looking after emotions and for doing the jobs in the home?

Conjugal roles

Families described in the past tended to emphasise the notion of segregated or separated conjugal roles. In this view of family, husbands and wives had different roles; men worked for family income and women cared for family and children. They spent little time together and men could dominate decision making because they controlled the finances. Functionalists argued that men and women had naturally different roles; men had instrumental roles because they took charge of family life. Women had expressive roles as they cared for family emotional life. Parsons viewed this as essentially a good thing, but by the 1960s and 1970s, feminists such as Gavron, Oakley and Firestone were challenging that description. They were conducting research and finding that women felt oppressed by family obligations.

Domestic labour

As this debate was taking place in sociology, social changes meant that more women were taking on jobs outside the home, and the fight for equal pay for men and women was a prominent political and social debate. Parsons believed that women could express themselves emotionally through caring for families. In the 1970s, Wilmott and Young suggested that men helped women in the home more. While they observed change, they still

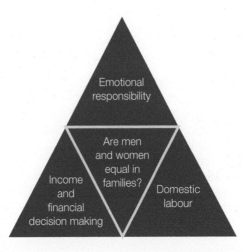

saw domestic labour as the job of women. Increasingly, feminists such as Oakley and Gavron, challenged this view and saw housework as being oppressive and dissatisfying. They described women experiencing boredom and loneliness, combined with excessive workloads. As women moved into the workforce, feminists described the triple shift. Women worked outside the home, but came home to housework and family support, thus taking on three jobs. Devine (1992) found that because women were working, men had to take on domestic work, but this was because it was necessary rather than because they wanted to or felt they ought to.

Decision making

There is a debate as to how much change was actually taking place within the family, and whether it occurred at the same pace across society. Stephen Edgell (1980) found that men made the infrequent important decisions in middle-class families even when wives earned money. Pahl (1989) found that men and women made decisions about different matters, so while women make frequent small decisions: what to have for dinner, men were responsible for bigger expensive issues such as buying a car. Hunt (1977) said that women make more decisions, but not the significant ones. Hardhill et al. (1997) studied families where both partners worked and found male domination of family decisions, but noted a shift towards more equal relationships. Gershuny (1992) talked about lagged adaptation; as more women were going into work, males were having to change but did this more slowly than women.

Emotions

One of the main criticisms of functionalism came from feminists who pointed out that there may be a dark side to the conventional nuclear family. The control of women was seen as natural, so male violence was not seen as a problem. Erin Pizzey set up the first refuge in London in 1971, but by the 1980s there were over 200. Hanmer (1983) and Saunders (1984) found that women's behaviour inside the home is constrained by fear of men.

Despite governments stating that tackling domestic abuse and violence is a priority, official statistics show that fear of domestic violence is justified. A Home Office document published in 2014 (*Strengthening the Law on Domestic Abuse - a Consultation*) defined domestic abuse as 'any incident or pattern of incidents of controlling, coercive, threatening behaviour, violence or abuse between those aged 16 or over who are, or have been, intimate partners or family members regardless of gender or sexuality'. It stated that in the previous year there had been 77 murders of partners. Statistics collected by Her Majesty's Inspector of Constabulary (HMIC) included:

Topic 6: Describing family relationships: conjugal relationships

Developing understanding

Watch the film *Made in Dagenham* (2010) to understand some of the changes that were taking place in the lives of women in the 1960s.

Are modern relationships more companionate and equal?

- ◉ 96,000 assault with injury crimes reported in 2013 were domestic abuse related.
- ◉ Every 30 seconds someone will call the police regarding a domestic abuse related incident.
- ◉ 269,700 domestic abuse related crimes were reported to the police in the last year.

> We can't destroy the inequities between men and women until we destroy marriage.
>
> Robin Morgan

Discussion point

- What arguments could you make for and against the view that domestic work is liberating for women because they have control over their work and can choose how to spend their time?

A more positive view is that relationships are becoming **companionate** with couples sharing interests and putting more time into their emotional lives. Anthony Giddens, for example, claimed that people now had 'pure relationships' where people only stayed together on the grounds that both were satisfied, rather than staying together out of necessity. He distinguished between romantic love, which was a myth that tied women to the home and family, and confluent love, which is for the mutual satisfaction of both partners. There is a claim that **joint conjugal relationships** are developing, where men and women have equal responsibility for making each other happy.

A controversial argument was developed by Catherine Hakim (1995). She suggested that women have less commitment to work because fewer of them have jobs than men. She claims that women have erotic capital and can control men through their desire for sex. She also believes that women can exploit men in the family and at work. Her argument is that the majority of women are happiest in the traditional family where they may prefer to be homemakers despite the fact that they have choices.

Sample questions

The Time Use Surveys (2000, 2005) show that at all ages women carry out about two-thirds of domestic labour. Gender affects which tasks are carried out, men are more likely to do repairs, and women the cooking, cleaning and shopping. When comparing household work and paid work, men and women do around the same. Men spend more time in paid work but women work part time and do more housework. This is **segregated conjugal roles**.

Source: ONS data Time Use Survey 2005

a) Describe the features of **segregated conjugal roles**.
b) Explain **two** reasons why there have been changes in conjugal roles in the contemporary England and Wales.

Extended writing

Discuss the view that conjugal relationships are equal in contemporary England and Wales.

Guidance: You will need to address a range of concepts in this essay: triple shift, dual burden, socialisation, domestic division of labour and conjugal roles. To get the highest marks you should question the extent to which change has actually taken place. You might claim that change has been exaggerated, or you might suggest that change is taking place more slowly. Refer to studies and evidence to support your views.

Write about 500-750 words.

Check your own learning
Match the terms to their meanings.

a)	Women work outside the home, do domestic work and also the caring role.	Segregated conjugal roles
b)	Women work outside the home and then do additional work in the home.	Joint conjugal roles
c)	Men and women take on totally different responsibilities in the home.	Dual burden
d)	Men and women support each other and share activities.	Dark side of family
e)	Men are taking their time to realise that they need to input more into the home due to their wives working.	Triple shift
f)	The feminist view that nuclear families are dangerous places for women and children.	Lagged adaptation

Research methods

How would you operationalise the term equality in conjugal roles for a questionnaire? There are many factors to consider, such as emotional work, income and decision making and the division of household labour.

Activity

Look at each of the possible reasons for changes in conjugal roles in the diagram. Explain each one and offer sociological evidence to describe what effect it has had on conjugal roles in the family.

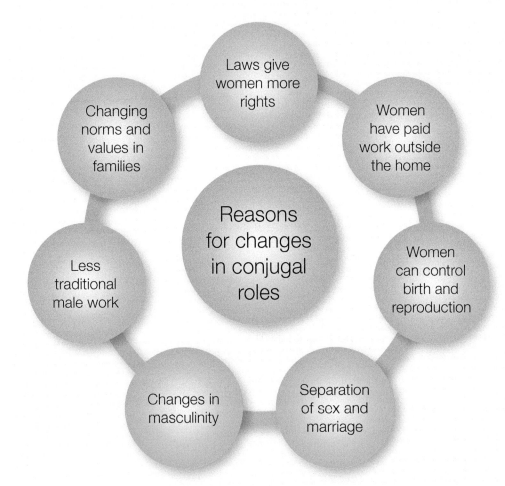

Reasons for changes in conjugal roles

- Laws give women more rights
- Women have paid work outside the home
- Women can control birth and reproduction
- Separation of sex and marriage
- Changes in masculinity
- Less traditional male work
- Changing norms and values in families

Aims

⊙ Over ten million people in the UK are 65 years or older and the numbers are likely to double by 2050. As the population ages, the impact of this on family relationships becomes more important to sociology and social policy

As people can expect significantly longer and healthier lives, the proportion of elderly people in the population is growing quickly. This is a major demographic change and combined with other changes in family such as child-freedom, divorce and the growth of beanpole family forms, there are serious implications for family relationships. Many grandparents are taking on parental roles, for example caring for children while parents work. However, they themselves may require care from their own adult children in later old age.

★ INTERESTING FACT

A growing proportion of single grandparents have children who are single parents themselves (31% in 1998 rising to 38% in 2007). These families are particularly at risk of financial hardship.

Topic 7: Describing family relationships: grandparents

Getting you thinking

What are the advantages and disadvantages to children of being brought up by older people such as their grandparents?

The social construction of age

In the past, life expectancy was short and few people expected to live beyond seventy or eighty. Many people would experience years of ill-health before death. In modern UK, we now talk of the third age. This is a period of active retirement when people may be fit and healthy, but no longer working full time. This may last for many years before people enter the phase of being elderly and perhaps physically dependent on other people.

Grandparenthood and family support

The emphasis that functionalists and the New Right have placed on the nuclear family means that extended families are often overlooked in terms of both their emotional and their financial importance to families. For example, grandparents are a significant and important source of childcare and child-rearing in modern Britain. Estimates of the average age at which people become grandparents vary between 47 and 54 but the data is not especially reliable. When families break down it is often wider family who take over some of the childcare or emotional support and this is increasingly the role of grandparents who are probably older but fitter than in previous generations. Increasing numbers of people are becoming step-grandparents as well. This is complicating family relationships.

It is estimated that grandparents provide between 40 and 70% of childcare. They may be bringing their grandchildren up. Both Hillman (2007) and Hastings (1997) found that in families with multiple disadvantages (for example, lone parents of disabled children); grandparents were providing emotional, practical and financial support, often at some cost to themselves in terms of time and earnings.

It is unusual for grandparents to be paid for their caring, so older people are providing financial support for their own children by taking on childcare. This level of care provision is complicated for many people, especially women, as they are also likely to be caring for their own elderly parents. They may also have jobs. Thus, the term **sandwich generation** has been applied to people who may be in their 50s, who are supporting elderly parents, their children and perhaps their grandchildren at the same time.

Caring for the elderly

As people grow older and more vulnerable, they may require support to enable them to continue to live in their own homes. Many older people experience loneliness and are vulnerable to depression. This can come about through ill-health and bereavement. This appears to affect older men who are less likely to have maintained social contacts with family. Bryan (2011) found that carers are most likely to be women and men in their forties and fifties. Most carers are in work, and there is an upward trend for retirement age due to pension changes. It is estimated that nearly 3,000,000 workers are also carers. People in late middle age are therefore under significant pressure and unable to offer as much help and support to their own elderly parents as they might wish.

Relationship between adult children and the elderly

There is a direct link between well-being in the elderly and the amount of social contact they receive from their children. Factors that may influence social contact may include geographical distance, hours worked, ability to use technologies such as computers and social networking.

Increasingly, there is awareness of elder abuse. Older people may be at risk of abuse from relatives or carers and may be exploited or harmed in a variety of ways. Victims tend to be over the age of 70 and often the abuser is a family member.

Sample questions

As many as 370,000 older people have been abused in their own homes by a carer, relative or friend in the last year, according to figures, exposing what has been described as a 'hidden national scandal'.

By 2020 the number is estimated to increase to 457,600; by 2030 the number is set to hit around 558,700. The projected increase in the number of people being abused correlates with the ageing of the country's population.

http://www.theguardian.com/society/2013/sep/08/elderly-abuse-carer-relative

a) Summarise the item on elder abuse in the UK.
b) Explain the growth in the proportion of elderly people in the population.
c) Using material from the item and your own sociological knowledge, explain **two** possible reasons why these figures may not be reliable.

Check your own learning

Match the beginnings and ends of the sentences.

a)	Elder abuse is where older	between 40 and 50, though carers can be all ages.
b)	The most usual age to be a carer is	the period between retirement and extreme old age when ill health is an issue.
c)	Probably up to 3,000,000 people have	caring for children and their own parents.
d)	Men are more likely to experience depression in old age	people are at risk of harm and exploitation from carers.
e)	The sandwich generation are people who have a dual role	full-time employment as well as caring responsibility.
f)	Third age describes	because they are less likely to maintain social contacts with friends and family.

What social and historical changes might a centenarian have experienced?

Extended writing

Discuss the view that grandparents are essential to the support of families in England and Wales.

Guidance: The evidence that grandparents are essential to the support of families is overwhelming, so answers that suggest they are not useful will probably not gain many marks unless very good evidence is provided. Given that, the question then is not asking you to consider the opposite point of view, but to look at ways in which grandparents may support families. You should look at a variety of options, both care of children and perhaps care for the elderly old as well.

Write about 300 words.

Aims

- To explain why functionalism remains influential despite the fact that many argue it offers a dated view of family

Functionalists see the family as a key social structure that holds society together. It argues that family structures have changed to suit the needs of industrial societies. Families exist to socialise children into the norms and values of society and to help people deal with the stresses of work and the pressures of society. The functionalist view of the family has been criticised because it is seen as being too optimistic. Whilst it has supporting studies, it overlooks the darker side of family life.

Public policy and family

Senior politician, Harriet Harman, said in 1997 that because the tax and benefit system had been changed, it marked 'the end of the assumption that families consist of a male breadwinner and a female helpmate in the home'.

Topic 8: Functionalist views of family

Getting you thinking

"STRESSED" is "DESSERTS" spelled backwards

To what extent is it true that the family is good for society and individuals within families?

What do functionalists say about families?

The functionalist theory of family suggests that the nuclear family has developed to suit the needs of modern industrial society. This idea is known as the fit thesis. The characteristics that make the nuclear family suitable for modern society are that people are no longer relying on wider family networks for survival and they are geographically mobile. They can move to where work is. The fit thesis has been challenged by historians of family on a number of points. However, Parsons argues that the family fulfils two functions for society:

- The socialisation of children.
- The stabilisation of the adult personality.

In this view of the family, it fulfils vital functions for society. Children are taught the rules for society from their parents, thus it is part of social control. They learn gender roles from their parents, thus are socialised to become future adults themselves. Women pass on expressive roles to their daughters, and so the welfare of family members is ensured.

Murdock studied families in a variety of cultures and claimed that not only is the nuclear family common to all cultures, it has four functions:

- Control of sexual behaviour of adults.
- Economic support for children.
- Reproduction of society through new members.
- Education of family members.

> All happy families are alike; each unhappy family is unhappy in its own way.
>
> **Leo Tolstoy**

Chester (1985) suggested that despite families appearing to have changed since the time that Parsons wrote, this was simply a surface change. He described the neo-conventional family. This is a dual-earning family in which both partners work. He claimed that the extent of family change had been exaggerated.

Strengths of functionalism as a theory of family
The main strength of functionalism is that it recognises the importance of family to people, and sees its importance in organising society. Furthermore, it sees how the

family is central to social structure and how it controls our behaviour. It explains why people follow social rules and emphasises the importance of social stability.

Weaknesses of functionalism

There are many criticisms from a theoretical point of view, especially from Marxism and feminism, which claim that the functionalists overlook the dark side of family life, the exploitation of women and the way that families are part of the ideology of capitalism.

The support of the nuclear family by politicians and functionalism implies that other family forms are lacking and unsatisfactory in some way. This has provided a theoretical base for the ideas and social policies of the New Right.

Much functionalist writing on the family is at a theoretical level and not supported by studies.

Sample questions

In 2014, an online survey of Welsh adults was conducted by YouGov for a leading charity. More than 2,000 people responded and 59% said family life was harder now than in the 1990s; 61% felt that families were let down by public services such as GPs and youth centres; 40% worried that their children would not have the opportunity for a good life. As a result of the survey, the charity has called for more **family-friendly policy** in government, more help with childcare and for flexible and part-time working including improved maternity and paternity leave.

a) Describe the meaning of the term **family-friendly policy**.
b) Explain **two** functions of the modern family.

Check your own learning

Sort out the following statements and decide if they are strengths or weaknesses of the functional view of family.

This theory shows how the family supports social structure and society.

The approach is very positive and overlooks the fact that families are not all good.

By stressing the importance of the nuclear family, it is critical of other types of family.

The approach shows a link between individuals and the whole of society.

It does not understand that other social structures can take on family roles.

The functionalist approach stresses the emotional importance of family life.

Extended writing

Discuss functionalist views of the family.

Guidance: In this essay, you should describe functionalist views of the family. Go back through the book and look for references to Parsons and functionalism to develop your descriptions. You will need to refer to other writers in the same perspective such as Murdock. When you have done that, you will need to mention the strengths of functionalism and back up your points with evidence. It is easier to criticise functionalism as you can then refer to other influential theories to pass comment on functionalist ideas.

Write about 500 words.

Discussion point

- Is the end of the assumption of female housewives and male breadwinners a good thing for our society? Refer to sociological evidence.

When considering theories, you should look back through the book and see what ideas and evidence you can use from other topics, for example the warm bath thesis is relevant here as it forms part of functionalist theory of family. See page 95.

Activity

Write a paragraph about functionalism and the family using all of the following words:

nuclear institutions

function breadwinner

values roles

expressive instrumental

Aims

- **To consider the view Marxism offers of the family: a critical and negative view of traditional family life suggesting it supports capitalism, traps men and exploits women and children**

In the 1970s, when many sociologists were critical of the optimistic and traditional view of families offered by functionalism, they turned to look at work on families written in the 1880s by Engels, a close friend of Marx. This argued that the family and marriage had evolved to control women and to pass on property. Inheritance was through the family, with property left to children; monogamy meant that men could be certain they left property to their children. This is essentially a negative view of families but it has been used by Marxists to analyse society, and as the basis of some feminist perspectives on family life.

STRETCH and CHALLENGE

Identify the similarities and the differences between functionalist and Marxist views of family.

Topic 9: Marxist views of family

Getting you thinking

With a study partner, consider the ways in which families and family life might act as a support to capitalist society.

Marriage is ... incontestably a form of exclusive private property.

What do you think Karl Marx meant by this statement?

What do Marxists say about families?

In many ways, Marxism and functionalism say very similar things about families: both recognise that the family passes on ideas and values and both see family members as part of an economic unit. The real area of difference is that while functionalists believe families are good for society, Marxists suggest that they are bad for people and for society.

Marxists tend to argue that the purpose of the family is to:

- Socialise children into the norms of capitalist society through their acceptance that the father is dominant and in control. Thus they learn that different people have power and they have none. Althusser, a French Marxist, argued that families taught children to accept inequality.
- Ensure that women are controlled. Their work is unpaid, but they support workers and that benefits capitalism.
- Work is stressful and unpleasant, so working men can relieve their frustrations in the family.
- The family is a unit of consumption; families purchase goods and services and this supports capitalism.

In the Marxist view of the family, the family is for the benefit of men, thus it is patriarchal. This is a point that was developed by feminists. Eli Zaretsky (1976) said that the family supports capitalism because it is the one place that working men can feel they have power. This helps them accept their lack of control in wider society. It has also been argued that men who have families are less likely to challenge employers or take risks such as political activity or strike action because they need to work and earn to support their families.

Strengths of Marxism as a theory of family

- Marxists explain the ideological role of families in society and suggest reasons people feel strongly about family structure and organisation.
- Marxism offers an explanation of why families first developed in society.
- Marxism points out the unpleasant aspects of family life and the inequalities of power within families.
- Feminist perspectives have based their analysis on Marxist views of family.

Weaknesses of Marxism

- Marxists are criticised for only looking at the negative side of family life and ignoring its positives. Perhaps family life is not as violent or unpleasant as Marxists assert.
- The family is seen in terms of its economic relationship to society and this is simplistic. It also operates on the basic assumption that capitalism is a bad thing. It may not necessarily be so!
- Catherine Hakim and others have pointed out that Marxist views of the role of the women in families are dated. Women now have choices, but many still choose conventional family life.
- In addition, it is similar to functionalism in that the female perspective on family life tends to be overlooked.

Sample questions

Althusser argued that within the family home, parents can pass on messages to children that encourage them to accept ideas about society without really questioning them. He called the family an '**ideological state apparatus**'. By this, he meant that the family supports the state oppression of people. For example, when parents insist that they are obeyed, then children learn not to question authority. If parents give pocket money in exchange for tasks, then children learn about how the economy works and accept that they must be good workers in the future.

   a) With reference to the item and sociological knowledge, explain the meaning of the term **ideological state apparatus**.

   b) Using the item and sociological knowledge, explain **two** ways in which children learn to accept social control from ordinary family life.

Check your own learning
Fill in the missing words.

Marxists believe that family life supports _ _ _ _ _ _ _ _ _ _. It does this in a number of ways. Marxists claim that families evolved so that men could pass on wealth and property to their _ _ _ _ _ _ _ _ and they could control _ _ _ _ _. Families act as a unit of _ _ _ _ _ _ _ _ _ _ _, because they buy the products produced by capitalism. Men control the family, this is known as _ _ _ _ _ _ _ _ _ _. They are able to release the stress and frustration of their paid _ _ _ _ in their homes.

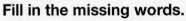

Public policy and family

Marx said that 'social progress can be measured exactly by the social position of the fair sex (women)'. What is the social position of women in our society?

Extended writing

Discuss Marxist views of the family.

Guidance: In this essay, you should start by describing Marxist views of the family. Ensure that you use language that is typical of Marxist analysis, concepts such as ideology, social control, capitalism, state and power. Show understanding of the link between the private lives of people in families and how this relates to the economic factors that govern society. You should be aware of weaknesses in Marxist views of society as well as any strengths.

Write about 500 words.

Marxists see influence going from parents to children through discipline. How true is this of normal family relationships in your view?

Aims

- Although the feminist movement was a feature of the second half of the 20th century, debates about gender inequality had been ongoing for many years before that. In the last century or so political campaigns have seen these issues challenged and women's rights and opportunities extended. Despite this, many feminists believe that changes in the family are essential if equality is ever to be achieved

There is a long history of female involvement in politics, art and society despite their generally low status and lack of power or political opportunity. In the 1960s, what we now call second wave feminism (the women's liberation movement) became a mainstream political and social force. Writers such as Betty Friedan and Germaine Greer popularised new ideas about the rights of women, and women could control their own reproduction. This had an influence on how new generations of women chose to live. Marriage became an option and not a life aim for these girls. However, the history of feminism is by no means an easy one, with many debates within the perspective as well as with other perspectives.

Topic 10: Feminist views of family

Getting you thinking

What do you think of when you hear the word feminism? What are the stereotypes of feminism in the media? Can a man be a feminist?

Feminisms

The underlying belief that all feminists share is that women experience injustice on the basis of their gender. Society works to favour men and this male domination of society is known as patriarchy. Most feminists agree that:

- Men oppress women, for example women work without pay in the home.
- Women are treated unfairly by men in law, so that violence against women is not always taken seriously by official agencies.
- Women are stereotyped in the media as being less efficient than men.
- Women are controlled through social perceptions of the ideal body image.
- Feminism should not be value-free, it should raise the consciousness of women as to their situation.

There are, however, a number of different feminisms. Here are the most common:

- *Liberal feminists* want to change culture and laws to make society more equal. They view gender socialisation as the cause of inequality.
- *Marxist feminists* see the family as the cause of inequality as women are domestic servants for men, and this mirrors the inequality of capitalist society.
- *Radical feminists* see men as the enemy and marriage as a fantasy into which women are drawn in order that men can control their behaviour.

Feminism and family

Given that feminism is not one single theory and not just a sociological movement, there is a huge amount of debate on the domestic situation of women. You need to be aware of the following key points, however:

- Different gender socialisation within the family is believed by most feminists to be the cause of social differences between males and females. Boys are taught to be aggressive and competitive whereas girls are encouraged to be domestic and obedient.

- Gender roles within the family mean that women have less freedom than men because they tend to earn less and spend more time on domestic labour.
- Men tend to control important decisions because they have financial power.
- Many men control women through the exercise or threat of domestic violence. Radical feminists, in particular, view men as potential rapists.

Strengths of feminism as a theory of family
- It has acted as a corrective to the very positive views of family life proposed by functionalists.
- Feminism has pointed out that much sociology of the family has a malestream bias because it views things from a male perspective.
- It has had a huge impact on the freedoms that ordinary women expect, even if they do not consider themselves feminists.
- Feminists have triggered research into areas of daily family life such as motherhood, food, housework and emotional life that were previously not seen as significant.

Weaknesses of feminism
- Hakim and others have suggested that women are not as entirely oppressed as feminists claim, and that many women do like domestic life.
- It fails to recognise that men may be just as constrained by socialisation into masculine roles as women are by feminine roles.
- Some feminist writing has been very extreme and hostile to men and assumes, for example, that all men are potential rapists.
- Feminism is not a united theory so therefore it is difficult to generalise from the various points of view.

Sample questions

Pantazis and Ruspini (2006) discovered that throughout the Western world, women do the majority of domestic work, although there is an increase in male participation in housework. Married women's health is generally worse than single women's, but married men enjoy better health. Lone women are wealthier than those who are married or single parents. Women are more vulnerable to domestic violence than men. Women are more likely to take parental leave than men. **Feminism** says that although women's situation in education and employment has improved, in the private sphere of family life, inequality is still a reality.

a) With reference to the item and sociological knowledge, explain the meaning of the term **feminism**.

b) Using the item and sociological knowledge, explain **two** ways in which men and women are unequal in family life.

Check your own learning

Match the terms to their meanings.

a)	Extreme form of feminism that views males as the enemy of women.	Malestream
b)	The domination of society by men.	Radical feminism
c)	Research that is from the viewpoint of men.	Liberal feminism
d)	Women need to address issues of culture and legal equality.	Marxist feminism
e)	Traditional families reflect the inequalities of wider society.	Patriarchy

Public policy and family

Feminists have pointed out that males control women through social policy in many ways. Tax allowances are offered for married dependents and children; for example, you can claim Married Couple's Allowance if all the following apply:

- You're married or in a civil partnership.
- You're living with your spouse or civil partner.
- One of you was born before 6 April 1935.

Extended writing

Discuss feminist views of the family.

Guidance: You will need to be aware of the various kinds of feminism, perhaps describing their differences as well as what they have in common. Remember that feminism talks about far more than the family, so keep your focus firmly on family life and patriarchy. Avoid drifting off topic.

Write about 500 words.

To what extent have women really challenged patriarchal views of society?

Family

Aims

◉ To outline the postmodern view of family structures and family life

Postmodernism is the most recent social theory to become popular; it suggests that people are now choosing family types that suit their individual emotional and social needs rather than strictly following any traditional pattern.

Tip

Postmodern views of family are useful for evaluating older theories such as functionalism and Marxism.

Discussion point

● Does postmodern sociology adequately explain *why* changes are taking place in family life?

Topic 11: Postmodernist views of family

Getting you thinking

With a study partner, draw a timeline of your life extending from birth, through your teenage years and into the future. Mark on the timeline all of the times in your life when you will have to make an important decision about family and family life (for example: to marry or cohabit, to stay or divorce).

Postmodernism

Postmodernism is the most recent social theory to become popular; it suggests that people are now choosing family types that suit their individual emotional and social needs rather than strictly following any traditional pattern.

Postmodernism suggests that the older traditional norms and values are giving way to a more individual approach to life. Traditional theories such as Marxism and functionalism do not explain these changes and are not relevant to people in contemporary society. Families are too varied to be generalised about, so ideas about families 'being good' for people and society are meaningless. People are adapting their families and family life in ways that suit their own personal needs at any particular moment in time, so there is no longer a single dominant family type. This is in direct contrast to New Right views of family life.

Postmodernist themes

There are a number of themes in most postmodern writing on the family:

◉ Gender equality means that traditional male dominance has been challenged and the nuclear family is no longer the only possible family type for most people.
◉ Individualism means that people choose to act on the basis of what is good for them and not on a sense of what others may expect or think.
◉ Modern society is fragmented. There are few connections between various groups or between some members of our society so the influence of society on behaviour has weakened.

We are encouraged from all sides to view our lives as being full of choices. Like the products on a supermarket shelf, our careers, our relationships, our bodies, our very identities seem to be there for the choosing.

Renata Salecl

What do postmodern theorists say about the family?

The Rapoports (1982) described and listed the variety of types of family diversity in modern society:

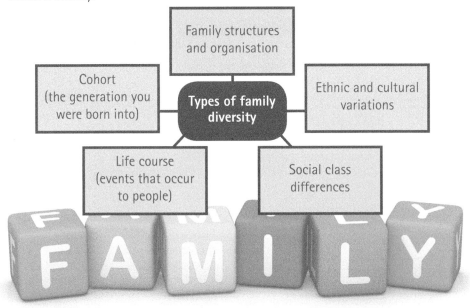

In 1993, Cheal theorised that the family has undergone major change because society is no longer predictable. People have choices in their lifestyles and exercise those choices. At about the same time, Anthony Giddens said that the cause of change in family and marriage was triggered by greater equality between men and women, but the cost of this equality was that personal relationships were less stable. Beck talked in terms of the **risk society**. By this, he meant that as tradition has less influence and people have more choices, we become aware of risks and rewards that come from decision making. Families are now **negotiated**; people decide what they want from relationships and if they do not get satisfaction, they leave. David Morgan (1996) claimed that it was the routines of family life that give us the sense of being a family member rather than relationships.

Discussion point

- How do postmodern views of family life contrast to the New Right or functional views of family?

Tip

When you revise previous chapters, look for postmodernist ideas that may be referred to. Giddens' ideas about confluent love could be used in an answer on postmodernism, for example. See page 120.

The postmodern approach is a sociological attempt to explain the public arrival/acceptance of new family types such as gay families.

Discussion point

- Is it possible to use post-modernist theory as the basis of research into the family? Make points for and against.

Judith Stacey (1998), who worked in California, found that women were drivers of family change because they had opportunities to create new and varied family structures. Women have these opportunities to create new family structures because it is usually women as mothers that families are based upon. Thus the new types of family (beanpole, blended) develop and form around women. In addition, it is changes to the roles of women, as there is some movement towards gender equality, that have contributed to many of the changes in family life. Weeks (2000) claimed that families tend to remain fairly traditional, but that acceptance of difference is growing. He claimed that one of the main causes of change was related to sexual behaviour. Sexual freedom is caused by the loss of religious values (associated with secularisation) and the loss of state power over individual choices.

STRENGTHS of postmodern views of family	WEAKNESSES of postmodern views of family
- It offers an explanation of family change and family diversity. - It acknowledges that different types of family exist, and offers us descriptions of some of those new family types and concepts to explain them. - It emphasises how emotions and choice are important aspects of family life. - Postmodernists have pointed out the role of government policy in imposing an ideology and judging what people actually choose to do (see the note on New Right thinking). - Postmodernists point out the importance of life course and decision making on family life.	- Many writers, including Chomsky, have claimed that it is vague and not based on evidence but theory. - The postmodernists overlook the persistence of the nuclear family and the importance of traditional marriage to most people. - It tends to overstate the amount of social change that is taking place in society. Hakim, for example, says that many women do not want to work and would choose domestic life if they could. - The language used to discuss postmodern theory can be very complex and difficult for people to understand. Critics claim that this is a way of covering up the weakness of the theory.

In the 1880s in Utah, USA, plural marriage of one man and many wives was acceptable. Is choice of family type a modern phenomenon? To research this use key words 'mormon' and 'plural marriage' in your search engine.

Sample questions

Postmodern sociology claims that the traditional theories of family do not take account of the reality of family life as it is actually lived by most people. Modern families are not generally nuclear, but different people join families at different times. Although the law assumes that legal and biological ties form the basis of families, postmodernists argue that in fact families are linked by tradition and choice. Changing gender roles, changing relationships and **individualism** mean that people have to make more and more decisions than ever before.

a) With reference to the item and sociological knowledge, explain the meaning of the term **individualism**.

b) Using the item and sociological knowledge, explain **two** reasons for increasing family diversity.

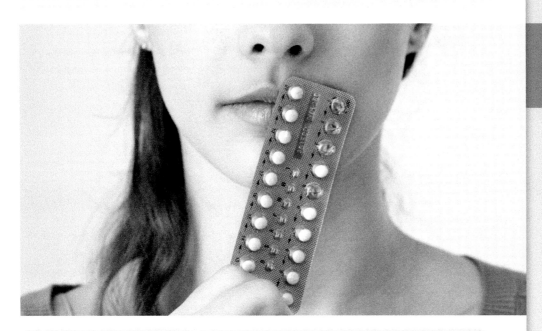

Is it the pill which means that sex does not necessarily result in pregnancy, or is it social change that caused people to re-examine traditional views of family?

Check your own learning
Match the terms to their meaning.

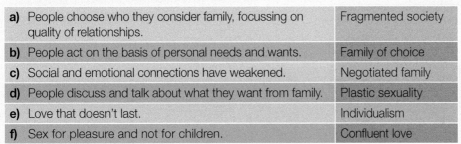

a)	People choose who they consider family, focussing on quality of relationships.	Fragmented society
b)	People act on the basis of personal needs and wants.	Family of choice
c)	Social and emotional connections have weakened.	Negotiated family
d)	People discuss and talk about what they want from family.	Plastic sexuality
e)	Love that doesn't last.	Individualism
f)	Sex for pleasure and not for children.	Confluent love

Tip

Go back and look at the Theory section at the start of the book, and revise the basic ideas of each theory.

Extended writing

Discuss postmodern views of family diversity.

Guidance: In this type of essay, a good basic plan is to begin by explaining the basic theory and summarise some of the key writers, using the terms that they developed to talk about new family forms and then summarising them with reference to strengths and weaknesses. The important marks are for AO3 analysis and evaluation, so don't leave that element to the end of the essay, but use evaluative language and linking phrases throughout your answer.

Write about 500-750 words.

Aims

⊙ **The New Right are hugely influential in terms of public policy regarding families, but many sociologists are doubtful about this approach to the understanding of family**

The New Right base their theories of family on functionalism. It is a controversial theory from a sociological point of view, but has been influential in terms of politics and policy in the UK since the late 1970s. The New Right offers a view of society that is very traditional. They tend to believe in a **golden age** in the past when things were better than they are now. They base their theorising on statistics that suggest that people who are seen as problems for society, such as those with mental illness or criminals, are often from single parent or broken families. They also believe that the welfare state encourages laziness and lack of personal social responsibility; for example, the benefits which support single parents or the unemployed encourage such behaviour.

Topic 12: New Right views of family

Getting you thinking

Is it true that young women deliberately become pregnant in order to gain benefits and housing?

New Right views of family life

Politically and ideologically, the New Right were at their most influential during the 1980s and 1990s when Margaret Thatcher was Prime Minister of the UK. The main sociological supporter for the New Right is Charles Murray, who claims that the traditional nuclear family is the best type of family. He went on to claim that the traditional nuclear family is threatened by the welfare state. He believed that young women had babies in order to gain money from the welfare state, which meant that young men did not have to take responsibility for fatherhood. The children of single parent families did not have a proper male role model in the family and in their turn grew up to be lazy, benefit dependent and criminal.

The New Right are particularly opposed to the growth of cohabitation because they argue that marriage strengthens family bonds so that cohabiting couples are more likely to split up than married couples. They see the growth of mothers in full-time

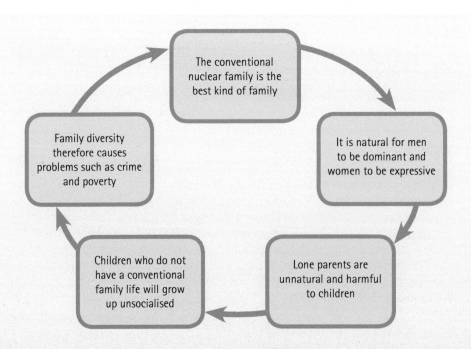

The conventional nuclear family is the best kind of family

It is natural for men to be dominant and women to be expressive

Lone parents are unnatural and harmful to children

Children who do not have a conventional family life will grow up unsocialised

Family diversity therefore causes problems such as crime and poverty work as unhelpful because it means, they say, that mothers cannot fulfil the expressive role of bringing children up to be good citizens. They believe that families should be heterosexual and oppose same-sex relationships because they believe that children need good role models of each gender.

Social problems and the single parent family

The New Right claim that the breakdown of the nuclear family causes social problems. Other sociological perspectives believe that the causes of social problems such as crime may also be what causes the breakdown of family relationships. Feminists would claim the problem in society that causes social problems and family break up is men, whereas Marxists would say it was capitalism. What might postmodernists and functionalists believe?

Discussion point

- Imagine that you are part of a New Right government policy group. You wish to try and solve the problems you believe are caused by family breakdown. What four solutions would you propose?

breakdown of traditional nuclear family → **CAUSES** → **social problems such as crime**

The New Right.

breakdown of family units and relationships ← **CAUSE** ← **problems in society** → **CAUSE** → **social problems such as crime**

Other sociological perspectives.

Frank Gallagher from the TV series Shameless, long-term unemployed and happy to live on benefits. How true is this view of society?

INTERESTING FACT

In 1996 the Economic and Social Research Council found that most unmarried mothers were in a regular relationship with the father of the child. Of those who were not, only 10% were living in social or council housing six months after the birth.

135

Family

These couples divorced and their children are now fully grown up. What impact on the children might experience of single parenthood have had, according to the New Right?

STRETCH and CHALLENGE

What would happen to our society if lone parenthood was made illegal?

Tip

To understand the New Right properly, it is advisable to make sure that you are familiar with functionalism as a theory.

STRENGTHS of the New Right theory	WEAKNESSES of the New Right theory
⊙ Arguably, the New Right have been very influential in terms of influencing government thinking. ⊙ The New Right emphasise the positive aspects of the nuclear family. ⊙ It appeals to 'common sense' ideas about society that many people share. ⊙ The approach corresponds to functionalist thinking on the family. ⊙ Children in lone-parent families are more likely to experience poverty than those raised by two parents.	⊙ Many sociologists have said that New Right theory blames the victims of society for their own poverty and deprivation. ⊙ It has had a negative influence on government policy so that it is more difficult for people to get benefits and the benefit-dependent are seen in a bad light. ⊙ Marxists see the New Right as reflecting capitalist ideology, and feminists see the New Right as eroding the hard-won rights of women to control conception and gain more equality in the home. ⊙ There is limited research to support the New Right and very little evidence that young women get pregnant for housing. ⊙ It does not take into account the varied experiences of people within non-traditional families, who value their relationships.

Sample questions

Charles Murray, a leading member of the **New Right**, has said, 'I think that the reforms of the 1960s jump-started the deterioration (in society). Changes in social policy during the 1960s made it economically more feasible to have a child without having a husband if you were a woman or to get along without a job if you were a man; safer to commit crimes without suffering consequences; and easier to let the government deal with problems in your community that you and your neighbours formerly had to take care of … a self-reinforcing loop took hold as traditionally powerful social norms broke down.'

a) With reference to the item and sociological knowledge, explain the meaning of the term **New Right**.

b) Using the item and sociological knowledge, explain **two** ways in which Murray believes that society has changed for the worse since the 1960s.

> *When it comes to effective socialisation, no alternative family structure comes close to the merits of two parents, formally married.*
>
> *Charles Murray*

Extended writing

Discuss New Right theories of family.

Guidance: This is an updated version of functionalist thinking. Functionalists analysed society when the nuclear family was the most common family form, but the New Right are reacting to social changes and fear them. They believe that the nuclear family is one that works best and that family values are important. This is an ideological view of family which begins from the perspective that standards in society are changing for the worse. Most sociologists are very critical of this idea, so you could usefully criticise the New Right from each of the other perspectives that you have previously studied.

Write about 500-750 words.

Research methods

How would you design a study to test whether young women in your area deliberately become lone parents so that they can have benefits? What practical and ethical problems might you experience?

Check your own learning

Answer the following questions:

a) When did the New Right first become influential?

b) Which British Prime Minister is most associated with the New Right?

c) What term is used to describe a past time that is better than the present?

d) Name the most important social commentator associated with the New Right.

e) Which type of family do the New Right believe is best for society?

f) What is the main reason for lone parenthood according to the New Right?

Discussion point

• Are single parents a problem for society?

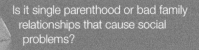

Is it single parenthood or bad family relationships that cause social problems?

Aims

⊙ To understand what is meant by the term youth culture and to consider what it is makes the behaviour of some young people different from the behaviour, actions and beliefs of those who are from a different generation

Many young people in Western society seem to go through a distinct stage in their lives when they have cultural values that are different from older generations. Their tastes, habits and behaviour may seem challenging because of their use of drugs, their fashions and music, criminal behaviours or attitudes to sex. The media present young people as a problem. Debates ask whether all young people go through this phase, what it means if they do and how significant it is. Youth culture may mean different things, so it may be a question of liking the styles or a statement of identity.

This may be a good point for you to return to Topic 1 of the Aquiring Culture through Socialisation section on page 10 and to revise culture.

Topic 1: What is youth culture?

Getting you thinking

Young people often behave in a way that older people find slightly different and challenging. Suggest reasons why this might be so.

Defining youth culture

Mainstream culture – This term is used to describe the cultural norms and values of the majority of the people in a society.

Peer groups – A peer group refers to those people who are of the same age and status. The term is often used when discussing young people as there is a common belief that young people are more likely to be influenced by their peer group than other age groups.

Adolescence – In the past, children were very much part of the adult world, but by Victorian times they began to be seen as different and special. It was not until early in the 20th century that the **transition** period between childhood and adulthood was given a name: **adolescence**. By the 1930s, the term 'teenager' also became current usage for people who were neither child nor adult.

Subculture – A subculture is a small group within a culture who have different norms, values and cultural beliefs from the mainstream culture around them. Subcultures are often viewed as being at odds with the mainstream culture, so Hebdige (1979) claimed that **youth cultures** are viewed negatively by others.

Youth culture – A youth culture is a term used to describe a set of norms and values shared by a group of **adolescent** people. It varies from the culture of older people, the mainstream culture, in a number of ways, having distinctive modes of dress, norms and values, and styles and interests.

Counter-culture – A **counter-culture** is a subculture that rejects the morality of the mainstream culture. Some youth cultures are seen as counter-cultural groups. The hippies of the 1960s are often described as a counter-culture as many of them chose to 'drop-out', which effectively meant to take a lot of mind-altering drugs and reject conventional society and its aspirations.

The history of the study of youth culture

One of the key issues for sociologists has been to explain why young people behave in a way that appears to be very different from the rest of their society.

⊙ Much early study of young people was linked to understanding young people and criminal behaviour. Albert Cohen said young people who became criminal shared similar problems of poverty and responded by committing crime.

- In the 1940s and 1950s, American sociologists such as Parsons claimed that youth cultures were just a way of young people having a good time while they were in transition (change) from being children to taking on adult roles.
- In the UK in the 1960s and 1970s, sociologists from the Centre for Contemporary Cultural Studies (CCCS) such as Paul Cohen and Hebdige said that youth culture was a rejection of capitalism.
- Feminist writers such as Sharpe and Garber in the 1980s suggested that girls and women had been overlooked.
- More recent writers such as Muggleton and Harvey say that young people no longer want to commit to specific youth cultures but are more concerned with style and taste.

What makes youth culture different from mainstream culture?

There are a number of characteristics that make youth culture distinctive in cultural terms from mainstream cultures:

Characteristics of mainstream culture	Characteristics of youth cultures
All groups in society contribute to mainstream culture	Are generally formed of people of a specific age
Mainstream culture is inclusive, we are all part of it	Are often exclusive and only people who conform to specific norms and values may claim to belong
A variety of forms of dress and behaviour is tolerated	These are forms of behaviour and dress that are only appropriate for the young. Old people who participate may appear faintly ridiculous
Antagonistic towards cultures that appear to challenge cultural values	Antagonistic towards mainstream culture
Mainstream culture changes over time but slowly and often without people noticing	Youth culture tends to be short lived and subject to change and fashion
People are part of mainstream culture for all of their lives	Being part of a youth culture is often, though not always, temporary
Resisting of change or challenge	Rebellious and challenging

Topic 1: What is youth culture?

Extended writing

Using sociological evidence and examples, explain the meaning of the term youth culture.

Guidance: You will need to point out that although youth is a biological stage in people's lives, it is also a social stage. Use the terms culture, subculture and counter-culture. Mention that young people may have norms and values that are different from (or reject those of) mainstream culture. The youth culture that we belong to may influence our tastes long into adulthood. Most youth cultures are short lived and last only for a generation or two before they change. Give some historical and recent examples of youth cultures

Write about 200 words.

Discussion point

- What is the difference between youth culture and fashion?

Check your own learning

Link the term to its meaning.

a)	Youth culture	The transition period between childhood and adulthood
b)	Peer groups	This term is used to describe the cultural norms and values of the majority of the people in a society
c)	Mainstream culture	Those people who are of the same age and status
d)	Adolescence	A small group within a culture who have different norms, values and cultural beliefs
e)	Subculture	A term used to describe a set of norms and values shared by a group of adolescent people

Sample questions

In the 1960s, many young people in the USA became politically active and joined social movements fighting for equality and justice for Black people, women and gays. They criticised the American involvement in the Vietnam War. In 1968, there were over 200 protests in American universities with more than 40,000 students participating in riots and demonstrations. Others joined a **counter-culture**, the hippies, and separated themselves from mainstream culture. They dropped out of college and many went to live in communes in the country or to live in San Francisco. There they participated in a culture which emphasised the use of mind-altering drugs and sexual freedom.

a) Using material from the item and sociological knowledge, explain the meaning of the term **counter-culture**.

b) Using material from the item and sociological knowledge, explain **two** reasons why some young people choose to reject mainstream culture.

139

Aims

- To understand that although youth cultures are often viewed as a relatively recent social phenomenon, there has been a history of youth groups who were seen to challenge mainstream values. You will identify reasons why large youth cultures developed in the UK in the 20th century

The idea of youth is a recent social construction, though historically, young people have always been seen as challenging by older generations. Early youth groups tended to take the form of gangs linked to criminal behaviour. The reasons for the development of such youth cultures were probably linked to the increased spending power of young people, the growth in employment, increased leisure time, delay in the age of marriage and the deliberate targeting of young people with products such as music and clothing.

Discussion point

- Which of the economic conditions for the development of youth culture still apply in contemporary Britain? How might the experience of youth be different for young people today and young people in the 1950s?

Topic 2: The history of youth cultures

Getting you thinking

How are these young Londoners of the 1950s who are looking at an American car, a rarity in Britain then, different from young people of today? In what ways is their behaviour similar to that of young people today?

The origins of youth culture in 1950s Britain

There is a historical debate regarding the development of distinctive youth cultures. Gardiner, for example, claims there were youth cultures in the 1920s. Others have suggested youth cultures occurred earlier, possibly even in the 19th century. However, most writers, including Marwick, suggest youth culture was a product of a set of social and economic circumstances particular to the 1950s.

In the early 1950s, Britain was emerging from the devastation of World War 2, which meant that people were still experiencing rationing of clothing and foodstuffs and the centres of many cities were bombsites. Imported American music and fashion captured the imagination of young people who watched American films, and enjoyed American popular music such as Rock and Roll, and who copied American fashions initially. This inspired the development of spectacular youth cultures that were very British but influenced by American fashion.

The earliest of these spectacular youth cultures was probably the Teds, or Teddy boys who can be seen in the picture above. They listened to Elvis Presley's music. Boys had elaborate quiffs in their hair and wore expensive fashion items such as crepe-soled shoes and drape jackets. Their drug of choice was alcohol. They were associated with flick knives and sometimes with guns left over from the war, so they were viewed with suspicion and fear by many people. The movement died away after racist rioting by the Teds in 1958 and was replaced in popular culture by Mods and Rockers.

What were the social conditions that enabled the Teddy boys and other early youth cultures to develop?

The earlier years of the 20th century were marked by war and economic depression. Young people were not therefore in a position to develop youth cultures or to rebel against society. However, by the early to mid-1950s, society was beginning to change and this meant that young people had freedoms and choices that had not been possible for earlier generations.

- *Growth economy* – Lewis (1978) has pointed out that the rebuilding of the country and the growth of the manufacturing industry for new goods such as cars, televisions and washing machines meant that young working-class people had jobs and money to spend on cultural products such as records and clothes.
- *High disposable income for young people* – Most people left school at fifteen, and most males did National Service, which meant that they were in the military for two or more years. They were in work and able to save, they were also away from the influence of family and were exposed to influences away from home.
- *Delayed adulthood* – People moved from school straight into employment, but the average age of marriage was the mid-twenties, so they had freedom to delay adult responsibilities such as family life, whilst at the same time having money and time for fun.
- *Leisure* – Hours of work were shorter and so people had more leisure time to themselves. They were able to go out and had the cash to afford to buy motorbikes and scooters and were able to travel around.
- *Targeting of teenagers* – Media companies realised that they had a whole new target market of young people with freedom and money. Films and music products, dance halls and coffee shops sprang up and all were pitched at the new teenage market. A myth of teen rebellion was portrayed in films such as *The Wild One*, *Teenagers from Outer Space* and *Rebel without a Cause* which had glamourous young actors such as James Dean as role models.
- *Multi-culturalism* – Fowler (2008) claims that people were aware of other cultures; there was immigration into Britain, so new music styles from the Caribbean were heard, people travelled and were aware of different cultures and there was more mixing between young people of different social classes.

Sample questions

The Teddy boys were described in national newspapers around 1953. At first they were described as a fashion trend known as the New Edwardian Look, but then the term Teddy boy was used in print by the Daily Express in 1953. It is probable that the origins of the Teddy boy style were earlier, among a group known as cosh boys, and that it was a street style in working-class areas in the late 1940s. Cross argues that working-class children began to have better expectations of life than their parents had, and wanted to challenge authority through their fashions.

a) Using material from the item and sociological knowledge, explain the meaning of the term **youth culture**.

b) Using material from the item and sociological knowledge, explain **two** reasons why youth cultures may have developed in the 1950s.

Check your own learning

Look at the following statements relating to the development of Teddy boy culture. Which are true and which are false?

a)	All sociologists agree that the first youth culture was the Teddy boys
b)	Teddy boys were generally wealthier middle-class boys who could afford the fashion
c)	Teddy boy culture was associated with violence and racism
d)	Media companies deliberately targeted young people with goods and services aimed at a teenage market
e)	The economy of Britain in the 1950s was booming and there were plenty of jobs for people
f)	Teddy boy culture at its most popular lasted for about five years

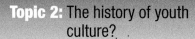

Research idea

Find out about the youth cultures which your parents and grandparents might have joined. What music did they enjoy? What were the fashions? What beliefs or ideas did young people have about society?

Extended writing

Using sociological evidence and examples, explain reasons for the development of youth culture in the 1950s.

Guidance: This response could be based on two or three reasons explained in detail with reference to studies, or a range of reasons discussed in less depth. Whichever approach you choose, you should note that you are required to refer to sociological evidence and examples, so specific knowledge of 1950s youth culture and reference to a study or two is necessary to do well. You might wish to talk about the specific social and cultural climate of the 1950s to explain why large numbers of young people bought into a style and also a set of cultural attitudes. You should point out the importance of economic factors in the development of youth cultures.

Write about 200 words.

Research idea

Find out more about recent Teddy boy style by searching the internet or reading *Teddy boys: A Concise History* by Ray Ferris and Julian Lord.

Aims

- To recognise that membership of a youth culture often gives people a sense of identity. People use their clothing and style to pass on a message about themselves. All youth cultures share characteristics that separate them from mainstream culture.

Young people who identify with specific youth cultures will tend to share certain ways of behaving, so, for instance, they may talk in a certain way. The group may be based around a leisure activity such as BMX or skateboarding, or a shared taste in music. As groups develop, many adopt a distinctive style of clothing. They may have shared attitudes that separate them from other people in society. When discussing and analysing youth cultures, sociologists start by identifying the common characteristics of all youth cultures; this provides a framework to explore differences between specific youth cultures or to understand why the cultures developed as they did. There have been a number of studies of specific youth groups which attempt to understand what the young people are attempting to communicate to society as a whole through their youth culture.

Topic 3: The characteristics of youth cultures

Getting you thinking

Which youth culture do you think this girl identifies with? What features tell you about her youth style? What do you know about how she probably behaves and her tastes from her choice of clothing? Would you be able to choose her as a friend?

Characteristics of youth cultures

The most obvious feature of a youth culture is the appearance of members: a particular style of clothing or a way of doing their hair. In cultural terms, what is also significant is that many members of youth cultures share norms and values which are different from those of mainstream culture.

For an overview of some of the ways in which cultures differentiate themselves, the diagram below shows many features of youth cultures:

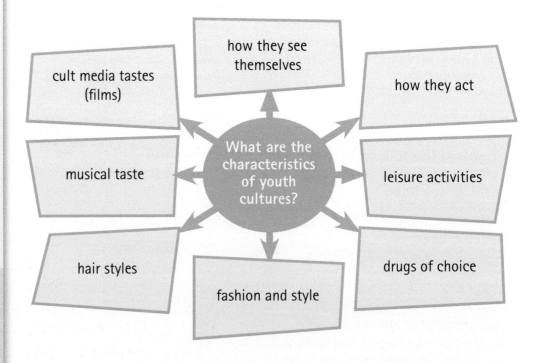

When comparing youth cultures, sociologists may describe how the cultures look and behave, before attempting to explain why they exist and what is particular about them. For example:

	Punks 1970s	Goths 1980s
Studied by	Frith (1978)	Hodkinson (2002)
Dress style	Ripped jeans, safety pins, tartan skirts over jeans, tight and ripped T shirts, paper clips, razors as jewellery	Black or dark red clothing. Tight trousers for males with buckles, long dresses and ripped black tights for girls, vampire look
Music	Groups who couldn't play their instruments and had offensive names, Sex Pistols	Death and sadness obsessed music such as Marilyn Manson or German techno rock, Joy Division
Body art	Safety pins in the face and ears	Piercings and tattoos of death imagery, make up for boys and girls including heavy eye liners and black nails
Drugs	Glue sniffing and anything else available	Alcoholic drinks such as Absinthe
Hair	Individual hairstyles with shaving, Mohican crests, spikes, hair dye in vibrant colours, lots of glue and hairspray to hold it in place	Dyed black and back-combed or long and straggling
Attitude to mainstream society	Angry, aggressive and deliberately shocking, promoting individual freedoms, anti-establishment	Withdrawn, peaceful, not out to annoy, but rather apart from society
Behaviour in public	Vandalism, squatting in other people's houses, aggressive graffiti, spitting at gigs	Creative, artistic, gender-bending behaviour, non-aggressive, gentle
Sociological conclusions	Subculture embodied reactions to high youth unemployment and the commercialisation of music	Not rebellious, but more concerned with shared interests, suitable for introverted people and intellectuals

Thus, while individual youth cultures may present themselves in different ways, they share a number of characteristics. However, these descriptions of youth cultures can be criticised for being too general because few youth cultures remain static in style; many evolve out of existing youth cultures and develop into new youth styles. Moreover, punk in the USA was different from punk in the UK. To complicate matters, some punk was aggressively neo-Nazi and adopted symbols such as the Swastika to celebrate racism, whereas other punks had very left-wing views. Modern theories such as postmodernism have pointed out the fluid and changing range of youth cultures. Each generation of young people appears to create a youth culture that reflects their own life and times, and which adapts the

Tip

Be careful in using chav as a name for a youth culture. Sometimes groups may call themselves by different names than those used by the media – hippies tended to call themselves 'heads', for example. Chav was a term of abuse used to describe a specific working-class style based on sports clothes, heavy jewellery and fake tan for girls. Few people would have called themselves by that name.

Thinking skills

Are youth cultures a way of life, a response from young people to their world or a statement of fashion and style? Discuss this point with people around you, including your parents. What do you learn?

I'm terrified of growing up. Once you become an adult, how do you step back from that? It's something that wakes me up at night.

Lorde, 17-year-old singer

Discussion point

- Frank Zappa, a famous rock star, once said of his audience, 'Everybody in this room is wearing a uniform'. What does this tell us about how the clothes we choose become part of our identity? Is it true that youth culture styles are a form of uniform?

David Bowie caused a sensation when he appeared in feminine styles on the TV programme *Top of the Pops* in 1972.

fashion of the cultures that have gone before. Some even readopt styles from previous decades, so the hippy look comes in and goes out of fashion regularly, but under different names.

Dominant youth cultures since the 1950s

1950s	Teddy boys
1960s	Mods and rockers, hippies
1970s	Skinhead, punk
1980s	New Romantic, goth, metal
1990s	Hip hop
2000s	Emos and club cultures
2010	Metalheads, straight edge

Note that this is not intended as a list of all of the youth cultures of each decade, just some of the variants that were available.

The glam rock culture of the 1970s was characterised by glitter, outrageous style, heavy cosmetics for boys and 'gender-bending' or androgyny where people experimented with traditional gender behaviour. It influenced many later bands but became commercial and marketed at young teenage girls and lost favour by the mid 1970s.

Glam rock may seem fairly mild to modern eyes, but in the 1970s it created a huge amount of shock because homosexuality had only been decriminalised for five years and homosexuality was still seen as shocking and abnormal by many. The Home Secretary in 1967, Roy Jenkins, famously described being gay as a 'disability' and 'a weight of shame'. It is argued by many that glam rock was part of major shift in attitudes to sexuality and made it possible for people to be openly gay or bisexual. Thus, it is argued, youth cultures can actually trigger change to mainstream social values. The dangerously sexual costumes worn by David Bowie in the 1970s to shock people became a popular museum exhibition in 2013.

DAVID

20. MAI – 10. AUGUST
MARTIN-GROPIUS-BAU
Tickets: DAVIDBOWIE-BERLIN.DE

Check your own learning

Revise your understanding of Teddy boy culture from the previous topic and then match the descriptions to the correct characteristics.

a)	Dress style	Being extremely well dressed and smart, threatening use of flick-knives as a fashion accessory
b)	Attitude	Pony tails for girls and quiffs for boys
c)	Music	Crepe shoes, draped jackets in pale colours, thin bootlace ties
d)	Hair	Rock and roll
e)	Evolved into	Aggressively racist in the later stages of the culture
f)	Attitude to mainstream society	Many Teds became the rockers of the 1960s, the look was revisited in the 1970s when it became associated with early punk and glam rock style

Sample questions

Police in Manchester have begun recording attacks on members of **subcultures**, such as goths, emos and punks, as hate crimes. But how do you define and protect these groups?

The problem of hate crimes against subcultures has been of mounting concern since the murder of Sophie Lancaster in 2007. The student and her boyfriend were set upon by a gang of teenagers in a park. The victims were targeted because they were goths. Previously, assaults have only been recorded as hate crimes when involving race, religion, disability, sexual orientation or transgender identity. These groups can usually be demarcated relatively clearly, but is it more difficult to identify what makes someone a goth, emo or punk?

The Oxford English Dictionary defines a goth as 'a performer or fan of [goth] music, or anyone who adopts a similar appearance, typically through the use of dark eye make-up and pale skin colouring, dark clothes, and bulky metallic jewellery'. 'They are not easy groups to define', says Paul Hodkinson, a goth himself and a sociologist at the University of Surrey, who specialises in **youth subcultures**.

Source: http://www.bbc.co.uk/news/magazine-22026044

a) Using material from the item and sociological knowledge, explain the meaning of the term **subcultures**.

b) Using material from the item and sociological knowledge, explain how people may show that they belong to a youth subculture.

Extended writing

Using sociological evidence and examples, explain reasons for the changing nature of many youth cultures.

Guidance: Not all youth cultures are short lived. Punk style has remained popular and has evolved, as has hip-hop. Many youth cultures spring up and die out very quickly. Brake, for example, said that young people have always been slightly separated from the adult world because of lack of experience. However, to be in a youth culture, young people require some money: for music, clothing styles and other accessories such as shoes, tattoos, jewellery, hair and make-up. Thus they must invest in the styles they adopt and as they gain responsibility, the up-keep of the style becomes difficult. The point of youth culture is that it is fashion, so the attractiveness of each youth culture will decline with its age. People are only adolescent for a short amount of time. Youth cultures often develop as a response to social events around them, so they change as society changes.

Write about 200 words.

Research idea

Find out more about hate crime directed at youth cultures by looking at the website of the Sophie Lancaster Foundation or searching her name on the Internet:

http://www.sophielancasterfoundation.com/

Activity

Choose one particular youth culture of the past or present and create a poster to describe the main features of it. Describe the features using the following ideas to help: age range of the people, their behaviours and how they spend their time, their art and creativity, fashion, language, music, ideas, values and views of the world.

Research idea

Not all youth groups are focussed on music or fashion. Some may have religion or sport in common. List types of youth groups that may exist by talking to students around you in order to discover what is important in their lives.

Aims

◉ To understand that some of the fashions and behaviours adopted by youth cultures are very extreme, and sociologists are interested in why such cultures form. They wish to discover the social pressures that lead to groups forming and social reasons why they attract young people.

Once youth cultures became identified as a separate topic of study, then why they arose and what purpose they served for the young people who joined them became the key questions for sociologists. They were interested in the group nature of such cultures. The answers that arose tended to reflect the perspectives that the sociologists were working in. Functionalists looked for the functions that youth cultures had for society, whereas Marxists looked for signs of working-class rejection of the capitalist system. These perspectives therefore influenced the style of research and the general findings.

Discussion point

● According to Russell Simmons, co-founder of Def Jam Recordings: 'The thing about hip-hop is that it's from the underground, ideas from the underbelly, from people who have mostly been locked out, who have not been recognised'. Which sociological theory does this view of hip-hop match?

Topic 4: Joining youth cultures

Getting you thinking

This woman was photographed at a Whitby Gothic Weekend. This festival is advertised as being attractive to punks, steampunks, emos, bikers, metallers and anyone else from 'the alternative lifestyle' who might be interested in shopping, dancing, drinking and music. Are shopping, drinking and dancing 'alternative'? Why might people be attracted to this form of lifestyle or dress?

Why do people join youth cultures?

Ceremonial function (rite of passage) – Functionalists suggest that youth cultures developed because in Western society, there is no clearly defined point at which a person becomes an adult. In some cultures, children pass through a ritual when they become fully adult. However, in Western culture, this function is served by youth culture.

Peer group pressure – Everyone else belongs to a youth style, so young people feel the need to participate so that they fit in with what for their age group is actually a mainstream culture as part of the process of learning friendship.

Establish an identity (a sense of self) – Interactionists say that membership of a youth culture helps people gain a sense of identity. They take on the values and morals of those around them. This may explain why people often hang on to the values of youth cultures long past the age at which anyone could consider them young.

Achieve a higher status (a higher place in the social hierarchy) – Interactionists suggest youth cultures are associated with young people who do not have a stake in society. Belonging to a youth culture gives them importance and alternative routes to self-esteem. Mac an Ghaill claims that young men join youth cultures in order to assert masculine values.

Media pressure – Stanley Cohen suggests that the media exaggerate youth cultures and offer an image of an exciting and attractive lifestyle option. Young people become attracted to the illusion offered and because young people consume media and are vulnerable to persuasion, they will buy items associated with the styles.

Rebel against the rules of a (capitalistic) society – Marxist sociologists look for signs of working-class resistance to capitalism so in the 1970s, there was a great deal of theorising about young people rejecting capitalist thinking and reasserting their social class identity through the development of youth cultures. This approach is particularly associated with the Birmingham University Centre for Contemporary Cultural Studies (CCCS). Stuart Hall, Tony Jefferson, Dick Hebdige and others all claimed that youth cultures were resistant to capitalism.

To consume the latest fashions, styles and trends – Postmodernists claim that youth cultures are consumer-orientated. Young people cannot distinguish between what they need and what they want and they are targeted by aggressive marketing. They are the age group most likely to spend their disposable income on clothing and fashion, as the age of marriage rises and fewer young people can aspire to home ownership. They may buy consumer goods that give them a sense of identity, personality or status, such as sports items, or they may feel a sense of belonging to society through ownership of consumer goods such as phones or cars.

Solution to a problem such as racism or sexism – Sociologists interested in the experiences of minority groups such as women or ethnic minorities point out that a youth group can be a form of safety against the aggression of dominant cultures. Young Black males, for example, may form a social group that understands and shares the problem of being in a racist society but also gives them the strength in numbers to fight back against racism. Girls may form **bedroom cultures** to share understanding of how to cope in a male-dominated, patriarchal society.

Check your own learning

Look at the following statements relating to reasons why young people join youth cultures. Match the descriptions to the correct theories.

a)	Being a member of a youth culture is just a stage of life that we all go through, and takes the place of a rite of passage.	Feminism
b)	Girls join bedroom cultures and girl gangs as a way of protecting themselves from boys and male expectations.	Postmodernism
c)	Membership of a youth culture gives people a sense of identity which they can buy alongside consumer products.	Interactionism
d)	Young people join youth cultures as a form of protest against capitalism and a rejection of capitalist values.	Functionalism
e)	Youth cultures offer people a route to self-esteem and self-identity.	Marxism

Sample questions

Read the passage written by an old hippie, Jim Greenlee.

First let me clear up a few misconceptions about what a hippie is. Long hair does not make a hippie. Clothes don't make a hippie and the use of drugs definitely doesn't make you a hippie. Being a hippie had nothing to do with being rebellious. It's a matter of respect. Allowing yourself to be who you are.

I'm not real sure when you might say I became a hippie. It kind of snuck up on me. There is a strong possibility I was a hippie years before I knew it. I've always had this thing about the mistreatment of animals and a strong fascination for nature.

I remember the first time someone called me a hippie. I was in college (1966) and after four years of dress codes in school I was free. I let my hair grow and wore cut-off jeans and sandals to class. Not for any sense of protest but just because I could. A fellow student (female) approached me one day and said 'you're a hippie aren't you'. I had never thought about it before but at that moment something in the way she said it made me say 'yeah I'm a hippie'. Well let me tell you, I had watched the bad boy biker types in high school always with women around them and wondered what the attraction was. All of a sudden I was a bad boy. The guy her father warned her about. I was a hippie.

Source: adapted from http://oldhippie.jimgreenlee.com/beingahippie.html

a) Summarise the item on becoming a hippie (hippy).

b) Using material from the item and sociological knowledge, explain **two** reasons why people may join a youth subculture.

Tip

This topic might well form part of the answer to two possible questions. The first is the more direct, 'why do people join youth cultures?', but you might want to use ideas to answer a second possible question about why youth cultures develop.

Extended writing

Assess reasons why young people may join youth cultures.

Guidance: This question is not just asking you to describe social reasons why people join youth cultures, but to consider how plausible you feel the explanations are. For example, if functionalists feel that youth cultures are simply a form of self-expression and a normal part of reaching adulthood, why are so many of them aggressively anti-mainstream societal values? If Marxist explanations of youth culture as a form of resistance to capitalism are true, then why are youth cultures so often about buying into fashion and music styles? The conclusions that you draw may be your own, but you should also refer to evidence from studies and from your knowledge of contemporary Britain.
Write about 500–750 words.

Aims

◉ To identify two contradictory ways in which young people are represented in the media. Youthfulness is considered beautiful, creative and desirable, but young people are also seen as a problem for society.

Youth is a social construction. This means that it is not a distinct stage in life and there is no clear definition of when it begins or when it ceases. The United Nations, for instance, defines any age under 18 as being childhood, whereas legally in the UK, people over the age of 16 may take on adult responsibilities such as marriage. Thus, youth can be seen as a period of transition; characteristics of adulthood such as maturity and independence do not always fully apply.

This ambiguity is reflected in wider social perceptions of youth: current media concerns include issues such as binge drinking, irresponsibility and crime. There is a perception of unregulated sexuality. At the same time, though, youth can be a positive characteristic, especially for women who, according to Mitra et al, are often chosen for public roles based on their attractiveness and sex appeal. So there is no single view of youth and youth culture. In government and policy terms, it would appear that the negative view of youth is one that is more powerful than the positive one.

Topic 5: The position of young people in society

Getting you thinking

According the a study published on the BBC website in 2014, more than two-thirds of people aged between 14 and 17 believe that negative images in the media are affecting their job prospects.

Use a range of newspapers. Look at the stories referring to younger people, how are they portrayed? Are they shown as positive and in a good way, or are they shown as being criminal and dangerous? Which view of young people do you think is closest to the truth, are they a problem or are they positive and good for society?

Social construction of youth

A social construction refers to an idea about something that is created by society. The idea of youth is a relatively recent one, and there is no actual age when one can no longer be said to be young, or when one has become a youth rather than a child. When applied to youth culture, this idea is of more significance because young people are often seen as a problem. Pearson has pointed out that each generation has a view of young people's behaviour being better in the past, remembering a 'golden age'; these complaints about the behaviour and culture of young people are not new: examples have been found in Roman literature.

Whilst there are some positive views of youth, and youthfulness and youth fashion are generally admired, generally, young people themselves are seen as problematic and dangerous. Part of the reason for this is because youth is a relational concept. This means that it only exists in opposition to adulthood. Adults have the social power to define what it is to be adult, so youth culture and young people are often seen in a negative light and as a problem.

Adults	Youth and young people
Grown up, mature, responsible	Not yet grown, immature, irresponsible
Arrived at an identity	Developing an identity
Powerful and controlling	Vulnerable and in need of control
Conforming to social norms	Rebellious and challenging social norms
Thoughtful behaviour with an awareness of consequences	Vulnerable to risky and dangerous behaviours
Full members of society	Threatening to forces of law and not really responsible for events

Activity

Consider all of the ways in which young people are viewed as a problem by society; for example, obesity, binge-drinking and knife crime. To what extent does this type of story reflect the reality of most young people's life experiences?

Problematic views of youth and young people

The view of youth and young people has led to a demonisation of youth and youth cultures, so that various areas of young people's behaviour have been subject to policies of control and punishment.

NEETS

During the 1990s, New Labour governments, and later Conservative governments were concerned about the number of young people who were Not in Education, Employment or Training (NEET). A range of policies was put in place aimed at reducing the number of NEETs because those who are NEET are more likely to remain benefit dependent throughout their lives. The focus is on encouraging NEETs to stay in school and to undertake training. The age at which young people may leave school or training has been raised to 18 to tackle this problem. However, many sociologists, such as Shildrick and Ruddy, have argued that focussing on NEETs as a problem overlooks the nature of the work available to young people: much of it zero hours contracts, temporary and very low paid. Young people have very limited opportunities and little support.

Young single mothers

Another key discourse which has demonised young people is the commonly held, but mostly mythical, belief that very young women have babies in order to obtain council housing. Prime Ministers, David Cameron (Conservative) and Gordon Brown (Labour) have at different times spoken about the problem of 'children having children'. In 2013, the Conservative Party, then the party of government, proposed that housing benefits to teenaged mothers should be cut. It was suggested that all benefits to teen mothers should be cut, unless the girls stayed in their own family homes or in supervised hostels. Fiona Weir pointed out that this was a stereotype, and incorrect, because teen pregnancy rates are falling and only 2% of single parents are teenagers.

Gang culture and crime

The association between youth and crime is long standing and there is some basis in fact, as young people are significantly more likely to be convicted of crime than older people. Gang crime is particularly associated with the young, so that in 2015, the ONS claimed that gang violence was associated with 22% of serious violence and nearly half of all shootings in London. However, this means that significantly more serious violence was not gang related. Moreover, London has the lowest murder rate in over 30 years according to Metropolitan Police statistics and there were only six fatal shootings in 2013. Nevertheless the government has introduced new offences to control gang violence including a range of new offences, and invested heavily in support for research into gang violence.

Research idea

Find out more about the relationship between young people and the legal system by searching the term 'young offenders and the law'.

STRETCH and CHALLENGE

Suggest reasons why adults have a negative view of teenagers and teen cultures. Create a mind map and then carry out your own research to support your ideas.

As a society, should we support or punish young women who become pregnant?

Mental health

A number of medical and social studies have suggested that young people have more mental health problems than previous generations. The ONS (2005) report that 10% of young people have mental health problems and 20% have experienced mental health issues within the previous years. It suggests that that there are higher rates of self-harm, anxiety and depression among young people than ever before. Research funded by the Nuffield Foundation in 2004 suggested that boys have higher rates of behavioural problems and girls are more likely to experience emotional problems but overall, boys are more likely than girls to experience mental ill-health. Carolyn Jackson found that the pressure for academic qualifications was placing a huge burden on young people. Charles Murray would suggest that the problem is poor parenting. Mental health issues are linked with poor behaviour in schools, risk behaviours such as smoking, drugs and alcohol abuse and with risky, promiscuous or abusive sexual behaviours. The government is investing money in health care for young people because it is argued that early support can prevent future mental health issues developing. Despite this, in Wales the Liberal Democrats in the Assembly claimed that 'mental health waiting lists are spiralling out of control' in 2015.

Sample questions

The term NEET is used to refer to those young people who are not currently in education, employment or training and vulnerable to being dependent on benefits or a problem to society in other ways. Recent data for Wales shows that at the end of 2013, 10.5 per cent of 16–18 year olds were NEET (11,800) compared with 10.8 per cent (12,300) at the end of 2012.

By 2014, 8.1 per cent of 16–18 year olds were estimated to be NEET, compared with 11.9 per cent at the year ending 2013. However, in Oct 2014, 3.1 per cent of Year 11 leavers were NEET compared with 3.7 per cent in 2013.

The position among 19–24 year olds is that at the end of 2013, 21.2 per cent of 19–24 year olds were NEET (55,300) compared with 22.9 per cent (59,600) at end 2012. By 2014, 19.7 per cent of 19–24 year olds in Wales were estimated to be NEET.

Michael Dauncey suggests that risk factors for becoming NEET include low educational attainment and low social class. However, he also suggests that some young people cannot see the benefit of being in work, or they lack family support and good information about work.

Source: adapted from Welsh Government data

a) Summarise the item on NEETs in Wales

b) Using material from the item and sociological knowledge, explain **two** reasons why young people may become NEET.

Check your own learning

Suggest ways in which young people are controlled by society. Use the headings as a guide to what you might put.

Area of life in which young people are controlled	Suggested example
Sexuality	
Work	
Freedom to live where you choose	
Politics	
Control over your body	
Leisure	

> The teenagers we 'despair' of today will, in due course despair of the children being born in future decades.
>
> **Martin Nairey, Chief Executive of Barnardo's**

STRETCH and CHALLENGE

Develop your understanding of the issues that face young people by looking at research into young people published as *An Anatomy of Youth* by Hannon and Tims: http://www.demos.co.uk/files/AoY_webfile.pdf?1270387139

Extended writing

Assess reasons why young people and youth cultures may be viewed as a problem for society.

Guidance: This question is asking you refer to evidence from studies and from your knowledge of contemporary Britain. As the question refers to young people as well as to youth culture, you have a wide range of ideas that you can use. Certainly, you should talk about youth cultures, but take a wide view and mention other ways in which the culture of young people can be seen as a problem. For example, you could consider the various ways in which young people may be demonised and portrayed as a problem for society. You can then link this to the idea that that the way young people are portrayed as a problem is part of a wider issue than just those people who are members of youth cultures.

Write about 200 words.

Research idea

In 2006, research by two youth charities, the British Youth Council (BYC) and YouthNet, suggested that 80% of young people felt the media gave a negative view of young people. How would you research the idea that the media do give a negative view of young people? What problems might you experience?

STRETCH and CHALLENGE

Read more about the government policies with regard to the mental health of young people online.

Topic 6: Youth culture in schools

Aims

- To understand that some youth cultures develop in school. Some young people form anti-school subcultures that reject education despite this negatively affecting their life chances.

There is a long history of Marxist and interactionist research into the development of youth culture within schools. Interactionists say that those who do not succeed in school form their own subcultures as alternative routes to status and recognition. It is a response to negative labels applied by teachers to some pupils. Marxists see a challenge to the capitalist structure of society by working-class pupils. However, it is possible that many sociologists, in their desire to find evidence of anti-school subcultures overlook the activities and needs of conventional young people.

Are boys more likely to form anti-school subcultures than girls?

Getting you thinking

Why might some children rebel against the values of schools and education? Consider how children might show their rebellion. What kind of norms and values do the rebels develop? How might being anti-school affect the rebel's future life chances?

Research into anti-school subcultures

Interactionism and school subcultures

Early educational research into the development of subcultures carried out in the 1960s and 1970s tended to focus on boys and was linked to concerns about the way that schools labelled and categorised children according to their perceived ability. Both Hargreaves (1967) and Lacey (1970) criticised functionalist ideas that suggested schools created shared norms and values by pointing out that children labelled as school failures actually gained high status from flouting school rules.

Marxist accounts of the development of school subcultures

In 1977, Willis carried out an ethnography, or detailed study, of twelve boys in school in the West Midlands. It was a secondary modern, a school for those who had failed exams at age 11 and been sent to a low status school. He concluded that the 'lads' developed a subculture as a deliberate act of resistance to capitalist oppression. His conclusion was that the lads deliberately chose to be anti-school and this contributed to their class oppression in work because they were likely to remain in low status, low pay work.

One criticism of Willis's work is that he was so concerned to follow the rebellious lads that he paid little attention to other groups within the school and may have overlooked what was happening among the non-confrontational pupils. Later studies, and particularly those interested in issues of gender and ethnicity, suggest that instead of one subculture, pupils within schools may form many groups, not all of them anti-school.

Subcultures and ethnicity

Sewell (2000), studied African-Caribbean subcultures and suggested that schools were openly racist, and African Caribbean boys were seen as threatening by teachers. Although not all became anti-school, a variety of subcultures developed, including conformist subcultures. Three main types of subculture were identified: innovators, who were for education but hated school; those who hated school but were non-confrontational; and those who formed an anti-school posse based on Jamaican cultural traditions. Sewell has since suggested that the failure of African-Caribbean boys is related to reasons that lie within their home culture.

Gender and issues of ethnicity

Many studies of youth subcultures in schools have focussed on boys, but more recent studies have looked at gender (both male and female) and ethnicity as cultural dynamics, so they acknowledge that the processes are more complex than labelling theory or Marxist analyses suggest. There is a complex interplay of factors that may include gender and ethnicity. Moreover, most acknowledge that school subcultures develop among those who support the aims of school or who support the idea of education although rejecting school values.

Safia Mirza (1992) identified a number of girl cultures in response to teachers who, in her view, displayed varying forms of racist behaviour. Although the girls were resentful, they developed anti-school attitudes that resisted racism through success and striving for high attainment.

Mac an Ghaill (1994) claimed that as girls have gained status in schools, and are now the gender achieving most educational success, boys have experienced a **crisis of masculinity**. They are unsure what male identity is or should be as traditional male jobs have disappeared from the job market. He identified four male subcultures including the 'macho lads'.

Shain (2003) studied Asian girl groups and discovered that there were various subcultural responses within the school. She identified subcultures that rebelled against racism, either through becoming anti-school or surviving by ignoring racism by conforming. A further group was pro-school and rebelled against the strict Asian cultures of their parents by succeeding and aiming for careers.

Carolyn Jackson (2006) identified a group she called ladettes. These were white working-class girls who were adopting masculine behaviours and norms, such as disruption, rudeness, swearing and open sexuality. However, this behaviour is not linked to school failure as many highly successful boys and girls subscribe to anti-school cultures in school, and cope by working very hard at home so that they can tread a fine line between outward rebellion and inward conformity.

Research in Wales

Truancy – Research into truancy carried out by Philippa James (2012) for the University of Wales and based on schools in Cardiff found that truancy and anti-school behaviours are not just confined to underachievers or anti-school subcultures. Many, if not most, children truant, and when they do, they are not particularly anti-school or anti-social. Mostly, the behaviour is so well-hidden that schools and other pupils are unaware of it. It is only when pupils are identified as truants by the schools that it becomes problematic.

Suggest a range of reasons why girls and girl subcultures in school may not be as widely studied as male subcultures.

Activity

Mind map different reasons why children may develop anti-school subcultures. Add your own ideas and those of the sociologists mentioned in this topic. Consider the strengths and weaknesses of each viewpoint.

Suggest reasons why young people in schools may be under particular pressure to join youth subcultures.

Sexuality and gender issues – Emma Renold (2013) carried out qualitative research in Wales for the NSPCC and the Welsh Assembly Government into childhood and sexuality. Focussing on pre-teen children (10–12) she discovered that looking older by wearing high heel shoes and make-up and participating in 'ladette' or sexualised behaviours among girls was more about looking older than about sexual behaviour. That there was a pressure on even pre-teen and primary school age children to form 'boyfriend–girlfriend' relationships which meant that normal friendships between girls and boys became almost impossible and left girls vulnerable to sexual harassment and bullying.

Conformity and young people – Williamson (1996) in a discussion paper on the status of youth work in Wales, concluded that despite negative reporting in the press and the focus of research into unusual and bizarre behaviour, most young people are conformist

and 'ordinary'. There is a growing number of, but still few, children who have complex family backgrounds and significant multiple disadvantages which leave them at risk of becoming involved in criminality or drug abuse. Much youth crime is 'expressive' or based on a desire for fun and excitement, but increasingly young people are involved in survival crime where they are looking for cash. He found that a third of young men have a criminal record.

Pro-school youth cultures – The Welsh language organisation for young people, Urdd Gobaith Cymru (2011), used qualitative research methods and found that young people required more activities and services. They found young people in Wales were proud of their ability to speak Welsh and wanted more opportunity for sport, arts and youth club activity.

Sample questions

In 1997, Valerie Hey conducted a detailed study of girls' friendships, collecting the notes they wrote in class, interviewing and observing the girls. She suggested that girls' friendships and subcultures were understudied. They often take place in secret so that while boys may talk and think 'dirty' in public, for girls this is a secret shared activity. Moreover, girls regulate and control each other's behaviour. She noted that middle-class and working-class girls responded to the pressures of male domination of social spaces in different ways, so that working-class girls would trade on their sexual appeal in order to get male attention. This then brought them into confrontation with teachers and schools and gave rise to **anti-school subcultures**.

a) With reference to the item and to sociological knowledge, explain what is meant by **anti-school subcultures**.

b) Using material from the item and sociological knowledge, explain **two** reasons why young people may become part of anti-school subcultures.

I pay the schoolmaster, but it is the schoolboys who educate my son.
Ralph Waldo Emerson

Check your own learning
Match the researcher to the finding.

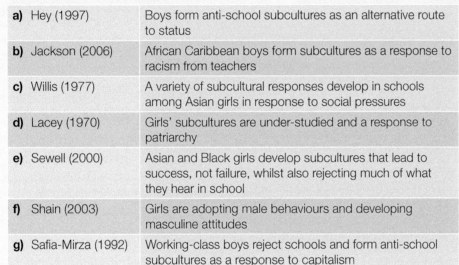

a) Hey (1997)	Boys form anti-school subcultures as an alternative route to status
b) Jackson (2006)	African Caribbean boys form subcultures as a response to racism from teachers
c) Willis (1977)	A variety of subcultural responses develop in schools among Asian girls in response to social pressures
d) Lacey (1970)	Girls' subcultures are under-studied and a response to patriarchy
e) Sewell (2000)	Asian and Black girls develop subcultures that lead to success, not failure, whilst also rejecting much of what they hear in school
f) Shain (2003)	Girls are adopting male behaviours and developing masculine attitudes
g) Safia-Mirza (1992)	Working-class boys reject schools and form anti-school subcultures as a response to capitalism

Discussion point

- Is it realistic to assume that youth cultures develop in school as a response to teachers and teaching, or do they perhaps develop outside school and affect the behaviour of teachers and schools?

STRETCH and CHALLENGE

Find out more about Valerie Hey's research into female friendships by researching online by her name and the title of her book, *The Company She Keeps*.

Extended writing

Assess the view that youth cultures may develop in school as a response to educational and social pressures on children.

Guidance: This area is significant in that the development of youth subcultures has been carefully observed in schools and that a variety of social processes have been identified as being contributory factors. However, much of this work has been carried out by educationalists, and currently there is little work continuing beyond school to see how youth cultures continue into early adulthood and late adolescence. If schools create youth cultures, it might be safe to assume that once the pressure of education is removed, then youth cultures will die away. The evidence, however, suggests that this does not happen. You will need to explain what we know about the development of youth culture in school but at each stage, consider that we do not know or understand what happens to these small social groups beyond education.
Write about 500–750 words.

Topic 7: Youth cultures and the media

Aims

- To recognise that the relationship between the media and young people is complex. Young musicians may create youth cultures, but equally, the media may create youth styles by informing young people about youth fashions.

In the 1950s, Teddy boys had money to spend on media products such as rock and roll music. Other youth cultures have been strongly associated with musical tastes; hip-hop is a culture associated with dance, clubbing and rap music. Often musical styles emerge from a 'scene' or exclusive group of people who have a strong cult mentality and exclusive knowledge of a particular style. However, if a style starts to become popular, it may be commercialised and then sold back to young people who happily adopt the fashions and music on offer. It can then be argued that youth cultures are a media creation.

Tip

You will be able to develop the content of this topic with theory drawn from postmodernism, Topic 17.

Getting you thinking

What role does the mass media play in your life? How does your use of mass media differ from the way your parents use it?

Youth culture, folk devils and moral panics

One of the first studies to link youth culture and the media was Stan Cohen's (1972) *Folk Devils and Moral Panics*, which studied events of the early 1960s. Cohen described how gangs of working-class London youths went to seaside resorts for bank holiday weekends. At first there was little to distinguish these groups. A dance hall scuffle between two groups led to some minor damage and fighting. However, newspapers reported it as a pitched battle. This led to a process of deviancy amplification whereby the violence was glamorised for the young who wanted to join in, and demonised for the older generations who were shocked. Young people become the folk devils and the response of authorities was moral panic.

The press described the gangs and suggested there were two groups: mods who were fashion conscious and rockers who were bikers. Gradually, young people began to associate with one side or the other. More of them began to go to seaside resorts with the intention of witnessing or joining in the rioting. British seaside resorts became dangerous places to be. Press interest moved on, however, to a newer youth trend, hippies, who were emerging in California by the mid-60s. They began to demonise those groups, and so the process started again.

Modern youth cultures and the media

Since the 1960s, when Cohen carried out his study, the nature and content of media have changed.

- People have more access to a wider variety of media types through the advent of new media technologies.
- People can create media more easily and make it accessible to a range of people through the growth of social media, starting with blogs and now moving through to an ever increasing range of apps, gaming programs and memes.

Youth culture and the consumption of media culture

David Buckingham (2010) says that in recent years, children and young people have become an increasingly important consumer market for media products and media technology. Music, films, television programmes, computer games are all produced for a youth market. Certain youth products such as sports goods, Nike, McDonalds, Starbucks and other large global companies encourage young people to buy into brands. Adorno, in the 1990s, suggested that the differences between consumer goods and products were largely artificial but they channelled particular goods to certain market sectors, so for example, some brands of jeans became 'cool' but other brands were seen as 'dad jeans'.

Kellner suggests that over the last twenty years, young people have bought into identities and presented themselves in roles and images through their purchases. Louise Archer pointed out that wealthier young people had a number of ways of expressing their privilege; they certainly enjoyed conspicuous consumption of designer goods and created youth cultures based on purchasing. They were able to do this in a number of arenas of cultural life, because they could buy into music or film and not just clothing. In addition, when middle-class people adopted working-class styles and fashions, they could be seen as cool and ironic. A working-class or Black person in a hoodie will be seen as 'dangerous' whereas a middle-class person may simply be seen as 'edgy' or fashionable.

Youth as creators of culture

Danah Boyd (2010) has pointed out that young people may develop a street style such as a new style of music. The media spot this and then market it to other young people. Companies seeking new ideas may promote a particular style long before it is widely seen on the streets. Hassan and Katsanis (1991) suggested that the growth of media technology is spurring the development of a global youth market for items of clothing, drinks and music. The popularity of the YouTube video of the 2012 Korean single *Gangnam Style* is evidence of this globalisation of youth markets. Globalisation is not a new phenomenon, though, the Beatles enjoyed worldwide success over 50 years ago; new technology has perhaps speeded up the process.

Sonia Livingstone suggests that as a result of technological change youth culture is qualitatively different in contemporary society because young people are able to develop global youth cultures. There is no single event or trigger that changes people. Something more complex is taking place. Young people are monitoring other young people from around the world and constantly adjusting their behaviour and beliefs in the light of what they see.

'New' bedroom cultures

The late 20th and early 21st centuries have been marked by massive changes in media technologies. In the 1940s and 1950s, most homes might have had a radio and perhaps a television but the primary media form would have been newsprint. Early youth might have bought records and record players but the speed with which media forms have developed and become obsolete has meant that each generation has had a new media form with which to access music and other cultural products such as film. Morley (1986)

What makes one brand of jeans appear 'cool' and others seem to be boring? Think about marketing and which celebs wear the styles. Find out more about celebrity endorsement and how this may make some brands attractive to young people.

STRETCH and CHALLENGE

Watch the YouTube video of *Common People* by Pulp and look at the lyrics. To what extent is working-class culture seen as something 'cool' that can be bought into by richer kids who are looking for 'cool'?

Research idea

Use the Internet to find out more about the cultures of the mods and rockers. Look at contemporary photographs and listen to the music.

157

Thinking skills

What links are there between popular music styles and the development of youth cultures?

Are these rappers youth rebels or are they subscribing to cultural values that encourage people to spend? What is your view?

Research idea

Ask people who are in their 60s if they were influenced by rock music based films such as *Easy Rider* or *Woodstock*. Are there other similarly influential films for people of a younger generation?

How much time do young people spend on media technologies in their own private spaces?

showed that family life has dispersed; in the past whole families might have gathered together to watch television or listen to radio programmes, now they watch or play in separate rooms. Media technologies have become cheaper, smaller and easier to access so there has been a process of individualisation in which people are encouraged to explore their own personal taste and traditional social groupings.

At the same time, outside spaces are seen as dangerous for children, they no longer play outside as they once did because of the increase in the number of cars and the perception of stranger danger by parents. The postmodernist, Beck, refers to the emergence of risk culture whereby people are anxious about modern society. Home is seen as 'safe'. Young people are now using the media in their bedrooms which are now a central location for leisure time. Livingstone (2002) discovered that many young people had so much access to the media that they frequently lost count of the televisions, computer gaming systems and products in their homes. For young people, their bedrooms are media-rich areas and are now the focus of life. **New bedroom cultures** are developing, not as spaces where young people gather, but where they organise their lives via social networking sites and use of media forms.

Sample questions

Andy Bennett (2007) has said that many forms of popular music that once were sold just to young people are now attracting much wider groups of people of different ages. This is not just true of styles such as punk and metal, which have groups of die-hard fans. Newer electronic styles are marketed to older people, encouraging them to adopt youth styles. The assumption is that people are part of youth culture till they feel too old to belong to it. Younger people are forced to move on to other forms of culture and style very quickly to feel credible and fashionable. **Globalisation** has meant that they are looking for cultural experiences that are different from their parents, so Japanese anime or Danish death metal are now significant parts of some youth culture.

a) With reference to the item and to sociological knowledge, explain what is meant by **globalisation**.

b) Using material from the item and sociological knowledge, explain **two** reasons why youth culture has become more global in recent years.

Check your own learning

Organise the stages in a moral panic in an order that makes sense.

The news story catches the public mood and people buy newspapers
Eventually the story is boring and the newspapers and media move on to the next thing
The media create a news story about the action which is sensational
Social control is imposed on the deviants, many of whom are seriously punished
New laws may be created
Deviants begin to live up to their label because of self-fulfilling prophecy
The media further exaggerate events and write more stories so deviants are seen as folk devils
A deviant act takes place
The public become very concerned and politicians and the police are put under pressure to act

Extended writing

Assess the view that the media may create deviant behaviour among young people.

Guidance: Clearly you will need to describe the process of deviance described by Cohen in his study of folk devils and moral panics. However, you will need to look at issues of the glamorisation of deviant behaviour; so, for example, you could consider the way that rappers and hip-hop portray gun crime and gang violence. Newspapers may talk about the young in negative terms and exaggerate the threat they pose to society. You might want to consider the influence of the new media forms, so for example, the use of the mobile phone to encourage people to join the London riots in 2011, or the fad for 'happy slapping' where young people would assault a victim, film it on their phones and upload it to YouTube. You could also mention the pressure young people are put under to have consumer goods such as phones leading to street crime and theft.

Write about 500-750 words.

Key People

Stan Cohen (1942–2013)

Cohen was South African, but came to London to work as a social worker in the 1960s. He opposed oppression and had Marxist principles. His concern was with the way that society tended to over-react and oppress minorities. He viewed the young mods and rockers in his study as having been victimised by organisations such as the media, police or magistrates who would benefit from the moral panics they provoked.

Activity

You may find it interesting to watch the film *Quadrophenia* (1979) about the mods and rockers riots of the 1960s.

Research idea

Ask your friends when and where they access different media forms such as music, film, social media and literature.

Discussion point

- Many parents worry that young people spend too much time alone in their rooms with various media forms. Should they worry that their children are too isolated or are wasting time?

Aims

- To understand that Marxists tend to see youth cultures as working-class resistance to middle-class values. However, some youth cultures such as hippies seem to have originated among middle-class young people.

Early 1950s American sociology viewed youth culture as being working class, making a link between youth gangs and crime. The view was that boys who could not attain status in socially accepted ways gained status through gang membership. British studies in the 1970s suggested that youth cultures were linked to specific social classes so that hippies tended to be middle class, but that skinhead culture was an attempt to 'magically' recover traditional working-class culture. Equally punk was seen as working class, but Laing (1985), when studying the lives of musicians, found that many were students, often from art schools. The link between class and youth culture remains complex.

Thinking skills

Reimer says that membership of youth culture is related to a desire for fun. Make points for and against this view.

Topic 8: Youth cultures and class

Getting you thinking

Early skinhead style was seen as a reaction to hippy culture. It was aggressively working class in terms of the symbols and styles. Although originally skinheads listened to West Indian and ska music, they later became associated with racism and violence, especially against Asian men but also against gay men. Suggest reasons why working-class young people may want to create youth cultures and styles of their own.

Social class and gang cultures

Albert Cohen suggested that because working-class boys could not gain status from the traditional routes to social success such as education and good jobs, they sought alternative routes through deviance and crime. Howard Becker said that working-class boys were victimised by the police and legal system leaving them labelled as criminal. They turned to gang subculture for their identity. Middle-class children, however, were treated leniently, any misbehaviour seen as acceptable 'high spirits'.

Walter B Miller suggested that deviant youth subcultures arise because the working- and middle-class cultures have different norms and values. Working-class focal concerns include:

- Toughness, which can manifest itself through violence.
- Smartness, so people try to outwit others through stealing in clever ways.
- Excitement, so people look for thrills and adventure.

These views therefore located the development of youth culture and gang culture as being working class in origin.

The Birmingham Centre for Contemporary Cultural Studies (CCCS)

Established in the early 1960s, this was a politically and socially radical approach to the study of sociology and popular culture based in Britain. A wide variety of research was conducted, much of it based on Marxism, feminism and critical theory of society. A number of significant studies emerged from the group:

- *Teddy boys* – Hall and Jefferson argued that the Teds were working-class boys who had been excluded from the new wealth of the country in the immediate post-war era. They aped the styles of wealthy people by adopting fashions of the middle classes of a previous historical era.
- *Skinheads* – Cohen and Clarke argued that skinheads were an exaggerated attempt to recover traditional working-class identity even as it was disappearing with the changes to industrial Britain. Their style was based on working clothes and they resented those who they felt threatened their community values, hence the racism that became associated with skins.
- *Punk* – Hebdige said that punk was a form of resistance to capitalism and set out to shock mainstream society. He said punk was short-lived because commercial companies adopted punk style so young people moved on quickly to other fashions.

In evaluation, it can be argued that some of these styles were adopted by middle-class young people. It is possible that because the sociologists were working within a Marxist perspective, they were simply reading youth rebellion into youth styles.

- *Middle-class youth culture* – Brake (1977) found that hippies were mostly middle-class students who lived on benefits or student grants. Whilst claiming to be anti-capitalist, they still spent a great deal on travel, expensive audio equipment and street drugs.

Subculture and choice

Postmodernists claim that the culture of young people is often a matter of personal choice.

- Hetherington found New Age travellers to be from a variety of class backgrounds. Bennett and Hetherington claim that young people opt for lifestyles and that class is not a dynamic.
- Reimer argues that the central feature of most youth cultures is the search for fun and excitement, not class.

Recent findings

McCulloch (2007) argues that youth cultures are class based. Interviews with young people in Edinburgh and Newcastle suggest that young people's membership of subcultural groupings is largely determined by social class, if only because of their existing friendship networks.

Sample questions

It has been argued that youth cultures are seen as working class in origin because many sociologists working in the field were Marxists who were looking for youth culture as a sign of working-class resistance to capitalism. Middle-class youth subcultures have existed, so hippies were largely a middle-class group, although many working-class young people participated. According to Brake, working-class youth cultures are an attempt to create a **magical solution** to their problems and to create a different world. This is in contrast to middle-class youth cultures which tend to be more concerned with self-development, individual understanding and romantic notions of withdrawing from society and making a new and better world.

a) With reference to the item and to sociological knowledge, explain what is meant by **magical solution**.

b) Using material from the item and sociological knowledge, explain **two** reasons why youth culture is often associated with working-class young people.

Check your own learning

Link the researcher to the findings.

a)	Brake	Punk is a form of resistance to capitalism
b)	McCulloch	Working-class culture has different values from middle-class culture, leading to youth cultures developing
c)	Reimer	Youth cultures are an attempt to find a magical solution to the problems of inequality in society
d)	Hebdige	Youth cultures are about fun and excitement not class boundaries
e)	Cohen and Clarke	Youth culture is an alternative route to success for working-class boys
f)	Gouldner	Skinhead style is loosely based on traditional work clothes for men
g)	Miller	Youth cultures are based on existing friendship networks
h)	Albert Cohen	Youth rebellion against the Vietnam war was carried out by those with most to lose by rejecting society

Extended writing

Assess the view that youth cultures are a working-class phenomenon.

Guidance: You will need to challenge the view in this essay. Whilst there is a lot of evidence that supports the view that youth cultures originate among working-class youth, and you can explore some of the reasons why, you also need to challenge this view. Most work in the UK has been carried out by Marxists and they are less interested in the middle classes, for example. Some youth cultures are associated with art school students, particularly the dramatic ones such as glam rock and the New Romantics who were interested in style and fashion rather than making a statement about themselves or society. Studies of popular bands, for example, tend to show that many musicians associated with youth cultures are, in fact, from middle-class homes.

Write about 500–750 words.

Research idea

Find out more about skinhead culture of the 1970s by using search engines. Useful sites are

https://www.pinterest.com/abegum0146/sociology-skinhead-subculture/ and

http://www.wikihow.com/Be-a-Skinhead

Topic 9: Youth cultures and gender

Aims

⦿ To understand that many youth cultures in the past were expressions of masculinity. Until feminism developed, young women were overlooked by sociologists.

Many youth cultures appear to be a male phenomenon led by boys, with the girls as an accessory to it. For example, early skinheads (70s) called themselves rude boys and treated girls with contempt. Hip hop refers to women as bitches. Some girls appear to be attracted to such youth culture, which is not easily understood. Feminists have pointed out that there is less study of female youth culture. This reflects malestream bias of much sociology but is also to do with the difficulties of accessing groups of young women to study. It was not till the 1980s and 90s that the idea of girl power promoted assertiveness among young women. Many youth cultures have a fluid concept of gender, so hippies (60s) glam rock (70s) and emo (90s) promoted styles where boys would adopt feminine characteristics and wear female clothing as a form of resistance to traditional morality and sexuality.

Getting you thinking

How are the identities of young men and young women shaped by youth culture? Do youth cultures reinforce traditional gender roles in society, or do they break them?

Girls in early youth culture

Girls were not considered in most early studies of youth cultures. There are a variety of reasons for this:

⦿ Girls had less freedom to express themselves and so may have been less likely to participate in some youth cultures.
⦿ Heidensohn pointed out that much of the work was carried out by male sociologists who therefore tended to overlook the development of youth cultures among young women.
⦿ The contribution of women to the development of youth cultures was overlooked; women were 'invisible'.
⦿ Barbara Ehrenreich (1983) pointed out that some youth cultures were anti-female. She claimed that the Beat world of the 1950s provided an opportunity for male bonding where women were unwanted.

Youth culture and masculinity

The first studies of youth culture began from a male point of view. Osgerby pointed out that before the 1950s, the traditional role of men was to look after women. However, youth cultures were often associated with males being both aggressive and sexist. Writers such as Albert Cohen explained this association of aggressively male youth culture as being linked to school failure and the attempt to gain status through exaggerated masculinity and criminal behaviour. In Britain, the work of the CCCS suggested that some youth cultures demonstrated an aggressive hyper-masculinity in order to exaggerate working-class masculine traits such as toughness and aggression. Thus their masculinity was an assertion of class resistance to middle-class behaviours.

Bob (now Raewyn) Connell (1995) suggested that male roles in society have changed and that many men feel threatened by the rise in power of women. They face uncertain futures in the job market as traditional male work has declined. Many sociologists have referred to this changing concept of what it is to be male as a crisis of masculinity. It is argued that some boys have responded to the challenge of female success by taking on a very masculine cultural form: homophobic, anti-women (misogyny) and macho. Diane Abbott, a politician, claimed in 2013, that easy access to pornography and psychological issues linked to drink and drugs mean that young men are more likely to turn to peer groups and remain immature for too long.

There is evidence being gathered relating to the theory of masculinity in crisis, much of it from work in schools:

- Mac an Ghaill (1994) claimed boys felt education to be a waste of time, so they coped by developing laddish behaviours.
- McDowell referred to redundant masculinity, claiming traditional male roles to be inappropriate to modern society.
- Griffin (2000) talked of boys experiencing a sense of loss of what it is to be male.
- Frith and Mahony (1994); Gilligan (1997); Keddie (2007); Robinson (2000) all suggested that boys demonstrate aggressively intimidating behaviour towards girls and even female teachers.
- Kimmel (2008) and Keddie (2007) suggested that boys still tend to feel that their natural position should be one of power and that laddish behaviour means they will attempt to undermine female teachers.

Women's participation in youth culture

Although girls participated in the Teddy boy cultures of the 1950s, they were not considered fully part of it. It was not till the 1960s that girls could really challenge traditional gender roles. Some young women embraced new youth cultures, by becoming feminists and challenging traditional male dominance. The contraceptive pill meant that girls could have sex without the risk of pregnancy, so girls were freed from pressures towards marriage.

Some girls began to embrace new forms of sexuality and one of the most controversial books of the decade, Germaine Greer's *The Female Eunuch* (1970) challenged male dominance over women's sexuality. It was commonly believed that a sexual revolution was going on, and this, according to Densmore, meant that women were placed under pressure to have sex rather than having the liberty to choose partners. However, while young women were challenging their traditional roles and seeking alternative lifestyles, youth cultures were still treating them with contempt. Much popular music performed by women centred on looking for and hanging onto a man. As Sheila Rowbotham pointed out, much of the male-produced popular music of the 60s and 70s was sexist and demeaning to women. Frith and McRobbie (1990) described the music of the Rolling Stones (70s) as being an example of 'cock rock' celebrating 'the rampant destructive male'.

A major criticism of the CCCS was that it consisted of male sociologists looking at male participants in youth cultures. An influential exception to this work was Angela McRobbie's (1978) ethnographic study of girls at a youth club. She argued that girls had a 'bedroom culture'

Mini Skirt
Designed by Mary Quant

different from the street culture of boys. She said that the bedroom was an exclusively feminine sphere, a place of safety from the rampant sexism of the streets. These 1970s teenagers were still focussing on getting and keeping a boyfriend. The impact of technology has changed bedroom culture. The television, the Internet and the growth of social media means that the bedroom is no longer socially isolated but a private sphere where girls are connected to the outside world.

Under my thumb, the squirmin' dog who's just had her day, under my thumb, a girl who has just changed her ways. It's down to me, yes it is, the way she does just what she's told, down to me, the change has come, she's under my thumb, ah, ah, say it's alright.

Lyrics to Rolling Stones hit (1966)

Changing gender patterns and youth cultures

Modern sociologists find that women are developing a role in youth cultures in public spaces. Sarah Thornton researched club cultures (such as rave, house). She claimed that we live in a more fragmented society and people have more choice. Girls are seeking space outside the home. McRobbie (1994) found Black Ragga girls used sexually explicit dance moves as a way ridiculing boys for their sexism. Garcia and others claim that dance and club culture first emerged in the LGBT communities of New York and London in places where gay people could be safe from homophobia. It was a scene, rather than a culture. People felt free to express gender and sexuality in a variety of non-straight ways. Skeggs pointed out that by the 1980s and 90s girls would go to gay clubs where they, too, could be safe from male harassment, and that straight boys followed them, which led to a wider club culture. Redhead, Hetherington et al., Bennett and Willis have all pointed to a blurring of sexuality and gender in modern youth cultures, with boys becoming more body and appearance conscious and girls becoming more assertive and sexualised in their behaviours.

Recent research into Straight Edge (sXe) in Australia and the USA supports the view that gender is fluid. Straight Edge is form of hard core punk that rejects drugs, meat, alcohol and easy sex. Many sXe have heavy tattoos. For men, tattoos are an expression of conventional masculinity, but for girls, tattooing is a political statement about conventional ideas of femininity. Haenfler found sXe girls adopt a masculinised femininity although they are not lesbian. An attraction is that they will not be taken advantage of, if drunk. Boys, however, may be hyper-masculine at shows but more progressive in other social settings.

Furlong and Cartmel have suggested that the movement of women into public youth culture is not as dramatic as sociologists have claimed. They point out that many public spaces are still male dominated and others have suggested that elements of youth culture, particularly adventure and shooting gaming are male dominated and male targeted. Women are portrayed in a sexualised manner. For example, there was an outcry in 2013 when the game makers for *Assassin's Creed* announced that it would not include women characters because 'they were too hard to animate'. Lads' mags and young people's television media still portray women in a highly sexualised manner.

Activity

Use the Internet to read the full lyrics to the song *'Under my Thumb'* by Mick Jagger and Keith Richards (1966). In contrast, look at the lyrics or listen to the song *'That's the Way Boys Are'* – Leslie Gore (1964). What do these popular songs of the 1960s tell you about youth cultural attitudes to women?

Why would many young people be attracted to a youth culture that is entirely based on clean living and traditional moral values? Can such a style be considered to be resisting mainstream values? Make points for and against.

Sample questions

According to a website aimed at retailers, www.labelnetworkds.com (2015), youth culture retail lines are moving away from selling items to either boys or girls and towards **gender** neutrality in terms of fashion and style. Gucci's collection in Milan in 2014 showed the same clothing being modelled on boys and on girls. Boys were shown in floral shirts, while girls wore tailored suits and masculine shoes. They are tapping into street style where girls and boys have been blurring gender lines for at least ten years. Selfridges fashion chain launched a new fashion line in 2015. Named Agender, it is targeted at what they call the post-gender generation. Selfridges' creative director said that they were tapping into a cultural shift so that 'people can select clothing freely without feeling they must buy gendered clothing'.

a) With reference to the item and to sociological knowledge, explain what is meant by **gender**.

b) Using material from the item and sociological knowledge, explain **two** reasons why young people may be moving away from traditionally gendered behaviour.

Check your own learning

Match the terms to their meaning.

a) Gender	Males assume exaggerated masculine characteristics and style
b) New bedroom culture	People blur the lines between gendered behaviours
c) Crisis of masculinity	Socially accepted patterns of behaviour for people of different biological sex
d) Gender-bending	Girls in the 1970s viewed bedrooms as places of safety
e) Misogyny	The view that boys no longer have a concept of what it is to be masculine
f) Hyper masculinity	Hatred and fear of gay people
g) Bedroom culture	People maintain social connections in a private space thanks to new technologies
h) Homophobia	Hatred and fear of women

Extended writing

Discuss the ways in which gender identity may be expressed through youth culture.

Guidance: You will discuss both male and female gender identities. You may need to identify what you consider to be traditional male and female patterns of behaviour before moving on to issues of youth culture and gender. There are a number of key issues that you may wish to consider, for example are boys becoming more like girls? Are aggressive behaviours among young males a response to feminism and the rise of girl cultures? You might even want to consider the idea that gender is becoming more fluid so that both masculinity and femininity are being challenged by youth culture. On the other hand, there are other youth cultures such as hip-hop which are aggressively misogynistic. Consider a range of youth cultures and refer to studies. You do not have to draw a definitive conclusion as to whether gender lines are blurred, the issue is more one of how gender identity is created.

Write about 500–750 words.

In 2014, 26-year-old Conchita Wurst (aka Thomas Neuwirth) won the Eurovision song contest. His appearance provoked strong reactions, so even the president of Russia, Vladimir Putin, made publicly critical statements. Conchita Wurst was not the first young artist to adopt a look that was neither fully male nor female (androgyny). Research David Bowie and his Ziggy Stardust persona of the 1970s, or Boy George of Culture Club in the 1980s.

STRETCH and CHALLENGE

For an insight into Beat culture, read Jack Kerouac's 1957 novel, *On the Road*, or watch the 2012 film of the book.

Aims

- To understand that there have always been serious issues of racism in British youth culture, whilst at the same time, young people have been drawn to Black music and borrowed from their street styles.

However, the first large groups of Black migrants arrived in the late 1940s and early 1950s, often from African Caribbean areas such as Jamaica. They moved into working-class areas of cities at the same time as large-scale youth cultures began to develop. White working-class youth were attracted to the styles and the music of Black culture, but they also felt threatened by the new migrants in terms of jobs and competition for housing. Migrants, who had been hoping for opportunities, experienced rejection, overt racism and prejudice. Their children, who had been born in Britain, developed cultural patterns based on resisting racism, only to see their cultural forms being adopted by white youth as evidence of 'cool', whilst at the same time, they were being rejected by those same youth cultures.

Topic 10: Youth cultures and ethnicity

Getting you thinking

Dreadlocks form when the hair is left without brushing or cutting. In many cultures, including West Indian societies, dreadlocks have deep spiritual significance. Why might Western young people adopt the style? What messages are they sending to others by adopting this look? How might African Caribbeans view this adoption of their style?

Formation of ethnic minority youth cultures

Cohen and early sociologists of youth cultures suggested that gangs and cultures were formed by young males who lacked social status. He called this feeling status frustration. The antisocial behaviour of young men was a direct attempt to gain status within the gang in response to lack of status in society. Thus, early sociologists could argue that Black subcultures in the USA and in Britain were a response to lack of social status. The problem for Black youths in Britain was far more than just status frustration. Clarke (1976) described early skinhead subcultures as violent, overly aggressive and both racist and homophobic. They were associated with unpleasant hate crimes which they described as 'queer-bashing' and 'paki-bashing'. Curiously, they were doing this while listening to Black popular music. It could be argued that these violent behaviours were just extreme manifestations of public attitudes among some sectors of mainstream society. Hall (1978) pointed out that Black young people were being presented as a menace to society and as muggers in the popular press.

The CCCS claimed that a more complex process was taking place. In 1966, Downes suggested that immigrant subcultures have to develop behaviours and a culture that have meaning and symbolism which are different from those of the culture around them. Hebdige said that all youth cultures developed as a form of resistance to dominant ideology and mainstream capitalist culture. He saw clothing and youth style as a symbolic form of resistance. The Black street culture that developed in Britain in the 1960s was a response to their specific problems of racism, discrimination and unemployment. He argued that the young African Caribbean men who felt excluded from dominant white culture, took an African centred identity based on Rastafarianism, a religious belief centred on the return of ex-slave cultures to Africa. Their dreadlocks were an important symbol of allegiance to Rastafari and a rejection of white capitalism because they are a reflection of African appearance and style.

Alternative suggestions regarding the development of Black youth cultures have come from sociologists working with young Black people in schools. Wright (1986) found that young Black people were often placed in lower sets in school where they became bored and disruptive. Gillborn (1990) found that Black children were treated differently and penalised more harshly by teachers where they retreated into youth cultures to avoid the racism of their education. The result of this was more conflict. Mac an Ghaill found Black and Asian students rejected school but not education but retreated into subcultures for safety. Sewell (1997) found that Black street style brought students into conflict with teachers who did not understand it.

The influence of Black street style on white youths

1950s Jamaican music had a range of interesting rhythms and styles, for example ska. This was popular with the mods in the 1960s and later with skinheads. White bands incorporated these rhythms into punk, developing Two Tone. Bands such as UB40 and Madness were also influenced by reggae music, which musicians like Bob Marley brought from Jamaica to wider prominence. As Black music forms were adopted by the white dominated music business young Black people moved on to new youth styles. Then in the 1980s ragga emerged as a new musical genre for Black youth; a throbbing form of electronic music. The clubs became the basis of early drum and bass sounds, and the clubbing and DJ crazes of the 1990s were white adaptations of Jamaican and Black American hip hop styles made acceptable for white youth culture. Black street culture was again being repackaged, commercialised and sold to white youth as 'cool'.

> How they brutalise the very souls. Today they say that we are free, only to be chained in poverty. Good God, I think it's illiteracy...
>
> **Bob Marley**

Asian youth culture and Bhangra styles

Hebdige points out that youth cultures only become seen and public when they are seen as breaking social rules. Asian youth cultures have been more discrete and less obvious, so they are less well studied. Nevertheless, Asian young people had to face their own issues of rejection, discrimination and racism. Alexander and Kim pointed out that many formed 'hybrid' cultures that fused elements of British youth cultures with traditional Asian patterns. Bhangra rhythms became popular in the 1980s and found their way into non-Asian popular music. A street style known as Brasian developed and has been adapted and commercialised for mainstream culture. For example, Asian women's dress style has been adapted and popularised among white women in the form of a tunic or dress worn over trousers and leggings. The wearing of scarves and bright jewellery is also Asian influenced.

Tip

Mairtin Mac an Ghaill's name is often misspelled by candidates who often think he is two people. For politeness and to show evidence of reading, if you quote his work, spell his name correctly.

$100
LEGEND – ADRIAN BOOT
50th Anniversary of the Birth of Bob Marley
JAMAICA

What Asian influences can you see in both male and female fashions currently? Remember that styles are usually adapted rather than copied directly!

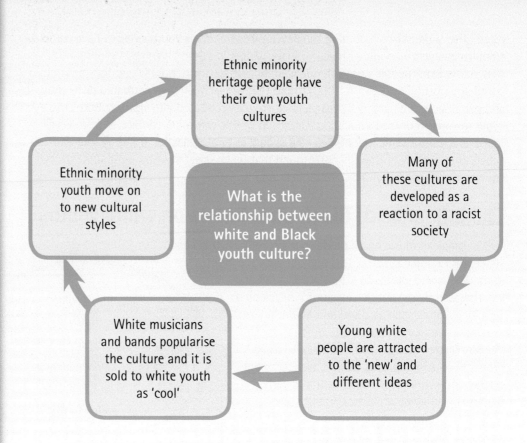

Ethnicity and gender

Black feminists have pointed out that females may experience sexism or a rigid gender divide within the family and then a dual challenge of sexism and racism in wider society. For example, in SE Asian families, decision making will generally rest with the males of the family. This means that young women may be understudied because of the complicating factors when conducting research. Thus, most research has taken

Sample questions

Tony Sewell, a Black university lecturer, who has just finished an inquiry into soaring levels of exclusions among Black pupils from a London school, claimed that too much concern with money and consumer goods was almost as damaging to Black pupils' chances as **racism**.

He warned that fashionable Black youth culture inevitably crossed over to white teenagers, and said tackling it would benefit all pupils. 'What we have now is... not only the pressure of racism, but Black peer grouping [which] has become another pressure almost as big as institutional racism was.'

Black children had gained much-needed self-esteem from their youth culture becoming part of the mainstream, he conceded. 'But that culture is not one that, for example, is interested in being a great chess player, or intellectual activity. It is actually to do with propping up a big commercial culture to do with selling trainers, selling magazines, rap music and so on.'

Adapted from an article in the Guardian newspaper
http://www.theguardian.com/uk/2000/aug/20/education.race

a) With reference to the item and to sociological knowledge, explain what is meant by **racism**.

b) Using material from the item and sociological knowledge, explain **two** reasons why young white people may be attracted to Black youth cultures.

place in schools. Safia Mirza found that Black girls resisted racism by succeeding in school and Mac an Ghaill found the 'Black sisters' succeeded by forming positive peer groups which supported each other in order to resist teacher labelling. The wearing of the hijab or other traditional clothing can be seen as reflecting a rejection of the mainstream culture of Western societies.

STRETCH and CHALLENGE

You may wish to read *Lives in Translation: Sikh Youth as British Citizen* (2002) by Kathleen Hall, much of which is freely available online.

Check your own learning

Match the term to the meaning.

a)	Ska, ragga and reggae	Young people form cultures that retain elements of their heritage culture but attach other cultural forms to create a new cultural form
b)	Racism	A belief in and actions supporting the view that one race (ethnicity) is somehow superior to another
c)	Rastafari	Traditional Jamaican musical forms
d)	Status frustration	A hybrid culture developed from a combination of Asian cultural forms and British and American youth cultural styles
e)	Resistance	People who cannot gain respect through the usual channels turn to alternative methods of gaining respect, such as criminality
f)	Hybrid culture	A religious and spiritual movement that looks to the symbolic return of those of Black African heritage to Africa and the rejection of materialism
g)	Brasian	People reject the dominant mainstream culture and fight against it by forming their own cultural styles

Activity

Mind map reasons why non-white young people would wish to develop separate youth cultures of their own. Start with these ideas and use your own knowledge and experience to map other ideas.

- Cohen and others suggest status frustration.

- Hebdige and others claim it is a response to racism and a rejection of white capitalism.

- Sewell, Wright and others suggest that it originates in racism in school.

- It could be a pride in a different cultural heritage rather than a rejection of white youth culture.

Extended writing

Discuss the ways in which ethnic identity may be expressed through youth culture.

Guidance: This question is not as straightforward as it looks. We all have an ethnic identity. The term is not reserved for those who have a minority cultural heritage. You could refer to white youth cultures, particularly the skinheads who reinforced their sense of ethnic identity in very unpleasant ways. Consider a range of youth cultures and refer to studies. You should certainly refer to the culture of the Rastas and also of British Asians who responded to racism and repression in different forms, but with music and style being a significant part of their identity. You might also consider whether there is a parallel between a religious response in terms of Rastafari and the return of strict Islamic codes among some young Asians.

Write about 500–750 words.

Topic 11: Youth cultures and nation

The overt nationalism and racism of some youth cultures such as the skinheads have not been studied fully. However, Nayak (1999) suggests they have a concept of whiteness and nationhood which is dangerous and racist. Other cultures, not especially racist in values only, appear to be attractive to white youth, for example goths or emos. They appear to be a white phenomenon. Sociologists have suggested that we need more understanding of the relationship between youth culture and whiteness if racism is to be challenged.

Research idea

Research a BBC documentary called *The Chelsea Headhunters* made by a journalist, Donal MacIntyre. You can view it on YouTube. It focusses on the activities of football hooligans with links to racist organisations and extreme nationalistic views.

Getting you thinking

In the 1930s the Hitler Youth (Germany) and the Young Octobrists (Soviet Russia) were government-run youth organisations. They were seen as important ways of establishing the ideologies of the ruling parties and encouraging nationalism. Young people were even encouraged to spy on their families and neighbours.

What might attract young people to such organisations? What methods could extremist groups use today to target young people?

White youth racism and ethnic minorities

Whilst many writers from the CCCS noted the basic racism of the cultures that they studied, these attitudes were not fully interrogated or explored. For example, Willis's Lads in the 1970s routinely used highly offensive language to describe non-white youth in a way that was casual and that most people nowadays would consider totally unacceptable. Other studies can be similarly criticised for not addressing issues of nation and racism: Parker's *View from the Boys* notes similar attitudes but doesn't really investigate them. Hebdige describes the use of the swastika by skinhead boys as being nothing more than an attempt to shock, but this is a rather kindly view of their attitudes. Gelder (1997) points out that the CCCS was so focussed on issues of symbolism, style and attitude that they overlooked what many of the youth cultures were actually doing. In the case of skinheads, for example, they were fighting at football matches, being sexual predators and aggressive with girls, picking fights with vulnerable people, drinking, being violent and abusing drugs. Many were engaging in actively aggressive racist violence. These anti-social behaviours were group activities and both threatening and dangerous for those who were targeted.

Race and 'other'

The concept of otherness is a useful one when discussing issues of nation and race among young people. The theory is that we build identities from what we are not – thus boys may assert masculinity by not being feminine and rejecting things they see as 'girly'. In the context of race and nation, young people may assert their sense of national identity by not being Black or Asian. This may lead to an assertive 'whiteness' and racist behaviours. For example, skinheads would use racist language to 'other' non-whites in order to ensure that their own bodies and behaviours were seen as normal and acceptable. Hebdige sees skinheads as asserting a specific type of white working-class masculinity.

Whilst racism is not geographically limited to some areas, it is noticeable that many youth cultures are an urban or former council estate phenomenon. Some of the youth cultures linked to racism are found in areas where migration patterns mean that there are also many non-white minority groups. Nayyar suggests that white ethnicity is therefore reinforced in such areas because white working-class youth choose to see Britishness as under threat.

Race and white nation

Riots involving racial elements have occurred at regular intervals in British cities since the end of World War 2. These have not always been white versus non-white. There have been occasions where communities have unified themselves against the police. Nevertheless, there is a common discourse of inner city rioting as being 'race-related'. Inner city areas have been targeted by racist groups and the Far Right for recruitment among white youth groups. Bagguley and Hussain (2001) found that rioting in Bradford had occurred after a group of white racists had marched through a multi-ethnic area of Oldham shouting racist slogans. When some appeared in courts for provoking the riots, they were not local people, but from a range of areas around the country. Modood (1997) has pointed out that in many areas of working-class poverty and deprivation; the poorest communities are often those of Pakistani and Bangladeshi origin. They earn roughly two-thirds the average pay of white men, well below the national average. Nevertheless, young white youth have often seen themselves as being the victims of poverty and deprivation and have been targeted by racist political groups looking for recruits.

Nation and youth subcultures

Within the context of New Zealand (Aotearoa), Lloyd Martin (2002), looking at Maori youth subcultures suggested that members of ethnic youth subcultures develop an identity linked with concepts of nation. By being 'good' at the subculture, individuals can gain respect. This can be an incentive to more extreme views and attitudes from subcultural members but lead to moral panics and over-reaction from those who object.

Consumption	Ethnic culture becomes a main source of identity so buys clothes and items associated with it
Social values	The subculture and knowledge of ethnicity become a source of cultural capital and status
Life styles	The individual can become a trend setter in the local community and subculture

Research idea

The 'Tebbit test' refers to the view of Norman Tebbit, a Conservative politician, in the 1990s. He said that members of ethnic minorities who supported India, Pakistan or the West Indies instead of the English cricket team were not properly integrated into British society. Do you agree?

Yeah, I mean... I did call him a 'paki' but it don't mean nothin I was just mucking about. I've got nothing against him we were just mucking about.

Terry (13 years old, male, white English)

From Les Back's 1990 study of racist name calling

171

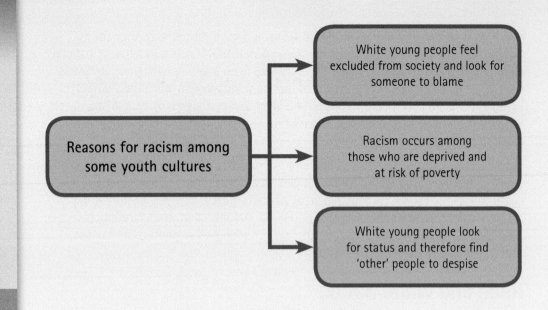

Reasons for racism among some youth cultures

White young people feel excluded from society and look for someone to blame

Racism occurs among those who are deprived and at risk of poverty

White young people look for status and therefore find 'other' people to despise

Reasons for youth cultural racism

Many of the songs of the Welsh band, the Manic Street Preachers were openly political and controversial.

Welsh nationalism and youth culture

Not all nationalism is necessarily a bad or dangerous thing. There has been a rise in nationalism in Scotland and Wales (the Celtic Fringe) in recent years. Welsh nationalism arose from working-class politics before the First World War (1914–18) but the Welsh Nationalist Party was not established till 1925. There was a strong socialist and Marxist element within it. Kellas suggests that most Welsh nationalism is a form of inclusive social movement which accepts inward migration as long as the migrants learn Welsh and become part of the community regardless of their heritage.

Wales has a thriving youth cultural movement, Yr Urdd, which is organises a national festival, the Urdd National Eisteddfod. This is one of the largest youth cultural festivals in Europe and there are competitions in the performing arts, music and literature through the medium of Welsh. The growth of the Welsh language among some sectors of the youth community has meant that there is a thriving popular music scene through the medium of Welsh. Many Welsh bands have gone on to more popular success outside Wales including Goldie Looking Chain, the Manic Street Preachers, Catatonia and Super Furry Animals. They have used Welsh in song lyrics and have referred to Welsh culture in their lyrics. Hill (2007) has pointed out that Welsh bands and musicians have also adopted musical styles from other cultures to produce music for Welsh-speaking audiences. Just as Black young people used reggae rhythms as part of their cultural identity, so Welsh musicians adopted the rhythms but sang Welsh language lyrics to emphasise their Welsh identity. Later musicians adopted hip-hop styles to produce protest songs for Welsh-speaking audiences.

Discussion point

- What associations does the flag of St George have when it is flown? Are they the same as or different from those for the Welsh flag?

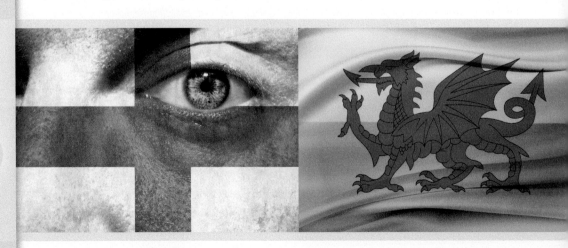

Sample questions

There was much controversy in Wales in 2015 when it turned out that a Labour Party candidate had previously written on a website in 2006 that cars in Wales displaying English flags should be vandalised. Huw Thomas was a student when he wrote that he was 'sickened' by the number of cars flying English flags in Wales to support the England World Cup football team.

According to Wales Online, he wrote: 'It truly shows the degree our society has been infiltrated by incomers who are not ready to integrate. Very often, from what I see, some flying English flags are young people, who have been brought up in Wales, but who are loyal to England. This raises questions about us as Welsh people as well.

It's true that the parents are at fault, but it's obvious that the education system has failed to create a Welsh Nationalism in these people, and I wonder also how many of us Welsh people, in our school days, tried to bring these people (aka chavs) into the Welsh circle.'

Adapted from an article on the BBC website
http://www.bbc.co.uk/news/election-2015-wales-32249455

a) With reference to the item and to sociological knowledge, explain what is meant by **nationalism**.

b) Using material from the item and sociological knowledge, explain **two** reasons why some youth cultures have racist attitudes.

STRETCH and CHALLENGE

Use a search engine to find out more about the link between football and English national identity.

Check your own learning
Look at these statements, are they true or false?

a) Many youth cultures have had a nationalist and even racist element to the culture and values

b) The CCCS expressed considerable concern at the racist and sexist attitudes of the groups that they studied

c) Most countries have ethnic minority groups who feel discriminated against and fearful of racist attack

d) Young white youth from poorer areas have often seen themselves as being the victims of poverty and deprivation

e) Racism among young people is a fairly new development since World War 2 ended

f) There were no ethnic minority migrants to the UK before 1946

g) Some ethnic minority young people have formed youth cultures for themselves as a form of protection against racism

Chelsea supporters were one of a number of football fan groups famous for their violence, racism and far right politics in the 1990s and 1980s.

Extended writing

Using sociological knowledge, explain what is meant by 'othering'.
Guidance: This is a fairly straightforward question and requires little more than a definition of the terms and some examples of how various social groups can be 'othered'. In the context of youth culture, groups who can be othered are those who do not belong or do not subscribe to the values of the group or those of a different generation. It can also refer to those of differing ethnicities who will 'other' both as a way of gaining an identity and of restricting access to the group for those who don't fit.
Write about 200 words.

Aims

⊙ To understand that Cohen used the concept of **spectacular** youth culture to describe the way that some **subcultures** appear to capture the public imagination and the mood of a time. Recent sociologists have said there has been a decline in the significance of such groups.

There is a debate within the study of youth which examines the issue of how far most young people actually have a culture distinct from mainstream society. The CCCS saw the development of youth culture as a form of resistance to mainstream society, so, they claimed that there was a cultural difference between youth cultures and mainstream society. Critics of this theory say that only dramatic youth cultures were studied by CCCS and that more mainstream cultures were overlooked. Most young people never identify with a specific youth culture. Youth cultures are so short-lived and evolve so quickly that they are more a statement of style and fashion that anything meaningful in cultural terms.

Topic 12: Spectacular youth cultures and neo-tribes

Getting you thinking

Look at the two images. To what extent is their clothing and style for each of these groups a public statement of their values and culture, or simply a statement of fashion? Is dress and style something that is only typical of young people?

Types of youth groups

Studies have suggested that there are many different youth groups and that many young people today may actually belong to one or more of these relatively casual groups, who nevertheless will have their own slightly distinctive styles and set of values. Some may be quite formalised such as religious groups, or fan-based groups, whereas others will be freeform in the sense that people will choose lifestyles or images and mix

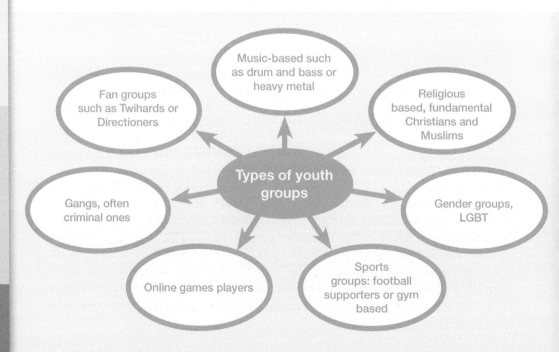

Can you think of other types of youth groups that could be added to this typology?

with others of the same world view. For example, New Age travellers or ecowarriors may drift in and out of the lifestyle.

Spectacular youth cultures

In the 1960s and 1970s, there were dramatic youth groups such as the hippies or punks that became global phenomena. Because they adopted fashions and behaviours that were so distinctive, they were described as spectacular youth cultures. Certainly, the appearance of hippies seemed very shocking and aggressive with their long hair at a time when many young American men were fighting in Vietnam. Long hair was a clear anti-War statement in contrast to the shaved hair of the military. Some sociologists argue that the social situations which created such a dramatic style have now ended. Looking back, postmodernists tend to suggest that the style and beliefs of hippies amounted to very little more than a few people taking to the lifestyle. The attention they received was excessive, given the numbers involved. For others it was little more than an issue of people wearing the clothes and self-identifying as belonging to the culture for reasons of fashion.

Punk is an example of a spectacular youth culture.

Hodkinson (2002) points out that for a substantial number of young people, membership of a youth culture is very significant, with people adopting a particular subcultural lifestyle, norms and values over long periods of time. Others have come to similar conclusions: Thornton (1995) and MacDonald in 2001. There are still recognisable elderly hippies and rockers. You may even find pubs and clubs where the music is played and the styles worn by people in their sixties.

Neo-tribes

By the 1990s, postmodernists suggested that youth cultures had become so commercialised that few young people would commit to any particular subcultural style. There were fewer boundaries between youth groups, so that whilst the difference between mods and rockers was clear and explicit, modern young people would simply choose a style that would suit them for a particular purpose. Feminists in the 1970s would have worn Doc Marten boots to signal a specific set of social attitudes and beliefs that others could have 'read'. Today, young people might choose them as a fashion item. Muggleton suggests that the speed with which fashions and styles change means that collective action by young people is no longer possible. It is no longer possible to be authentically part of a rebellious subculture when others are accepting and tolerant of style differences. It is also the case that the 'rebellious subcultures' are being marketed by commercial interests, for example punk bands like the Sex Pistols were signed up by major record labels.

By the 1990s, sociologists were investigating trends and styles. For example, Alix Sharkey (1993) attended a summer rave in a field. He identified five 'tribes', each of which had an identifiable style and a taste in music. These he describes as being: Hardcore Nosebleed, The Trendy-Trance, Eurotechno-Ambient, Young Crusties and Hippy Nouveau. Clearly, these descriptions are subjective but it suggests that young people no longer subscribe to one set of behaviours forming a single youth culture, but that it is a collection of youth subcultures, which are known as neo-tribes. These descriptions, though subjective, suggest not a single youth culture but a collection of different co-existing youth subcultures, or neo-tribes.

Discussion point

- Have young people ever all belonged to one set of behaviours known as youth culture, or have there always been collections of co-existing groups?

Activity

Use the internet to find out about the Manchester Peacock Society, a Teddy boy group of men in their 60s.

Research idea

How many different tribes can you identify in your college or school? What problems do you have putting people into categories?

Discussion point

- What specific meanings can be read into a woman's choice of footwear today?

Postmodernism and neo-tribes

Both Bennett and Hetherington reject the view that class or social background shapes the behaviour of young people. Hetherington (1998) studied New Age travellers and found they were from a range of backgrounds and it was their beliefs and behaviour that unified them. They had made an active choice to assume the lifestyle. The term neo-tribe was probably coined by Maffesoli but used by Bennett, among others, to describe modern youth cultures. He says they have a loose structure based on lifestyle and consumer choices. They share a common world view rather that a class position. Bennett is therefore being critical of the CCCS and also pointing out a significant shift in behaviour among young people saying youth culture is now less meaningful and more consumer led.

> You have your way. I have my way. As for the right way, the correct way, and the only way, it does not exist.
>
> *Friedrich Nietzsche*

Sample questions

To be honest, we're a bunch of about 70 hippies, some of us 'originals'. Tipi Valley is high in the Welsh hills, on 200 acres that we have bought bit by bit together over 40 years. The idea is that we are part of nature, living within nature as part of our survival **lifestyle**. Thus all our homes are low-impact dwellings such as tipis, yurts, domes and thatched or turf-roofed round houses. We are a village, not a commune, and everyone is responsible for their own economy. We do not have regular business meetings, only necessary ones, and we never vote. It works by consensus and personal relationships. Dogs are not welcome. And cats have a very negative impact on the environment. Village spirituality is natural, the simple paganism of celebrating our total dependence on Mother Earth, mostly expressed in chanting and drumming at the sweatlodge (sauna) and at Big Lodge social get-togethers, and Saturday night music jams.

Adapted from a website guide to alternative living
http://www.diggersanddreamers.org.uk/communities/existing/tipi-valley

a) With reference to the item and to sociological knowledge, explain what is meant by **lifestyle**.

b) Using material from the item and sociological knowledge, explain **two** reasons why some sociologists believe that we no longer have spectacular youth cultures.

In the past, young people would need to gather together to listen to music, at home, in dance halls or discotheques (now clubs). Records and cassette tapes were very expensive so people saved up to buy them and listened to them with friends. What effect do you think the easy accessibility and availability of music had on pop-cultures and youth subcultures?

Check your own learning

Answer the following questions with one-word answers.

a)	Which sociologist was probably the first to use the term neo-tribe?	
b)	What term is used to describe a collective youth culture with its own set of norms and distinctive behaviours?	
c)	Who identified five 'tribes' at a 1990s rave in a field?	
d)	Who said that that the speed with which fashions and styles change means that collective action by young people is no longer possible?	
e)	Who wore Doc Marten boots to signal a fight against patriarchy?	
f)	Who claims that youth cultures are totally commercialised?	
g)	Who said that all elements of youth cultural style had meaning?	

Research idea

Find out how many people in your year group describe themselves as being 'fans' of bands, comics or other cultural items. Ask the fans how much they spend on their fandom. What does this tell you about the role of young people as consumers of products?

> Young men with shaved heads and pigtails, stripped to the waist, are executing vaguely oriental hand movements. Freeze-framed by strobes in clouds of dry ice, revivalist hippies and mods are swaying in the maelstrom. Rastas, ragga girls, ravers there is no stylistic cohesion to the assembly, as there would have been in the golden days of youth culture. So what is this noise that has united these teenage tribes?
>
> T. Willis, 'The Lost Tribes: Rave Culture'. Sunday Times 18 July 1993

Extended writing

Using sociological knowledge, explain what is meant by the term neo-tribes.

Guidance: This is not entirely a simple question, because mention needs to be made of the concept of a spectacular youth culture which is an oppositional theory. Be careful not to spend too long on the explanation of spectacular youth cultures but move on swiftly to describing the characteristics of a neo-tribe and linking it to the ideas of postmodernism and some relevant research. You could talk about technological change and commercialisation of youth cultures. Mention that young people now have a choice of styles so that they can take their pick of which style they may choose on any particular day.

Write about 200 words.

Discussion point

- Reimer (1995) says that the central feature of modern youth cultures is the desire to have fun. To what extent do you agree or disagree with this viewpoint?

Aims

- ⊙ **To understand that the earliest studies into youth cultures look at their link to delinquency and gangs. Youth groups are often the subject of moral panics because of criminal activity.**

Many American inner cities are marked by gang violence. The gangs exist as subcultures with different norms and values from those of wider society. Studies of gangs show that there are characteristics of criminal youth cultures that can be identified. In recent years there have been more studies of female gangs. Other gangs may be based on religion, class or ethnicity. Evidence suggests that the activities of youth gangs are exaggerated to create moral panics in order to provide a scapegoat for wider social problems.

STRETCH and CHALLENGE

Read the report on girls and gangs produced by the Centre for Social Justice online at http://www.centreforsocialjustice.org.uk/UserStorage/pdf/Pdf%20reports/Girls-and-Gangs-FINAL-VERSION.pdf

Topic 13: Youth cultures and deviance

Getting you thinking

To what extent is it true that young people are more criminal than other sectors of society?

Characteristics of criminal youth gangs

- ⊙ *Territory* – Gangs are often associated with a particular area and see themselves as having ownership of a specific geographical area. They may use graffiti tags to warn off other young people.
- ⊙ *Loyalty* – Gang members follow gang rules and may even have specific signs and tattoos to show membership of the gang. Some gangs require members to have passed a test of some kind to join the gang. This may be to commit an act of violence or to experience pain.
- ⊙ *Hierarchy* – Some studies such as Venkatesh's *Gang Leader for a Day* suggest a clear leadership structure, but not all gangs are so well organised. They appear to have a more fluid structure.
- ⊙ *Delinquent subculture* – Criminal gangs such as Patrick's *Glasgow Gang* appear to have different norms and values, for example selling drugs or stealing cars. Membership can be linked to excitement, risk and money.
- ⊙ *Family and sense of belonging* – There is some suggestion that gangs become like families to members who will be looked after. Miller said young people need to fit into a social groups and youths form gangs in order to fit in. Underclass theorists such as Marsland and Murray support these ideas. It may be dangerous in some areas not to be a member of the gang because then there is the risk of victim status.
- ⊙ *Shared taste and social networking* – Sometimes the media report normal youth behaviour as being gang related, when actually this is overstated. Williamson's study of the Milltown Boys (1997) suggested that although there was territory and hierarchy, it was not particularly criminal, more social networking.

What causes youth gangs to form?

A famous American study by Cloward and Ohlin (1960) identified three different types of criminal youth gangs. These were:

- ⊙ *Crime-oriented gangs* which are influenced by adult professional criminals and which act as a form of training and apprenticeship system.

- *Conflict-oriented gangs* which use violence to gain status in an area.
- *Retreatist gangs* which turn to drugs and have contempt for mainstream society.

Whilst this may be a useful way of understanding gang behaviour, the functionalist Travis Hirschi (1969) pointed out that most delinquent boys become law abiding citizens so that criminality is simply a phase which many working-class young people pass through.

High delinquency areas of cities

Shaw and McKay (1969) said that there are definite patterns of youth crime in cities and it is concentrated in areas of poverty and deprivation such as heavy industrial areas and inner city estates. They claimed that youth crime was a response to social disorganisation and local norms that value crime and antisocial behaviours.

Miller and cultural explanations

Miller, in 1958, suggested that the problem of youth crime was triggered by six focal concerns, or values, held by young men. These are: staying out of trouble, toughness, quick-wittedness, thrill-seeking, trusting to luck and the need to feel in control of oneself and one's area.

British studies of gang cultures

The previous theories were based on work in the USA, but there is a tradition of ethnographic studies of youth gangs in the UK which are more descriptive of what the gangs do and how they behave.

- Howard Parker (1974) *A View from the Boys* describes a culture in Liverpool where boys are not looking for trouble, but will not back away from it if it starts.
- Willmott (1966) *Adolescent boys in East London* found young men in boring jobs who used deviance to get some excitement in life.

Recent work on British gang cultures

Criminal gangs and gang culture have become a recent moral panic. A Home Office report of 2008 suggested that youth gangs were linked with problems of urban violence and rising rates of weapon use. Specific cases of young people being killed as a consequence of street violence have fuelled fears that such crimes are gang related. There are some arguments to suggest that the issue of gang violence is exaggerated. For example, there are claims of rising participation of young women in girl-gangs. Increasingly, gangs in the UK are being represented in terms that are similar to the way that American gangs are seen as drug-fuelled and dangerous murderers. Much of the discussion has been based on secondary sources. However, there are problems with such material as it tends to be dated and not necessarily valid, because much crime is unrecorded and unreported. Comparisons with the USA are not necessarily valid either, because culturally, the UK is different and guns are not as easily accessed. However, gang cultures can be seen in terms of:

- *Masculine identity* – Many researchers view the existence of gangs and aggressively deviant youth cultures as being linked to the crisis of masculinity where gang members are asserting their male status.
- *Educational failure* – Pitts (2008) suggests that young men find respect in gangs and in street culture. In addition they can make money through criminal activity.
- *Style and resistance* – This echoes research by the CCCS which suggests that gang-related activity rises at times of economic stress when working-class youths become aware of their lower position in the social structure.

Activity

Although it is very dated now, a stylised and interesting depiction of street gang behaviours can be seen in the musical, *West Side Story*. Alternatively, you might watch *The Wire*, an excellent series set in Baltimore, which examines gang culture in some detail.

Discussion point

- Many youth gangs use graffiti to 'tag' their area as a warning to other young people. What reasons would they have for doing this apart from just warnings?

Research methods

What practical and ethical problems would you experience in trying to understand youth criminal gangs? Discuss this with a group.

⭐ INTERESTING FACT

There is a possibility that criminal activity has become mainstream to youth culture. In 1999, research by Edinburgh University showed that drug use was common, with more than half of young people surveyed using drink and drugs and a quarter driving under the influence. There were 222 respondents and more than 75% reported using drugs; 93% of the drug users mixed substances. If almost everyone is breaking the law, who is the deviant?

Why might it be dangerous to view all youth groups as being gangs?

STRETCH and CHALLENGE

Enter the term **UK Government Youth Crime Prevention** into a search engine. What do you learn about government attitudes and beliefs about youth crime?

Modern gangs – are they a problem?

The Centre for Social Justice (CSJ) (2009) argues that modern youth criminal cultures are a serious problem for British society because whereas in the past, most young men grew up and got wives and jobs, now this is not an option. Wilson and Murray both claim that an urban underclass of young people from difficult home circumstances who rely on benefits is developing. These people who live in deprived areas can find opportunities for status and wealth through crime. There is no reason for them to cease this lifestyle.

Feminists such as Batchelor (2009) argue that young women who become involved with such gangs are at risk of sexual exploitation. There is little hard evidence to suggest that aggressive girl gangs are developing, but there have been recent examples of gangs grooming and exploiting young and vulnerable girls. The CSJ claimed, in 2014, that gang members use rape as a weapon against young women, so they can be bullied into carrying drugs or guns. Often the young women are vulnerable because of difficult home lives and poverty. They become attracted to the excitement of fast cars, drugs and sex. The CJS found evidence that a school girl was abducted and sexually assaulted for criticising gang members. As the police usually stop and search males, more girls are drawn into gang life and use pushchairs to smuggle illegal goods. Regan, one of the authors of the research report, suggested that the full scale of the problem was not known.

> Every society has the criminals it deserves.
>
> *Emma Goldman*

Kinsella (2011) in a Home Office report found that young people feel negatively labelled by the media. This suggests that the possibility of a self-fulfilling prophecy in terms of youth crime is plausible. Young people are seen in a negative light, there are over-reactions to perceived deviancy among young people, and there is pressure from the media on the government to 'take action'. In 2011 there was additional funding from government in order to tackle the problem of youth crime despite statistics which show that violent crime is declining. GANGBOs were introduced that year which prevents individuals from 'wearing gang colours' or 'walking aggressive dogs'. The question remains whether gangs are a social problem, or the social environment that condemns some young people to deprivation and dysfunctional families is the problem.

Hierarchy of gang types

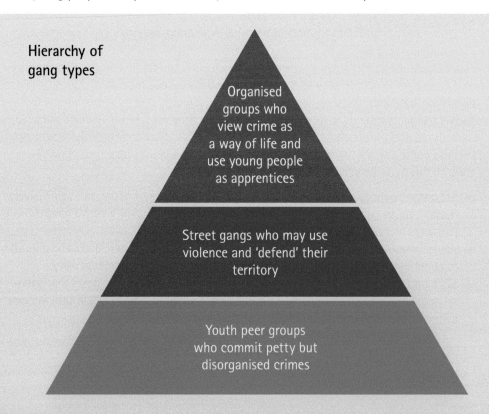

Organised groups who view crime as a way of life and use young people as apprentices

Street gangs who may use violence and 'defend' their territory

Youth peer groups who commit petty but disorganised crimes

Sample questions

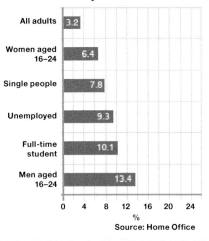

RISK OF BEING A VICTIM OF
VIOLENT CRIME
British Crime Survey 2007/08

Source: Home Office

a) Summarise the content of the bar chart showing the risk of being the victim of a crime in 2007/08.

b) With reference to the item and to sociological knowledge, explain **two** reasons why some young men may be attracted to join criminal subcultures.

When quoting research, it is advisable to consider who has produced the reports. For example, the Centre for Social Justice was established by a Conservative politician and Cabinet minister, Iain Duncan Smith, who has views that are typical of the New Right. How might this influence the views in the report on girls and gangs?

Research idea

Use the words **London street gangs** in a search engine to explore some sites related to youth crime and violence.

Check your own learning

Link the research finding or theory to the name.

a)	Young women involved with gangs are at risk of exploitation	Centre for Social Justice
b)	Gangs have a hierarchy and a leadership structure	Kinsella
c)	Young people are negatively labelled by the media	Batchelor
d)	Boys don't look for trouble, but they won't back away if it finds them	Miller
e)	Youth crime is a very serious problem for society	Venkatesh
f)	Youth crime is concentrated in areas of poverty and deprivation such as heavy industrial areas and inner city estates	Parker
g)	Young people need to fit into social groups	Shaw and McKay

Use the Internet to find some sociological research into girl gangs, for example:
http://britsoccrim.org/volume1/002.pdf

Extended writing

Assess the view that there is a link between youth subcultures and criminal behaviour.

Guidance: There are a lot of possible responses to this question. At one level, there clearly is, because you can point to the fact that many youth cultures are associated with violence, aggression and drug abuse. The London riots of 2011 were believed by the government to be caused by gangs using mobile phones to go out and loot property. Many early studies pointed to the link between youth cultures and crime, so you can talk about the American subcultural and delinquency studies. However, for the better marks, you should bring this up to date and mention some work carried out in Britain. You might want to question whether the link between youth culture and crime has been over-stated and whether we are in fact experiencing a moral panic.

Write about 500-750 words.

Research methods

Suggest ways in which you would set about researching the experiences of gang members? What problems might you experience?

Aims

- To learn that functionalists view youth cultures as being part of a transition from childhood to adulthood. Tribal societies may have a rite of passage, but Western society has no clear point when adulthood starts.

Functionalists suggest that our views of adulthood and childhood are socially constructed. This means that, although age appears to be real, it is actually something that exists in a social context. The social role of young people is fluid, this makes them uncertain and they need the support of peer groups to help each other through that period of time when they are no longer considered to be children but not old enough to be treated as fully adult. Most young people do not join youth cultures with values that are different from mainstream society but adopt styles and fashions as part of normal development.

> I am convinced that most people do not grow up... We marry and dare to have children and call that growing up. I think what we do is mostly grow old.
>
> *Maya Angelou*

Topic 14: Youth cultures and functionalism

Getting you thinking

The Hamar tribe in Ethiopia are cattle herders in an area that is near desert. The men raid the cattle of other people, often killing in the process. When they have killed another man, an elephant or a lion, they are scarred on the body. Once they have 'hero scars', they are seen as part of society and may take a wife. Suggest reasons why a culture living in a challenging environment might develop such traditions for its boys and men. At what stage would a British child consider him or herself to be fully adult?

The social construction of youth

Biological youth

All young people go through a range of hormonal changes at puberty. These result in the body changes that make them become physically adults. This is a relatively slow process that may last a couple of years. In many cultures, girls are deemed ready to marry not long after their first period and this marks adulthood. Hormonal changes will affect the behaviour of young people and they may become irritable or unsure of themselves.

Social transitions to adulthood

- *Laws* – Each culture has different rights and responsibilities for young people. Thus in the UK, a person must be 17 to drive and 18 to vote and buy alcohol. In many American states, people may drive at 15 or 16, but not buy alcohol until the age of 21.
- *Accepted behaviour* – It is believed in the West that young people are emotional and unsteady. This may not be true for all cultures. Chinese young men are expected to remain cool. Mead described Samoan young people as calm.
- *Normative behaviour* – Social customs vary. Many cultures expect girls to marry and bear children in their teens. In Western cultures, the age of marriage is rising to the late 20s and the age for bearing first children is rising rapidly, too.
- *Rites of passage* – Many cultures mark a specific point at which a person can be considered to be adult. This is marked by a ceremony which celebrates the end of childhood and start of adulthood. In Western cultures, childhood has been extended because of the complexity of our culture. People pass through a series of **rites of passage**, but no one point marks them as fully adult. They may vote, for example, but still be dependent on their parents for money and a home.

Functionalist theorists and youth cultures

Many cultures mark the change in status from childhood to adulthood with a ritual of some kind, known as a rite of passage. This may be dangerous, as it is in Hamar society, or something religious such as confirmation into a religious group, but once the person has experienced the rite of passage, they have left childhood behind. Functionalists claim that people need to feel part of society in order to belong. They call this, integration. Without integration, society will break down, and social breakdown is known as 'anomie'. If too many people lack a sense of belonging then no-one knows the rules, so levels of crime and suicide rise. Western culture has no particular rite of passage, so people may be fully physically adult, but still depend on their parents for money and a home. Thus, without youth culture they will experience anomie.

Parsons (1954) says that young people try to detach themselves from their parents and achieve their own independent sense of integration to wider society. He says youth culture provides a bridge between childhood and adulthood and is a 'rite of passage' that all young people go through. He sees youth cultures as no more than a passing phase of life. Children learn to establish their own identities in youth cultures and can develop ideas and values that are different from those that they learned in the home. Children take on responsibilities of adulthood but in a milder form, so they learn about work and money management from taking part-time work whilst they are at school. Youth culture is a gentle way for young people to integrate fully into their adult lives. Eisenstadt (1956) supports this and suggested that as youth is a time of stress and anxiety caused by the changing norms of becoming an adult. Young people had to rely on each other so youth culture provides an outlet for tensions and it binds young people together.

A famous critic of Parsons' theory was Theodore Roszak (1969) who argued that a huge social divide was emerging between older and younger people. He called this the generation gap. He claimed that age was becoming more significant than social differences based on class, race or gender. He has since claimed that the same generation who challenged their parents should now be working to challenge their children in order to make a better society.

Assessments of functionalism

- ⊙ Functionalists point out that much public response to the behaviour of the young is over-dramatised and exaggerated.
- ⊙ Most young people genuinely are quite conformist and do not want to overthrow society.

Refresh your understanding of functionalist theory by returning to Topic 2 of the Theories section.

Discussion point

- Do you think that youth cultures are functional and useful for society as a whole?

Research methods

Berger (1963) said that most young people go through life without being involved in any specific teen culture and without being particularly deviant. How might you set up a study to find out more about conformist 'straight' youth?

How rebellious and non-conformist are this group of young people at a festival? How does the image support functionalist analysis of youth cultures?

Jewish boys undergo a ritual known as bar mitzvah when they are thirteen in order to become adult men. Girls have a similar rite known as bat mitzvah.

How true is the statement on the right for a young person in British society?

Discussion point

- Do all young people belong to youth subcultures? How would you describe the ones who do not belong to groups or gangs?

Research idea

Enter the phrase 'rites of passage' into a search engine to discover more about different cultural traditions which mark the end of childhood.

18

You are now leaving the child zone

- ⊙ Feminists such as Oakley have pointed out that family life is not as ideal as Parsons would suggest so that the anxieties and fears of young people which may attract them to youth cultures should not be underestimated or seen as 'just a phase'.
- ⊙ Feminists such as Sharpe and Hey say that the role of gender in youth groups is ignored.
- ⊙ Functionalism doesn't take account of the forms and varieties of youth cultures. Hippies, for example, can be seen as a direct response to American involvement in the Vietnam War. Punk was a response to high unemployment and the decline of industrial areas in 1980s Britain.

Sample questions

The legal situation with regard to the rights of young people as they enter adulthood can be confusing; for example, ten year olds can have ear piercings and choose their own religions. Fourteen year olds are allowed in pubs as long as they do not drink alcohol. Sixteen year olds can be prosecuted for sex with under 16s but they can marry or cohabit with parental permission. They may not watch films with explicit sexual content. Seventeen year olds may be considered adult under some parts of the criminal justice system so the police can interview them without an appropriate adult. A person's 18th birthday is often seen as a **rite of passage** into adulthood, but even then young people do not have full adult legal rights, such as the right to the national minimum wage or to drive a heavy goods vehicle.

a) Summarise the content of the passage describing the legal situation of young people in the UK.

b) With reference to the item and to sociological knowledge, explain the meaning of the term **rites of passage**.

- Marxists argue that social class is a key dynamic in the development of youth cultures. Functionalists overlook its importance in the variety of forms that youth cultures take.
- Functionalism tends to describe the culture of middle-class white America and claim that it is both normal and correct for all societies. Thus it does not understand the social pressures placed on minority and working-class groups.
- Polemus, a postmodernist, says there is no such thing as a single youth culture, but a variety of styles.

> When you become a teenager, you step onto a bridge. You may already be on it. The opposite shore is adulthood. Childhood lies behind. The bridge is made of wood. As you cross, it burns behind you.
>
> *Gail Carson Levine*

Check your own learning
Link the theoretical perspective to the statement.

a)	Public response to the behaviour of the young is over-dramatised and exaggerated	Marxist
b)	Youth culture provides a bridge between childhood and adulthood	Feminist
c)	The role of gender in youth groups is ignored	Functionalist
d)	Social class is an important dynamic in the development of youth cultures	Functionalist
e)	Youth is a time of stress and anxiety caused by the changing norms of becoming an adult	Marxist
f)	Punk was a response to high unemployment and the decline of industrial areas in 1980s	Functionalist
g)	Family life is not ideal and the anxieties and fears of young people which may attract them to youth cultures should not be underestimated	Postmodernist
h)	There is no such thing as a single youth culture, but a variety of styles	Feminist

Research idea
Find out about your legal rights as a person under 18 by searching the websites of either the NSPCC or Childline.

Extended writing
Evaluate functionalist views of youth cultures.
Guidance: You will need to describe functionalism as a theory, and to think about how it then applies to functionalist understanding of youth cultures. Use some of the key concepts such as consensus and socialisation. You will need to describe youth culture as a rite of passage and explain why that is necessary in modern societies. When you are evaluating functionalist views of youth culture, refer to previously learned knowledge that you have gained through your study of youth cultures, so if you refer to Marxist criticisms of functionalism, you could refer back to your studies of youth culture and class and name some key writers. To be a balanced discussion, you should consider the insights that functionalism brings to an understanding of youth cultures.
Write about 500-750 words.

Tip
Whilst functionalists tend to be relaxed about the idea of youth cultures, the New Right, who normally are closely associated with their ideas, tend to see the behaviour of the young people as being a serious problem.

Aims

- To understand that Marxists view society as being dominated by class conflict. Young people experience the world according to their class position and respond to social pressures according to their class.

Functionalists tend to talk in terms of a youth culture as a whole, seeing it as a phase all people pass through. Marxists tend to identify youth cultures and subcultures and to link the behaviours of those cultures to social class. Much of the work in this area carried out in the UK was by members of the Centre for Contemporary Cultural Studies (CCCS) who looked at specific youth cultures in order to find evidence and examples of resistance to capitalism expressed through style and music. The basic argument is that young people are reacting to social oppression, poverty and deprivation by forming anti-social youth cultures. They were aware of their class position and their position in society but could not express it formally so they did it through subcultural styles and symbols which could be 'read'.

Topic 15: Youth cultures and Marxism

Getting you thinking

The Rolling Stones were once a symbol of rebellious youth culture, despite having fairly comfortable backgrounds. Now, they are elderly multi-millionaires who can command millions for a concert. To what extent can their cultural style be said to be an expression of youthful resistance to capitalist culture?

Marxism and youth culture

Functionalism was the dominant social theory until the 1970s. However, many sociologists rejected functionalism because it did not explain social conflict or the spectacular youth cultures of the time. Conflict theories such as feminism and Marxism became more popular as an explanation for social relationships. The CCCS was formed in Birmingham University in 1964 and gave rise to a number of influential theorists and studies. The Centre closed in 2002 but original material can be seen online.

Marxism

Marxists see society as being based on the domination and exploitation of the working class by the capitalist economic system. They argue that capitalism is able to maintain its domination through the use of power and legal systems. They suggest that the working class accept their class position because of the way that capitalism passes on values and ideology about society through social control via agencies such as the media and education.

Marxism and neo-Marxism

Traditional Marxism explains social behaviour in terms of the economic system. Traditional Marxists claim that inequalities of wealth are the mechanism which holds society together, because they lead to class conflict and differences in power between various groups of people. Clearly, however, this is too simple an explanation for the social processes that we see around us. Many modern writers use Marxism as a starting point, but instead of looking at the economy to explain behaviour, they look at culture and ideas as well. Writers who use Marxism as a starting point are known as neo-Marxists. Most modern writers on youth culture are part of the neo-Marxist style of sociological thinking.

Neo-Marxists look at classes, but suggest that people from different social classes view the world in different ways. They

> *Rebellion cannot exist without the feeling that somewhere, in some way, you are justified.*
>
> **Albert Camus**

experience different social pressures and so respond in individual ways. Writers using this approach have also looked at symbolism as being an important part of people's social responses. The study of social symbolism is known as semiology. Semiologists believe that there are hidden meanings in everyday objects and behaviours, so an item of clothing could just be used to cover the body. We are all aware that clothing has more significance than that, so Goths use black clothing because it is associated with funerals and death in Western culture. Phil Cohen (1972) first used semiological techniques to look at subcultural styles in the East End of London. He claimed youth cultures were a response to a loss of traditional community life and their styles could be 'read' as responses to that loss. Mods, for example, were adopting the styles of the wealthy, but skinheads rejected middle-class style to become traditional working class in style. Other members of the CCCS who were also neo-Marxists used similar techniques to explore class and youth culture.

Tip

Refresh your understanding of Marxist theory by returning to Topic 3 of the Theories section.

Explaining youth cultures

Marxists tend to agree that youth cultures share certain characteristics despite their different styles:

⊙ They are a form of resistance against capitalism.
⊙ They exaggerate working-class values.

The reason that youth cultures vary so much is because each generation is facing a different set of problems and challenges caused by capitalism.

Resistance theory

During the 70s and early 80s, the focus of study was on deviant subcultures. The general perception was that working-class youth resisted the ideology of capitalism through anti-social behaviour. Stuart Hall claimed that young people joined subcultures with norms, values and dress codes that were antagonistic to mainstream cultures.

Anti-capitalist rioting

Discussion point

● For many young people in the 1960s and 1970s, rebellion against capitalism took the form of active political participation in groups such as women's, anti-racist or gay rights movements, pro-abortion rallies, support for striking workers or membership of mainstream and far-left political parties. What does this suggest about the view that youth culture was a form of resistance to capitalism?

⊙ Hall and Jefferson (1976), for example, looked at Teddy boys and claimed that their style was an expression of contempt for middle-class values.
⊙ Both Cohen (1972) and Clarke (1976) looked at skinhead gangs, and they argued that the aggressive racism of skins was simply an attempt to preserve a traditional but threatened working-class identity.
⊙ Paul Corrigan's (1979) study of aggressive and hooligan working-class males in Sunderland suggested they were looking for excitement because they were bored in school. Thus, violence was a way of expressing frustration with capitalism.

Magical solutions

Mike Brake (1984) claimed that youth cultures provided magical solutions to the lives of their members. Young people are relatively powerless in society and cannot alter their social world. However, membership of a youth culture allows people to believe that they will be different from their parents' generation. It is a magical solution because it has no basis in reality. Further writers within the Marxist tradition used the idea to suggest that some youth cultures 'magically' or symbolically recreated working-class culture through their styles and symbolism.

Assessments of Marxism and the CCCS

⊙ Len Barton (2006) and feminists in particular have criticised the CCCS for romanticising some rather unpleasant youth groups, seeing evidence of working-class resistance to capitalism among young people who would not have recognised themselves in the descriptions made by the writers. Groups such as the skinheads were overtly and violently racist, sexist and homophobic; points that were noted in the studies but not really explored.

⊙ Feminists have complained that the CCCS had a **malestream** bias. This means that they only looked at youth cultures from a male point of view. This is probably a fair criticism because most of the youth cultures studied were white, male and working class.

⊙ It is possible that the attraction of violent youth culture is that it is exciting and fun to participate in. Many of the CCCS authors noted this in their studies, but again it is an idea that is not explored in detail.

⊙ The extreme subcultures were described and explored so that conformist young people were overlooked. This gives a cultural importance to some quite small peer groups such as the 12 'lads' Willis studied as the basis of his book, *Learning to Labour*.

⊙ Muggleton points out that the CCCS assumes most of the youth cultures of the 70s and 80s were working class in origin. Some certainly were, but many youth styles originated in art schools and among wealthier young people who could invest in clothing, style and music and thus gain cultural capital from their knowledge of youth style.

⊙ Postmodernists have found that recent neo-tribes and subcultural groups come from a range of backgrounds. Sarah Thornton even goes so far as to suggest that class is irrelevant because most youth cultures are media-generated anyway.

STRETCH and CHALLENGE

You can read some of the original research by members of the CCCS online by looking at Birmingham University website or entering Centre for Contemporary Cultural Studies into a search engine.

Is racist behaviour simply an attempt to preserve traditional working-class culture, or is something more dangerous happening among some youth cultures?

Are groups like the English Defence League simply English nationalists, trying to preserve English values or do they represent a racist response to changes in society?

Research idea

Frith (1978) claimed the creation of subcultures was a reaction to high unemployment and poverty among council estates where youth were often bored, and looking for something to focus on. How could you design a study to test this idea? What problems might you experience?

Sample questions

Teenage rebels are not what they were. There is less evidence of **resistance** to mainstream cultures. In 2012, national statistics suggested that adolescents are increasingly turning their noses up at drugs, booze and fags, with consumption by young people the lowest at almost any time since we started measuring these things. So what is going on? When it comes to smoking and drinking and taking drugs, British teenagers are behaving better than their parents. That's not to say there are not still real challenges, of course, but the trends are encouraging enough to question whether the teen is evolving. Since the 1950s, Teddy boys, bikers, mods, rockers, hippies, punks, ravers and grungers put two fingers up at authority in their own fashion and took delight in watching the grown-ups flinch and frown. Today, though, where are the rebellious subcultures? Could it be that teenage rebellion needs to look different from what your mum and dad did?

Adapted from an article by Mark Easton on the BBC website
http://www.bbc.co.uk/news/magazine-19786264

a) With reference to the item and to sociological knowledge, explain what is meant by **resistance**.

b) Explain **two** weaknesses of the Marxist view of youth cultures.

Check your own learning

Link the writer to the statement.

a)	Class is irrelevant. Youth cultures are media creations	Muggleton
b)	Youth cultures are magical solutions to working-class youth problems	Corrigan
c)	The CCCS were wrong in assuming youth cultures are a working-class phenomenon	Mike Brake
d)	The CCCS romanticised some nasty youth groups and overlooked their racist behaviour	Sarah Thornton
e)	Working-class youth behave violently for excitement as a reaction to the boredom of capitalist education	Hall and Jefferson
f)	Teddy boy style was an expression of contempt for middle-class values	Len Barton

Extended writing

Evaluate Marxist views of youth cultures.

Guidance: You will need to describe Marxism as a theory, and to think about how it then applies to Marxist understanding of youth cultures. Use some of the key concepts such as resistance, conflict and ideology. You will need to describe youth culture as an act of rebellion against mainstream culture so you may wish to return to earlier topics to refresh your knowledge. When you are evaluating Marxist views of youth culture, refer to your studies of youth culture and class and name some key writers. To be a balanced discussion, you should consider the insights that feminism and postmodernism bring to our understanding of youth cultures. You could mention studies of neo-tribes, for example.

Write about 500-750 words.

Activity

Key events of 1982 included: a war between Britain and Argentina, massive rises in unemployment, mass protests against American nuclear weapons on British soil at Greenham Common and IRA bombings in Hyde Park and Regent's Park.

Watch the 1982 video of Dexy's Midnight Runners, *Come on Eileen*. Read the lyrics online. What references to issues of social class and politics can you see in the styles of the band and its video?

Discussion point

- Traditional Marxists believe that individuals are passive and controlled by society so they cannot change their identity. More recent neo-Marxist writers suggest that individuals can and do change elements of their identity. Which viewpoint do you agree with? Give reasons.

Topic 16: Youth cultures and feminism

Aims

- To recognise that feminists say that the majority of writing on youth cultures is focussed on the behaviour and experiences of males, and the experiences of girls are understudied and less well understood.

Feminists say that women have been marginalised and ignored by malestream (masculine) sociology. Feminists are concerned to bring women to the forefront of research and raise a number of problems. Do girls create youth cultures that are different from male youth cultures? Were girls participants in the earlier youth cultures and simply overlooked by male researchers? Has it been particularly difficult to research girls because their behaviours were less public in the past?

Topic 16: Youth cultures and feminism

Getting you thinking

Are girl gangs and posses in schools and colleges different from male gangs? With others, make a list of the key differences and the similarities between the ways that girls and boys behave when in same-sex groups.

Malestream sociology

Photographs and images of youth cultures of the 1950s and 1960s certainly show women as participants in youth cultures. As World War 2 ended, girls had paid jobs. Despite the fact that they earned significantly less than men, they still formed a significant market for cosmetics, clothing, magazines and music. McRobbie has pointed out that most of this material was still focussed on the process of getting and keeping a man and becoming a domestic housewife. So although women were enjoying more economic independence than before, the way they spent their money reflected the social expectations of society.

Male sociologists looking at youth cultures tended to overlook girls or to view them as passive participants, just girlfriends rather than active members of the group. Willis studied motor cycle gangs and noted that girls were unwilling to talk to him.

- Frith (1986) says girls were present in youth cultures but overlooked because most of the ethnography was carried out in public areas by males. Girls were more controlled by their families therefore not present in street cultures.
- Feminists such as Garber have suggested that the problem of the invisibility of girls from research into youth culture was that much of the research was carried out by men, and at the time, girls would not or could not open up about their lives and experiences.
- It is difficult to rely on contemporary accounts of the role of women in youth cultures because much media material reflects the moral panics of the time. When violence is discussed, girls are described as victims or bystanders. When sexuality is seen as a problem, female promiscuity is the main story.

Girl subcultures

McRobbie and Garber reported on girl cultures in the 1970s and described girls as being marginalised in youth culture and dominating their bedrooms where they would gather to discuss boyfriends, make-up and clothes. Girls were described as being the passive receivers of media pressure to buy into ideas of 'pop stars' and romantic love.

More recent studies of female involvement in youth culture suggest that because the 'street' is not a safe or respectable place for girls, they have not participated in much youth culture. However, subcultures located in clubs, such as rave and dance culture, have a large female involvement. McRobbie (1994) suggests that female competence at dance is significant in rave culture. She also suggests that modern feminism has affected how girls are portrayed in popular magazines and in popular culture because young women are not quite so willing to be represented as passive.

Ladette cultures

Osgerby (1998) claimed that women were always present in youth cultures, but that they were generally passive. This suggestion is supported by Garber who developed the point by suggesting that the more girls are ignored, they more they behave in the predicted fashion, so there was an element of self-fulfilling prophecy in their passive nature. Evidence comes from images of all youth cultures where girls are present and often actively involved, perhaps dancing or partnering boys in an activity. However, young women in the 1950s and 1960s would have been constrained by their need to attract a husband and to have a 'good' reputation. Girls would have been financially dependent on men because of their relative lack of education and low pay in the workplace. The change came in the 1960s when effective female-controlled contraception in the form of the pill gave women the opportunity to be sexual without the risk of pregnancy and legislation meant they could earn the same as men in the workplace. The rise of feminism in the 1970s gave women and girls unexpected freedoms to act in the same way that boys and men always had.

More recent discussions have suggested that some girls are changing their behaviour dramatically. It is claimed that a new form of femininity is developing and this is the ladette, a girl with the morals and values of boys. Jackson identified this behaviour in her study of eight schools and reported the negative response of teachers to the activities of girls who took on the worst elements of masculinity. It is claimed by the media that ladette culture is alcohol fuelled and consists of fun and irresponsible behaviours among young women. However, concern about the 'bad girl' can be seen as a form of social control because it is linked to a whole set of social notions of the correct behaviour expected of women. Media stories tend to focus on three main areas:

⊙ Concepts of socially accepted feminine behaviour, girls should not drink or have sex.
⊙ Girls are placing themselves at serious risk in terms of their health, their safety and risk of sexual harassment.
⊙ Girls are engaging in the kinds of public crime and anti-social behaviour which were once a male preserve.

This debate has spread into the media and is being seen as a relatively sudden change in society. A typical story from the *Daily Mail*, in 2013, claimed that heavy drinking among women, who were now behaving as badly as men always did, had given rise to an increase in the number of broken noses being reset in hospitals! Carolyn Jackson and Penny Tinkler (2007), however, point out that complaints about girls behaving as boys do can be found in the popular press of the 1920s and suggest that the existence of the ladette is a moral panic rather than a recent phenomenon. It has serious consequences for women though, because it:

⊙ Reinforces traditionally passive female roles.
⊙ Stigmatises young women as being somehow 'bad'.
⊙ Influences the behaviour of people who should be supporting young women, such as teachers, the police and doctors.

Activity

Jackie magazine was studied by McRobbie. It was aimed at younger teenage girls and was first published in 1964. Its 50th anniversary was marked by many retrospective articles; find out more about the content of the magazine by looking for relevant articles on the Internet.

Discussion point

● How much do modern girls owe to the work of feminists in the 1970s?

Discussion point

- To what extent can the media presentation of ladette culture be seen as 'anti-female' moral panics?

The Spice Girls of the 1990s were a manufactured singing group who claimed to stand for girl power, a new assertive femininity. Was 'girl power' meaningful or a marketing tactic?

Is this picture of the pop star Madonna an expression of female dominance or of a woman dressing to please men? What does this picture tell you about the role of powerful women in the popular media?

I'm tough, I'm ambitious, and I know exactly what I want. If that makes me a bitch, okay.

Madonna

Young women and music in popular culture

Simon Frith in the early 1980s emphasised the masculine nature of hard rock, claimed that it was an exploration of male sexuality, so hard rock was for boys and ballads were for girls. This has led to a response from feminists. Mavis Bayton (1998) conducted an ethnographic study of women in rock and pop music from the 1970s onwards. She suggests that young men and women learn gender through rock musicians, and imitate their behaviours and styles. Women's music has been overlooked by a male-dominated music industry and those who do get media attention tend to offer a traditional, passive and sexual view of themselves. Women who challenge gender roles tend to be overlooked by commercial companies either as producers or consumers of music. Girls who focus on mainstream popular music are unaware of other possibilities for themselves, so girls are denied a form of self-expression through music creation.

There is now more representation of alternative sexuality in the mainstream media; however, people portrayed are still conventionally rich, thin, white and beautiful and don't really represent the full range of human experience. Susan Driver (2007) makes the point that lesbians (queer girls) have developed a separate and flourishing youth culture based on creating and listening to music. Girls who objected to the portrayal of femininity in hip-hop in the 1990s had little choice but to listen to hard core punk rock riot grrrl music.

Assessments of feminism

- ◉ Feminists have pointed out that girls are overlooked and under-represented in studies of youth culture. The reasons for this are varied and there is debate within the perspective about which is most significant.
- ◉ Many studies are of small mixed-sex groups or of girls and thus may not be representative or generalisable to wider populations.
  - ◉ Feminists tend to be concerned with issues of gender and so may overlook issues of class and race. However, not all females have the same experiences, so Black girls may have different perspectives from white girls and working-class girls experience youth culture differently from middle-class girls. Skeggs, for example, pointed out that poor young women cannot risk being seen as scruffy, as richer women do, because it will be suggested that they cannot afford goods.
    - ◉ Issues of gender in youth cultures remain under-studied. The fragmentation of youth styles means that it will become difficult to generalise about girls and women and their role in youth cultures simply because youth cultures themselves are so varied.
- ◉ In the current social climate it is difficult to criticise feminism from a masculine point of view, possibly because for so long, many women have been and still are victims of gender inequality.
- ◉ Feminism itself can be seen an act of resistance and so is worthy of discussion in subcultural terms.

Who runs the world? Girls..

Beyoncé Knowles

Sample questions

The **ladette culture** is being blamed for an alarming rise in the numbers of women in their thirties and forties dying from alcohol-related conditions. The death rates have more than doubled in the last 20 years even though they have fallen among men and for other age groups, research has shown. Experts blame the 'ladette culture' which began in the 1990s and has seen women increasingly going out and drinking similar amounts to men. The availability of cheap alcohol was also a factor. Because women are smaller than men, alcohol has a greater effect on their bodies. The findings, researchers said, should be an 'early warning sign' for the government. But just this week David Cameron dropped plans for a minimum price for alcohol claiming there was not enough evidence it would reduce excessive drinking.

Adapted by an article by Sophie Borland (2013) in the Daily Mail

source: http://www.dailymail.co.uk/health/article-2370951/Ladette-culture-blamed-rise-booze-related-deaths.html#ixzz3cg9ZGbaN

a) With reference to the item and to sociological knowledge, explain what is meant by **ladette culture**.

b) Using the item and sociological knowledge explain **two** reasons why women have been understudied in youth cultures.

Check your own learning

Match the definition to the term.

a)	Patriarchy	Youth cultures are located in a domestic setting such as the home rather than on the streets
b)	Malestream	The idea that males no longer know what it is to be a man and feel threatened by the rise of women
c)	Feminism	A social system where males hold the power and control society
d)	Crisis of masculinity	A range of ideologies linked to the idea that women and men should be more equal in society
e)	Invisible women	Research that is carried out from the point of view of the male
f)	Bedroom cultures	Women and girls are overlooked and missing from much academic writing despite their presence in society

Extended writing

Evaluate feminist views of youth cultures.

Guidance: You will need to describe feminism as a theory; however, feminism is not one single theory but a set of perspectives united by the belief that men dominate society. Many of the key debates are within feminism rather than against it. Thus there are different explanations for the causes, processes and results of patriarchal society. When you are evaluating feminist views of youth culture, refer to your studies of youth culture and gender and name some key writers. For a balanced discussion, you should consider the impact of feminism on society itself, so consider how the roles and expectations of men and women have changed. Much feminist writing is situated in the 1970s when sexism was far more explicit and overt than it is today.

Write about 500-750 words.

Discussion point

- Do men need feminism? Make points for and against.

Research methods

How might you set up a study to find out more about girls' youth subcultures?

Activity

Use a search engine to find stories about ladettes in the media. What themes emerge from the coverage? What image of women and girls is presented?

Rock and pop music have been notoriously male dominated and women musicians marginalised or judged on their looks rather than their playing skills.

Topic 17: Postmodernism and youth cultures

Aims

- To understand why postmodernists claim that there is no such thing as youth culture, just personal style.

Postmodernists say that it is not possible to have one theory to explain youth cultures as the Marxists do, because modern society offers too much choice. Because the media are so important in our society, reality very much depends on your point of view. We gain identity through what we buy and consume, so we can change our identities to suit ourselves and our circumstances. There is a variety of youth styles and cultures for young people to buy into; people may belong to more than one social grouping. They may have one taste for a style of computer gaming but listen to a different style of music. Social media mean that we are more aware of tastes, style and fashion in other countries. Maffesoli says that people no longer identify with a single youth culture, but may belong to a number and switch from one group to another. This idea is known as tribalisation.

Getting you thinking

What has been the impact of the mobile phone and other communication technologies on modern youth cultures, styles and fashions?

Postmodernist approaches to youth cultures

According to Bennett and Hetherington, class, ethnicity, gender and social experiences are irrelevant in cultural terms for young people. In this, they differ from most of the earlier subcultural theorising. Along with functionalists, they claim that youth is a social construction; social and economic changes mean that 'youth' lasts far longer than it did in the past. This is because people may be dependent on families, attend university, travel or put off settling down until their thirties. They can pick and choose their friendships and social groups based on a need to fill time and enjoy their leisure. These associations can change according to a person's needs at a given time.

Neo-tribes

Much of the cultural work of the 80s and 90s was into the club cultures which formed in cities such as Manchester and Newcastle. Clubbers were found to be more interested in dance than anything more substantial in terms of politics or meaning. Whereas young people in the 70s and 80s appeared to have a deep commitment to a particular single set of styles and values which they would identify themselves with, for example punk or skinhead, now young people's tastes are more variable. Bennett found that clubbers in the 90s might be binge drinking or leisure drug using at the weekends, but would slip back into boring predictability on Monday when they went to work. Bennett describes this loose grouping of people as a neo-tribe, using Maffesoli's concept of modern tribalism. A neo-tribe is united by shared tastes and styles. Neo-tribes share consumer choices, and have a similar state of mind and lifestyle. This is supported by Hetherington (1998) who found that New Age travellers shared moral convictions rather than social class background.

Ted Polhemus refers to the supermarket of style. We all have a wider range of choices than ever before and often we create cultural fusions; for example, Chicken Tikka Masala is a fusion of Indian cooking style with British tastes. Polhemus uses this term to describe the way that styles can be joined together to form new styles, so Britney Spears used Bhangra beats in her music.

Is modern youth culture meaningless?

Reimer has claimed that what youth cultures and neo-tribes have in common is a single-minded pursuit of fun and excitement that is more significant than issues of class and gender. Not all postmodernists agree that youth cultures are meaningless and empty styles. Kahane argues that fusion styles are meaningful because they represent an attempt to make something new and original from the subcultures of the past and the choices of the present. Thornton argues that, although modern youth cultures are often commercially produced for mass consumption by the media, some young people deliberately change them and make them original in ways not thought of by music and fashion interests. However, they need to move fast to keep ahead of commercial interests, as Louise Archer points out, because often these industries look to street style for inspiration.

Globalisation, postmodernism and youth cultures

Hebdige has moved on from the Marxism of the CCCS and argues that the Internet has resulted in virtual youth cultures developing where ideas from a number of cultures are adapted according to local tastes and ideas. These youth cultures are interesting because there may not be much physical interaction between individuals. Luke and Luke suggest that cultural influences are global and cite the significance of American culture on young people around the world.

Tip

Refresh your understanding of postmodernist theory by returning to Topic 6 of the Theories section.

McDonalds burgers can be bought in almost any country in the world. This one is in Russia. What does this fact tell you about the global nature of youth cultures?

Assessments of postmodernism

⦿ Not all sociologists are convinced that class no longer shapes the lives of young people, as postmodernists suggest. Archer (2007) found significant and meaningful style differences between middle-class and working-class youths in her study in London. Middle-class young people aped the style of the working classes to look more streetwise whereas working-class youth did not copy the middle class, recognising that the style was aspirational and beyond their means.

Discussion point

● Does class still influence a person's identity and status in modern society?

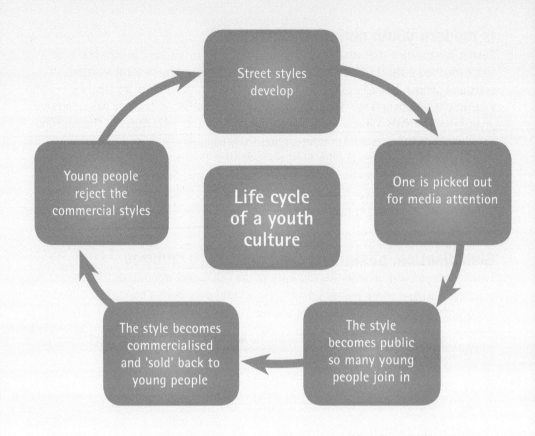

Life cycle of a youth culture

- Street styles develop
- One is picked out for media attention
- The style becomes public so many young people join in
- The style becomes commercialised and 'sold' back to young people
- Young people reject the commercial styles

Discussion point

- As groups, think about and discuss the question of how you define what is stylish. What makes some activities and modes of dress really interesting and fashionable and others just pointless and stupid?

Adam Ant was one of the style leaders of the fairly short-lived glam rock style in the 1980s. Find out what you can about glam rock and then consider whether the idea that style is more important than meaning is a new idea in youth culture.

Research methods

How might you set about researching the idea that young people no longer belong to youth cultures, they just adopt a style?

- ◉ Harriet Bradley (1997) makes a similar point when she says that postmodernists ignore the fact that there are structural differences in what people can afford, which limits their style and lifestyle choice. Marxists such as Marshall (1997), Westergaard (1997) and Hall agree that postmodernists ignore statistical evidence that economic and class interests still shape people's lives.

- ◉ Postmodernism has no value because all it can do is describe society and social problems, it cannot actually help us to solve some of the issues young people face in the modern world.

- ◉ Chomsky, among others, has criticised postmodernism for being vague and difficult to understand. Hebdige, for example, says it is simply a buzzword (or fashionable term) for almost anything including art, literature, home decoration or a style. Because it is so unclear what the basic points being made are beyond issues of style and taste, then it has no value because it cannot be used as the basis of research, especially in something so fluid as youth cultures.

- ◉ Marxists say that postmodernism doesn't address the very real issues of inequalities of class, ethnicity and gender that lead to the formation of youth culture and youth rebellion so it ignores issues such as racism and sexism in society, pretending that they do not exist.

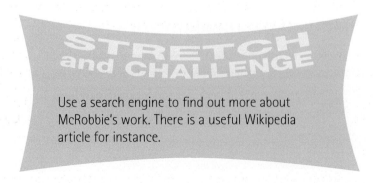

STRETCH and CHALLENGE

Use a search engine to find out more about McRobbie's work. There is a useful Wikipedia article for instance.

Sample questions

They're everywhere: Young Alts down one end of the high street; skaters pulling moves in front of the town hall; trendies ignoring everyone else as they march towards a Saturday shopping spree. The UK tribe project, commissioned by Channel 4, created by Crowd DNA, takes you to the heart of young Britain and into the **neo-tribes** that make up youth culture.

Tribal alliances are less hard and fast than they once were. The exchange of ideas is more fluid; the social glues that unite people more varied – you might disagree on which band is best, but you could still share a loyalty for Topshop, Sony PlayStation or Channel 4. Thus, understanding the dynamics of tribal UK is essential for commercial brands and companies who wish to engage and, vitally, become part of the conversation. Using modern talent, we quiz young people about their lives, their media, their aspirations and their brand preferences. The results are exciting and revealing; we have a look at UK youth culture from the street up.

Source adapted from https://www.uktribes.com/about-uk-tribes

a) With reference to the item and to sociological knowledge, explain what is meant by **neo-tribes**.

b) Using the item and sociological knowledge explain **two** features of postmodern society.

Check your own learning
Link the writer to the discussion point.

Is being a 'chav' a lifestyle choice as postmodernists might argue or is it related to class and position in the social structure?

a)	Louise Archer	People no longer identify with a single culture, but may belong to modern tribes
b)	Reimer	Fusion styles represent an attempt to make something new and original from choices of the present
c)	Ted Polhemus	There are significant and meaningful style differences between middle- and working-class young people in Britain
d)	Maffesoli	We can now choose what identity we wish from a supermarket of style
e)	Kahane	The Internet has resulted in virtual youth cultures developing where ideas from a number of cultures are adapted according to local tastes and ideas
f)	Hebdige	What neo-tribes have in common is a single-minded pursuit of fun and excitement

> The secret of theory is that truth doesn't exist. You can't confront it in any way.
>
> **Baudrillard**

Extended writing

Evaluate postmodernist views of youth cultures.

Guidance: You will need to describe postmodernism but not as a theory, more as an approach to understanding the dynamics of contemporary society. Describe the key concepts of the neo-tribe, the supermarket of style and the global and fusion cultures. When you are evaluating postmodernist views of youth cultures, refer to Marxism and feminism because they contrast most strongly with postmodernism. For a balanced discussion, you should consider whether poorer people and women really can participate on an equal footing with richer white males in youth cultures and styles. One fairly straightforward criticism of much postmodernism is that it is written in a complex style and difficult to understand so it is difficult to recognise the key issues.

Write about 500-750 words.

Aims

- To understand why interactionism believes that subcultures arise out of labelling; and to understand the impact of interactionism on research processes used by all sociologists.

Interactionists suggest that deviant behaviour is group activity. People develop norms and values at odds with those of mainstream society. It is concerned with the process by which this happens and the results of the creation of a deviant subcultural group. Once a behaviour is labelled as criminal or deviant, people who are associated with that behaviour take on an identity as a criminal. Other people will stereotype the group as being 'bad' and behave as though it were a social truth. The main style of research is ethnography. This is a particularly appropriate method for studying small groups and has been adopted by cultural theorists and writers such as the CCCS who have studied youth cultures.

Topic 18: Interactionism and youth cultures

Getting you thinking

What would be the repercussions of an arrest and a conviction for a serious criminal offence such as drug dealing, theft or violence on your life chances and lifestyle? Think about things such as job chances, but also how ordinary people such as potential partners and your family might react to you.

Interactionist approaches to youth cultures

Interactionism is a name for a range of approaches to the research of social phenomena. It is based on small-scale study and is sometimes called social action theory.

Labelling theory

Interactionists say that no action is deviant or not deviant. The definition of an action as deviant depends on issues of time, place and situation. Howard Becker (1963) said that society creates deviance by creating rules. People who break those rules become 'outsiders'. Once people are labelled as outsiders, they are then treated as such by others and criminalised. They mix with other outsiders and become part of a deviant subculture because they are rejected by others. Youth subcultures and gangs develop because agencies of social control, such as the media, education and the legal systems, label them as criminal or deviant. Being labelled as deviant leads to a crisis for the individual's sense of identity and may lead to a self-fulfilling prophecy. It reinforces the individual's sense of being an outsider and rejected. Thus the outsiders form a subculture that is deviant where they have alternative role models, support and may even gain a deviant career.

The impact of labelling on society

In the 1970s, Chambliss studied two groups of American High School boys to follow their careers. The Saints were middle class and well off. The Roughnecks were from poorer backgrounds. Both groups of boys behaved in a similar fashion, but the Saints were seen as 'just mucking around' whereas the Roughnecks developed reputations as troublemakers. Most of the Saints ended up having a good education and career, whereas some of the Roughnecks ended up in prison or not amounting to much in economic terms.

Many studies, including classic work in the USA by Cicourel, Lemert and Chambliss, have suggested that police decisions tend to be based on stereotypes of age, gender, class, ethnicity and dress. Reiner (1994) found that ethnic minority youths and the working class were targeted more by the police. In the UK in 2013, an Equality and Human Rights Commission report found that Black and Asian young people were up to 29 times more likely to be stopped and searched by the police than others.

Recent studies into youth behaviours

◉ Briggs (2013) used ethnographic methods to understand what happens to young people on holiday in Ibiza who get involved in criminal or risky behaviours. He argues that the holiday groups tend to behave in the way that is expected of them by the social expectations of commercial resorts who make money from their behaviours.

◉ Densley (2013) studied youth gangs and looked at the social processes of recruitment and the motivations of the gang members including the process of 'retiring' from active gang membership and the dangers inherent in ending their relationship with other gang members.

◉ Blackman (2010) claims that for many groups of young people, the use of drugs is normalised. They are part of everyday culture. Current policies for dealing with drug use and abuse cannot work because people do not consider the careful leisure use of drugs to be a problem. He presents an argument for the decriminalisation of leisure drug use.

Ethnography

As most interactionism focusses on deviancy and criminality and on subcultures rather than on youth cultures as such, it has not had a very direct effect on our understanding of youth as a separate stage in life. It is important though because it offers a method that can be used to study youth groups. Ethnography is an interactionist approach to research which is based on an in-depth study of everyday life. Because of the fluid and disorganised nature of youth cultures and youth groups in general, qualitative research methods are more appropriate. Ethnography became the preferred method used by the CCCS and some more recent research into youth because a variety of different techniques can be used to gain information. There may be interviews, focus groups, observations and media research. Work has been done with youth groups in schools and with youth subcultural groups to understand their relationships and values. In 2003, Bennett argued that ethnographic study of young people was challenging but essential because they are at 'the cutting edge of social change'.

Refresh your understanding of interactionist theory by returning to Topic 5 of the Theories section.

Key People

Jock Young

Jock Young (1971) studied cannabis smokers in the UK. He described the way that hippies used cannabis as part of their lifestyle. However, the use of cannabis became a moral panic and many 'smokers' felt threatened by public reactions. Once they became labelled as users, they mixed with others, harder drug users and the use of cannabis became a symbol of defiance against mainstream culture rather than a social activity.

The action is less significant than the social response to the action. For example, before the 1970s, homosexuality would have resulted in a prison sentence in the UK. Nowadays, while there is still homophobia, public reactions would be less hostile and have fewer consequences for the individual.

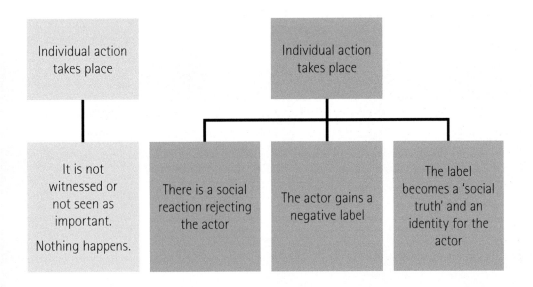

Discussion point

- Is it likely that being labelled a trouble-maker is enough to make someone turn into a criminal?

Our responses to people can be affected by what we know about them.

Tip

Any study of youth culture that you come across which is described as an ethnography can be useful in a consideration of interactionism because ethnography is a methodological approach developed and widely used by interactionists.

Assessments of interactionism

- ⊙ The ideas of the interactionists have been very influential in British sociology, so concepts such as moral panics and folk devils, which were used by Stan Cohen, can be traced back to this type of theorising.
- ⊙ The methods used by interactionists have been useful in understanding the beliefs, behaviours and values of youth cultural groups. The CCCS relied on these methods.
- ⊙ Interactionism has tended to focus on lower status or outsider groups, often approaching them in a sympathetic way. This can lead to biased accounts, for example seeing skinheads as victims (of social change) rather than as violent racist aggressors.
- ⊙ Although it describes how youth cultures may develop, it doesn't really explain why people acted in an anti-social or deviant manner in the first place.
- ⊙ It ignores capitalism and issues of social power and inequality in society, so class, race and gender are not seen as an important dynamics in youth cultures.

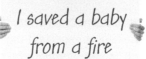

Sample questions

Read this extract adapted from a book by James Densley (2013) *How Gangs Work*, he describes how it was to be an Englishman working as a teacher in New York. In this extract he writes about the experience and gives **ethnographic data** about his students.

> My students were distracted. The source of their distraction was gangs. The symbolism of the graffiti on their desks and in their notebooks, the tattoos on their necks, and the clothing on their backs was visible even to the untrained eye. The airport-style metal detectors and small army of police officers that greeted me each morning suddenly made sense. In the weeks that followed, I separated fights, mediated conflicts, and learned about children dealing drugs out of backpacks and carrying weapons in playgrounds. I witnessed first-hand how events outside the school disrupted the learning process inside the school. It was an education.

http://www.palgraveconnect.com/pc/doifinder/10.1057/9781137271518

a) With reference to the item and to sociological knowledge, explain what is meant by **ethnographic data**.

b) Using the item and sociological knowledge explain **two** reasons why many researchers have used ethnographic methods when studying youth cultures.

Check your own learning

True or false?

a) Interactionists say that statistical data is essential for understanding society

b) Becker studied the Saints and the Roughnecks and found that despite similar behaviours, their later lives were different

c) Becker says that society creates deviance by creating rules

d) Black and Asian people are more likely than white people to be stopped by the police

e) The CCCS used methods devised by the interactionists

f) Interactionists focus on crime and deviance more than youth groups

Activity

Find out how a criminal record can affect your future. For many jobs you have to disclose details of any convictions, even if they are many years in the past. For more information check the website of the Disclosure and Barring Service.

> Social rules define situations and the kinds of behaviour appropriate to them, specifying some actions as 'right' and forbidding others as 'wrong'.
>
> **Howard S. Becker, Outsiders**

How might the social rules for a young person at school or college be different from the social rules for the same person at a party?

STRETCH and CHALLENGE

Howard S Becker has a website if you would like to read more about him and his work.

Extended writing

Evaluate the usefulness of interactionism to the study of youth cultures.

Guidance: You will need to describe interactionism, but the focus is not on the theory but how useful the theory is. You will therefore need to describe how interactionism has been applied. There are various research studies you can use; for example, in this topic you have Becker and Chambliss. However, if you return to your previous topics, almost all of the references to the CCCS can be used as well. You will need, therefore, to focus on the value of the theory, which is useful but not without flaws, and the value of the methods. The methods are probably more significant in many ways because it is difficult to look at a specific subculture using quantitative methods, although youth culture in general is often studied in this way. However, the issues of representativeness and generalisability will apply to interactionism here because what does a 13 year old in Aberystwyth share in cultural terms with a 20 year old in Inner London?

Write about 500–750 words.

INTERESTING FACT

Nick Glynn, a Black Leicestershire police inspector, claims to have been stopped and searched by fellow police officers from other forces over 30 times when he was off-duty.

Topic 1: Why do we educate children?

Aims

- To understand that that there are a variety of reasons why countries develop education systems

The education systems followed in various countries around the world are quite different and the reasons for these differences are generally historic. Systems have arisen out of specific needs at specific times; for example, the teaching of reading is linked to the development of industry and the need for workers to be able to follow written instructions. However, there are also ideological reasons for the development of education, based on the beliefs current at the time about the needs of children. Many sociologists have been critical of the education system, believing it to be associated with control more than educating children.

Getting you thinking

Design, with a study partner, the perfect school. Imagine you have complete freedom to design the best and fairest education system possible, one that would support all pupils well: what should be taught and for how long? Would there be examinations? What facilities should there be?

What is education?

Education is the process by which the collected knowledge of a culture is passed on to people, usually children. In the UK, all children between the ages of 5 and 16 (18 for those born after 1 September 1997) must receive an education, but they do not necessarily have to go to school. They may be educated at home.

Informal education

All societies educate children; in the past this would have been done by parents in the home, or through normal daily activity. This type of education into the skills of adulthood is known as informal education.

Formal education

Modern societies have highly developed education systems with professional educators working in complex institutions and often preparing pupils for public examinations. There is significant debate at all levels of society as to the purpose of education and what essential knowledge should be passed on. These debates are very much influenced by the beliefs of the people who are in power and their beliefs about what children need to know.

The youngest Nobel Prize winner Malala Yousafzai. In 2012 she was shot in the head by terrorists for demanding the right to an education. Find out about her campaigning and why she was willing to risk her life.

Historical reasons for the development of education systems

There are a number of historical and social reasons why we have an education system and why governments fund schools and colleges:

- ⊙ *Child labour* – If children are in school then they are protected from exploitation by employers of child labour.
- ⊙ *Vocationalism* – Children can be trained for work and the needs of employers.
- ⊙ *Public health* – Children from poorer families can be offered basic nutrition and encouraged to maintain a healthy lifestyle.
- ⊙ *Economic trade* – British manufacturing and business requires a trained workforce if it is to maintain its position as a world leader in trade.
- ⊙ *Military capacity* – Historically, Britain was a military nation engaged in frequent wars abroad. It required soldiers with a basic education and a good standard of health.
- ⊙ *Training in cultural values* – The requirement of schools to promote the well-being and culture of children is explicit in most educational legislation.
- ⊙ *Religious reasons* – It was thought that if children could be taught to read the Bible, it would improve their moral behaviour.

Theoretical debates

Structural theory viewpoints look at education in terms of the role it plays in society rather than the mechanics of how it takes place.

- ⊙ **Functionalism** is not critical of the education system. It sees education as a tool by which society sorts out children so that the most able will take on the best jobs. It sees education as meritocratic in that it provides a ladder of opportunity for the best students to achieve well.
- ⊙ **Marxism** views education as a source of social inequality and a tool of an unequal social system. The inequality in educational opportunity socialises people into accepting that some people have more access to power and wealth than others.
- ⊙ **Feminism** views the education system as oppressing women and suggests that it exists to socialise children into traditional gender patterns which perpetuate gender inequality.

Social action theories have little to say about the organisation of the education system and instead focus on the relationships within the school and how these influence the attainment of children.

- ⊙ Interactionism looks at the relationships between teachers and pupils, and between pupils. In particular, it is interested in how teachers label pupils as successful or not successful and the impact that this labelling has on the self-identity and self-esteem of pupils. Interactionism can appear to be deterministic, if it it suggests that children are not active participants in this process.
- ⊙ Postmodernists are similar to interactionists, focussing on what happens within schools. They see teachers and pupils as 'constructors' of knowledge. This means that in schools realities are constructed for pupils and this is how values are passed on.

STRETCH and CHALLENGE

What would happen to British society if all schools were closed and education became the responsibility of parents? Find out about home education from the Education Otherwise website: http://www.educationotherwise.net/

> Britain requires a National Curriculum that promotes the spiritual, moral, cultural, mental and physical development of pupils at the school and of society.
>
> *Educational Reform Act 1988*

In the 19th century the Welsh language was vigorously discouraged in schools. The Welsh Not, or Welsh Knot, was used to force Welsh children to speak English at school. A child heard speaking Welsh would be given a stick or plaque which they handed on to another pupil they heard using the language. At the end of the day, the child left with the Welsh Not would be punished.

How would the Welsh Not be explained by:

a) Functionalists and

b) Marxists?

Discussion point

- How different from the British education system is the education experienced by Finnish children?

The UK has spent approximately £45 billion on rebuilding and updating schools: would you say it was money well spent?

204

How may education systems vary from British education?

When considering the role and function in contemporary society, it may be useful to consider a highly successful education system that is very different from the one that British children experience. The education system in Finland is viewed as being one of the best in the world. The scores in international tests of maths, science and reading are often the highest, beating nations such as the UK and the USA by a long way. The underlying principle of the Finnish education system is that all citizens should have access to high quality education. Education is free; all children have the right to educational support if is required and the same opportunities should be available regardless of wealth, ethnicity or age. Financial support is offered to all pupils if they require it and many children have access to free meals and free transport to school. Children attend schools that are closest to their own homes.

It is believed by the Finns that the education system should encourage children to be active participants in society and that education is a way of helping them become good citizens. Finns believe that people should be lifelong learners so that the whole child is cared for: health, music, art, special education and sports are all equally important. It is believed that this will not exclude anyone from learning and will encourage people to give of their best to education.

Teaching is a high status profession and well-paid, so there is serious competition for places on teaching courses. Only the top graduates apply for teaching training and they are given free training. There may be up to 1,000 candidates for jobs, however. Teachers only teach for four hours each day and are allowed two hours each week to train and update their skills. There is little homework, though children are actively encouraged to read for pleasure. Schools are relaxed and very clean.

The example of the Finnish system of education is relevant to an understanding of British society because education is seen as central to the development of the whole society. Patterns of attainment for all children are good and teaching is viewed as an important job.

To develop your understanding of education and education systems, consider the following questions:

- Is success in education due to hard work or to natural ability?
- Is it more important to remember facts or to understand how to use them?
- Should children have more individual attention in school or should they learn to get on without it?
- Should class sizes be small or large?
- Is it important for children to enjoy school?
- Is it more important for children to be creative or to pass examinations?

Sample questions

Wales has a population of around 3,000,000 people. Expenditure in 2011 on education was around £4.162bn. State schools funded by government educated around 465,000 children aged 5 to 16; 65,000 students aged 16 to 19 were at further education institutions or in vocational training. Some students attend private fee-paying schools. Many pupils are taught entirely or partially in Welsh, and Welsh medium education is available to all age groups, including nursery pupils, universities and adult education.

a) Summarise the content of the item on education in Wales.
b) Explain **two** sociological reasons why governments spend large sums of money on providing an education system for their citizens.

Check your own learning

Match the terms to their meaning.

a)	Functionalism	Teachers and pupils work together to construct knowledge.
b)	Marxism	Children are labelled by teachers in schools and learn to act according to those labels.
c)	Feminism	The education system is a ladder of opportunity for the best people to get to the top.
d)	Interactionism	The education system exists to ensure that children learn to accept inequality as normal and acceptable.
e)	Postmodernism	The education system exists to ensure that male power and dominance over women is maintained.

Extended writing

Assess reasons why modern Britain requires an education system for its young people.

Guidance: If you are required to assess something, then you must judge the value of it. Make a decision about whether the theory or evidence that you are assessing does the job it is designed to do. In this case, you will need to look at all of the various reasons why we have an education system and then to choose which you think is the most or least useful in terms of explaining why we have a system. In this case, social action theories do not really offer a good explanation because they tell us what happens, but structural theories are useful and so are historical reasons, if they still apply.

Write about 500-750 words.

Tip

Education is a major employer and huge numbers of people are part of the system. The BBC has an education news page and the better quality papers have education supplements. Keep up to date with recent news stories so your knowledge is current and you can develop your examination responses.

Research idea

Find out about the home education approach to schooling in the UK. Is it a good system of educating children – what are its strengths and weaknesses?

Activity

Design an interview schedule to ask teachers how they would improve the education system in the UK. Ask your teachers if they would like to participate and, if they are willing, take their answers.

Aims

⊙ **To understand that that the education system may carry out a number of functions for society**

Functionalists have a great deal to say about education, they view it as a way of socialising children into the norms and values of society, thus it contributes to social cohesion. Children are expected to learn the rules of their society. Marxists and functionalists would agree that a great deal of what happens in school is concerned with social control. Functionalists, however, would see this as essentially positive, whereas Marxists see it as a form of class control, oppressing the working class. Functionalists also emphasise the examination system as being a sorting process enabling the best to do well in life, whereas Marxists see the same process but claim that it favours the middle classes.

These issues are important because the theories and debates that people have about functions of the education system will affect the quality and type of education that children in England and Wales receive.

Topic 2: Functions of the education system

Getting you thinking

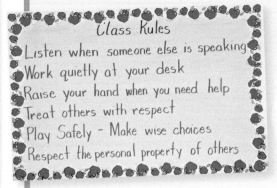

Class Rules
Listen when someone else is speaking
Work quietly at your desk
Raise your hand when you need help
Treat others with respect
Play Safely - Make wise choices
Respect the personal property of others

Take a trip around your school or college, look at notice boards and corridor signs. How many of them are telling you what to do? How much of your life at school or college is governed by sets of rules? If you could choose your own rules, what would they be? Why would you choose those rules?

What are the functions of the education system in England and Wales?

Sociologists and political thinkers are not necessarily agreed on the functions of the education system; however, some themes do emerge from most public policy. These are that education should:

⊙ Provide opportunities for children, though Marxists would tend to put more emphasis on equality of opportunity than functionalists do.
⊙ Sort children in terms of their ability to learn and then to provide the correct type of educational opportunities. Functionalists would prioritise this function.
⊙ Prepare children for adult life, most particularly for work, this is known as vocationalism.
⊙ Help children to become active participants in society and to live healthy and productive lives as citizens of their country.

Socialisation and education

Emile Durkheim claimed that the education system was an important agency of secondary socialisation. Its primary role was to ensure social stability and social cohesion so that society could be well-ordered with different people filling appropriate roles to ensure society survived. For functionalists, education bridged the gap for children between the close personal relationships of family life and was their first introduction to the less emotional and more universal relationships of adulthood. Children would be introduced to the shared cultures of their society and thus would learn their place in the social world. Marxists see this socialisation as part of brainwashing children into accepting inequality.

You might be able to recognise how this type of thinking affects contemporary education by looking at how much socialisation into the rules of wider society takes place within schools and the education system. The National Curriculum is a basic outline of what you need to know about your own culture. Much of the education that takes place in nurseries and primary schools is concerned with teaching children how to get on with their peer group and with teaching them the basic rules of social interaction, as well as teaching them more formal skills.

Economic functions of education

There is a strong link with the idea that children need the skills for employment, this is known as vocationalism. Societies require a workforce with advanced skills in order to develop economically. Durkheim and the functionalists suggest that schools ensure that students are equipped with the skills needed by the economy of the country. Talcott Parsons said that schools allocate roles to the more talented and that the education system has a sorting and sifting function. This idea is known as meritocracy. Marxists are more critical, however, as they see the education system purely in terms of reproduction of class inequalities.

Within your own education you will have seen that there are two basic themes to all your work. The first is knowledge, and children are taught facts which the government feels are needed. However, students are also taught transferable skills, which should help them in the workplace. Quite a lot of education is focussed on encouraging children to learn more about work and careers.

Social control

Much of what happens in education is about social control. Children learn to follow rules and to behave in the way that the schools require. Marxists such as Althusser believe that schools form part of the ideological state apparatus because they teach the ideas of the ruling class. Children are taught to obey teachers, and this reproduces the world outside the classroom where they will obey their employers. Durkheim, however, was very much in favour of very strict discipline in schools. His logic was that offenders

> ### Tip
>
> Children in the UK belong to four different education systems, depending on where they live. Historically, Scotland and Northern Ireland have had differing systems from the rest of the UK for a long time. More recently, since devolution, there has been a widening gap between England and Wales, particularly with regard to examination systems and curriculum content.

> We want to create an education system based on real excellence, with a complete intolerance of failure. Yes, we're ambitious. But today, we've got to be. We've got to be ambitious if we want to compete in the world.
>
> **British Prime Minister, David Cameron, speaking in 2011**

How much of what happens in schools is about teaching children to conform to social rules?

affected the whole social group, so by strict punishment they would learn to act in the interests of society. They needed to understand that offences have a major impact on society.

Consider the rules that pupils in school are subject to, for example school uniforms or fashion regulations. What purpose do these serve in educational terms? Durkheim sees them as reinforcing social cohesion and group norms whereas Marxists see them as part of the process of training children not to be rebellious.

Functions of education in contemporary society

What other functions of the education system can you think of?

Research idea

Interview a range of people, including teachers and parents, and ask them what they think is the main purpose of schools in Britain and how well British schools achieve those aims. To what extent do parents and teachers agree?

Functions of Education

- Agency of secondary socialisation
- Allocation of children to different social roles
- Transmission of cultural heritage and knowledge
- Preparing children for adult work
- To provide training in logical thinking
- Provide opportunities for children
- Instilling social values in children

> *Don't these schools do enough damage making all these kids think alike, now they have to make them look alike too?*
>
> George Carlin

Sample questions

The link between beliefs about the purpose of education and the type of education that children actually receive can be seen in practice. For example, many policymakers believe that the role of education is to train students for adult work so they encourage schools to focus on job training or **vocationalism**. British governments since the late 1970s have argued that the main aims of education should be to encourage economic growth, encourage competition, increase choice for parents and raise standards in schools by setting them up as competitors for the best students.

a) Explain the meaning of the term **vocationalism**.
b) Using the item and sociological knowledge, explain how education prepares students for work.

Check your own learning

Identify which theory is associated with each of these views of the education system:

Functionalism   Feminism
Functionalism   Marxism   Functionalism

a) The education system exists to control the children of the working class and make them accept a worse position in society.
b) The education system exists to control females and make them accept a worse position in society.
c) The education system provides a ladder of opportunity for the brightest and the best to reach the top of society.
d) Education trains children to accept cultural norms and social cohesion.
e) Education sorts children and prepares them for their future roles in society in the process known as role allocation.

Extended writing

Using sociological evidence and examples, explain the role and functions of education in contemporary society.
Guidance: If you see the word **functions** in an essay title, this is an indication that the focus of your answer should be on functionalism. However, you will need to show that other theories may also have insights into the role and functions of education, and in this case, Marxist views are very similar to functionalism, though the conclusions that Marxist draw about education are negative whereas functionalists are positive. Choose three or four functions of education for society and explain each one with reference to the education system and how it may affect society or children.
Write about 300 words.

STRETCH and CHALLENGE

Should schools have the right to exclude children permanently if they refuse to follow uniform regulations? Make arguments both for and against.

For each of the functions of education that you can identify or which are mentioned in this topic, look for examples in your own life and see how they impact on your experience of education.

Discussion point

• What do you think are the most important functions of education? Give reasons for your views.

Aims

- To describe the current education system of England and Wales and to look at some of the factors that have led to the system of education that we have

From the 1940s through to the 1970s it was possible to describe the education system of England and Wales in a straightforward way. Although there was some local variation, school organisation was similar across the two countries. There was an emphasis on promoting equality of opportunity, though there were disagreements about how best to achieve this. More recently government policies and devolution have resulted in a wide variety of school types and organisation. While equality of opportunity remains an aim, recent changes have reflected the influence of the New Right and a belief that the education system should reflect the needs of employers.

Tip

Keep up to date with education debates and if you are asked about schools or educational change, talk about things that have taken place since the 1980s. Anything earlier is out of date.

How well you did in the 11 plus examination determined which secondary school you went to. Research showed the exam tended to favour middle-class pupils.

Topic 3: The education system of England and Wales

Getting you thinking

How similar is this image from the 1950s to your experience of education? How different is it?

A brief history of state education until the 1980s

- Before World War Two, most children in the state sector remained at 'elementary schools' until the age of 14. A secondary education was available only to those who paid for private (or independent) schools or who had passed selection examinations to council-run grammar schools.
- The 1944 Education Act introduced secondary education for all from the age of 11, different types of secondary school were established and pupils were allocated on the basis of their results in the 11 plus examination. Those with the highest marks attended grammar schools offering an academic curriculum; most of the rest (around two-thirds) went to secondary modern schools and were not expected to take any examinations. In some places technical schools existed, sitting between the grammars and secondary moderns.
- From 1965, many local authorities developed comprehensive secondary schools which all children attended; this was partly a response to what was seen as an unfair system of selection which favoured children from middle-class families.

Surname .... Candidate number ....

First name ....

Current school ....

Grammar School Entry Exam
11+

30 minutes

- Since the 1970s, there has been continuing debate about the quality of state education. New teaching methods, changing attitudes towards behaviour and punishment and young people's readiness for the world of work are amongst the concerns. This has resulted in a variety of school provision.

Educational change since 1979

The Conservative government elected in 1979 under Margaret Thatcher introduced a series of Education Acts which had a massive influence on schools. Many of the ideas have been continued by subsequent Labour and Conservative/Liberal governments.

- The introduction of parent governors.
- Financial control being taken from local authorities and given to head teachers and governing bodies.
- More frequent inspections of schools.
- The development of the National Curriculum.
- Increased examination of children at various ages.
- The introduction of competition between schools for pupils.
- The concept of educational choice for parents who would pick the school they felt was most suited to their child, rather than having their child allocated to a school.
- Better performing schools were given additional funding.
- Some schools were allowed to select up to 10% of their pupils on the basis of ability.
- Grants to students at universities were replaced by loans to be repaid when employed.
- Fees for higher education rather than public funding.
- Some schools have become data driven, so that pay and income depend on examination results.

Overall direct central government and local authority control over individual schools has declined. At the same time, though, the introduction of league tables, and the increased role of inspection systems means schools and head teachers are subject to more external scrutiny.

One significant result of the changes has been an increased variety of school types: including academies, city technology colleges, free schools, faith schools. In some areas, selection remains; Trafford and Kent still have grammar schools; in Wales, most children still attend comprehensive schools.

Supporters of the education reforms

Supporters of educational reform have said that education has improved for children:

- They argue that there is better teaching in schools.
- Schools are more responsive to the demands of parents.
- Competition forces weaker schools to improve, as if they do not they will lose pupils.
- There are better links between employers and universities and schools.

Critics of the changes to education system

There are many critics of the changes to the education system who argue that:

- Changes in funding arrangements mean there are gaps growing between schools with some lacking resources.
- The emphasis on league tables encourages schools to favour more able students. As there is a link between social class and educational success, this can disadvantage some pupils.

> **Research idea**
>
> Interview a range of people, including teachers and parents, and ask them about their experiences of education. Did they have a better or worse experience in school than you? What were the most significant differences between schools in the past, and schools now? How many exams did they take? At what age?

Conservative education policy 2015: more free schools and academies.

211

- Schools have become so examination focussed that the idea of education for its own sake has been squeezed out. The requirements of the examination drive lessons, not pupil interest.
- Some of the new school types have freedom to adapt their curriculum; this has led to concerns that children may have a narrower education, for example not being taught about scientific ideas such as evolution.
- The ideology of equality of opportunity for all children, which characterised education up to the 1960s, has been replaced by an emphasis on competition and division.

The academy programme

During the 1990s, local education authorities were seen by the Labour government as a barrier to school improvement. The response was to force failing schools to leave local authorities to become 'academies' sponsored and managed by boards or 'trusts' led by business and local universities and colleges. Some schools choose to become academies and do not need a sponsor. Academies are funded directly from central government and there has been huge investment in such schools. The argument is that independence and new ideas will produce better examination results.

The changes have not been welcomed by everyone. The evidence about examination performance is difficult to interpret so researchers are not sure that changing to academy status has any long-term impact on performance. Other concerns have been expressed. As the state sector is broken up, and there is freedom to adapt the curriculum, it means that children in different parts of the country will be having different educational experiences. As the gap in resources widens it is possible that some schools will have unfair advantages when it comes to recruiting teachers and pupils. As local authorities lose schools they will also lose money and the ability to support their remaining schools.

Diversity and devolution

Scotland and Northern Ireland have always had different education systems from England and Wales. Until 1998 there was little difference between Welsh and English schools; although the Welsh had more grammar school places in the 1950s than England, reflecting the value placed on education as a route to success. Since devolution of power to the Welsh Assembly, the differences between England and Wales have widened. From 2016, England and Wales will have different A level systems of examinations and Wales has not followed the academy path.

Independent and private schools

Alongside the state-provided education system, there is also a system whereby parents can pay for their children to attend independent schools. These are schools which charge fees. The most prestigious are known as 'public schools', but not all independent schools offer the same kind of facilities, history or tradition as schools such as Eton or Cheltenham Ladies College. Many of these independent schools operate as charities, so although they are in fact businesses, some schools are very wealthy indeed.

Arguments in favour of independent schools are that:

- Parents can choose how to spend their money and if they choose to spend it on education, that is their right.

- By educating around 7% of pupils, independent schools are saving the state sector money; parents have paid taxes which support the state system and then pay again through fees.
- Examination results are good.

Arguments against independent schools are that:

- People are able to buy privilege for their children at the expense of all children, thus increasing social inequality in UK.
- Many independent schools enjoy favourable tax treatment as charities, so rich parents are subsidised through the tax system.
- Those who use the independent sector have little or no concern for the state system, if more influential parents used the state system there would be more pressure for it to improve.

Sample questions

Supporters of the academy programme, and politicians, have claimed that academies are a huge success and have transformed weak comprehensive schools into powerful and achieving schools. The data, however, is not quite so clear cut for all academies. They appear to be teaching alternative courses such as BTEC rather than GCSEs so that it is easier to get their five A*–C grades by studying one subject rather than a range. They are also less likely to teach traditional subjects such as history, geography and languages. Academy schools appear to improve examination results, but results are improving in all types of schools.

    a) Summarise the item on the academy programme in the UK.
    b) Explain **two** sociological reasons for changes to the education system in the UK.

Check your own learning

Identity the school type from the description:

    a) All children attend the same secondary school in order to have equality of opportunity.
    b) An elite fee-paying school attended by the children of the very wealthy and powerful.
    c) A school which taught children a traditional curriculum, many were set up by the 1944 Education Act.
    d) A school which has left local authority control to be run by a trust.
    e) A school that is controlled and run by people who share a religious belief in common.

Extended writing

Using sociological evidence and examples, assess the view that children in Britain all receive a similar form of education.
Guidance: This is a slightly tricky question in that there really is not a powerful debate about this issue. Arguments in favour of the view suggest that schools offer broadly similar curricula, that the teaching styles do not differ that much and that much education is broadly familiar. However, in opposition are points such as the variety of different schools, so that in places there are legacy schools from the reorganisations of the 1940s and the 1960s but recently there has been a far greater range of school type. Alongside all of this is the independent system which educates up to 10% of children depending on geographical area.
Write about 500-750 words.

STRETCH and CHALLENGE

Should independent fee paying schools be banned? Make arguments both for and against.

INTERESTING FACT

In 2014, 36% of the leading members of the government, the Cabinet, were people who had been educated in private schools. A third of all MPs attended a private schools, compared to just 7% of the general public.

Developing understanding

It is very easy to believe that your own experience of the education system is typical of all schools. Talk to people from a range of different schools and cultures to find out how your own school experiences may be similar to or different from theirs.

◉ To recognise and explain why, despite many years of government intervention, the most significant determinant of how well a child will do in school is social class

Despite very many changes to the education system over the years, it is clear that the most significant influence on educational attainment is not intelligence but social background. Intelligence is pretty equally spread amongst classes, genders and ethnicities. However, the working classes, boys, and people from certain ethnic groups will generally achieve lower results than the children of professional people, girls, and people from other ethnic groups. This is not to say that individuals cannot do better or worse than expected, but that patterns and trends show educational success to be closely linked to social background.

Developing understanding

Underachievement and under-attainment
These terms are used interchangeably. They refer to the *average* level of achievement of a group, compared to another group. Thus, in the material that introduces this section, children receiving free school meals underachieve compared to other pupils. Not all children receiving free school meals achieve lower results than others, and not all others achieve better results than all the FSM children.

Topic 4: Educational attainment and social class

Getting you thinking

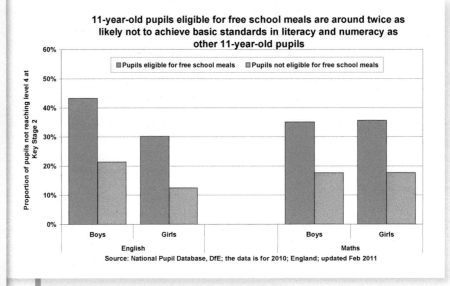

11-year-old pupils eligible for free school meals are around twice as likely not to achieve basic standards in literacy and numeracy as other 11-year-old pupils

Source: National Pupil Database, DfE; the data is for 2010; England; updated Feb 2011

Why do you think that children who have free school meals tend to do less well than other children at age 11 in England? Make a list of suggestions to explain this pattern of data.

Social class

Britain is a class-based society. Whilst many people would like to believe that everyone has an equal chance in society, this is certainly a myth. Those who are born into the lower and poorer sections of society have limited chances of escaping from lives of relative hardship, and those who are born into wealthy privileged families will tend to succeed in life. Sociologists are not entirely agreed on definitions of social class or what categories to create, but generally accept that people who are professionals, educated and in good jobs make up the middle classes and those who are less well educated, or highly qualified in practical skills, and who work for other people are working class. Of course it is not as simple as that, but the link between parental education and work and children's success in school is absolutely clear. Those who are very poor, perhaps in receipt of free school meals (FSM) affect the outcomes of schools in terms of expected examination results, and this is so well known that it is factored into data analysis for schools by governments.

Parents and attitudes to school

It is probable that most parents want their children to do well in school. They recognise that there is a link between a good education and good chances in life for children. Although it is a huge generalisation, people with higher levels of education generally have better health, live longer, occupy better quality housing and have more

> **Research methods**
>
> What ethical issues would you have in conducting research in a school to find the link between free school meals and low educational attainment?

opportunities. Parents are anxious to see their children do well in life, and qualifications are a route to success. The government is anxious for pupils from all backgrounds to do well because there is a wastage of working-class talent, and industry requires a highly skilled workforce. The issue for sociologists is to ask why, despite most people supporting equality of opportunity in education, it still is not happening in the modern UK.

Causes of under-attainment among working-class pupils

Sociologists have offered a range of theories to explain working-class underachievement. The conclusions that they draw depend on their perspectives about how society works:

- ⊙ Functionalists: claim that the working class fail because schools are meritocratic, and thus they must not be the best pupils.
- ⊙ Marxists: believe that the education system exists to legitimise ruling class power, so the education system is biased against the working class, existing only to oppress poor pupils.
- ⊙ Interactionists: tend to the view that schools are middle-class institutions and that teachers label working-class children as failures. The children live up to their labels by failing.

Other reasons to account for working-class failure

Material deprivation

Material deprivation refers to the lack of money to buy possessions. There has been a huge amount of research that links poverty with low attainment. For example, Smith and Noble (1995) found that poor parents cannot afford additional resources such as books, computers and space to work. However, the impact of lacking money and material resources is more significant than that. Poor housing quality means that poorer children take more ill-health absence and have limited space to work. Leon Feinstein (2003) suggested a link between poor nutrition, particularly during pregnancy, and educational underachievement. Government data on *Deprivation and Education* (2009) suggested family stress was a significant contributor to school failure.

Cultural deprivation

Many modern sociologists have a problem with this type of theory because it is based on the assumption that the working classes are not only 'different' from, but also not as good as, the middle classes. The theory is that working-class children have less culture than middle-class children. In very controversial work, Basil Bernstein suggested that the problem is caused by language: working-class children have lower language skills and do not think as well as richer children as a result of this. Douglas, in the 1960s, said that working-class parents do not value education and do not read to their children.

Cultural capital

This is a Marxist theory, put forward by Pierre Bourdieu in the 1970s, and is similar to cultural deprivation theory. The claim is that middle-class people possess knowledge and use it to benefit their own children. This use of knowledge can be things such as how to influence school policy, which schools get the best examination results, how to talk to teachers to gain advantage, how to use education systems and play the game. Working-class people do not have access to these skills and cannot support their children in the same way.

Cultural reproduction theory

This is another Marxist theory. Bowles and Gintis (1976) suggested that schools are middle-class institutions and that they pass on the norms and values of capitalist society. Thus schools socialise children, but only to produce workers for society.

Are all parents equally concerned their children do well in school?

Research idea

The government concern with white working-class underachievement can be seen on the Parliament website where a whole raft of reports and findings are available for an Inquiry between 2010 and 2014. Google 'Parliament', 'committees', 'education', 'working class' and see what there is.

> The dice are loaded against the child born into a disadvantaged family. It is the language used in the home, diet, the capacity to borrow, clothes, housing, quality of schools and the availability of work ... You can work like a Trojan to get out of these traps, but still be stuck.
>
> **Will Hutton**

Education

Activity

Practise your evaluation skills for AO3. For each of the theories described, suggest one or more strengths or weaknesses of it. If you can refer to a theory, concept, piece of evidence such as research or refer to contemporary educational policy in some way, you are more likely to achieve mark band 4 on the assessment criteria of the mark schemes.

Policy point

The government do not measure social class as a factor in school attainment, instead they use eligibility for free school meals (FSM) as their indicator of low income.

Tip

There are two ways that this material could be used as the basis of questioning. The first is through the data analysis question where you will be asked to suggest two or more reasons for working-class underachievement. The second is in extended writing, where you may be asked to assess or evaluate the various theories to explain the causes of it.

They call this theory, the **Correspondence principle**. Thus, the organisation of the school mirrors the organisation of the workplace and trains working-class children for subordinate, unpleasant boring work.

School organisation

Government policy and recent government-funded research by a Parliamentary Select Committee (2014) suggests that the problem lies within schools themselves. Working-class children in schools rated as outstanding are twice as likely to gain 5 A*–C GCSE grades than similar children in schools rated as satisfactory or 'requiring improvement'. They suggest schools should aim to recruit high quality teachers, and currently, schools in poor areas have less funding than schools in rich areas. They claim that teachers have low expectations of poor pupils. They argue that teachers need to improve their skills and that the school day should be longer. Obviously, this type of thinking has been heavily criticised by teachers themselves, who claimed the issue was material poverty.

Labelling theories and self-fulfilling prophecy

While the government has taken on the concept of labelling theory, possibly because it is easier to blame teachers for low expectations than to address issues in wider society, these theories are dated in sociology. The claim is that children gain identity from schools and that teachers label working-class children as failures. Becker (1952) supported labelling; Ball (1981) said that schools stream children on the basis of behaviour rather than ability. Goodacre, (1986) found that working-class children tended to be under-marked by teachers. The children then accept their labels. This theory has been heavily criticised by Safia-Mirza and others who claim that children can and do reject negative labels.

Subcultures and peer groups

Many interactionists have worked with groups of children within schools and found that children who find it difficult to succeed on the terms that the schools set, form social groups that reject the norms of the school. They can gain status by being 'bad' rather

Check your own learning

Match the terms to their meanings.

a)	Children and parents cannot afford the basic essentials to support educational success.	Cultural capital
b)	Working-class people do not have cultural knowledge and their culture is inferior to middle-class culture.	Material deprivation
c)	Working-class people do not have knowledge of the system and how to play it to support their children at the cost of other people's children.	School organisation theory
d)	Schools reproduce and prepare children for the inequalities of wider society.	Sub-cultural theory
e)	The problem lies within schools and with poor teaching.	Cultural deprivation
f)	Teachers have low expectations of working-class pupils who internalise these low expectations and subsequently fail.	Cultural reproduction
g)	Children cannot gain status in school from being clever or passing exams so they look for other routes to gaining self-esteem by forming peer groups that reject school.	Labelling theory

than feel inferior because they are challenged by teachers. Jackson (2002) suggested that laddish, clowning behaviour among both boys and girls (ladettes), is a form of self-worth protection strategy as a response to over-testing and over-emphasis on educational success in modern schools.

Sample questions
GCSE results and deprivation in Wales

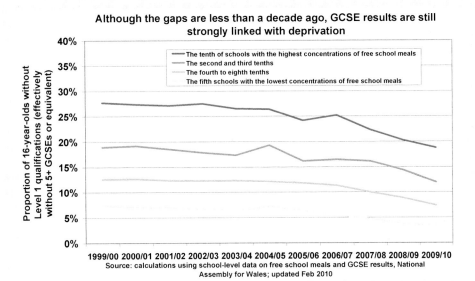

Although the gaps are less than a decade ago, GCSE results are still strongly linked with deprivation

Legend:
- The tenth of schools with the highest concentrations of free school meals
- The second and third tenths
- The fourth to eighth tenths
- The fifth schools with the lowest concentrations of free school meals

y-axis: Proportion of 16-year-olds without Level 1 qualifications (effectively without 5+ GCSEs or equivalent)

x-axis: 1999/00 2000/01 2001/02 2002/03 2003/04 2004/05 2005/06 2006/07 2007/08 2008/09 2009/10

Source: calculations using school-level data on free school meals and GCSE results, National Assembly for Wales; updated Feb 2010

Source of data: http://www.poverty.org.uk/w26/index.shtml?2

a) Summarise the content of the table showing the link between schools with highest concentrations of pupils receiving free school meals and number of pupils who do not have five or more GCSEs A*–C.

b) Explain **two** sociological reasons for the relationship between high levels of free school meal take-up among pupils and lower levels of achievement at GCSE.

Extended writing

Assess the relationship between social class and attainment in education.

Guidance: If you are asked to assess, you are making a specific judgement as to whether something is fit for purpose. If you simply repeat the various possible explanations of working-class under-attainment, you will gain high AO1 marks but cannot score highly on AO2 or AO3. For those marks, you should be commenting specifically on whether the theory is a good explanation of working-class under-attainment. Your best conclusion is that they all have merit, but none answer the question fully. You may even suggest that some theories are better than others. To gain the highest marks, you should develop your answer with recent evidence drawn from contemporary England and Wales.

Write about 500-750 words.

Tip

In your examination, you will be asked about a table, graph or piece of data. Take care and read everything, because often it is easy to misunderstand graphical data if you do not check all of the writing and the labels. This is a skill that you should practise.

STRETCH and CHALLENGE

What strategies would you put in place to improve educational outcomes for the working class if you were in government? What opposition might you expect from teachers, parents and the popular press?

What barriers to learning and succeeding in school might children who live in flats like these experience?

Aims

- To recognise and explain the complexity of the relationship between gender and educational attainment

In the 1940s and 1950s, boys tended to do significantly better than girls in school. The most general viewpoint was that it did not really matter as girls were only going to get married and have children anyway. The common belief was that men were naturally more talented than women. In the 1960s and 1970s, feminists challenged this perception and provided ample research evidence to show that girls and boys received very different education even within the same classrooms. As a result there have been many strategies introduced to tackle gender inequality. Now girls are outperforming boys in examinations; that has come to be seen as the problem for public policy.

Tip

If the question is about males, then you should focus on male attainment and just mention girls as a way of commenting about males. If the question is about females, the opposite is true. If the question mentions gender, then you should focus on both genders equally or you will not be producing a balanced argument.

Topic 5: Educational attainment and gender

Getting you thinking

Pupils achieving five or more GCSE grades A* to C or equivalent [1,2] by sex

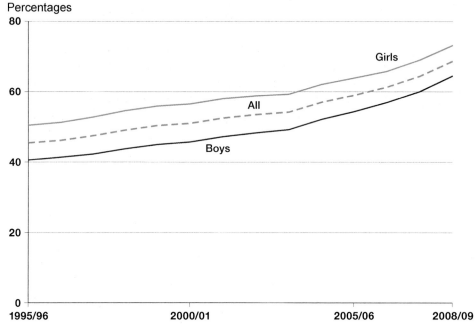

1 For pupils in their last year of compulsory education. Pupils aged 15 at the start of the academic year; pupils in year S4 in Scotland. From 20004/05, pupils at the end of Key Stage 4 in England.
2 From 1990/91, National Qualifications[xv] were introduced in Scotland but are not included until 2000/01.

Source: ONS/DFE

What can you learn from this line graph about patterns and trends in educational attainment and gender in recent years?

Gender

Gender is a social construction. Many sociologists, such as Bob Connell, suggest that the biological differences between males and females are overstated. The differences between individual men and women are far greater than the differences between the genders as a whole. Nevertheless, assumptions are made about men and women that overlook individual differences and assume that everybody of the same gender is similar. In the past, this resulted in women being placed in an inferior position in society, and there are still many who believe masculinity is somehow 'better'. By the 1990s, challenges to this type of thinking and changes in society were so difficult to ignore that Helen Wilkinson (1994) coined the term genderquake to describe the massive shifts that were taking place in traditional gender patterns.

When sociologists first started to study gender and education, boys were more successful than girls. Early studies identified sexist practices in schools that depressed girls' attainment. Now studies are concerned with boys under-attainment and the idea of 'masculinity' as a barrier to success is an issue.

In addition to differences in levels of achievement, another concern is the way that subject choices tend to be heavily gendered with boys and girls opting for different types of subject, which has implications for job opportunities in the future.

Causes of under-attainment and gender

There is a link between theory and the type of research that is carried out. Feminists began to research girls' underachievement in the 1960s. Before then the main concern had been class inequality and gender differences were largely overlooked. The explanations for gender differences offered by different theories reflect the basic assumptions of those theories:

- ⊙ *Functionalists*: see gender as being linked to male and female social roles. What happens in education is a reflection of society.
- ⊙ *Marxists*: are concerned with class and so gender inequality tends not to be seen as important.
- ⊙ *Interactionists*: studies within schools show that teachers and pupils share ideas about gender roles and so traditional gender patterns tend to be reproduced in schools through the formal and hidden curriculum.
- ⊙ *Feminists*: showed how patriarchy extended into schools from the wider society. They looked for and found evidence that girls systematically lost out in the education system. Now male underachievement in school is seen as the problem, rather than the continuing inequality that exists after school in the world of work.
- ⊙ *The New Right*: agree with functionalists, but are concerned about the recent perceived failure of boys and seek policies to overturn this pattern.
- ⊙ *Postmodernists*: tend to see gender as a choice, and so suggest that the way that children are forced into identifying with a gender in schools is an unpleasant and aggressive form of social control.

Discussing gender attainment in education

Genetic theories of gender difference

Sociologists are generally not keen on biological and genetic explanations of differences in attainment. However, some educationists believe that boys and girls learn differently. One solution that is often applied to male underachievement is separate classes for boys and girls. Some commentators favour single sex education for such reasons. However, if differences in attainment are based on biological factors, how can the changing patterns be explained? Clearly if genetics were the cause of differences then patterns and trends would be static.

Gender socialisation

Feminists such as Sue Sharpe (1976) suggest that gender differences at school reflect the creation of gender identity; this begins in the home and is reinforced by secondary socialisation in education and the media. This accounts for the boys and girls opting for 'masculine' or 'feminine' of subjects when options are chosen. The National Curriculum attempted to break down some of these gendered assumptions about subjects, but some subjects are still associated overwhelmingly with males or females. Interestingly, a number of studies, such as that by Clarricoates, have pointed to social class as a factor in subject choice with middle-class girls more likely to opt for male-dominated subjects, but working-class girls having a more traditional view of careers.

School organisation

Recent studies have suggested that changes to government policy and examinations favour girls. The teaching profession has become increasingly dominated by women.

A level choices

Boys are twice as likely as girls to study A level Maths, three times as likely to study Further Maths and more than four times as likely to take A-levels in Physics. On the other hand, twice as many girls as boys study English.

What other gender differences in A level choice would you expect to find? Use the Internet to see if your ideas are accurate.

Are male and female brains really different? Consider nature/nurture arguments on page 14.

Activity

Subject choice differences

There have been many reports discussing the differences in subject choices at GCSE and AS/A-level between boys and girls. Girls are much less likely to study STEM (science, technology, engineering and maths) subjects than boys; boys are outnumbered in subjects such as sociology and psychology.

Use the Internet to investigate subject choices and gender differences.

What explanations are there for the differences?

What are the implications of these differences for future options for boys and girls?

This offers boys fewer male role models in schools. As success in education becomes associated with femininity, then males concerned will need to reject educational success to assert their masculinity. The emphasis has tended to be on helping girls do better and to take up traditionally male subjects; less has been done to encourage boys to challenge stereotypes. WISE (Women in to Science and Engineering) does not have a 'boys into childcare' equivalent. It is suggested that the introduction of course work in the 1980s and 1990s benefited girls' learning styles more than boys; this is linked to the idea that girls are more willing to sit and listen whilst boys prefer active learning. Boys' behaviour is seen as more challenging by teachers. Government data shows that boys are three times more likely to be excluded than girls.

Hegemonic masculinity

There is evidence from writers such as Willis (1977) and others that some boys are likely to reject the values of education and form anti-school subcultures. This was linked to a form of masculinity linked to male work in traditional industries, work that often required few qualifications. According to Francis (2000) males feel threatened and so distance themselves from femininity as girls move into traditional male areas of achievement. This leads them to reject the strategies that lead to educational success. Such attitudes can be seen as self-defeating as employment patterns have changed. Poor school achievement has long-term consequences when qualifications are demanded by most employers.

Feminism

One of the strongest arguments to explain the change in male and female success rates in school is linked to feminism and its impact on girls' expectations. Increased opportunities at work and the accompanying economic independence mean girls no longer have the expectation of finding a husband who can support them for life. With the possibility of careers, girls have become more committed to their education. Sharpe's study in the 1970s found that girls were focussed on finding a husband, but when she repeated her research in the 1990s, their orientation had changed to finding a career. As this was happening within school, traditional male work in industry was more difficult to find; more jobs were demanding communication skills and the ability to get on with people, attributes traditionally associated with women.

The New Right

The New Right have claimed that changes in the family and especially the increase in single mothers mean that boys do not have good male role models in the home. Boys look to the media, sport and entertainment for their role models; often the men portrayed have achieved their success without doing well in school. Thus boys make little effort in school and this leads to poor achievement and poor employability. This is a simplified view, and the New Right often link it more specifically to working-class boys, as middle-class boys still do better in school than working-class girls.

> *Achieving gender equality requires the engagement of women and men, girls and boys. It is everyone's responsibility.*
>
> **Ban Ki-moon**
> **(Secretary General of the United Nations)**

Sample questions

There has been a persistent and widening gap between the attainment of girls and boys at school. The Welsh Assembly Government found that in 2006:

- 9% more girls than boys reached the expected levels in the core subjects in primary school.
- At 16, 58% of girls got five or more good GCSEs in 2005 compared with 46% of boys.
- At 18, 70% of girls got two or more A levels (grades A–C) compared with 64% of boys.
- 3.3% of boys left school with no qualifications, while for girls it was 2.1%.

Welsh Assembly Government 2010

a) Summarise the content of the item showing the link between gender and educational attainment.

b) Explain **two** sociological reasons for the relationship between gender and attainment in education.

Check your own learning

Match the theory to the concepts.

a)	Traditional gender patterns are reproduced in schools and gender is taught through social interactions.	Feminism
b)	Girls are victimised in the educational system and undervalued.	Hegemonic masculinity
c)	There is a very serious issue related to male under-attainment and this is caused by single parenthood and bad mothering of boys.	Genetics and biology
d)	Gender is a choice and forcing children into gender patterns is a form of social control of children.	Feminism
e)	Men and women are genetically different, and schools cater for females at the expense of males.	Postmodernism
f)	Gender identity creation begins in the home and is reinforced by secondary socialisation.	New Right
g)	Boys and girls have different learning styles and males are not catered for in schools.	Gender socialisation
h)	Males need to create a gender identity that is separate from females.	School organisation theory
i)	Male failure has been over-stated in order to disadvantage women.	Interactionists
j)	Males have inadequate mothering and a lack of acceptable male role models.	New Right

Research idea

Look for recent stories on the issues raised in this topic by using Google to look up 'gender gap', 'education' and 'evidence'.

Extended writing

Assess the relationship between gender and attainment in education.

Guidance: You will need to describe the patterns and the trends of gender attainment, looking at males and females equally. Refer to recent legislation, for example the Equality Acts and school equality policies. Look at the various theories and suggestions for gender inequality and assess them by referring to how well they explain the current patterns. You may wish to comment on the idea that perhaps there are other inequality patterns that are more significant and that focus on gender means that real problems are being overlooked. You might want to raise the point that boys and girls can make active choices, and that girls may choose to work well, whereas boys have other priorities that make them vulnerable to failure in school.

Write about 500 words.

Research methods

Design a study to find out what influences subject choices between boys and girls. See how you would discover what subjects are seen as 'male' and 'female'.

Aims

- To recognise and explain the complexity of the relationship between ethnicity and educational attainment

Variations in attainment between children of different ethnic groups are marked. Some ethnic groups over-attain against the average, but other ethnic heritage groups do rather badly against the average, and against children of similar ethnicity in the home country. This suggests that there are serious issues with culture and with the education system.

The most obvious solution to the problem is to suggest that the education system is institutionally racist and there is evidence for this. However, if that was the sole reason for under-attainment, it would not explain why some under-performing groups are not actually from visible minorities. Other explanations may lie with home culture or with poverty, as ethnic minorities often experience issues of class and deprivation.

Topic 6: Educational attainment and ethnicity

Getting you thinking

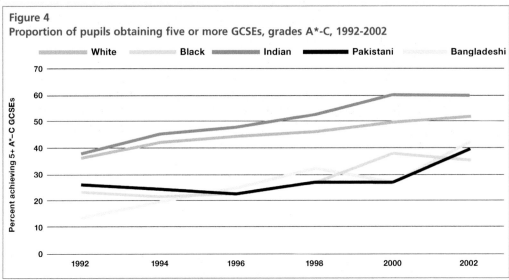

Figure 4
Proportion of pupils obtaining five or more GCSEs, grades A*-C, 1992-2002

Source: figures from Statistical First Release, Youth Cohort Study: the activities and experiences of 16 year olds: England and Wales 2002

Look at the table above showing the proportion of children from differing ethnic backgrounds who obtain 5 or more A*–C grades. What patterns and trends can you identify? Suggest reasons for the patterns that you can see.

Ethnicity

Britain is a multicultural society with a long history of immigration of minority ethnic groups. Non-white people have long been part of the population of Britain, for hundreds of years. Historic migrations from Ireland, the Netherlands, France and Poland were linked to war and religious upheaval in the home country; non-white migrants such as the Somali community and the Chinese arrived as sailors in the 1830s and onwards. Slavery was an important part of the economy of the country until 1833 so there is plenty of evidence of African and West Indian origin people in the population.

More recent migrants arrived in the UK after the Second World War, and often from former British colonies. The need to rebuild Britain after the devastation of the war meant that British companies advertised abroad for workers to come to the UK, many of them former soldiers who had fought for the Allies. Later migrations into the country were educated people from African countries which

Research idea

The Joseph Rowntree Foundation produces regular reports on many social problems in our society. Google 'JRF' and then enter 'ethnicity' and 'education' in their search engine to find recent reports to develop your notes.

expelled their Asian populations as they had worked for the British Empire. There have been recent migrations from Eastern European countries as a result of the free movement of labour among Member States of the European Union.

The link between attainment and ethnicity

In all ethnic groups, there are children who are high achievers and committed to education, just as there are those who remain indifferent. White children can be accepted as the average or norm, but only because the vast majority of children in schools are white.

- *Functionalists:* tend to see some ethnic minorities as pre-disposed to fail in school and look for cultural and genetic explanations.
- *Marxists:* are concerned with class and so ethnicity tends to be overlooked in favour of the class status of ethnic minorities.
- *Interactionists:* tend to look at labelling, teacher racism and institutional racism as being the causes of school under-attainment.
- *Feminists:* suggest that girls from ethnic minorities experience a double disadvantage, that of sexism (possibly within their own communities) and of racism.
- *The New Right:* agree with functionalists, but are very concerned about the recent perceived failure of boys, claiming that West Indian boys in particular lack suitable role models because single parenthood is more common in that community.

Explaining ethnic attainment in education

It is probable that most of the factors discussed below may play a part in ethnic variations in attainment. However, the most significant impact on attainment is almost certainly low socio-economic status and social disadvantage.

Genetic theories of ethnic difference

There is little or no evidence to support the idea that some ethnic backgrounds are more or less intelligent than others, though this has been proposed by New Right thinkers such as Murray, Herrnstein, Eysenck and others. The basis of such theorising is the belief that intelligence tests are a valid measure of ability, a theory that is no longer seen as valid. Further complicating the picture is the way that Black African children tend to over-achieve compared to white children whereas Black Caribbean pupils tend to under-achieve.

Poverty and class

Strand (1999) found that in primary and secondary schools in London, both Black and white able children from disadvantaged backgrounds failed to make the expected progress; however, Chinese and Indian heritage pupils tended to do better than predicted. There may be many reasons for this, over and above the known effects of social class. Suggestions include the fact that ethnic minority children tend to attend low-performing schools, have low expectations placed on them by teachers, are perceived as having problem behaviour. However, the worst performing ethnic groups in education are white Traveller groups and white working-class British pupils. This suggests that whilst issues of racism are significant, they do not explain why some pupils from ethnic backgrounds underachieve.

English as an additional language

Government data suggests that approximately 10% of children in English schools have English as an additional language (EAL) and use a different language in the home. Over 90% of Bangladeshi children qualify as EAL whereas only 7% of Black Caribbeans use a different language in the home from their school; 31% of EAL children are from low income families whereas only 15% of non-EAL qualify for free school meals. EAL pupils are often at a low starting point in infant school, but appear to make greater progress as they catch up with the language through school.

Research idea

Google 'Black History Month' to learn about the cultural diversity and heritage of non-white British people. How representative is this site of all ethnic minority heritage groups?

STRETCH and CHALLENGE

What would the effect on the country be if everyone from an ethnic minority cultural background was forced to leave the country, even if they were born here? Where would they go? What would the impact be on the economy, including the Health Service?

Tip

Remember that everyone is a member of an ethnic group. The term does not simply apply to members of visible ethnic minorities.

> Families of Chinese heritage see taking education seriously as a fundamental pillar of their Chinese identity, and a way of differentiating themselves not just within their own group, but from other ethnic groups as well.
>
> Becky Francis

Policy point

What strategies and policies would you put in place to ensure that children of lower attaining ethnicities are able to improve their school performance? Why do you think that this might be important to society?

Research methods

What ethical and practical problems would you have in researching links between ethnicity and attitudes to educational success?

Cultural differences

The case of Gypsy/Roma or Traveller children shows that culture may impact on educational attainment. These groups tend to be from the most disadvantaged families. A curious detail from the figures shows that far more Traveller children attend primary school than secondary school, which suggests that many families do not register their children at school. It is thought that this may be for child care and work reasons. However, Chinese children are consistently among the highest attaining children and it is thought that Chinese parents strongly encourage or even demand high educational attainment of their children. At GCSE, Chinese children on FSM perform better than the national average for all pupils. Chua described the Chinese parents as 'Tiger Parents' who cannot accept failure.

Racism

The Swan Report of 1985 recommended that schools should promote the idea of multicultural Britain because many schools were institutionally racist. Sociologists and ethnographers such as Gilroy, Sewell, Modood and Safia Mirza have pointed to racist attitudes among schools and teachers. Cecile Wright (1992) found that although teaching staff opposed racist views, they often had stereotypical attitudes which saw some children as problematic. She said that Asian girls tended to be seen as submissive and so were overlooked, whilst Black Caribbean boys were seen as of low academic potential which resulted in poor behaviour from the boys. Childline reported that in 2013, there were 1,400 children reporting incidents of racist bullying in schools, and evidence that young Muslims are being called offensive names linked to terrorism and Islamophobia. This is an increase from 802 in the previous year, though it is difficult to tell whether there is more bullying or more open reporting of issues. Childline claimed that teachers were unable to help pupils. Stuart Hall suggested that racism in schools led to a rejection of schooling by Black Caribbean boys which he called a culture of resistance.

Ethnocentric curriculum

Ethnocentricity is the view that one's own culture is central to an understanding of the world. Sociologists have claimed that the National Curriculum is ethnocentric and overlooks the contribution of non-white groups to British history. When Black people are considered, it is often in the context of negative stereotypes such as slavery so the contributions of non-white British people are frequently overlooked. This results in damage to the self-esteem of non-white pupils.

Single parenthood and the New Right

African Caribbean communities tend to have relatively high levels of lone parenthood. Lone parenthood can mean that families face financial challenge, which is a known factor in low school attainment. The New Right have been very critical of single motherhood and see it as contributing to huge social problems among the poor in our society. Conversely, Wright and others have pointed out that single mothers can be

Check your own learning

True or false?

a) All members of ethnic minorities achieve less well than white children in British schools.

b) Among the lowest attaining groups in British education are white Traveller (Gypsy) and Roma children.

c) The sole cause of underachievement among ethnic minority groups is racism.

d) Poverty is an issue affecting the school attainment of many ethnic minorities.

e) Among all ethnic groups, girls attain better grades on average than boys.

f) Many people believe that the English and Welsh education systems are ethnocentric and do not pay enough attention to other cultures.

positive role models for young women who perform better in education knowing that they may raise a family on their own. This may account for the relatively high rates of achievement among Black Caribbean girls compared to Black Caribbean boys.

Sample questions

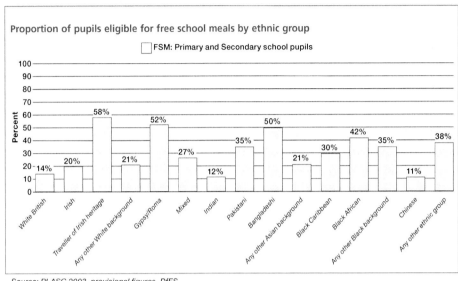

Proportion of pupils eligible for free school meals by ethnic group

☐ FSM: Primary and Secondary school pupils

White British 14%, Irish 20%, Traveller of Irish heritage 58%, Any other White background 21%, Gypsy/Roma 52%, Mixed 27%, Indian 12%, Pakistani 35%, Bangladeshi 50%, Any other Asian background 21%, Black Caribbean 30%, Black African 42%, Any other Black background 35%, Chinese 11%, Any other ethnic group 38%

Source: PLASC 2003, provisional figures, DfES

a) Summarise the content of the item showing the link between free school meals and ethnicity.

b) Explain **two** sociological reasons for the relationship between ethnicity and educational attainment in England and Wales.

Extended writing

Assess the relationship between ethnicity and attainment in education.

Guidance: You will need to describe the patterns and the trends of ethnic attainment, looking at over and under-attainment equally. Refer to recent legislation, for example the Equality Acts and school equality policies. Look at the various theories and suggestions for ethnicity inequality and assess them by referring to how well they explain the current patterns. Whilst racism of various kinds may well be a contributory factor in school under-attainment, cultural misunderstanding and poverty are also significant parts of the picture. Cultural attitudes may well be very significant as well.

Write about 500-750 words.

Tip

The important issue about ethnicity and attainment is that many groups over-achieve compared to like groups of white working-class pupils. Essays that focus on ethnic under-attainment are likely to only answer half the question.

Activity

What explanations for the differential attainment of different ethnic groups do you find most satisfactory? Give a strength and a weakness of each one.

INTERESTING FACT

Government figures in 2008 showed that only 15% of white working-class boys in England got five good GCSEs including Maths and English. This compared with white boys from more affluent homes, of whom 45% achieved that level of qualification. Poorer pupils from Indian and Chinese backgrounds achieved higher results than white middle-class boys with 36% and 52% gaining 5 A*–C grades.

- To look at how home circumstances may affect the educational attainment of poorer children

Over the past 40 years or so, Britain has become an increasingly divided society in terms of the distribution of wealth. Traditional working-class male work such as mining or manufacturing has declined and unemployment and deprivation are typical of parts of the UK which were formerly industrialised. Work has generally become low paid, casual and linked to service sector work in supermarkets, for example. Even this work is less easy to obtain as mechanisation takes over working roles. There are many people who rely on benefits, which have been deliberately kept low, but many of the poor are those who work for low wages because they have few qualifications or because better paid work is not available. Their children are those who are least likely to benefit from education.

Note that many children may be vulnerable to multiple risk factors, such as membership of an ethnic minority and lone parenthood.

Topic 7: Material factors and deprivation as a cause of under-attainment

Getting you thinking

Renée works as a mental health support worker. Her hourly pay is just above the minimum wage so she takes as much overtime and night shift work as she can to increase her earnings. The family struggle to get by. The family haven't been on a day out for three years due to lack of time and money. Renée owes money on rent and other bills. Renée's long working hours mean that she has very high childcare costs. Renée spends £115.80 a week to keep her three-year-old daughter, Zennisha, in nursery, and pays £32.50 a week in after-school care for her 8-year-old son, Tyrone.

Source http://www.poverty.ac.uk/living-poverty/personal-experiences/renee-low-paid-worker

Look at the item, what effects might Renee's family life have on her children's ability to do their best in school?

Leonard Feinstein, material poverty and deprivation

In 2003, Feinstein analysed data from the 1970 Birth Cohort Study. He found test scores at 22 months predicted educational attainment at 26 years and were related to family backgrounds. Children from poor backgrounds who achieved well at 22 months were often overtaken by the poor attainers from wealthy backgrounds.

Which children are likely to experience material deprivation?

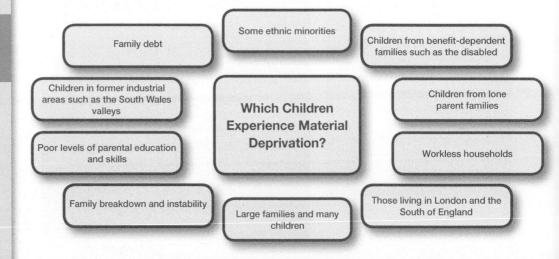

Poverty and policy

Government data shows that there is a clear link between childhood poverty and adult poverty. People find it difficult to escape from the effects of poverty in their childhood home lives. The link between educational qualifications and high earning potential is unarguable. Whilst some people undoubtedly do well despite lack of formal education, this is very rare. The largest single predictor of adult poverty is the educational qualification level of the father. The ONS suggest that children have a 7.5 higher chance of poor educational attainment if their fathers also did badly in school. For most people, the best route out of poverty is through education and so governments have seen the issue of tackling child poverty and improving education as being priorities for the country.

Environmental factors contributing to low educational attainment

The New Right would argue that the key issue affecting low school attainment is lone parenting, but other sociological perspectives would tend to claim that the issue is linked to poverty and material deprivation based on the evidence of a range of studies.

- ◉ Parental qualifications may impact on children in a number of ways. These could include limiting children's ambitions and encouraging them to leave school early or to resent school discipline. Homes may lack books and reading matter.
- ◉ Housing stock in many cities is poor and children experience poor health as a result. Scottish government data in 2010 found that over-crowding and homelessness affect health and social behaviours. The link is a complex one, because areas of poor housing often have high crime, poor transport, few public play areas and a general lack of resources such as youth centres or health centres.
- ◉ In addition, poor health behaviours such as smoking in front of children or lack of exercise may be typical of poorer parents.
- ◉ Poor nutrition may also contribute to lack of attainment in school. There is a link between obesity and poverty, for example, and this suggests poor nutritional practice and bad diet. The Avon Longitudinal Study (2011) found that there was a link between a diet high in fat and reduced intelligence in children.
- ◉ In the UK, there is also a known relationship between the number of people living in a household, the economic position of the parents and the financial situation of the family. Lone parents tend to be poor as much housing is expensive and easier to maintain in dual income families. Thus government statistics suggest that for the children of lone parents, there is a one and a half times higher chance of low attainment than for children of dual income families.
- ◉ Recent research into child poverty and education by Goodman and Gregg for the Joseph Rowntree Foundation suggested that poorer families tend to have weak learning environments so that there is little reading matter and few computers available for children because these are expensive items and viewed as luxuries.
- ◉ There is evidence that the poor are vulnerable to bullying from their peers because of the poor quality of their clothing or lack of fashion items. Louise Archer (2007) pointed out the significance of clothing and style in the culture of young people. Failure to attain style

> Children who grow up in poverty all too often become the parents of the next generation to live in poverty. Where a child starts in life should not determine where they end up.
>
> *Government Report – Measuring Child Poverty 2012*

Activity

With a study partner make a list of different problems that you might experience through your school life, examples such as having difficulty in a subject or joining in activities. How would having a good income help you to solve your problems?

What do parents need to spend to ensure children have what they need to do well? List the items you can think of.

left young people without status, so often the poor worked long hours in order to purchase consumer goods. However, street style set up the poor in confrontation with schools who demanded middle-class standards and styles of dress.

Research methods

What ethical and practical problems would you have in researching reasons why poverty might affect the education of children?

Activity

Scotland, central London and the north of England and Wales have significantly higher rates of poverty than other areas of Britain. Research 'child poverty statistics' and your geographical area to find out the extent of deprivation in the various countries of modern Britain.

Discussion point

- Material deprivation refers to those whose living conditions are affected by not being able to afford certain items. These might include being able to pay rent or mortgage, bills and loan repayments or to keep their home adequately warm. Are there other things families require? How would you define material deprivation? What particular and special needs do families with school-age children have?

Sample questions

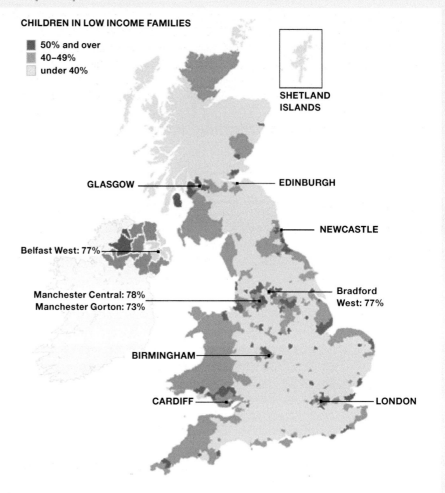

CHILDREN IN LOW INCOME FAMILIES

- 50% and over
- 40–49%
- under 40%

SHETLAND ISLANDS

GLASGOW — EDINBURGH

NEWCASTLE

Belfast West: 77%

Manchester Central: 78%
Manchester Gorton: 73%

Bradford West: 77%

BIRMINGHAM

CARDIFF — LONDON

a) Summarise the information on the map showing the link between where children live and poverty.
b) Explain **two** sociological reasons for the relationship between material deprivation and low educational attainment in the UK.

Source: http://news.bbc.co.uk/1/hi/uk/7642689.stm

Check your own learning
True or false?

a) According to government statistics, in 2013, one in six UK children lived in poverty.
b) The government estimates that any family with an income over £250 a week is not experiencing poverty.
c) The Conservative government and the New Right believe the solution to poverty is to increase benefits to the poor.
d) The head of Gingerbread, a single parent charity, suggested that one in three children with a single parent in part-time work was experiencing poverty.
e) Leonard Feinstein suggested that children's educational attainment at 26 years could be predicted by family background at 22 months.
f) Research suggests that many poorer children experience obesity problems as they live on cheap but inadequate diets.

Extended writing

Assess the relationship between material deprivation and attainment in education.

Guidance: The issue is more complex than simply one of poorer children being unable to afford key necessities for school. There are issues of self-esteem, ill health, bullying and poor learning environments that affect the attainment of the poor. This topic is very difficult to disentangle from cultural deprivation, so in order to fully evaluate material deprivation as an explanation of school failure, you will need to ensure that you understand both material and cultural explanations of school under-attainment. You can also link this material to issues of class under-attainment, because clearly poverty and class are linked.

Write about 500-750 words.

Tip

If the question refers to material deprivation, then avoid the temptation to write about cultural deprivation. You will not be answering the question.

Policy and material deprivation

Historically, various governments have tried to tackle issues of material deprivation and its impact on the educational attainment of the poor. Some of the best known are listed below and might be worth researching. Policies that you could refer to in answers include the following:

- Sure Start
- Learning mentor schemes
- Specialist schools
- Operation Headstart
- Raising of the school leaving age
- Education Maintenance Allowances
- Maintenance/fees/loans and grants for higher education
- Lotteries to allocate pupils to secondary schools
- Vocational education.

To attain the highest grades, you might want to assess their effectiveness.

Why would material poverty leave children vulnerable to bullying in schools?

Aims

- To consider whether cultural factors are a cause of differential attainment between children

Most people would find it easy to recognise that there are cultural differences between ethnic groups in Britain, but there are also some cultural differences between people from different social classes. Although advertising and marketing target different products, it is politically and socially sensitive to discuss class cultural differences. It is easy to slide from identifying differences between classes to suggesting that the culture of one class is superior or inferior to others. There have been a number of theoretical approaches which suggest that the success of the wealthy and the relative failure of the poor are due in part to cultural differences and attitudes among the poor which pre-dispose them to failure.

Key terms

Cultural deprivation – working-class culture is seen as inferior to middle-class culture.

Cultural difference – schools are middle class and do not understand the cultural differences between themselves and working-class pupils.

Cultural capital – working-class culture is not valued and the middle class have access to knowledge of social systems and structures that give them advantages.

Topic 8: Cultural differences as a cause of under-attainment

Getting you thinking

A night at the opera or eyes down for bingo? Does everyone in Britain have a similar lifestyle or are there cultural differences? Consider issues such as norms, values, clothing habits and ways of thinking.

How advertisers see us

Social grade	Social status	Occupation
A	Upper middle class	Higher managerial, administrative or professional
B	Middle class	Intermediate managerial, administrative or professional
C1	Lower middle class	Supervisory or clerical, junior managerial, administrative or professional
C2	Skilled working class	Skilled manual workers
D	Working class	Semi and unskilled manual workers
E	Those at lowest level of subsistence	State pensioners or widows (no other earner), casual or lowest grade workers

Working class underachievement and aspirations

In 2014, the Association of School and College Leaders presented evidence to Parliament that working-class underachievement was linked to social factors. They suggested that young people spend more time outside school than in school and so social factors outside school can significantly influence school attainment. These factors include aspirations (or ambitions), cultural knowledge, quality of parenting and time spent doing homework. The Joseph Rowntree Foundation, a poverty charity, said that the issue was not aspiration but knowledge of the routes through education and employment to achieve ambitions. It is this that is more likely to be missing in low-income families.

Whilst sociologists from most perspectives agree that there are cultural differences between the rich and the poor, the nature and impact of those cultural differences is a matter for debate.

- Functionalist views tend to suggest the poor fail for reasons to do with their own cultural values and lack of ambition. It is suggested that in some ways, working-class children are culturally deprived.
- Marxists claim that the cultural issue is one of power and influence: the culture required for educational success is middle-class culture. Working-class culture is not deprived, but different and not as highly valued.
- Interactionists tend to suggest that teachers favour those pupils who resemble the teachers in terms of culture and class.

Working-class culture and education

There is an argument that the culture of the working class is a major contributory factor to underachievement through two main issues:

1: Inappropriate norms and values.
2: Linguistic deprivation.

Norms and values

It has been suggested that working-class culture does not support the development of children's education. For example, working-class homes tend to have fewer books and parents spend less time reading with their children; as a result, by the time children start school there is already a gap between middle-class and working-class children in terms of their readiness to benefit from education. Much of this type of thinking is based on the work of Oscar Lewis. His studies of very poor people in Mexico in the 1940s and 1950s identified what he called a 'culture of poverty'. He concluded that they had a fatalistic approach to life: what happens is seen as outside their control. This view develops as a way of coping with poverty, but it helps keep them in poverty. This culture of poverty focusses on the present rather than planning for the future and they do not take control of their own lives. By the age of six or seven, children have absorbed the social values of their families and are on a path to repeat the lives of their parents.

This idea was very powerful in American sociology and influenced functionalist accounts of poverty. It remains a controversial issue because it was reinterpreted to mean that:

- The poor were seen as responsible for their own failures, known as 'blaming the victim'.
- Parents were seen as offering poor socialisation to their children.
- Policymakers could argue that interventions to help the poor, such as education, were of no value.
- It influenced the thinking of New Right policymakers who claimed that the culture of the urban poor created crime and social problems.

Current government thinking in Britain still offers suggestions that working-class failure is due to working-class parental inability to support their children. In 2011, the Children's Minister, Sarah Teather, announced free parenting classes in areas of high to medium levels of deprivation. Among other things, parents would be taught to provide stimulating learning environments, to eat meals as a family, and to insist on proper bedtimes and consistent discipline.

Linguistic deprivation

Some writers such as Basil Bernstein, have suggested that there are different ways of using language. Restricted code is a type of spoken shorthand, using short sentences and a limited vocabulary; meaning is implicit, relying on the context. Elaborated code is more explicit and less dependent on the context; a wider vocabulary is used. Restricted code is used within families or groups of friends who share an understanding of the context. Elaborated code is a more formal way of using language.

According to Bernstein, working-class families and their children rely on the restricted code, unlike the middle class who can make use of the elaborated code when that

The influence of parents, places and poverty on educational attitudes and aspirations

Tip

Be careful to distinguish explanations based on 'cultural deprivation' (which tend to blame working-class underachievement on working-class culture) from those based on 'cultural differences' (which look to inequality in society and in schools as the issue).

Use ideas about culture from throughout your previous learning to develop your understanding of this topic.

Is eating family meals really likely to solve the problems of inequality in British education?

Culture and policy

The idea that the culture of the working class contributes to educational failure has prompted a number of policy initiatives to 'correct' the problem such as:

⊙ New Labour's 1997 target of encouraging working-class participation in universities through setting a 50% participation rate for all young people.

⊙ The targeting of Able and Talented pupils in all classes.

⊙ Policy documents relating to raising the aspirations of children.

Research methods

Are middle- and working-class cultures actually very different? How could you set out to find evidence to test the theory that middle-class parents are 'better' than working-class parents?

is required. Bernstein suggested that working-class children could not access the information in schools because teachers use an elaborated code. Schooling demands the elaborated code much of the time. It is also suggested that the restricted code limits cognitive development; the restricted vocabulary that is used does not allow for the exploration and expression of abstract ideas.

Other versions of this theory have developed, some based on language use by some ethnic minorities. They share the basic point that the quality of thinking of which a person is capable is influenced by the language they habitually use. The evidence for this theorising that Bernstien offered has been heavily criticised. For example, Labov studied language patterns among Black Americans and said that language does not limit thought. The implication that the working class are somehow to blame for their own 'failure' because they do not use complex language makes this an interesting contribution to the cultural debate.

Cultural difference theory

This remains a very sensitive area of study and debate despite ethnographic studies which do suggest that some groups do have a culture which does not support educational achievement. Willis, for example, in the 1970s suggested that working-class boys were not interested in education.

In reaction to the functionalist view that working-class culture is inferior, many Marxists and others denied that the culture of the working class causes failure. Keddie, for example, claimed that working-class culture is not inferior, but different; the response to the culture by teachers is the problem. Others, including Rose, 1999; Gerwitz, 2001; Francis and Hey, 2009; Reay, 2009; and Bauman, 2005 have pointed out that by looking at cultural failings in the working class, the government can safely ignore issues of funding, social deprivation and material deprivation. Interactionists suggest that the focus on cultural deprivation also directs attention away from school processes that contribute to working-class failure.

Cultural capital

Some types of knowledge are regarded as more useful or important than others. Within the education system, governments, teachers and examiners decide what knowledge is worth having and this forms the basis of the curriculum.

Marxists see this control of knowledge as a form of social control and is linked to social inequality. Those who have the approved knowledge gain qualifications that lead to higher rewards and more power than those who do not. Developing this thought, Pierre Bourdieu pointed out that some children enter education already having access to the approved knowledge: middle-class families possess 'cultural capital' which helps ensure the success of middle-class children. They know how the system works; they have already succeeded in it.

This theorising was supported by Gillies (2005) who found parents with high levels of qualifications are able to use their knowledge and influence to benefit their children. They focussed on teaching social skills and used their professional knowledge to prepare their children for the demands of schools and teachers. In contrast, Gillies found working-class parents were more likely to offer strategies to cope with disadvantage and bullying.

... there is a lot of evidence that working-class families have high aspirations. What they do not have is the information and the understanding as to how you might mobilise that aspiration effectively for outcomes for your children. Money makes a big difference here [...] but also understanding the rules of the game

Prof. Becky Francis

Research idea

Look at the lyrics of the 1995 hit song Common People by Pulp which describes 'class tourism'. You can see the video on YouTube. What differences between the culture of the rich and poor are described? Can the girl in the song ever understand the culture of the poor? Why not?

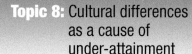

Culture of masculinity and laddishness

A further development of cultural theory is applied to gender rather than to social class. Many commentators have argued that males and females experience different cultural pressures and that boys are the victims of cultural pressure to fail. Typical cultural suggestions include:

- Mitsos and Browne who suggested that boys are less inclined to be conscientious in schools.
- Mac an Ghaill who said that masculinity is no longer clear for boys, as girls have challenged their assumption that to be male is to be superior. In addition, changes in the workplace mean that boys no longer know what it is to be a man, and so experience a **crisis of masculinity**. This involves a rejection of what can be seen as femininity, such as success in school.
- Ruddock found that boys tended to have a different approach to examinations, preferring not to be seen to work. Thus examination revision is left to the last minute, a recipe for disaster for many children.
- Recent work by Carolyn Jackson refers to **laddishness** and the tendency of boys to be more disruptive in class. They feel pressured by examinations and respond by becoming part of a macho culture that undervalues education.

> *The poverty of aspiration is as damaging as the poverty of opportunity and it is time to replace a culture of low expectations for too many with a culture of high standards for all.*
>
> **Gordon Brown (then Prime Minister 2007)**

Sample questions

In 2013 a leading teaching union, the NASUWT, surveyed more than 13,000 teachers. The findings suggested that children were lacking in discipline and that parents were part of the problem: 85% reported they experienced verbal abuse by a pupil in the last year. More than a third had been abused or insulted by parents; 69% of teachers agreed that there is a 'widespread problem' of poor behaviour in schools. The respondents believed that 'lack of parental support, pupils not coming to school ready to learn and the **low aspirations** of families and students' were the biggest causes of indiscipline. Low-level disruption was seen as the main form of bad behaviour, with teachers complaining of chatter in class, failure to complete work and the inability of pupils to follow basic rules.

Source: adapted from NASUWT website: http://www.nasuwt.org.uk/Whatsnew/ NASUWTNews/PressReleases/WidespreadConcernOverPupilBehaviour

a) With reference to the item and sociological knowledge, explain the meaning of the term **low aspirations**.

b) Explain **two** sociological reasons for the relationship between culture and low educational attainment in the UK.

Extended writing

Assess the relationship between culture and attainment in education.

Guidance: There is a link between culture and attainment in education; for example, in your study of the link between ethnicity and education, you will have met the concept of the Chinese tiger mother who has very high expectations of her children. This attitude is believed to contribute to the relatively high achievement of Chinese students in schools. You will also have considered New Right theories of lone parenthood causing educational failure. The debate is made more complex by the suggestion that working-class failure is caused by working-class culture; despite the support of government for this theorising. The issue under discussion therefore is the importance of the link, not whether a link exists or not. **Write about 500-750 words.**

Check your own learning
Match the terms to their meaning.

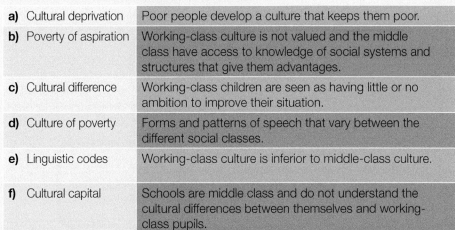

a)	Cultural deprivation	Poor people develop a culture that keeps them poor.
b)	Poverty of aspiration	Working-class culture is not valued and the middle class have access to knowledge of social systems and structures that give them advantages.
c)	Cultural difference	Working-class children are seen as having little or no ambition to improve their situation.
d)	Culture of poverty	Forms and patterns of speech that vary between the different social classes.
e)	Linguistic codes	Working-class culture is inferior to middle-class culture.
f)	Cultural capital	Schools are middle class and do not understand the cultural differences between themselves and working-class pupils.

Aims

◉ **To consider the impact of schools themselves on the educational performance of children**

In England and Wales, children spend over 15,000 hours of their life at school and it is reasonable to assume that this has a significant impact on the educational attainment of children. What is taught, to which pupils and the relationships within schools have all been identified as important. Interactionists have looked at the relationships between pupils and teachers and identified social processes that can affect the self-identity of pupils and their subsequent performance in schools. Other interactionists have looked at how schools are organised and the effect of selection, setting and streaming on pupils. More recent sociological research has tried to identify the characteristics of successful schools, partly because government funding is available for this kind of study. The main thrust of this research has been to look at what makes a successful school in order to develop a model that 'failing' schools can imitate.

The process of teacher labelling of children.

Topic 9: Factors within schools that impact on success

Getting you thinking

PISA (Programme for International Student Assessment) is an international study of education systems and uses standardised tests to measure the performance of students across the world. In 2012, the PISA report found that the better performing education systems were those that discouraged social selection, paid teachers well, allocated resources equally across all social classes and groups and had well-equipped schools. Good discipline is an important part of school success. The PISA research is carried out for the Organisation for Economic Co-operation and Development (OECD), an international body which aims to foster economic growth and reduce poverty.

To read the reports for yourself, Google OECD and PISA.

Use the findings of the PISA study of global education systems to suggest changes that could be made to improve the school systems of the UK.

What factors might affect both the reliability and the validity of the findings of the PISA study?

Labelling theory and the self-fulfilling prophecy

Labelling theorists describe a social process that involves a person being given a label by others; this label then affects interaction and behaviour, with the label becoming part of an individual's identity. A number of studies in the 1970s described the way that teachers form an impression of a pupil and then perceive the behaviour and ability of that child in the light of the label. Hargreaves et al. (1975) described this process as consisting of three stages. Hargreaves went on to suggest that teachers may be subject to the Halo effect, so behaviours from pupils labelled as 'good' will be accepted. Similar behaviours from 'challenging' pupils will attract punishments.

| Speculation – forms initial impression | Elaboration – tests the impression | Stabilisation – acts according to the beliefs about the pupil |

According to Hargreaves and other sociologists, those labelled as failing or naughty tend to form friendship groups with similar students; they form groups with a **counter-school culture**. In these subcultures status is gained by challenging teachers and not conforming to their expectations.

One important element of the process is identifying pupils as clever and likely to do well, or as less able and unlikely to succeed. A widely discussed study by Rosenthal and Jacobson (1968) suggested that teachers could affect pupil attainment, in some way favouring those they thought of as intelligent who would then go on to succeed. This study has been widely criticised, in part because it was based on an experiment that could not be repeated on ethical grounds. However, it was influential, suggesting that teachers could have a powerful influence on educational outcomes.

Concern about the effects of labelling contributed to the campaign to end selection at the age of 11, and to introduce mixed ability teaching. School inspectors OFSTED (in England) and Estyn (in Wales) have said that teachers should have high expectations of all pupils, regardless of their background.

There is evidence to support labelling theory:

- In the 1970s studies by Becker (1971) and Rist (1970) found teachers making educational judgements on the basis of social class and appearance and favoured middle-class children.
- Careers teachers gave different advice to working- and middle-class pupils, according to Cicourel and Kitsuse (1971).
- Pupil behaviour was a factor in placing children into ability streams in the comprehensive school studied by Ball (1981).
- Ethnicity also seems to affect judgements: Wright (1987) found teachers viewed Black Caribbean students negatively.
- More recent research by Boaler in Britain and the USA has found students taught in mixed-ability classes outperform those taught in streamed classes.

Boaler J (2002) Experiencing School Mathematics
http://www.theguardian.com/education/2011/aug/08/streaming-pupils-limits-aspirations

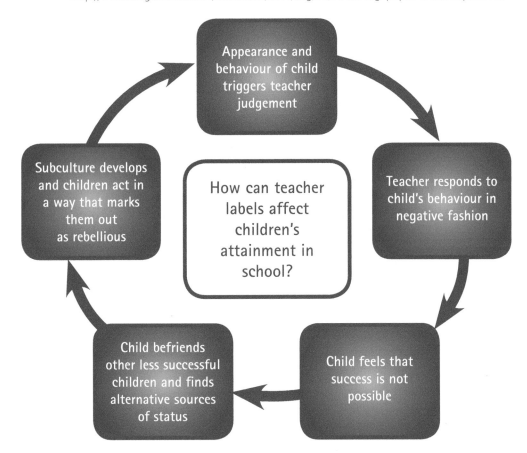

Appearance and behaviour of child triggers teacher judgement

Teacher responds to child's behaviour in negative fashion

Child feels that success is not possible

Child befriends other less successful children and finds alternative sources of status

Subculture develops and children act in a way that marks them out as rebellious

How can teacher labels affect children's attainment in school?

The 11-plus examination effectively labelled pupils: those successful in the 11-plus went on to grammar schools, those who went to secondary modern schools were seen as '11-plus failures'.

INTERESTING FACT

Exclusions from school: in 2012 the Children's Commissioner for England was concerned that some groups of pupils were over-represented in school exclusions. Pupils of Black Caribbean origin were almost three times more likely to be excluded than the rest of the school population. Pupils on free school meals were nearly four times more likely to be permanently excluded and three times more likely to get a fixed-term exclusion. Boys were about three times more likely to be excluded than girls and were more likely to be excluded at a younger age.

Tip

Labelling theory can be used to explain class, gender and ethnic attainment patterns in schools and is therefore a very useful theory to use in essay writing. Remember that it should be used critically because although it is appealing, it does not answer all our questions about why children succeed or fail in education.

Developing understanding

A YouGov opinion poll in November 2014 found that 54% of respondents favoured the opening of more grammar schools, based on selection at 11.

If the question had been 'Would you like to see more secondary modern schools?', do you think the result would have been the same?

Sociologists such as Ball, Keddie, Lacey and Hargreaves have said that the practice of selection can be unfair, with the working classes and ethnic minorities being more likely to be allocated to lower sets where they are offered less challenging work and are entered for fewer examinations. This process also helps the development of anti-school cultures. It seems that labelling theory can be applied to whole groups of students as well as individuals.

Criticisms of labelling theory

Many find labelling theory convincing as it seems to relate to their experiences of schools; however, there are some problems with it:

- Many of the studies are based on small-scale observational studies and so the evidence is not reliable and may not be generalisable.
- The theory does not explain why the labels develop in the first place; it may be that teachers are acting on years of experience to recognise difficult pupils.
- The theory is deterministic, implying that once labelled, children will act according to their labels. There is evidence that many children, especially ethnic minority girls, actively reject teachers' labels and decide to prove them wrong. Fuller and also Safia Mirza found evidence of resistance to teacher labels.
- By blaming teachers for children's poor performance, it ignores the fact that children are also active in making choices to work or not work.
- Marxists point out that it overlooks the importance of social structures such as class, racism and sexism in creating school inequalities.

Institutional racism in schools

Labelling takes place when teachers individually respond to individual pupils and spark a process whereby anti-school cultures develop. However, there is also evidence of institutional racism in schools, despite equality policies. Institutional racism is when the school as an institution acts in a way that disadvantages some groups of people. For example, the National Curriculum is seen as ethnocentric, because it reflects the experiences of the white majority and is accused of presenting non-white people in a negative way. Gillborn and Youdell found that Black minorities are more often found in lower sets in schools. The Swann report found systems in schools disadvantage some ethnic minorities. Exclusion rates are significantly higher for Black Caribbean children.

Schools and gender

As discussed in the section on gender and attainment, schools and teachers often have different expectations about girls and boys. They may be expected to behave in different ways and to take different subjects. These stereotypical ideas can form part of the labelling process, which reinforce the attitudes found in wider society. One effect of this labelling is on career aspirations; a report by OFSTED in 2011 found that, although girls were aware of the equality agenda, most schools were not doing enough to encourage girls and young women to challenge vocational stereotypes.

(OFSTED 2011 Girls' career aspirations)

Setting and selection debates

In the 1950s, children were selected by the education system for different types of secondary education. The comprehensive system of the 1970s was intended to put an end to selection; however, within schools many children were placed in bands, streams and sets. This meant that they would be placed in groups with children judged to be of similar ability and taught different topics and in a different way. Opinions among teachers and parents on this practice are divided. Many are strongly in favour, especially those parents whose children will probably be in the top sets. Some schools with a specialism, such as music, are allowed to select 10% of their pupils. If the labelling theory is accurate then the benefits for those in top sets are obvious in terms of educational opportunity and self-esteem development.

School improvement research

In the short term, governments can do little about the material and cultural issues that may contribute to school failure. However, they can influence what happens in schools, and recent policy has had the aim of making more schools effective. Politicians have drawn on recent sociology of education research which has helped identify the characteristics of successful schools. As more data is collected on school performance and individual pupil targets as a result of the changes in educational practice since the 1980s, it can be seen that schools which have broadly similar intakes of pupils often have rather different examination result patterns. The conclusion is that some schools underperform and that they need to reform themselves, and become better at encouraging disadvantaged children to do better.

The effect of school organisation on pupil attainment was the focus of much research in the 1990s. Poor organisational structure and low teacher expectation were identified by Stoll and Fink (1998) as characteristics of sink schools. It is noticeable that these schools are generally found in areas of poverty and deprivation. Many of these sink schools have since been turned into academy schools as part of government policy to remove schools from local authority control.

Some critics have said that the reforms have led to unequal provision and a fragmented education system. There is also a debate about how much actual difference schools can make when the social problems of some of their pupils, such as poverty, are so desperate.

Is it possible that sociologists have over-emphasised the role of the teacher in pupil performance and that pupils make active choices whether to try and do well or not?

Developing understanding

What makes a good teacher?

Barber (1996) constructed a list of characteristics of a good teacher, including: strictness, fairness, enthusiasm, sense of humour, and careful marking of work. Teachers with these traits appear to gain better results for pupils. This type of work has affected teacher training and it is claimed that recent teachers are better trained than older ones. However, given these characteristics are personal rather than trained, it is arguable how effectively young teachers can be trained to take a joke.

Activity

List the basic characteristics of a school that is good for all pupils equally. What is the ethos? How do children and teachers treat each other? How are visitors received?

INTERESTING FACT

Rossi and Springfield (1995) identified ten characteristics of a good school including:

- Shared vision
- Shared sense of purpose
- Shared values
- Acceptance of diversity
- Good communication
- Participation
- Care
- Trust
- Teamwork
- Respect and recognition.

How reliably measurable are these characteristics?

Research issues

How would you design a quantitative study to research whether teacher labels affect school performance? What practical and ethical issues might you experience with your work?

INTERESTING FACT

The UKIP political party said in 2014 that they would re-introduce grammar schools to the UK. The Green Party are opposed to them.

Sample questions

2013 PISA reading scores for selected education systems

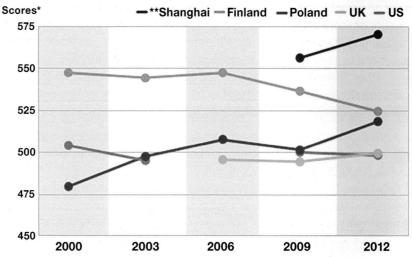

*Data not available for every year

**China does not participate as a country, but is represented by cities such as Shanghai and Hong Kong

Source: OECD

In 2013, OECD PISA tests showed that the UK failed to make any progress in catching up global rivals in school tests taken by teenagers in maths, reading and science – and is no longer in the top 20 for any subject. The results of the OECD's PISA tests are particularly poor for Wales, which trails behind the rest of the UK. Wales has fallen below average in tests taken by 500,000 pupils. In science, the UK has slipped downwards, from 16th to 21st place, in a downward trend for results in the subject. The UK remains stuck among the average, middle-ranking countries, in 26th place for maths and 23rd for reading, broadly similar to three years ago. Wales is the worst performing country in the UK. In maths, Wales fell three places to 43rd of the 65 countries. In reading, the nation is now ranked at 41 down from 38 but the biggest fall came in science where Wales dropped six places to joint 36th.

Source: adapted from BBC website
http://www.bbc.co.uk/news/education-25187998

a) Summarise the item on the findings of the PISA tests for UK.
b) Explain **two** sociological reasons for the relationship between schools and educational attainment in the UK.

Check your own learning

Which researcher or research team made the following findings?

a) The United Kingdom is behind many developed countries in terms of success at international tests.
b) Teachers prefer to teach pupils with middle-class social characteristics.
c) Careers teachers offer advice along social class lines.
d) Teachers view Black Caribbean students in a negative fashion.
e) Children are often placed in teaching groups on the basis of behaviour rather than ability.
f) Sink schools have poor organisational structure and low teaching expectations.

School inspection

Estyn, in Wales, and OFSTED, in England, are external agencies that have responsibility for reporting on schools and judging how effective they are. Although there are some differences in how they perform their role, they share important features. Both organisations base their approach on the assumption that schools and teachers can make a difference to how well children learn and that this has an impact on the opportunities available for pupils. Judgements about schools are based on a range of evidence including examination results (quantitative data) and observations of lessons (qualitative data). They also consider the quality and effectiveness of school leaders.

Extended writing

Assess the relationship between schools and attainment in education.

Guidance: The bulk of this essay should probably be about labelling theory, but you should be critical of the theory because it leaves a great deal about school attainment unexplained. To bring the work up to date, then research into what makes an effective school is essential. Link the discussion to ideas that you have already discussed when learning about class, gender and ethnicity. You can focus entirely on schools and address the issues, but to show depth of knowledge and high level evaluation, then reference to alternative theories can be made, but only in order to address the question directly.

Write about 500-750 words.

The relationship between society and school attainment: areas of debate

Social variables: gender, class, ethnicity

The nature of the school: academies, grammar, private

Cultural factors: language, aspirations, cultural capital

Processes that take place within schools themselves: labelling, quality of teaching

Material factors: poverty, deprivation

Research idea

Ask a teacher whom you trust if you can observe a lesson with a young school group. What evidence do you see of labelling? For ethical reasons, you must explain what you are doing and obtain the teacher's consent.

Activity

Find out more about the work of Estyn (www.estyn.gov.uk) or OFSTED (www.gov.uk/government/organisations/ofsted).

Activity

For recent research on schools and education, go to the website of the National Foundation for Education, www.nfer.ac.uk. Go to publications and browse.

The issue for you to decide is which of these factors is most significant in affecting children's attainment and to provide evidence and theoretical back-up for your point of view.

Aims

◉ **To assess functionalist theories of education**

An important theme in functionalist views of education is meritocracy, the theory that the main purpose of education is to allocate people to positions based on their ability and talent. Inequality in education is not a problem because if people compete, it helps ensure that the most talented will rise to the top. Society benefits as it means the most talented fill the most important positions. People who are at the top of the society deserve to be there, they are talented and have worked hard. Others fail either because they did not work hard enough or because they are not very talented. This theory is challenged on a number of grounds, but it has been influential in the past.

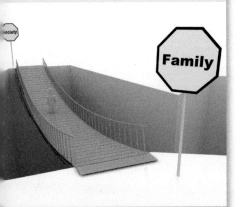

Functionalists see the education system as a bridge between the home and wider society.

Topic 10: Functionalism and meritocracy

Getting you thinking

Do you agree that the education system is a ladder of opportunity? Are there any barriers to success for some children?

Functionalism and education

Education is a form of socialisation

Role allocation is not the only function of the education system. Durkheim offered the view that education is essential to society because it helps build social cohesion. It links people to their culture; so, for example, the teaching of the Welsh language in Wales maintains a cultural tradition that gives people a sense of their identity. Ultimately, for Durkheim, the role of education was socialisation.

One criticism of this viewpoint is, as Stephen Gorard and others have pointed out, that modern schools are too concerned with individual examination results and competition to be concerned with social solidarity. The emphasis on league tables reflects an individualistic, competitive approach.

Education acts as a bridge between the home and society

Talcott Parsons believed that the education system acted as a bridge between a child's experience of life in a family and his or her experiences of the wider world. He claimed that families socialise us into their own familial values (**particularistic values**) and schools operate according to the values of the wider society (**universalistic values**). He did point out that these values can clash, so that parents may offer advice that goes against that of the school. One of the values taught in schools is that of 'achievement'; children achieve status in school through their hard work and talent. Children are thus encouraged to work hard.

One criticism of this view is the evidence that many children do not conform to the expectations of school. Recent research by Mac an Ghaill, Jackson, Connolly and Francis has suggested that anti-learning laddish attitudes are adopted by boys and girls as a reaction to the pressure of examinations. Social success in school is not always associated with academic success: the geek or nerd is a social stereotype that links academic talent with social ineptitude, it seems that you can either be clever or popular, but not both.

Sheldon Cooper from The Big Bang Theory: academic achiever, social oddball.

Education is meritocratic

Davis and Moore (1967) argued that the education system helps to allocate people to appropriate job and career roles. Because some jobs require more training and commitment, and have greater responsibilities, they are rewarded by high pay and good working conditions. The education system sifts and sorts children to take on those roles, by identifying the most talented people. Role allocation thus requires inequalities in educational outcome for children. Those with the best examination results and highest qualifications are able to enter the highest paid and most prestigious occupations.

However, the link between academic qualifications and earnings is not consistent. For example, girls gain better grades in schools than boys but by the age of thirty or so, they tend to be lower earners. Ability itself is not an easily measurable characteristic, and so proving a link between intelligence and earning levels is difficult. Further, as we have seen in earlier sections, it is far from clear that all children have the same chance of developing their talents.

> We need to believe in absolute mobility – the ability of every single person in this country, regardless of what anybody else is doing, to shape their own success through hard work and diligence.
>
> **Elizabeth Truss (Education and Healthcare Minister 2014)**

Thinking skills

Promoting fundamental British values through spiritual, moral, social and cultural development.

Schools should promote the fundamental British values of democracy, the rule of law, individual liberty, and mutual respect and tolerance of those with different faiths and beliefs.

Schools should:
- Enable students to distinguish right from wrong and to respect the civil and criminal law of England.
- Encourage students to accept responsibility for their behaviour, show initiative, and to understand how they can contribute positively to the lives of those living and working in the locality of the school and to society more widely.

(Extracts from Government guidance to schools in England, November 2014)

How would this guidance be explained by functionalists?

Thinking skills

Do you agree that the most important jobs in society are the best paid? How can the importance of jobs be measured?

241

Evaluating functionalism

There are two main areas of weakness in functionalist views of education and meritocracy.

- The first is that functionalism is too accepting of the inequalities that are apparent in the education system. It sets out to explain the need for inequality, accepting that there is such a need. It does not adequately explain why whole social groups involving large numbers of children from some ethnic minorities and the working class (and in recent years, boys) appear to underachieve. Functionalists appear to suggest that these children lack talent and/or a willingness to work hard.
- The other criticism concerns socialisation. If education exists to pass on norms and values, Marxists and feminists ask, whose norms and values are being passed on? Functionalists assume that there is a set of shared values to be transmitted. An increasingly diverse society contains many cultures and subcultures. Who decides what cultural values are to be transmitted? Marxists and feminists suggest that there is an ideological element in education, based on class or patriarchy.

Summary of the main functionalist viewpoints and the criticisms that can be made

Functions of education	Criticisms of the functionalist theory
It transmits culture to children through socialisation	Marxists say that it passes on ruling class values which make inequality acceptable
It bridges the gap between the values of home and school, and people gain status on their own efforts	Most of the powerful people in society come from wealthy and privileged backgrounds who had access to opportunities not available to most people
It provides a good and highly trained workforce	Most people 'learn on the job'. Schools teach obedience and not skills
Davis and Moore said education is meritocratic and sorts the most able for the best jobs	Given the power of middle-class white men in society, are we to assume that ethnic minorities, the poor and women lack talent?

Tip

You might be asked to assess or to evaluate functionalist views of education, or you may be asked to consider whether education in the UK is meritocratic. In either case, you will be following much the same grounds for discussion, so make sure that you understand the two ideas are linked.

Activity

Look for news stories about the notorious Bullingdon Club to which some of our senior politicians belonged whilst they were still at university.

Sample questions

Just a glance at today's political elite and it is clear the **meritocracy** is in trouble. Nobody can deny that our current crop of political leaders is bright. But the pipeline which produces them has become narrower and more privileged. Cameron (Prime Minister), Clegg (formerly Deputy Prime Minister) and Osborne (Chancellor of the Exchequer) all went to private schools with fees now higher than the average annual wage. Half the cabinet went to fee-paying schools – versus only 7% of the country – as did a third of all MPs. After falling steadily for decades, the number of public school MPs is on the rise once more, 20 of them from Eton alone – five more MPs than the previous Parliament.

a) With reference to the item and sociological knowledge, explain what is meant by **meritocracy**.
b) Explain **two** sociological reasons for the relationship between a wealthy and privileged background and a well-paid influential job.

Source: Adapted from bbc.co.uk/news/mobile/magazine-12282505 Jan 2011

Check your own learning

Identify the sociological perspectives linked to each of the following statements:

a) The education system is a ladder of opportunity for the talented and able.

b) All children have an equal chance to do well in the modern British educational system.

c) The education system reflects the class inequalities of wider society.

d) If the education system was purely meritocratic, women would earn more on average than men.

e) Education exists to sort the most talented for the best jobs.

f) People who are at the top of the society deserve to be there, others fail because they did not work hard enough.

Extended writing

Assess the view that the British education system is meritocratic.

Guidance: There are two plausible approaches to this question, both of them equally valid. The first is to look at this discussion from a purely theoretical level, talking about the functionalist view of education and then presenting opposing viewpoints showing the strengths and weaknesses of the view. The second variation is to present the functionalist point of view and then to show how various social groups are advantaged or disadvantaged in education. Remember that if you *do not* show knowledge of the British education system, you will not have addressed the question, so evidence of knowledge of the system is essential for the top mark bands.

Write about 500-750 words.

Research idea

Find out more about the 11+ examination which is used in some parts of the UK to select children for different types of education. Find out why many people are bitterly opposed to this examination system, while others are firmly in support.

STRETCH and CHALLENGE

Suggest reasons why so many powerful people in our society believe in meritocracy and the idea that you are where you are because of what you have done rather than because the structures and institutions have given you and your family life chances that are not available to other people.

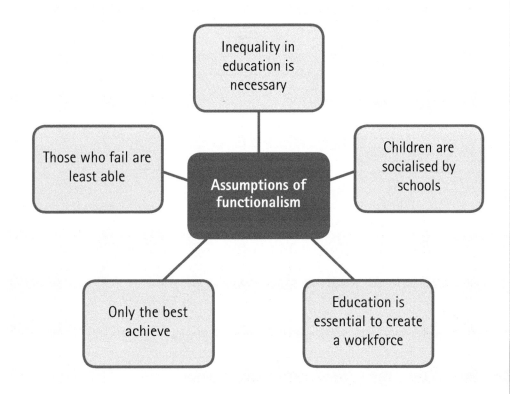

How far can you agree with these assumptions? Give reasons for your views?

Topic 11: Marxism and ideology

In addition to being a social theorist, Karl Marx was a revolutionary and a political theorist. He predicted that capitalism would be overthrown within his own lifetime or soon after his death, which occurred in 1883. Whilst revolutions occurred in many countries, they didn't occur in England or Germany which is where Marx suggested the first revolutions would appear. This has left writers in the Marxist tradition with a serious problem, which is to explain why the working classes continue to tolerate a social situation whereby they experience unequal access to power and wealth. One of their solutions has been to explain this in terms of **ideology** (beliefs) – the education system is part of a process whereby people are taught that inequality is not a problem and that they should accept capitalist ideas.

Tip

Many famous studies, such as Paul Willis's study are used uncritically by candidates in examinations. It was certainly a famous and influential study, because it used new methods and suggested interesting ideas, but if you refer to these famous studies, mention when they were written and perhaps offer criticisms of their findings to show evaluation skills.

Getting you thinking

Is it true that in your experience of education teachers oppress and bully children or prevent them from thinking for themselves? Be prepared to justify your point of view, but do not refer to individuals in public, for ethical reasons.

Marxism and education

Education is a form of social control

Marxism is a conflict theory. It assumes that different social class groupings in society are in competition for power and wealth. Marxists view education as a means of oppressing the working class. There are a variety of mechanisms described by Marxist writers to explain how this may actually happen within schools. Some see this in terms of passing of ideology and beliefs, whereas others look at social structures and processes. Whatever their approach, Marxists are generally hostile to formal school organisations and to teachers.

Correspondence theory

Bowles and Gintis see schools as a mirror to society, so just as society is a **hierarchy** with workers being oppressed by bosses, so schools oppress children and children learn the obedience that they need to be a docile workforce. Those children who succeed in school are those who are obedient and who accept authority.

This can be criticised, because their approach was theoretical. Bowles and Gintis see schools as a conspiracy against the working class, but in practical terms, schools as organisations are not going to find those who challenge authority make good students. This does not mean that they are deliberately oppressing the working class.

Counter-school cultures

Many theorists have pointed to the existence of counter-school culture as evidence of revolutionary potential among the working class who misbehave in school because they are resisting the values of capitalism promoted by schools. It is argued that only the working class form a counter-school culture, even though there is little evidence to support this.

One of the foremost writers in this tradition was Paul Willis, who studied twelve working-class boys in a secondary modern school in the 1970s. Whilst the study is often quoted, many writers have criticised Willis and the concept of the counter-school culture itself; these boys were seen as 'working-class heroes' because Willis was a Marxist, whereas in reality they displayed rampant sexism and racism and were very anti-social.

School as an agency of repression

Althusser, a French philosopher, argued that schools transmit capitalist ideology and that education is an ideological state apparatus which justifies capitalism. This is possibly an over-simplification of the position, given that schools do a great deal more than oppress children and brainwash them.

Money plays the largest part in determining the course of history.
Karl Marx

What messages are children given by being asked to wear formal school uniform? For example, why are girls expected to wear a white shirt and a tie?

Hidden curriculum

The hidden curriculum is not specifically a Marxist idea. Functionalists agree with Marxists that schools teach social ideas without a conscious knowledge that they do so. Marxists differ from functionalists as they see this process as negative and oppressive. Pupils have little control over their work; this reflects most adult work. Thus pupils are prepared for the boredom of adult life. Ivan Illich said that schools kill creativity and children learn to accept authority without challenging it, thus they accept what governments tell them in an unthinking fashion.

Formal curriculum and hidden curriculum

Formal intentional messages taught in schools

Hidden, unintended messages taught informally in schools

Activity

Create a table showing differences between Marxist and functionalist thinking using the following subheadings to help: Purpose of education, vocationalism, agency of socialisation, purpose of the curriculum, meritocracy, view of society.

Criticisms of this approach suggest that children may not be engaged in conscious rebellion against school rules, and that it implies that children cannot judge for themselves the worth of what they are told by teachers.

Cultural capital

Pierre Bourdieu was heavily influenced by Marxism and his claim was that capital was more than money, it extended to the kinds of knowledge that people have access to. He identified three types of cultural capital:

⊚ Embodied capital refers to class indicators such as accent, culture and manners.
⊚ Objectified capital refers to ownership and access to social markers such as knowledge of music, access to art and books.
⊚ Institutionalised capital is capital that signifies authority and power, for example a high-power job or educational qualifications.

Again, this is highly theoretical and unsupported by much direct research evidence based on quantitative methods.

Evaluating Marxism

The strengths of Marxist views of education:

⊚ It challenges the functionalist view that the education system is meritocratic, showing that some pupils have greater opportunities to succeed than others.
⊚ It provides an explanation of class differences in educational attainment.
⊚ It highlights the ideological role of formal education.

There are some areas of weakness of Marxism:

⊚ The first is that it overlooks structural inequality relating to ethnicity and gender.
⊚ It ignores the fact that for many children, education is a route to better standards of living than their parents enjoyed.
⊚ It sees teachers as agents of the middle class; this is a naive generalisation.
⊚ If education is designed to serve the needs of employers, why do employers so often complain about the lack of work-readiness in school leavers?

Sample questions

In 2003, a Scottish teenager called Freya MacDonald took her local education authority to court because she was given eleven detentions in seven months. She had broken school discipline by using a fire door to get into school, and drank fizzy drinks in lessons. Scottish law says that every child has a right to an education. However, Freya claimed that the detentions were affecting her right to learn and were a form of **social control**. In addition, she claimed that the school could not insist on keeping her in detention as a punishment after school because it is illegal to detain children without their permission. She claimed compensation for psychological distress.

a) With reference to the item and sociological knowledge, explain the meaning of the term **social control**.

b) Using the item and sociological knowledge, explain **two** ways in which schools control how pupils think and behave.

Check your own learning
Identify the term from the definition.

a) The kind of knowledge that people have access to.
b) The things that are taught in school unintentionally.
c) A belief system about how the world should be run.
d) An economic system that prizes profit above everything.
e) A group of children within a school who reject education.
f) Schools are a mirror to society.
g) Groups in society are in competition for wealth and power.

Extended writing

Evaluate Marxist theories of education.

Guidance: You can evaluate Marxism on its own terms, by looking at and criticising the various Marxist viewpoints that you will have studied, or you can evaluate Marxism by looking at other theories and comparing them to Marxism. One of the main points made by Marxists can also be used to evaluate functionalism, and that is the idea that schools legitimise social inequality. There is some evidence to support that view. However, the key point about Marxism is that it probably over-states the idea that teachers dominate and control children, given that most people enter the profession with the idea that they are offering help and support. Not all teachers are from middle-class backgrounds either and many self-identify with the working classes.

Write about 500-750 words.

Activity

Find out more about anti-school theorists Paulo Friere and Ivan Illich. Can you agree with their ideas?

Who will benefit more from the education system: the rich child or the poor one? Why?

Topic 12: Feminism and gender

Feminism did not become a mainstream perspective till the 1960s and 1970s when mostly female researchers began to point out that most research and academic thinking was **malestream**. They argued that the contribution of women to society had been overlooked and that most research was conducted from the point of view that to be male was normal. They claimed that differences between men and women were either wildly overstated, so women were seen as naturally less intelligent, or totally ignored so that their experiences were not seen as important or relevant. Feminists challenged traditional value-free methods of research, claiming that they were in fact biased against women, and developed modern methods that were fuelled by anger and intended to raise the consciousness of women in order to make them aware of their own oppression.

Most female work tends to be in the traditional areas of cooking, cleaning, child-care and check-outs.

Getting you thinking

In the 1850s and 1860s, middle-class girls were frustrated by the lack of opportunities available to them. A campaigning group known as the Langham Place group developed a form of Liberal feminism because they believed that good education was a means to change women's lives and give them the same opportunities as men. They faced hostility and ridicule. The first women's colleges at Oxford were founded in the 19th century, but women were not allowed to be full members of the University until the 1920s. It was not until 1974 that five previously all-male colleges accepted men and women on equal terms. It was only in 2008, when St Hilda's College, originally female only, accepted males that all colleges had equal access rights for both genders. In 2010, 15 male members of Hertford College, Oxford were suspended for compiling a list of 'fitties', women in the college that they graded by appearance.

Even if men and women have equal rights under the law, to what extent can it be argued that attitudes have changed and they do in fact have equal status?

Feminism and education

Lack of education is a form of social control

Much feminism drew its theoretical framework from Marxism, substituting gender for Marxist analyses of social class as the key issue. Thus, feminism is a conflict theory. For feminists, education is one of the most significant areas where women can gain social justice. Their argument is that because women are disproportionately likely to be involved in childrearing and in taking on female work such as the four Cs: cooking, cleaning, caring and check-outs, they remain vulnerable to poverty and deprivation. Education that prepares women for the challenge of taking on traditional male work offers them opportunities. Lack of education leaves women vulnerable to exploitation by men and by patriarchy.

> Extremists have shown what frightens them most: a girl with a book.
>
> **Malala Yousafzai**

Liberal feminism and education

Liberal feminism can be recognised by its concern with concepts such as equality of opportunity, socialisation into sex roles and gender discrimination within schools. A particular area of focus for liberal feminists was the way that the curriculum discriminated against women, so until the 1980s and the introduction of the National Curriculum, it was common and completely unremarkable for girls to be taught entirely different subjects from boys. The girls would study domestic sciences and boys would be taught carpentry and sciences such as physics. Many subjects remain heavily gendered even though children have more freedom to choose what they study. Feminists argue that attitudes are changing slowly and that many girls are dissuaded from 'masculine' study whereas boys, if they find themselves in traditional feminine roles, often progress quickly and are viewed in a more positive light. A 1998 report on careers in nursing found men were twice as likely to be promoted.

Criticisms of the liberal feminist explanations of educational attainment suggest that it is not critical enough of the entrenched masculinity of education systems, particularly in higher education where women opt for courses leading to less well paid work. In 2014, it was found that men were more likely to get top level degrees at Oxford University despite women being more likely in general to apply to universities.

Socialist and Marxist feminist views of education

There is a more obvious link in Marxist feminist thinking between economics and education, so Marxist feminists are more likely to look at cultural reproduction, power and ideology. They would argue that gender socialisation in the home is reproduced in schools and education. They tend to look at why women accept a lower social status than men and then, because they are also interested in the idea that some women are willing to challenge masculinity, will look for signs of resistance. Areas of concern include:

- Gendered language used in schools (Oakley).
- Gendered roles in books and in the hierarchy of the school (Kelly, 1987).
- Gendered stereotyping in reading schemes.
- The invisibility of women in the curriculum, which is known as symbolic annihilation (McCabe, 2014).
- Girls being made to feel uncomfortable in male subject areas (Culley, 1986).
- Lack of positive role models.

This perspective can be criticised because many of these issues have been addressed as a result of equality legislation in schools, and yet gendered attitudes and behaviours still persist among boys and girls. The key issue for educationalists tends to be the under-performance of boys, particularly the white working class.

Activity

Make arguments based on sociological knowledge for and against single-sex education in schools.

INTERESTING FACT

Harvey Goldstein, in 1986, found that at age 11, there was systematic discrimination against girls who were achieving higher marks than boys in tests, by being allocated to the secondary modern schools because more grammar school places were available for boys. It was thought that because more girls than boys passed the exam, 'many teachers feel the system is unfair to boys'.

Many feminists have protested about male violence.

INTERESTING FACT

Henry Maudesley wrote a book in 1874 claiming that women experienced 'menstrual disability' which caused women to become thin and weak if they had intellectual challenge during their periods. He and many other doctors believed that education would cause infertility and other serious health problems if women studied. Many women were concerned and in the 1880s carried out their own research to prove the theory to be incorrect. In the 1910s and later, Herbert Spencer argued that female intellectual evolution stopped before that of the male in order to preserve the reproductive organs from strain.

Discussion point

- *The Invisible Woman* (1996) is the title of a book by Joanne Belknap that argues that women are overlooked in society, in particular with relation to being the victims of crime. Do you agree?

Many feminists criticised children's reading books as being part of the hidden curriculum that teaches children gender.

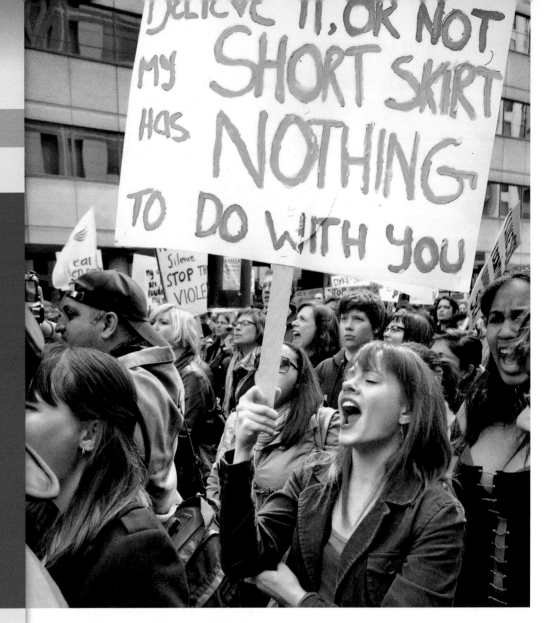

Radical feminism and education

Radical feminists have tended to point out that males monopolise knowledge and teacher time. They dominate social spaces in which both genders occur and are aggressive towards transgressive women, who challenge male dominance. Currently in the USA, there are huge public debates about the frequency of sexual violence by male college students and the failure of universities to deal with the problem, choosing to tell girls how to avoid rape and thus implying that the victims 'brought it on themselves'. Radical feminists tend to favour single-sex classrooms, arguing that women's needs should be put first.

Critics of radical feminism tend to suggest that it is too general, and that all men are not rapists and all women are not victims. It is deterministic, implying that women do not exercise choices but are suppressed in male society. It overlooks the speed of social change.

Feminists and the hidden curriculum

Feminists claimed that the hidden curriculum acted as a powerful reinforcement for gender stereotyping in schools. The argument was that the textbooks provide messages about gender as they offer information about the world to children. In the 1970s and 1980s, study after study showed that story books portrayed boys as active and girls as domestic or invisible. There were fewer female characters and often they existed to be rescued by males. Maths and science books showed boys in images or used male-appropriate examples. A recent study by Janice McCabe of books published between 1900 and 2000 found that 31% had female central characters and even books about animals focussed on male animals. The former children's laureate, Anne Fine, complained that even in modern books, where positive images of race are shown, gender stereotyping is seen as acceptable.

Sample questions

Children's reading books are dominated by male characters, despite the way that reading tends to be a more feminine activity. Janice McCabe (2014) looked at over 6,000 children's books published in the last century and found that males are central characters in over half of the stories. Only 31% had female central characters. Nearly a quarter of animal-based stories have male heroes, whereas females star in 7.5% of books. McCabe argues that this sends children a strong message that women and girls are less important in society than boys and men. She said, 'The disproportionate numbers of males in central roles may encourage children to accept the **invisibility of women** and girls and to believe they are less important than men and boys, thereby reinforcing the gender system.'

a) With reference to the item and sociological knowledge, explain the meaning of the term **invisibility of women**.

b) Using the item and sociological knowledge, explain **two** ways in which schools may discriminate against girls.

Check your own learning

True or false?

a) In 2014, boys got a higher proportion of A* grades at GCSE than girls.

b) In 2014, girls were 8% more likely to get an A*–C grade at GCSE than boys.

c) The A* to C rates for boys and girls have tended to rise each year at GCSE.

d) Boys tend to do slightly better than girls in Physics.

e) Girls tend to do better than boys at subjects involving coursework.

f) Boys and girls tend to achieve similar grades in English.

Extended writing

Evaluate feminist explanations of educational attainment.

Guidance: You should use a range of evidence from throughout the course to support your writing and show knowledge of the fact that feminism is not one single theory, but is an approach. Feminists are as likely to criticise each other as to challenge the other sociological perspectives. You can criticise feminism in general, but you really need to focus on linking your points to educational attainment. This question does not specify which gender is being considered. In this case, you might want to point out that feminists do not offer an account of the recent relative failure of boys to do as well as girls.
Write about 500-750 words.

STRETCH and CHALLENGE

What would be the effect on society if education for girls was banned?

Discussion point

- What has been the effect of educational opportunity for women on modern society?

Research methods

How would you design a project to investigate the view that children's reading books favour males and boys?

Topic 13: Interactionist accounts of educational attainment

Interactional accounts of educational attainment focus on the quality and type of relationships that occur within schools. Interactionists have little interest in social structures or organisational practice. This is both a strength and a weakness. Interactionism gives us a keen sense of process within schools in classes and between individuals, but overlooks the much bigger picture of the structural reasons that may explain school failure for some groups of students.

Tip

You have already covered some of this type of thinking in your studies on the processes that take place within schools and affect performance, so you should be revising that at the same time as looking at this topic. Look back at gender, class and ethnicity, too.

Getting you thinking

Functionalists view education as a race for success and achievement. Interactionists believe success and failure to be just a label. Cassen and Kingdon (2007) attempted to define low attainment in education and listed four separate measures of school failure. These include: no passes at GCSE, no passes above a grade D at GCSE, failure to attain a pass in either English or Mathematics, failure to gain at least five passes at any grade including English and Mathematics.

How would you define low attainment in education? How useful is it for people to think in terms of success and failure in education? How would the less able respond to a negative label?

Interactionist explanations of school failure

Interactional accounts of school failure focus on the view that children are labelled by teachers individually and by schools as organisations. These labels are absorbed by children into their sense of self and children accept these labels. If they are labelled as failures, they will form anti-school subcultures but if they are labelled as a success, then they will go on to achieve good results and become approved of by the schools.

Ability grouping, resources and class size

One of the prime areas of debate centres on selecting, banding and streaming. Some British schools are able to select candidates on the basis of ability or talent and according to government regulations may set entrance examinations. Those areas where grammar schools still exist will accept only those who score highly at the 11+ exam. Interactionists would criticise this on the basis that those in the top streams gain confidence and do well, whereas those in lower streams absorb the message that they are failures.

Curiously, it was discovered by more than one study that the top sets in secondary modern schools often out-performed the lower sets in the grammar schools, which supports labelling theory. Ireson et al. (1999) found no link between ability grouping and performance. Duckworth et al. (2009) suggested that the effect of ability grouping on pupil attainment is limited; however, they also note that it is policy in large numbers of English and Welsh schools to set children.

In the past, British schools used heavy physical punishment. What messages would this pass on to children?

Tip

Avoid using the word 'prove' in sociology answers. Few studies can offer absolute proof of any facts because research methods all have limitations.

This is a powerful argument to support the idea of labelling theory and suggests that:

⊙ Children do absorb teacher labels.
⊙ Working-class children are more vulnerable to the labelling process.
⊙ Low expectations of pupils can result in poor teaching and preparation.
⊙ Selection on the basis of ability can damage a child's self-esteem.

However, even in schools which do not set, band or select, there are still differences in attainment between the various social groups that are generally seen as disadvantaged, so a single explanatory theory such as labelling offers insight but doesn't fully explain the problem of under-attainment.

Teacher practice and behaviour

Rosenthal and Jacobson (1968) self-fulfilling prophecy

Rosenthal and Jacobson administered an intelligence test to a number of children in a deprived inner-city neighbourhood in California. They picked names at random and then told the class teachers that those children would experience a sudden boost of intelligence and perform better. When tested a year later, some of the children did perform better on the test. The argument was that teachers believing something to be true, made it happen. Despite some very obvious problems with reliability, ethics and validity, this became an enormously influential study. It was taken to 'prove' that teacher expectations affect the outcome of children.

Research methods

Use the Internet to find out more about the Rosenthal and Jacobson study, which goes by the name of *Pygmalion in the Classroom*. Be careful, because many websites are very uncritical of the study. You will need to exercise your own skills of evaluation. What are the obvious problems with reliability, ethics and validity that you can discover?

The self-fulfilling prophecy

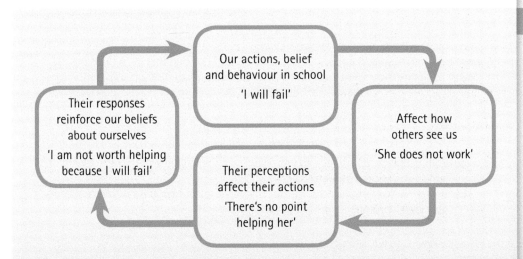

Our actions, belief and behaviour in school
'I will fail'

Affect how others see us
'She does not work'

Their perceptions affect their actions
'There's no point helping her'

Their responses reinforce our beliefs about ourselves
'I am not worth helping because I will fail'

Interaction and gender

When labelling theory was at its most popular as an approach in sociology in the 1970s, feminists often used the techniques to look at gender and labelling. They discovered quite significant differences in the behaviour of teachers towards boys and girls:

- Jones and Dindia (2004) found that teachers praise boys more, sending out unconscious messages to girls that they were not valued.
- Stanworth (1983) found careers teachers offering strongly gendered advice.
- However, Becky Francis recently found that boys were less positively labelled in schools.

The evidence is inconclusive and again, it may have an influence on school attainment but cannot explain it fully.

Interaction and ethnicity

Many studies suggest that teacher racism is the cause of ethnic minority failure. Teachers have low opinions and label some cultural groups as failures. A great deal of evidence has suggested teachers are racist: Coard (1971), Mirza (1992) Sewell (1997) Gilbourn and Youdell (2000) However, when most of the major studies were carried out, attitudes to race in general society were very different from today and most modern schools are highly sensitised to the issues. In addition, some of the work was conducted by researchers from ethnic minorities.

Evaluating the interactionist approach to education

A strength of the interactionist approach is that it is based on evidence collected from inside schools and classrooms. The results of this research can then be used by schools and teachers to change what they do and provide a better experience for their pupils. Its basis in evidence is in contrast to the theoretical emphasis of structural approaches, which aim to show how the education system fits in with their overall view of how society operates.

However, critics of interactionism suggest that many studies are small scale and may not be representative of the education system as a whole. Furthermore, schools are not isolated from the wider society and it is likely that teachers and pupils create social constructions that do not reflect the ideas of society. For example, the labelling of boys and girls reflects gender stereotypes that exist outside schools.

> Keep away from people who belittle your ambitions. Small people always do that, but the really great, make you feel that you too can become great.
>
> Mark Twain

Research idea

Find out what you can about the psychological concept of the Halo Effect. How might some children benefit from it?

Sample questions

In Kent (2003), there is a pattern of **educational selection** whereby able children are selected for grammar schools, but others attend comprehensive schools. Labelling in such an environment is very real. My own school (non-selective girls) borders the local girls' grammar. They share fences, entrances, and in some cases barbed wire and anti-vandal paint! Girls who pass the 11+ wear green uniforms and girls who fail wear brown. Thus a child's basic IQ is communicated publicly to all by clothes she wears. One can only imagine the extent of the negative effect on self-esteem and aspiration such a daily reminder can have and I trust that many will be duly horrified that such practices still exist. Remarkably it is also common practice for secondary modern schools to further set and band their students. The bottom set of the bottom school must be quite a dreadful place to be!

Adapted from a webpage by Andy Walker
http://www.schoolhistory.co.uk/forum/index.php?showtopic=1289

a) With reference to the item and sociological knowledge, explain the meaning of the term **educational selection**.

b) Using the item and sociological knowledge, explain **two** ways in which schools may label children.

Check your own learning

The following evidence came from a 2006 study by Diane Reay into interactions in school. Which support labelling theory and which do not?

Setting processes continue to operate to the disadvantage of working-class students.	Teachers may label working-class pupils negatively and middle-class pupils often receive preferential treatment.
Teachers may also use informal 'ability' groupings within formally mixed ability classes.	Teachers demonstrated prejudicial views of working-class parents. 'I'm afraid some parents are just pig ignorant.'
When asked: 'If you had a choice what would you choose to learn?' students responded as follows: Jamie: 'Nothing'. George: 'Nothing'. Andy: 'No idea'. Paul: 'Definitely nothing'.	Class cultural factors also influence pupils' attitudes to school. Peer pressure among many working-class boys was a significant factor inhibiting their educational achievement.
Interactional theories do not explain the origin of the labels.	Some teachers are well informed sociologically and show sympathetic concern for working-class students or feel themselves to be working class.

Extended writing

Assess interactionist accounts of school failure.

Guidance: The conclusion that you should probably arrive at is that labelling theory is useful and helps us gain an insight into school processes, but it doesn't answer the question of why some children fail. Given that you have already learned that some children are able to resist labels and choose to succeed despite them (Mirza, 1992) this should give you some clues. This essay probably is easier if you use structural theories such as Marxism, feminism and functionalism to assess labelling theories because they will give you more recent studies to refer to. Most of the significant studies which established labelling as a theory are now very dated indeed and describe a far different education system and society than the one that we now live in.

Write about 500-750 words.

Discussion point

- Should some children be labelled as 'gifted and talented' in school? What effect does this have on the able child? What is the effect on other children?

Activity

List ten characteristics of a good student in school. Ask your teachers if they can do the same – if they are willing.

What does this tell you about the kind of person that teachers prefer to teach?

◉ **To assess postmodernist theories of education**

Postmodernism is a very new approach to sociology and there is virtually nothing available from before 1991 when this approach to sociology became more widely known. In terms of describing modern life, postmodernism is generally quite useful. However, it is a complex theoretical approach written in difficult terminology and many of the ideas have not yet become widely known or applied to educational theory. The research methods arising out of the postmodern approach have been very influential.

Key terms you might come across in wider reading

Postmodernisation describes the way that society has become increasing technological in recent years.

Postmodernity is a condition of society where there have been changing patterns of consumption, globalisation, changes in work and leisure.

Postmodernism is the study of postmodernity and social change.

Postmodernists is how the researchers describe themselves.

Topic 14: Postmodernism and education

Getting you thinking

The picture on the left represents a piece of traditional art. The fork is an example of postmodern art in Geneva. In what ways does the sculpture piece of art break the traditional idea of art?

Modernity

The word 'modern' comes from the mid-nineteenth century and describes the movement of society towards a better and more civilised world characterised by progress, truth, certainty, social freedom and the presence of pure facts. Postmodernism is a rejection of that idea, saying that nothing is certain except that change occurs.

Living in a postmodern world

Whether you accept postmodernism as a theoretical analysis of society or not, most people agree that it describes a number of recent aspects of modern culture linked to highly advanced capitalism and technological advances:

◉ We have a cultural 'pick and mix', so we choose ideas, products and clothing from a variety of sources.
◉ Image and impression management are very important to people.
◉ We interact with highly developed technologies which are changing regularly.
◉ We take spiritual and cultural ideas from a variety of sources.
◉ We tend to be individualistic and look after our own and ourselves.
◉ We are far more concerned with consumerism and labels than with making things.
◉ We tend to be absorbed in 'virtual worlds' on television and through computer games.
◉ Society has become more unpredictable.
◉ We live in information-rich societies that gather vast amounts of data about people.

Postmodern research suggests that researchers should be looking for different identities and different voices, methods should be varied and different media should be used to present findings. Researchers themselves influence their results and should be aware of that.

What does postmodernism tell us about education?

Knowledge
Teachers and educators are biased. Together with children they construct knowledge. Therefore the creation of knowledge is an active process. The knowledge of one generation of people may well be incorrect in another. Take, for example, gender. The knowledge of feminine biology a hundred years ago suggested that women should not read at certain times of the month in case they strained their bodies and became infertile. This was a fact. Now we think differently, but it is possible that people in the future will look at our ideas with equal disbelief. This construction of knowledge is known as a discourse.

Culture
According to postmodernists, the functionalist goal of unifying society leads to oppression and persecution because a unified society is based on one dominant point of view. Not only are truth, knowledge and cultural belief entirely relative and dependent on your beliefs, but imposing your views on another is not acceptable. Children from minority ethnic groups have the right to assert their own cultural identity against modern British culture.

Societal values
Given that all truth is relative and personal then it is to be expected that teachers offer their own values or social agendas. Schools should be offering children access to a variety of opinions. Important cultural values should include a tolerance of diversity, emotional intelligence and creativity. Children need to learn quickly that schools are not value free.

Identity and understanding
Each individual is a personal construct. We are all engaged in an active process of developing an identity, so none of us can say with any logic, 'This is who I am'. Who a person is, changes in each situation. The role of education then is to help individuals decide who they want to be and to empower them in order to achieve their own personal goals.

Postmodern street fashion in Japan

One feature of postmodern approaches to style is known as bricolage. Combining and assembling familiar things to make something new and extraordinary is typical of postmodern style. The Tokyo district of Harajuku is famous as a centre of street style based on postmodernist ideas of bricolage.

> We live in a world where there is more and more information, and less and less meaning.
>
> Jean Baudrillard

257

Critics of postmodernism

- Chomsky argues that postmodernism offers no factual or empirical evidence to support it. Given that, it makes it difficult to actually use the theory effectively to support action.
- It understates the diversity within society in the past.
- There is no explanation in postmodernism, it simply describes society.
- Dawkins suggests that it is empty of meaning, using complex language to obscure its emptiness.
- If knowledge is relative, then what is the value of postmodernist theory?

> In our postmodern culture which is TV dominated, image sensitive, and morally vacuous, personality is everything and character is increasingly irrelevant.
>
> **David F. Wells**

Modernist theory of education	Postmodern theory of education
Teachers pass on knowledge to children.	Teachers and children construct knowledge together
Culture is something children should learn in school. Children from ethnic minorities need to be taught dominant culture.	All cultures are of equal value so children from ethnic minorities should be taught to question Western culture and explore their own cultures.
Teachers should train children in social values such as truth and science.	Values very much depend on culture and there are no universal values that everyone agrees with.

Postmodernism involves a 'pick and mix' approach which is where people take ideas from a variety of different belief systems and combine them to make something new and different. It is a challenge to traditional ideas. It could be argued that the variety of schools and the breakdown of a single state education system is an example of postmodernism in operation in education policymaking.

Postmodernists believe that we create an identity for ourselves and make active choices in who or what we are. How might schools help us in this process? Revise education and socialisation for some ideas.

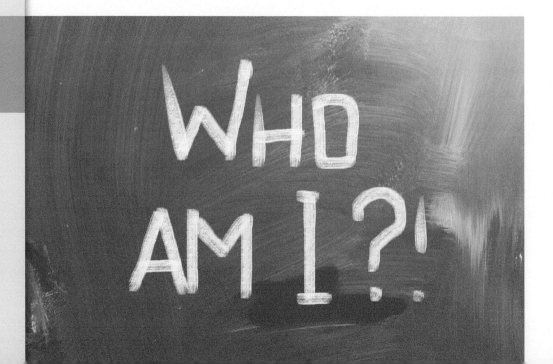

Marxists and postmodernism

Marxists have been particularly critical of the influence of postmodernism on educational theory and practice. Marxists say that because postmodernism assumes that the social world is fragmented, and all problems are local ones, it is encouraging researchers and policymakers to overlook structural issues that divide society such as class, gender, ethnicity, race and disability. Marxists suggest that despite postmodernists claiming to be critics of the education system, they cannot offer a clear education policy direction for government and they make no suggestions about how to improve the experience of education for young people.

As Marxists, they are clearly more concerned with issues of class and power than other inequalities in education, so Hill et al. (2002) claim that some schools are actively making teacher and support staff union members redundant and targeting them when they are critical of education policy.

They also make specific criticisms of current education policy. These are based on statistical data showing class to be the most significant factor in attainment at GCSE and acceptance to university. They suggest that postmodern education policy means that individual schools are targeted and expected to 'improve' rather than problems of inequality in society being addressed fully.

Sample questions

One form of evidence of postmodernism in British education can be seen in the variety and **social diversity** of different schools that children can attend. Societies are becoming increasingly fragmented so that children are no longer a part of a unified state system of education but may go to one of a variety of types of schools. For example, community schools are run by a local authority, but Trust schools are run by a governing body which has formed an educational trust. Academies are set up through business or faith sponsorships but funded directly by government. More recently, Free Schools have been set up in a similar way to academies but they are brand new schools, whereas academies are usually rebranded state schools which are deemed to have failed.

  a) With reference to the item and sociological knowledge, explain the meaning of the term **social diversity**.
  b) Using the item and sociological knowledge, explain **two** ways in which the culture and experience of school children has become postmodern.

Check your own learning
List six characteristics which describe postmodern society.

Extended writing

Discuss sociological reasons why many sociologists have claimed that society is postmodern.
Guidance: First you will need to explain what modernism is, because postmodernism is a rejection of modern culture. This question is asking you to consider whether society is postmodern or not, so you will need to provide some supporting evidence including the increased diversity of modern culture and the way that few people follow single unified belief systems.
Write about 500-750 words.

Discussion point
- Do you think that the problems of inequality in educational attainment are the result of schools or of society?

Activity

How postmodern are you? Check the influence of other cultures and places on your personal daily life. Where were your clothes designed? Where were they made? Where did you buy them? How influenced were the fashion designers by ideas from other cultures? Do you have tattoos? Where did the design idea originate? What foods did you eat today? Where were they grown?

Aims

⦿ **To assess New Right theories of education**

During the early 1980s, there was a move in political life in the UK towards the New Right led by the Conservative Government of Margaret Thatcher. This type of thinking suggests that the most efficient way to run a society is by encouraging competition and choice. Conservatism argued that taxation should be reduced, allowing people to keep more of their own money and to spend it as they wished. Thus services supported by the state for the benefit of citizens were encouraged to become competitive and led by market forces. The implications of this for the educational system were contradictory because, although schools took charge of their own budgets, they were also subject to checks by a government that introduced the National Curriculum and heavy examination and inspection routines.

Topic 15: The New Right and education policy

Getting you thinking

Are examination results a good indicator of the quality of a school or of a teacher? What factors might influence examination results that are beyond the control of your school or teachers?

New Right perspectives on education

There are broad similarities between the New Right and functionalism. The New Right believe in meritocracy and see the failure of children to attain as being due to lack of ability or the will to succeed. They also have a commitment to the concept of social competition or market forces. The New Right view is that the state cannot run a good education system because there is not enough competition to power school improvement schemes. Their focus is entirely on schools, and other causes of under-attainment are overlooked.

New Right explanations of school failure

In the 1970s a range of criticisms of the comprehensive system and of education in Britain in general was made even as comprehensive education was being introduced:

⦿ It was argued that schools had declined as a result of the loss of grammar and secondary modern schools in the UK. Selection was believed to be good for children. In the USA, Chubb and Moe found that poor children in fee-paying schools achieved better than in state run schools. They suggested that this was because private schools are responsive to the needs of parents who are paying customers.

◉ There was also a claim that school discipline had got worse, especially as it became more difficult for teachers to physically punish children.

◉ Lack of accountability caused by the fact that schools were not responsive to parents, pupils or employers, thus they had no incentive to improve and were satisfied with mediocrity and poor performance.

◉ New teaching methods involving children in more active learning were deemed to have failed.

◉ Teachers were said to be indoctrinating children into Marxist and left-wing attitudes.

◉ There was a belief that schools and local authorities were inefficient and wasteful of money because they are not as focussed as businesses. It was believed that this was a cultural problem caused by dependence on the welfare state.

Not everyone agreed with these criticisms; the school inspectorate said that problems in education were caused by comprehensive schools becoming too examination oriented and too much like the old-fashioned grammar schools. Nevertheless a huge range of reforms and changes were introduced that have affected the British education system to this day.

New Right solutions to the perceived problems included:

◉ Encouraging competition between schools and pupils.

◉ Reducing the power of local councils in the running of schools and allowing schools to make many of their own financial decisions.

◉ Encouraging employers into schools.

◉ Increased testing, inspection and publication of results.

The three strands to policy making

The education reforms of the 1980s and subsequent Labour and Conservative/Liberal governments followed a broad trend of:

◉ Central control of assessments, the National Curriculum, examination systems and funding. These were taken away from regional centres and put in the hands of government departments.

◉ Earmarked funding for specific projects, so governments allocate money to certain key targets and money should be spent on achieving those government aims. These have included lifelong learning, or the inclusion of deprived children. Schools and education have had to become clever at applying for and gaining funding.

◉ Assessments by outcome, which means that target setting, performance criteria, league tables and payment of teachers by results has become the norm.

STRETCH and CHALLENGE

What would be the effect on the education system if there were no public or school examinations?

Research idea

Use Google to find out more about educational reform and policy since the 1986 Education Reform Act.

Should schools be spending more on buildings or on teaching staff? What is your view?

Discussion points

- What do you think the aims of a successful education system should be?
- Do you think that the British education system has achieved those aims? If not, what are the barriers to success?

Academy and free schools reflect the influence of the New right on educational policy.

Evaluating the New Right

- Examination results appear to have improved, so if examination systems are reliable and valid, New Right changes to the education system have been a success. However, there are many reasons to account for changes to results, such as the possibility of grade inflation.
- Gorard and also Gerwitz argue that the middle classes can get their children into more desirable schools, so failing schools that became academies attracted more middle-class parents because initially, these schools were better funded and had newer buildings.
- Teachers and school managers claim that the low standards of some state schools are a reflection of general poverty and poor funding. If a system has schools in competition, then in addition to winners, there will also be losing schools who attract only challenging pupils.

> The keys to school improvement are excellent teaching and leadership and a relentless determination to stamp out failure.
>
> **Brian Lightman**

The main aims of education, according to the New Right are:

- Encouraging competition and market forces to ensure that schools are run efficiently and in a business-like manner.
- Meeting the needs of employers so that there is a skilled and effective workforce to meet the needs of industry.
- To improve educational standards for all children, especially the most able who require challenge.
- To create equality of opportunity between children and to encourage a meritocratic society.
- To allow freedom of choice, so that parents can choose the education that they believe will be best for their children.
- To make teachers and schools accountable for their performance so that if children fail to progress, teachers should change their practice and improve.
- The performance of a school and of teachers can be measured by success rates in public examinations.

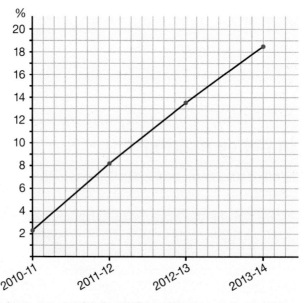

Mainstream academies & free schools as a percentage of all mainstream state-funded schools

Source: Dept for Education November 2014

Sample questions

Academy schools were originally set up by Labour governments of the 1990s as a strategy to improve underperforming schools in poor areas. Since 2010, more schools have become academies. They have considerably more freedom from central government control than state schools despite having their funding direct from central government. One of the advantages to schools is that if they become academies, they are better funded because they are given money directly that would normally go to the local authority to pay for services such as special needs support. They have control over the selection process for pupils. academies can set their own curriculum, do not have to follow pay and conditions guidelines for teachers or even to employ qualified teachers. Currently, in 2015, Wales has no academy schools and Welsh Assembly government is resisting the policy.

a) Summarise the item on the academies programme.
b) Using the item and sociological knowledge, explain **two** ways in the New Right have affected educational policy.

Check your own learning

Theories of educational disadvantage summarised.
Link the theory to the explanation.

a)	Some children are just less able than others, and these tend to be working class and from ethnic minorities.	Cultural deprivation
b)	Children who fail in school are badly socialised.	Structural views
c)	Children from poorer families experience worse health and poor home conditions.	Individual failure
d)	Disadvantages are caused by poor schools which are unresponsive to pupil needs. Teachers have low expectations and schools are badly managed.	Poverty and material deprivation
e)	The structure of society itself is to blame for school failure because the education system fails many children and reflects social inequalities.	School factors

Extended writing

Evaluate New Right policies on education.

Guidance: The focus of your answer should be on policies, so you will need to discuss what problems the policies were intended to solve and what the underlying ideology of the policymakers was. In terms of evaluation, you may need to consider whether the claims that are made for the success of the policies can be justified. Politicians seem to be enthusiastic, but their views are not always equally supported by researchers.

Write about 500-750 words.

Tip

The Marxist idea of cultural capital is relevant to the debate about parental choice. Why might middle-class parents benefit more from choice than poorer parents?

Policy points

▶ In 2015, the Prime Minister, David Cameron, pledged that there would be a massive expansion of the academy programme as part of his election manifesto.

Activity

Ask your teachers what they think are the strengths and weaknesses of league tables of school performance.

What do they really tell you about schools and the quality of teaching?

The Sociology exam

WJEC EDUQAS WJEC and Eduqas papers have very similar markschemes and similar questions. There are some variations in terms of the wording of the questions and how the marks are allocated. Much of what follows applies to both qualifications. We have used Eduqas and WJEC tags and colours to help identitfy the bespoke exam guidance you need according to which specification you are following.

What do examiners in Sociology want to see?

Sociology examiners are looking for candidates who show interest in and understanding of the social world around them. This means that they expect you to refer to current events or recent research findings. You should understand that there are theories that account for the way that the world is organised and you should be able to make intelligent and informed comments on those theories. Moreover, you should know something of what others have said previously about society and be able to comment on the basis of previous studies.

You should understand how evidence is gathered through research and be able to comment on it critically and be aware of the strengths and weaknesses of the various research methods available to social scientists. This may seem a challenge, but can be done if you understand how you need to prepare for the examination papers. Leaving it to the last minute and hoping for the best is a very poor strategy for success. The more you study, the more you understand and that will be the key to being successful and enjoying sociology.

What are examiners looking for on scripts?

There are clear guidelines to the examination system; these are open so that candidates, teachers and examiners know what is expected and what will be rewarded. These can be seen on specimen assessment materials and on previous markschemes for past papers and consist of a range of skills and knowledge.

Displaying skills requires the ability to write clearly and to the point. Long rambling responses are not welcomed. It is better if you display knowledge and use the skills indicated by the markschemes and then move on rather than to write all that you know about a topic. Each type of question will require a different range of skills; however, all of them demand that you can hit specific parts of the assessment objectives for that question.

Write a clear and logical response to the question or command

This means that your response has a structure; this should be absolutely clear to whoever reads it. Short response questions generally require that you explain something, so keep your explanation focussed and short. Extended response essays require a slightly different technique, whereby your essay consists of an introduction, five or six paragraphs and a conclusion. Every single point made should refer directly to the question. This takes practice because it is a high-level skill. Reading books and newspapers will give you some idea of how it can be done.

> Making points relevant to the question is described in the markschemes as 'providing context'.

Provide depth and breadth

An extended response essay may be quite open in terms of what is required. Take for example:

> Assess feminist explanations of family change.

There are a number of possible ways to answer this:

- You might describe and assess the various feminist explanations of family change. There are at least three that you could write about: Marxist, liberal, radical. Such an approach requires depth because you are not discussing many theories, but you should be able to talk about each of them in detail and perhaps offer strengths and weaknesses of each approach with reference to studies and theory.

Your conclusion would offer a judgement as to the usefulness of feminist explanations.

⊙ You could also describe and assess feminism in the light of what other theories of family change have to say. This means that your response will have breadth because there is more that you can write about in terms of theoretical understanding and as long as your response is completely focussed on assessing feminism in relation to family change, it will be credited.

The higher level skill is to have breadth and depth, and show that you have a good overview of the key points and enough sociological detail to back up your views.

Answer the question

Examiners are only allowed to credit material that is made specifically relevant to the question. All the skill levels of all of the markschemes refer to the *context* of the question in some form.

Take the previous example:

> Assess feminist explanations of family change.

Responses that just describe changes to the family or only talk about feminism without relating it to family change cannot reach the top mark bands. Again, this is a skill that needs to be rehearsed and it is advisable that when you complete a paper under examination conditions, you read what you have written before you hand it in and make sure that you have linked each point that you have made to the topic of discussion. You should allow for this when planning how you will use your time in the examination.

Assessment

Markers will be looking for specific sociological skills and these are known as assessment objectives. Learners must:

AO1 Demonstrate knowledge and understanding of:

⊙ Sociological theories, concepts and evidence.
⊙ Sociological research methods.

AO2 Apply sociological theories, concepts, evidence and research methods to a range of issues.

AO3 Analyse and evaluate sociological theories, concepts, evidence and research methods in order to:

⊙ Present arguments.
⊙ Make judgements.
⊙ Draw conclusions.

In simple terms:

AO1 – Knowledge and understanding of sociology (make clear points and use evidence in responses)

AO2 – Application of sociological knowledge (show how the knowledge can be used in a new **situation or scenario**)

AO3 – Analysis and evaluation of sociological knowledge (make judgements as to the value of evidence or theory)

Success in exams is more than a matter of luck. You need to prepare carefully and practise examination techniques.

Understanding markschemes

There are various elements to a markscheme and these tell markers what they should be looking for in candidates' responses:

Descriptor

This is a description of an expected response. It indicates what is expected in a top markband response. The descriptor will vary according to the command words used in the question.

Skills weighting

In each part of the markscheme, you will see how many marks are available for each assessment objective. In the example above, from a WJEC AS level, there are more marks for AO1 (knowledge) than for AO2 (application). This tells you that the markers will have more marks to allocate to factual information than they will allocate to application. Thus, you will need to offer detailed knowledge to hit the top markband and gain the 5–6 marks available. Application only has 4 marks available, so your focus should be on giving information and then applying it. In other parts of the markscheme for the same qualification, the weighting (numbers of marks available for each skill) will vary considerably. So you may have other questions on the paper where the knowledge carries fewer marks than application and evaluation.

Question

The question is always given to remind markers what the command and the key terms in the response will be.

SOCIOLOGY Specimen Assessment Materials 26

2. (a) (ii) Statistics and research have shown that the average age of first time marriage for women has increased.

Explain **two** sociological reasons for this. [10]

For band 3 AO1 there should be two reasons with supporting evidence/examples for both. For band 3 AO2 a clear explanation of the reasons and supporting evidence/examples should be present.

Indicative content
- Legislation such as; 1975 Equal Pay Act, 1975 Sex Discrimination Act, 2006 Equality Act, abortion laws and divorce laws.
- Feminisation of the workforce: the growth in service sector jobs and career opportunities for women.
- Female independence and opportunities linked to work and career – Scase.
- Marriage and remarriage are more common.
- Changing values: cohabitation is seen as acceptable.
- Less stigma attached to childlessness and single parenthood.
- Secularisation means people delay marriage.
- Cost of formal weddings prohibitive.
- Creative singlehood Hall et al.

Band	AO1 elements 1a & 1b	AO2 element 1a
3	5-6 marks Answers demonstrate detailed knowledge and understanding of sociological theories/ concepts/ evidence relating to the context of the debate/question.	4 marks Answers demonstrate a detailed ability to select, apply and interpret appropriate sociological theories/ concepts/ evidence in the context of the debate/question. There will be appropriate use made of the item to demonstrate understanding.
2	3-4 marks Answers demonstrate some knowledge and understanding of sociological theories/ concepts/ evidence relating to the context of the debate/question.	2-3 marks Answers demonstrate some ability to select, apply and interpret appropriate sociological theories/ concepts/ evidence in the context of the debate/question. Some reference will be made to the item.
1	1-2 marks Answers demonstrate basic knowledge and understanding of sociological theories/ concepts/evidence relating to the context of the debate/question.	1 mark Answers demonstrate a basic ability to select, apply and interpret appropriate sociological theories/ concepts/ evidence in the context of the debate/question.
	0 marks NRSP	0 marks NRSP

The indicative content

Indicative guidance is for markers so that some probable content is illustrated. You are not expected to mention every item on this list. You may even mention things not on the list. The list is often added to in markers' conferences to take account of the variety of responses offered by candidates. You will always be rewarded for relevant points.

The banded markscheme

This tells the marker what skills should be rewarded and describes the skills that should be demonstrated in answers. This is a restricted response question, so only AO1 and AO2 are requested of the candidate. In an extended response question, there will be a column for AO3.

In advance of the examinations, it would be advisable for you to look at the banded markschemes with some care because they do vary according to the marks awarded for each assessment objective and depending on whether you are taking an AS and/or A2 paper.

The descriptions within each box in the banded markscheme do not vary much. The strongest answers will be ***detailed***. This means that there will be reference in responses to theories, concepts and evidence and these will be linked to the context of the question. Examiners will be expecting to see the language of sociology used with accuracy. The weakest responses will be ***limited*** or ***display no knowledge or skills***.

The levels within the banded markscheme for Eduqas/WJEC Sociology will remain the same throughout all papers:

- detailed (strongest responses)
- some
- basic
- limited (weaker responses)
- none (no marks awarded)

Levels of demand

Candidates often let themselves down because they do not develop the skills of evaluation fully. It is not enough to use lots of evaluative language such as: *however, therefore, strengths, weaknesses,* even though examiners like to see such writing. The strongest responses will use the language effectively to make serious points about the work. Sometimes the difference between one markscheme band and another will be in the way in which evaluative language is used.

Look at how this could be applied to a point made in a response to the extended response question:

Evaluate Marxist explanations of working-class failure in schools:

◉ No marks

> In my opinion, Marxist explanations of working-class failure in school are good because they show that working-class children do not succeed as well as they could.

Notice that despite the use of evaluative language, no actual point has been made, and no evidence is used. Moreover, the candidate referred to his or her opinion. This fails to work because sociology should be evidence based.

◉ Weaker evaluation

> One possible important cause of working-class failure in schools is the hidden curriculum.

Evaluation is present but not much has been done with the idea here. It lacks development and detail. In addition, the focus is not on the context of the question which is about Marxism and not working-class failure.

◉ Stronger evaluation

> One **strength of Marxism as an explanation** of working-class failure in schools might be that Marxists point out that children from different social classes have different experiences within school as a result of the working of the hidden curriculum.

Evaluation here is explicit and applied to the context of the question which focuses on Marxism rather than on working-class failure in schools as the response above does.

Types of evaluative language

Comparisons – 'good evidence to support this theory comes from a study by xxx'

Contrasts – 'this can be contradicted by findings from xxx which show that xxx'

Criticisms – 'a weakness of this theory is that xxx' or 'a strength of this viewpoint is xxx'

Linking phrases – 'on the other hand' or 'Although dated, evidence from the xxx study suggests that…'

Avoid talking in terms of evidence 'proving' something. This is acceptable in sciences but not generally so in sociology where writers talk in terms of supporting evidence.

Evaluation is a higher level thinking skill and essential in professional life. By evaluating social theories and concepts you can decide whether they are useful and relevant to our society.

The format of the exam

If you are studying sociology in Wales, then you are probably entered for WJEC papers. In England, candidates will almost certainly be studying for the Eduqas qualification. Check which examination you are entered for with your teachers because there are differences in the papers and the expectations for each vary a great deal.

The separate examinations are known as 'components' (Eduqas) or 'units' (WJEC). At AS level, there are two units/components in both WJEC and Eduqas papers.

WJEC papers in sociology

If you are studying for a WJEC paper, then your AS paper is a building block for A2. Your marks for AS will contribute to your overall examination grade. The AS papers offer slightly less challenge than A2 papers, so the skills you display at A2 will be at a higher level. There will be reference to Welsh examples on examination papers and you will need to show some specific understanding of Welsh society for the top mark bands, where there is data or evidence available for study.

WJEC Units for AS level Sociology

Unit 1: Acquiring Culture through Socialisation – This requires you to study themes related to concepts and processes of socialisation, culture and identity. You will have a compulsory question on the Core theme of socialisation, and then you will answer one further question from a choice of options. In this textbook, the options that are offered are Youth Cultures and Family. The examination will last 1 hour 15 minutes, so you will need to develop the skill of time planning to make sure that you manage to write enough to satisfy the markers.

Unit 2: Understanding Society and Methods of Sociological Enquiry – This focusses on methods of sociological enquiry together with another question from a choice of options. In this textbook you will be prepared for answers on Education. This examination lasts two hours, so you will need to plan your time, so that you think about what you are writing and plan your responses.

WJEC assessment weightings for AS

Unit	Unit weighting	AO1	AO2	AO3
AS Unit 1	37.5%	20%	10%	7.5%
AS Unit 2	62.5%	33%	17%	12.5%
Total	**100%**	**53%**	**27%**	**20%**

Eduqas papers in sociology

If you are studying for an Eduqas paper, AS is an entirely separate qualification from A level. You will study for half the content of a full A level but will show the same level of sociological skill as for a full A level.

Eduqas components for AS and A level Sociology

The separate examinations are known as components. At AS level, there are two components. For the full A level, there is a third component, Power and Stratification, which is not covered in this book, although evidence from material you have studied for this year is relevant to the full A level and useful to your understanding of Power and Stratification. The components are:

Component 1: Socialisation and Culture – This requires you to study themes related to concepts and processes of socialisation, culture and identity. You will have a compulsory question on the Core theme of socialisation, and then you will answer two further questions from a choice of options. In this textbook, the options that are offered are Youth Cultures, Families and Education. The examination will last 2½ hours, so you will need to develop the skill of time planning to make sure that you leave yourself plenty of time to think about and develop your extended response essays.

Component 2: Methods of Sociological Enquiry – This focuses on methods of sociological enquiry. For Eduqas A level. The examination is more challenging than for Eduqas AS level because a research project will be designed. More time is allowed for the A level component than for the AS component.

Eduqas assessment weightings for AS only

The table below shows the weighting of each assessment objective for each component and for the AS qualification as a whole.

	AO1	AO2	AO3
Component 1	35%	21%	14%
Component 2	15%	9%	6%
Total	**50%**	**30%**	**20%**

Revision tips

Motivate yourself

Sometimes, candidates write messages on scripts to the effect that they have not done as well as they thought they could because they did not get on with their teacher or some such reason. Examiners take a dim view of this type of message. The only person who really gains from you doing well is you, so you should take responsibility for your own learning. Studying is very hard work; this can't be avoided, but the harder you work, the easier it gets. Don't put off revising, do it, and then reward yourself later for a job well done.

Understand your work

It is easier to learn if you think deeply about your work rather than if you try and simply remember it. This means that if you are struggling, you should talk to your teachers and view them as a resource. Read your notes carefully and make a point of checking things that you do not understand.

Use a variety of revision techniques

People are often trained in a variety of techniques for learning. Different styles of learning suit different people, but all methods probably work. The trick is to keep yourself interested and so using index cards, making notes, creating posters or simply talking about and writing about work all help.

Develop relevant skills

Sociology requires that you are able to write clearly and at speed. If you cannot write enough in the allocated time or your work is illegible then you are at a disadvantage, no matter how much you understand and know about sociology. Practise writing clearly and quickly for ten minutes a day. Try speaking out loud in good paragraphs. Read as much as possible and improve your literacy skills.

Work intensively for short bursts

The study of psychology tends to show that people have limited attention spans. Study is more effective if you take a short break to process your work before trying to learn more. Regular exercise, such as walking, can help you to recall more and will reduce stress, another barrier to effective learning.

Revisit work

Again, the study of psychology shows that little and often works best for learning, so re-reading material on a regular basis will help you to retain it. It is not possible to learn absolutely everything for an examination, so leaving revision to the last minute is a weak strategy. Creating index cards or posters and looking at them regularly is a stress-free and easy way of reminding yourself of key points.

Using study partners and talking through work

Working closely with another sociology student is an effective way of making sure that you both understand key points and ideas. It is difficult to spot the errors in your own work and easy to see them in someone else's so if you check your partner's essays and they check yours, then both pieces of work can be improved. Talk through key ideas with your study partner. One of the reasons why teacher subject knowledge is usually so good is because they spend all day talking about their subject to people who know and understand much less. If you explain and talk through your work with a willing parent, sibling or friend, it will become much clearer to you.

Be well-prepared

When you know what examinations you are entered for, look for Specimen Assessment Material (SAMs) on the examination board website, and past papers and past examiners' reports. This gives a clue as to the type of questions asked, the markschemes and how previous candidates have succeeded or perhaps failed to do as well as they might have done. Look at the banded markscheme to see how the weightings for the skills are allocated. Check how much time you are allowed and how many questions you are expected to answer and then work out how much time you need for each response. When you enter the examination room do not spend more than your allocated time on short response answers because it will leave you short of thinking time for the extended response questions, which are worth more marks.

Skills weightings

Look at specimen papers and markschemes to understand how skills weightings are applied to individual questions and then tailor your responses to demonstrate the particular skill that is being sought by the examiners for that particular question.

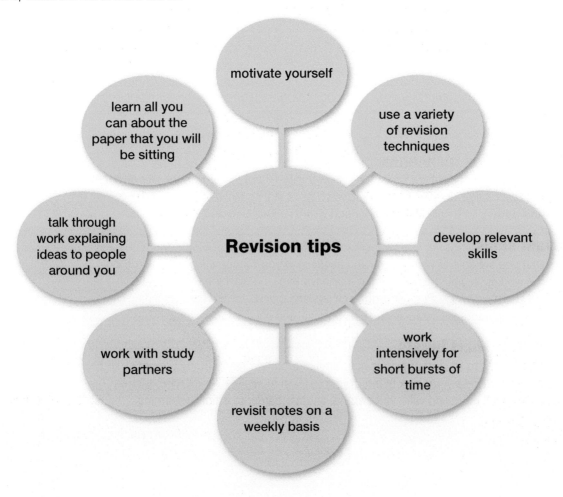

motivate yourself

learn all you can about the paper that you will be sitting

use a variety of revision techniques

talk through work explaining ideas to people around you

Revision tips

develop relevant skills

work with study partners

work intensively for short bursts of time

revisit notes on a weekly basis

Updating sociology

The new criteria emphasise contemporary social policy/society throughout. This means that you should be trying to bring your work up to date, referring to recent issues in the news and to recent studies written or published since 2000. Classic studies are still relevant, especially if there is little recent work in the same area of study but you should demonstrate awareness of the limitations of the older material and make it apply to the questions in front of you.

For example, look at how the classic 1970s study by Paul Willis, which was conducted in a secondary modern school, could be used in response to an extended response question:

> Evaluate Marxist explanations of working-class failure in schools.

◉ No marks

> Paul Willis shows that working-class children fail in school against middle-class children because they do not like school.

This is not entirely accurate in terms of who Willis studied. He didn't look at middle-class children, he looked at working-class boys. Although working-class boys did not like school, that was not the reason for their failure, according to Willis. The word 'shows' suggests that Willis is talking about the present, but this is incorrect, Willis's work is now almost fifty years old.

◉ Weaker use of study

> Paul Willis showed that most working-class boys reject school and therefore do not work as hard as they could.

This is a far better response, but it lacks the specific detail that shows understanding of the importance of the study. Although Willis's work is a classic study, it has been criticised because he only focussed on twelve boys in one school in one part of the country. Therefore, can it be generalised to all children now?

◉ Stronger use of study

> Paul Willis's classic study of working-class boys in the 1970s is still relevant today, despite changes to the education system and to work practice, because he shows how working-class males may reject school as a way of resisting a system that makes them feel like failures.

In this way, adding a little detailed knowledge and criticism of the study is adding to evaluation marks, because the Willis study has been evaluated and also it has been applied to the question.

Update your own knowledge by looking at websites. There are many referred to in the pages of this book. Google media sites with the key term you want to discuss + 'recent research studies show' , e.g. 'ethnicity and educational attainment + recent research studies show'. Exam board resources and materials are also easily accessible and you should be looking to see what is available for you in order to develop your understanding and higher order skills of evaluation and application.

Useful websites for updating AO1

British Sociological Association – www.britsoc.co.uk

The Fawcett Society – www.fawcettsociety.org.uk

Economic and Social Research Council – www.esrc.ac.uk

Sociological Research Online – www.socresonline.org.uk

NatCen Social research – www.natcen.ac.uk

Joseph Rowntree Foundation – www.jrf.org.uk

Office for National Statistics – www.ons.gov.uk

Wales Institute of Social and Economic Research Data and Methods –
www.esrc.ac.uk/research/research-methods/wiserd.aspx

Assessment

A range of assessment types with differing skills weightings can be seen on question papers. Each requires a slightly different technique in order to write stronger responses and maximise marks. These types of assessment questions consist of:

- Short, open response questions.
- Restricted response essays.
- Extended response essays.

Short, open response questions

These questions are often focussed on an item or piece of data and you are usually expected to use the information in the item to support your response, even if you are not actually told to in the question. Look at the following examples, which are similar to the style of A level papers:

A study carried out for the Joseph Rowntree Foundation in 2013 found that half of all children in Wales who are poor come from families where their parents have jobs but are on low pay. This report is based on a **quantitative** approach because the research was based on an analysis of secondary data. It used official statistics produced by government bodies. The research team was therefore able to identify patterns and trends in family wealth over past years.

Q 1 (a) Using material from the item and your sociological knowledge, explain what is meant by the **quantitative** approach to research. (5 marks)

Q 1 (b) Explain **one** reason why the researchers may have wanted to use official statistics in their research. (5 marks)

1 (a) Skills weighting based on AS SAMs

A01 Knowledge and understanding (3 marks)

A02 Application (2 marks)

1 (b) Skills weighting based on A level SAMs

A01 Knowledge and understanding (2 marks)

A02 Application (3 marks)

A strong response will refer to the item, use evidence or examples and offer some explanation to reach the higher mark bands. However, there are only five marks available so it does not have to be a long answer. Question 1 (b) asks for one reason only, although on AS papers, similar questions ask for **two** reasons and carry more marks. In each case, offer the number of reasons requested and do not expect to get marks for more reasons.

Your possible answer
1) Explain the meaning of the key term in the question. This addresses A01.
2) Refer to the item, so that you are addressing A02 and the question command.
3) Expand on your response with some additional sociological knowledge used in evidence to consolidate your marks. If A01 is your focus, add a fact. If A02 is your focus, develop your reasoning and link it to the question.

A stronger response can be quite short if there is detail and understanding:

The quantitative approach to research is based on numbers, statistics and data gathering to answer questions about society. In the item, the data used was based on official statistics, which are usually gathered in numerical form by government agencies which monitor society. The earliest piece of social research was carried out by Emile Durkheim and it was quantitative because it was based on government data on suicide figures. It aimed to be scientific and reliable.

Restricted response essays

All questions of this type are compulsory on any paper. Note that there is variation in weightings between the questions and between AS level and A level but the descriptors in the banded markscheme remain similar. Markers will be trained to look for evidence of the skills according to the weightings of the paper.

An example of a possible restricted response essay in **Eduqas** 'A' level. You could use evidence from the family and from education to answer this full A level question.

Identify evidence of gender inequality in **two** areas of life in the contemporary UK (20 marks)	**EDUQAS** Skills weighting based on A level SAMs **A01** Knowledge and understanding (14 marks) **A02** Application of knowledge (6 marks)

An example of a possible restricted response essay in **Eduqas** 'AS' level:

Explain **two** sociological reasons why some people choose to join youth cultures. (15 marks)	**EDUQAS** Skills weighting based on AS level SAMs **A01** Knowledge and understanding (10 marks) **A02** Application of knowledge (5 marks)

An example of a possible restricted response essay in WJEC 'AS' level:

Statistics and research have shown that the average age of women when their first child is born has risen. Explain **two** sociological reasons for this. (10 marks)	**WJEC** Skills weighting based on AS level SAMs **A01** Knowledge and understanding (6 marks) **A02** Application of knowledge (4 marks)

In each of the above examples, the focus is on A01, with some assessment of your ability to apply knowledge and understanding to the question. The questions will provide structure and offer a framework for responses. In these questions you are asked to provide two pieces of information. You will therefore write two paragraphs and in each case highlight both reason 1 and reason 2. If you are told to write about an item, then you should do so. How much you write in answers depends very much on the amount of allocated time that you have for the paper that you are sitting.

Extended response essays

These will appear on all papers, and they test your ability to construct a straightforward argument about a view, or a theory or some sociological knowledge in a limited amount of time. The demand and the mark weightings for skills vary, but in all extended response essays the focus is on application, analysis and evaluation rather than on knowledge. The skill in these responses is to structure and frame a response, selecting appropriate supporting evidence and creating a sensible and realistic conclusion based on that evidence.

Planning extended response essays

One of the most depressing things a marker can read is a 'stream of consciousness' response. Some candidates simply write all they know in a disorganised manner. It can be very difficult to find marks, so the trick for you is to create six or so good, clear paragraphs which demonstrate the skills that are being assessed.

A very rough guide to essay writing skills would suggest that you should be able to manage 1,000 to 1,500 legible and grammatical words in an hour. A page of A4 is about 250–350 words depending on the size of your writing. So, if you have an hour, aim for 3–4 sides of A4. If you write very much less, your essay may lack depth and breadth. If you write a great deal more, then it is possible that your essay has wandered away from the point and lacks focus.

Steps towards creating a good extended response essay plan

A good essay plan probably consists of 100 words or fewer but it will mean that you do not have to stop and think once you are writing your response, you can refer back to your plan and keep writing.

1) Read the question, because this tells you exactly what it is that you should do. There are a variety of command words that can be used. Each has a slightly different meaning:
   - **Assess** – this means that you should make a judgement as to the value, effectiveness or usefulness of an idea. Thus, in your answer and your conclusion, you will write about how valuable, effective or useful that idea is. Does it explain what it is supposed to explain about society?
   - **Evaluate** – this means that you should make a judgement as to the strengths and weaknesses of the idea or theory under question. Is it a good theory?
   - **To what extent** – this asks you to make a judgement as to how far an idea is true or not. Is it a correct theory?
2) Decide what your basic conclusion will be. This then helps you to create a starting position and an end to your essay. There are only three possible conclusions: you agree, you disagree or you take a position near the midpoint, seeing both strengths and weaknesses. Most sociology essays should take a mid-point view. Very few theories and concepts are either all good or all bad.
3) Make some points for and against your conclusion.
4) Review your work. Does what you have written fully answer the question? Are there any ideas that you want to add, or points which are not fully relevant?

Starting your essay

Introductory paragraphs should always define the terms of the question. If a theory is mentioned, explain it. If a concept is part of the question, then say what it means and who suggested it. If a debate is part of the question, then say what the two points of view might be. Make sure that the introduction makes it clear to the marker that you know what you are talking about and where the essay is likely to end.

Tip

Avoid starting essays with phrases such as 'in this essay I am going to …'. Your answer hasn't actually begun till you have said something. Start with a phrase such as, '… is a key debate in sociology because…' or '… is a concept used to explain …'. Get on with your writing rather than stating your intentions.

Paragraphing

A good paragraph has a very simple structure. If you construct your paragraph carefully, you should be able to hit every assessment target easily. For example, in a question such as: *Assess the relationship between gender and education,* you are being asked to make a judgement as to the significance of gender as an explanation of educational attainment. Is it a strong relationship or is it a weak relationship? Each paragraph should address that question and hit the assessment objectives at the same time. Look at how a possible opening paragraph has been created:

- **Identify your key point** for each paragraph or for the essay from your basic plan. Make sure that it is clear exactly what it is you want to say about the theory, concept or idea in the question. For example, you make a statement.

   In recent years, girls have tended to do better than boys on average in the education system.

- **Elaborate on your point** by adding factual detail, theoretical knowledge or a concept. This is your evidence and can be used to demonstrate AO1.

   Examination boards and government data show that increasingly girls are the gender of attainment as females tend to have higher numbers of GCSE passes and at higher grades than males.

- **Link this point to the question with evaluative language** to demonstrate both context and AO3.

   Thus there has been a changing relationship between the genders and education. Whereas in the past, boys were expected to do well, now, it is girls of all ethnicities who achieve better than boys.

Sometimes people forget to use basic punctuation and sentence structure under exam conditions. This makes their ideas difficult to understand. Avoid using the word 'and' to link very complicated ideas. Keep most of your sentences short and to the point.

This now creates a basic opening paragraph, and you can make a range of other points linking back to this paragraph, the most obvious being to explain reasons why girls tend to be the gender of achievement in education, and why boys on average have lost their top position in the education system. Use the same basic structure for each paragraph, and you should have an essay that is a pleasure to read.

Coping with the examination process

Before the examination

- It may seem obvious, but try and avoid stressing yourself before the examination. Don't try last-minute learning of new material, the skill lies in using what you know effectively. Look over your revision notes if it makes you feel better. Don't panic if you don't recall something; this is a normal stress reaction. Often it will come back to you when you relax. Hopefully, this is not after you leave the examination room and it is too late!
- Make sure you have all your equipment. You should have a pen and a spare pen, too. Make sure you know what paper you are sitting, where the examination room is and then what time it is. Arrive early.
- As some of your papers will take quite a long time, eat a good meal with plenty of protein and carbohydrate to keep you going.

In the examination

- Read the paper. Breathe carefully and read it again. Note down key words and key ideas on your paper as you think of them.
- Choose the questions that you will answer with care. Decide the order in which you will answer the questions. Start planning responses.
- Choose your option topic from Section B, either Families or Youth cultures. Do not attempt an option you have not studied on the basis of your GCSE knowledge, it will lack sufficient depth.
- Answer the questions with an eye to the clock. If you are going past your allocated time, leave a question and come back to it. Leave space between each answer and each paragraph so that if you have something to add, you are not adding little arrows or writing in margins.
- Five minutes before the end of the paper, stop writing. If you have left yourself short of time, it is unlikely you will gain many marks by scribbling a sudden conclusion. It is far better to go back and check your extended response essays and if any paragraphs do not link to the question, add a sentence to make that link explicit.

Have a look at some responses that follow and see how these skills have been applied, or how the responses could have been improved with just a few words.

Key strategies for examination success

1) Listen to your teachers; view them as a resource.
2) Revise and understand the work.
3) Look at the specification.
4) Look at past papers, mock papers, markschemes.
5) Calm down, take exercise, avoid caffeine and control your negative emotions.
6) Plan your time in the examination.
7) Write good English and use sociological language.
8) Answer the questions that have been asked.

Although there are separate instructions and examples given for the different qualifications, we suggest that you look at all of the questions and responses provided because the sociological and examination skills are the same whichever qualification you are being assessed for. Thus, points made about a paper you are not sitting may nevertheless still be highly relevant in terms of guiding you in your examination responses.

Although the questions used in this section of the book are taken from the Specimen Assessment Material (SAM) published by WJEC/Eduqas, the answers and associated commentary are from the authors. The responses are not the work of AS students but have been written by the authors to provide a framework for the commentary. The commentary reflects the opinion of the authors alone and has not been produced by the examination board.

WJEC/Eduqas AS papers question 1 a)

All papers for the introductory core begin with a short, open response question. Thus, the type of question below could appear on the introductory core of unit/component 1 of all qualifications. In this case, because the question is requesting the meaning of a term, the skills weighting will be in favour of knowledge. Thus the weighting is AO1 – 3 marks, and AO2 – 2 marks. Examination guidance says that responses should include accurate knowledge points for AO1 in band 3. This means that points should be supported with examples and/or evidence. For AO2 band 3 a clear explanation of the examples or evidence should be present.

1 Read the item below and answer the following questions:

British people of whatever background all have a culture, but there is more than one British culture. Rich white people from the South of England may have a different culture from the people of North Wales, with slightly differing norms and values. Aspects of culture might include dress, language, food and music. These aspects of culture will all affect a person's sense of social identity.

a) With reference to the item and sociological knowledge, explain the meaning of the term aspects of culture.

(5)

Stronger response to 1 a)

A culture is the way of life shared by a group of people and an aspect of culture might be a way in which they express their shared ideas and traditions. For example, people in North Wales may speak Welsh but people from the south of England are unlikely to speak it. Aspects of culture contribute to how people see themselves and therefore Welsh people may have a different sense of identity from English people.

Commentary

This response has the strength of referring to the item throughout. It explains culture and also explains what an aspect of culture is. It offers an example based on the item. It might have been improved with a little extra sociological knowledge or language applied to the question. Key terms such as socialisation could have been used.

Weaker response to 1a)

Aspects of culture refer to the culture that people share so that they have different beliefs and values. People in Wales have a different culture from people in England and that means that there are aspects of their lives that are different so they have a different aspect of culture.

Commentary

This response probably justifies some marks for understanding the meaning of culture, but there are no explicit references to the term 'aspects of culture' which is used in the question. It would have been improved by clear examples and evidence as is specified in the descriptor part of the markschemes.

WJEC/Eduqas AS papers question 1 b)

The second question for the introductory core will ask for two specific explanations of social behaviour. The wording may vary slightly each year and between WJEC and Eduqas papers. However, the strategy for success remains similar. The weightings will be similar, too, so there are 6 marks for AO1 and 4 marks for AO2 on both papers.

---

1 b) Using the item and sociological knowledge, explain how any **two** agents of socialisation pass on culture. (10)

WJEC
EDUQAS

To reach the top mark bands, then two specific examples should be clearly seen by the marker. You should refer to the item and you should use key terms to show AO1 Knowledge and understanding. You can show that you have met the terms of the question by writing two clearly identifiable paragraphs which describe processes of socialisation.

Revision suggestion

You might want to refer back to pages 8 and 9, where key terms are identified and then to look through your notes on the family and education as well as part of your preparation for this part of the examination.

Stronger response

One agency of socialisation that can pass on culture is the family. Functionalists such as Parsons point out that socialisation is a major role of families. Families are agencies of primary socialisation where children are taught social skills through watching and imitating their parents who act as role models. Children will be encouraged to behave like their same-sex parent and will learn gender roles. Sanctions are used to punish children for incorrect behaviour and they are praised within families for following appropriate norms and values.

A second agency of socialisation is education. Education systems may act as agencies of formal and informal control. For example, within school, there may be formal control where children are punished by teachers for breaking school codes of behaviour. Equally there may be informal control where teachers socialise children through praise and rewards. One process of socialisation is the hidden curriculum where children are taught assumptions and beliefs unintentionally by teachers. Marxists view the hidden curriculum as a means of control but functionalists tend to see it as being a good thing.

Commentary

Whilst this is a very strong response for using technical language, showing lots of use of theory and concepts and answering the question directly, a serious weakness is that there is little or no reference to the item, so the AO2 target of application is not fully met. A sentence such as 'For example, children will learn their language in the home so North Wales children may speak Welsh whereas English children will learn English' would make a lot of difference in terms of the marks available.

Weaker response

Families and education are agencies of socialisation where children are taught social skills. Adults act as role models and children will imitate them to learn gender roles. Sanctions are used to punish or praise children. Socialisation takes place in the following way so that they learn through role models and imitation. For example, in the home, children learn through the media where they may see violence, psychologists did a study and found children copied violence on television in the home and in school children learn to mix with people of their own age group and they develop a playground culture. Peer groups in schools can be influential so children may fit in with a bad crowd and get into trouble and teachers will punish them. They may start to smoke or take drugs. In families, children watch television and get their ideas and norms from that so they get their ideas on how to act from people around them and their friends and they are punished if they do the wrong things. This is how they are socialised.

Commentary

There are exactly the same number of words in both the stronger and the weaker responses. The problem with the weaker response is that it is not clear which two agencies of socialisation are being discussed. Markers are only required to give marks for two agencies as this is what is specified in the question. It starts well enough, so gains some AO1 marks but the processes are not linked to specific agencies so it does not merit many AO2 marks.

Eduqas A level paper question 1 b)

The second question for the introductory core will ask about social behaviour in general terms so a range of ideas will be expected. The wording may vary slightly each year. The weightings will be 9 marks for AO1 and 6 marks for AO2 on both papers.

EDUQAS   **1 b)** Using the item and sociological knowledge, explain how culture is transmitted by families.

Stronger response

The item points out that aspects of culture might include dress, language, food and music. These aspects of culture will all affect a person's sense of social identity. They will be taught within the family where children will be expected to conform to their cultural norms such as festivals such as Eid or Christmas. Ann Oakley said that one way in which this may be achieved is through parents and other adults within the family acting as role models. Children will see how their family members behave and imitate them. This is one way in which children acquire gender roles, for example if girls are given dolls by their parents they will learn that this is an expectation within the family. Families will teach norms and values as the family is an agency of primary socialisation. Children will learn language, dress, traditions, customs and beliefs. For example in North Wales, many children will speak Welsh in the home. In addition, children may be sanctioned if they do not follow family norms; this may take the form of punishment or praise. Thus as Parsons pointed out, the family is a significant way in which culture is transmitted to children.

Commentary

It is not essential to refer to theory in this question, but relevant reference to theory shows that the question is fully understood and it will score highly for AO1. Another sensible technique used by this candidate is to use the item in two different places, though without over-describing what the item says. The focus of the response is on the family throughout and nearly every sentence uses the words family or parents.

Weaker response

There are many agencies of socialisation that transmit culture and these include the media, peer groups and education. Culture can be passed on in a number of ways so people pass on their culture by sharing it with their children. For example, there are festivals such as Christmas and Chinese New Year and children learn their culture through taking part in these traditions. Children learn from their parents by watching them, so Bandura did an experiment to show how children learned from copying people on the media. Children learn important traditions and gain cultural knowledge from looking at what their parents do, and doing the same things. Culture is the language and belief of people so that it is a way of life of a group of people and children learn culture through socialisation. Families pass on socialisation because they are an agency of primary socialisation and they teach children what the culture is and pass on norms and values.

Commentary

This response would gain some marks for AO1, but it is disorganised. The key point is overlooked. If a question asks 'how…?' it means that you should focus on the process of something. In this case, the process that is required is that of how families pass on or transmit culture to children. The candidate has spotted role models and mentioned tradition, but these are not really described.

Wisely the candidate has defined culture and mentioned socialisation, which is the most important point in the question, but it reads as though it is an afterthought. These two sentences should have been the opening to the response. It is typical of weaker responses that people tend to write what they know before planning what it is they want to say.

WJEC/Eduqas AS papers question 2 a(i)

The introductory question on the family will be similar between the two papers and will focus on AO1, Knowledge. If you look at the examples below, you will notice that the Eduqas 2 a(i) demands more detail than the WJEC question. If you look at markschemes available on the WJEC/Eduqas website, you will notice that reference to terminology and studies is expected for top band responses.

---

2 a(i) Explain the meaning of the term single parent family.   **WJEC**

(5 marks available: AO1 3 marks, AO2 2 marks)

'Explain' requires you write in simple terms about how something works. In this case, what the term is used to refer to in sociology.

Stronger response

A single parent family refers to a family where the children are brought up by one dominant parent in a single household. There may be another parent, but she or he takes a lesser role in the lives of the children. The Office for National Statistics (ONS) shows us that in Britain, approximately 25% of all families are single parent households. The majority of single parents are mothers, though approximately 10% are fathers.

Commentary

There are only five marks available so responses should be succinct and full of facts. The meaning of the term is correctly identified. In this case, the response merits AO2 marks for correctly identifying a source of information about single parent families.

---

2 a(i) Describe the features of a single parent family.   **EDUQAS**

(10 marks available: AO1 6 marks, AO2 4 marks)

'Describe' requires you to offer a short account of what the key features of something are. In this case, how a single parent family may be formed, what it may look like and some facts about single parent families.

Stronger response

A single parent family refers to a family where the children are brought up by one dominant parent in a single household. There may be another parent, but she or he takes a lesser role in the lives of the children. Single parent families have a number of key features that have been identified by data produced by the Office for National Statistics (ONS) who point out that that about a quarter of all British families are headed by a single adult. Most single parents are in their thirties and very few are under 21. Most single parents became single parents because of relationship breakdown or the death of a partner. Single parenthood is often a short period of time as people find new partners and form blended families. Single parents are more likely to be female, though probably between 10 and 12% are males. Single parents are likely to experience poverty for a variety of reasons, including the high cost of childcare and the difficulty of obtaining work.

Commentary

The meaning of the term is correctly identified. In this case, the response has focussed on offering facts about single parenthood and has referred to one source of evidence. To be certain of AO2 marks, this candidate could have referred to feminism or to the way that single parents are sometimes described by the media is not always an accurate picture.

2 a(i) Explain the growth in single parenthood in the contemporary UK.

(15 marks available: AO1 9 marks, AO2 6 marks)

The command, 'explain', requires you write in simple terms about how something works. In this case, what the term is used to refer to in sociology. Here you are expected to give a range of reasons for the growth in single parenthood and so some reference to theory and policy would be expected.

Mid-range response

A single parent family refers to a family where the children are brought up by one parent. There was a big rise in the number of single parents throughout the end of the last century and at the start of the 2000s, but for the last ten years or so, the number appears to have stayed the same according to Gingerbread.

There are a number of reasons for the rise in single parenthood in contemporary Britain, one of the most important being the changes in the role of women in society. For example, legal changes mean that women are no longer dependent on men to look after them so they can leave unsatisfactory relationships and choose to become single parents. Divorce laws have made it easier.

Women have the right to earn their own money so they can leave unsatisfactory relationships and have their own income. This leads to single parenthood as they can bring up their children without help from men. There are more jobs for women so they can get work more easily.

Changing norms and values mean that it is acceptable for women to bring up their children on their own. This gives them the freedom to leave bad relationships or to plan families without fathers. They can also have sex outside marriage and keep their children if they want to and this causes single parents.

Conservatives and Charles Murray say that there are more single parents because there are benefits available and that some women choose to have babies and stay at home rather than get a job.

Commentary

Challenging the term of the question by saying that the growth in single parenthood has slowed down displays clear evidence of both AO1 and AO2. However, it is a bit vague in places, for example, naming a specific law would have added AO1 marks. Some of the reasons are not fully linked to the question, so why is easier divorce leading to single parenthood? The link needs to be made explicit all the way through. The reference to theory is very useful at the end, but an alternative viewpoint might have been offered.

WJEC/Eduqas AS papers question 2 a(ii)

This number question will only arise on AS papers and does not appear on full A level papers. It takes the form of a small piece of information followed by the command to write about **two** things. This will probably be to explain two reasons why a particular social change has taken place or to describe two features of a social phenomenon. For WJEC, 10 marks are available, AO1 is 6 marks and AO2 is worth 4 marks. For Eduqas, more detail is required because AO1 is worth 10 marks and AO2 is worth 5 marks.

> More than 1,400 same-sex marriages have taken place in the UK since the law was changed in March 2014. Explain **two** reasons why there is more social acceptance of same-sex relationships in contemporary Britain.

WJEC
EDUQAS

In this question, the item tells you about same-sex marriage, but the command asks about same-sex relationships. Be careful, because you must follow the command. The item is useful, because it gives one good reason why there have been changes to social attitudes.

The example offered below is for WJEC. To meet the needs of Eduqas or to hit higher bands for WJEC, then more detail will be required. You might want to work on this example to see how it could be improved to meet the assessment objectives with as few alterations as possible. Alternatively, write your own response.

Weaker response

There is more acceptance of same-sex marriage as more people of the same sex get married. Thus, same-sex marriage is becoming a norm in our society and more people marry people of the same sex rather than people of other sexes. In the item it says that in 2014, 1,400 people married people of the same sex which shows that same-sex relationships are more popular and it is acceptable.

In addition, famous celebrities have same-sex relationships and some have had children as well. Research by Yougov shows that most people supported gay marriage and there are lots of gay people on television so that shows that same-sex relationships are acceptable. Thus same-sex relationships are a norm in contemporary society.

Commentary

There are some obvious factual errors and misunderstandings in the first paragraph, for example, 2,800 people married people of the same sex, there were half as many weddings! This is down to carelessness, rather than lack of understanding, but it certainly means that both AO1 and AO2 assessment targets are not being met. It is not necessary to refer to the item because that is not part of the command. Only one point is made, which is that same-sex relationships are seen as normal. This would gain few marks in an examination.

WJEC/Eduqas all papers question 2 extended response essays

In all papers, you will be given a choice of two extended response essays for your option on the family. You will write one essay on this topic. Despite the fact that the essay questions will be very similar in style and level of demand, the number of marks available for the essays and their weightings will vary hugely according to the paper that you will be sitting. See the table below:

Qualification	WJEC AS level	Eduqas AS level	Eduqas A level
Marks available	30	25	35
Weightings AO1, AO2, AO3	14, 4, 12	9, 4, 12	12, 11, 12

The types of command words that you might be given could include the following. Each will require you to do something slightly differently and sometimes they may be combined in one essay.

- **Discuss** – Present key points and raise important issues with them.
- **Evaluate** – Judge from available evidence the strengths and weaknesses of an idea.
- **Explain** – Set out purposes or reasons why something is as it is.
- **Identify** – Name or pick out key features of something.
- **Outline** – Set out main characteristics.
- **Assess** – Weigh up or make balanced judgements as to whether a sociological idea is true or has value.

WJEC EDUQAS Assess sociological reasons for increased family diversity in the contemporary UK.

The command for this question requires you to suggest a variety of reasons for increased family diversity and then to make informed judgements as to whether they are useful or not in order to explain family diversity in the contemporary UK. You will plan your essay by listing five or six possible reasons for increased family diversity and then offer a short assessment of the value of each when you write the essay.

These might be, in no particular order:

- Medical changes
- Legal changes
- Families of choice (Giddens)
- Demography and life span changes
- Ethnic diversity.

There are other reasons for increased family diversity and each might be equally useful on which to base an essay, but you have a limited amount of time and will therefore need to be selective in what you choose to write about. This is the skill of selection.

Stronger response

Family diversity refers to the variety of different family types in the contemporary UK. Over the past fifty years or so, there has been an increase in the different types of families that exist. For example, in the 1950s, the most common family types were nuclear and extended families. In modern society, there is a much wider range of family types that have been identified.

One reason for increased family diversity could be the range of legal changes that have taken place which affect family life and increase diversity. For example, recent legal changes make it acceptable for same-sex couples to marry, whereas until the late 1960s, gay people could be imprisoned for expressing their sexuality. Divorce laws have eased, so couples can find it easier to end unacceptable relationships. Whether this legal change is a cause or a result of increased family diversity is difficult to know, it might be that the law has changed as a result of changing social attitudes rather than legal change actually causing family diversity.

One of the most significant reasons for increasing family diversity is probably down to changes in society itself impacting on families. Social action theorists suggest that people can choose their families. Anthony Giddens (1982) suggested that in the past, people married for economic reasons and because it was a social expectation. Modern couples can cohabit or marry as a matter of choice. This has led to family diversity because people are not controlled by social expectations and can form 'families of choice'. This may be a good explanation of why there is family diversity as it shows that traditional views of marriage have broken down and people make their own arrangements.

Weeks (1999) pointed out that there are many more openly gay and lesbian families now than in the past as laws and traditions have changed and people become more accepting. Weeks says such relationships are founded on commitment and may include friends, who then form 'families of choice'. Even though such families are accepted, they are not the majority of families though. Most people still live in heterosexual relationships.

Another cause of family diversity might be that there are now new types of medical technology that allow for same-sex parents or much older parents. Macionis and Plummer suggest that IVF allows women to make more choices over their bodies and this increases family diversity. However, such technologies can be very expensive and so are probably only available to the very rich so this may not be a big factor in family change.

Modood has pointed out that Britain is a multi-cultural society with people from a range of ethnicities. Often family types reflect the cultures of the origin country. Black Caribbean families tend to be matriarchal and single parenthood is quite common, whereas Asian families are extended, traditional and patriarchal. They have lower rates of divorce and low rates of single parenthood. Oakley found that Cypriot families tended to have strong relationships even after children married. This may explain family diversity among migrant groups but does not account for reasons why the general population has a variety of family types.

Other social factors that affect family diversity could include social class, because inequality has increased in Britain. Regional differences may be a factor, so that on the South Coast there are elderly retired people and in poorer areas there are more single parents and single people living alone after divorce. In contrast, however, Chester points out that although we do have more choice, most people still live in fairly traditional relationships.

In conclusion, there is a variety of causes of family diversity in the contemporary UK and they are linked to general social change and attitude change. It is difficult to pick on one particular cause of family diversity as being the most significant. Even though there are different types of family most people live in traditional family types.

Commentary

This response does not really demonstrate knowledge and understanding of the various types of family in contemporary UK; types such as single parent or gay families. It is vague about legal change as well, reference to specific legal change is expected for the top mark bands. These are weaknesses. However, key terminology has been used. There is understanding of the various causes of family diversity and there are examples and concepts present. The response does assess the value of the theories, and discussion is generally effective. There is also reference to one argument that suggests that although family diversity is increasing, it is not as significant as some think because most people still live in traditional families. Thus, it should be awarded high marks for AO2 and AO3.

Exam questions: Youth cultures

WJEC/Eduqas AS papers question 3 a(i)

The introductory question on youth cultures will be similar on the two papers and will focus on AO1, knowledge. If you look at the examples below, you will notice that the Eduqas 3 a(i) demands more detail than the WJEC question. If you look at the mark schemes available on the WJEC/Eduqas website, you will notice that reference to terminology and studies is expected for top band responses

WJEC **3 a(i)** Explain the meaning of the term youth cultures.

(5 marks available: AO1 3 marks, AO2 2 marks)

The command word 'Explain' requires you write in simple terms about how something works or to offer a description. In this case, what the term youth cultures refers to in sociology.

Stronger response

Youth is generally used to refer to the period of life when a person is neither a child nor an adult. Youth culture is the idea that people of a similar age tend to have similar habits, norms and values, which make up a distinctive and separate cultural form from that of adulthood. The term youth cultures refers to subcultures within youth culture, groups such as hippies, goths and straight edge. These may be more distinctive in terms of dress, music and language and are often the subject of moral panic.

Commentary

There are only five marks available so responses should be succinct and full of information. The meaning of the term is correctly identified. In this case, the response merits AO2 marks for correctly using a range of terminology and noticing the question specifically mentions the plural word, cultures. This shows that not all young people are part of youth cultures.

EDUQAS **3 a(i)** Describe the features of a youth subculture.

(10 marks available: AO1 6 marks, AO2 4 marks)

The command to 'Describe' requires you to offer a short account of what the key features of something are. In this case, how you would recognise a youth subculture, what it is that makes it very different from mainstream and general youth culture. Keep your response factual.

Stronger response

Youth subcultures have a number of features in common although there will be specific differences between them in terms of characteristics, for example hairstyles may vary. Hippies were known for growing their hair long, but skinheads, who emerged slightly later than hippies in the 1970s, had shaved heads in a style known as buzz cut. The common characteristics of youth subcultures would include specific styles of clothing: shops may cater for groups such as goths. Often there is a musical style, a mode of dancing to the music and drugs of choice, such as alcohol or illegal high. They may engage in specific activities, such as break-dancing which emerged from the streets of the USA in the mid-1970s. There may be specific language, world view and philosophy, and a set of values. More importantly in terms of culture, the subculture can be a source of personal identity and people identify themselves by belonging, for example, to a group such as the Beliebers (fans of Justin Bieber). Youth subcultures can be music, religious, sport, fan and style based. Thus, it can be argued that young people form a specific subcultural form.

Commentary

The meaning of the term is correctly identified. This answer will be credited for recognising and showing full understanding of what a culture and a subculture actually are. The candidate has not just focussed on obvious aspects of youth subculture such as style, but mentioned different youth cultures and different types of youth culture.

Eduqas A level papers question 3 a(i)

Explain reasons why young people may choose to join youth cultures.

(15 marks available: AO1 9 marks, AO2 6 marks)

The command, 'Explain reasons' usually requires you say **why** or **how** something happens. Look very carefully because if you do not spot what is required you are not answering the question. If the question is **why**, then you should focus the purpose of something, what use it is. If the question is how, then you focus on the process that happened. In this case, the question is **why**, so you will look at the social forces that push or pull young people towards creating their subcultures. There is a whole range of possible reasons you could write about, so be selective and choose just a few to write about and develop.

Stronger response

Sociologists have offered a whole range of possible reasons why young people join youth cultures. There can be personal reasons, so membership of a youth culture will offer a young person specific social benefits such as a sense of identity or belonging to a group. They may internalise the values and norms of the group so that they gain a sense of self-esteem and security, so they join youth cultures.

Social theorists have offered different reasons for young people joining youth cultures. Each perspective takes a different view. Functionalists see youth culture as a rite of passage, a phase that young people must pass through if they are to emerge as fully functioning adults in our society. Thus young people join youth subcultures as part of a normal process of growing up.

Marxists such as the CCCS see the reason for young people joining youth cultures to be linked to resistance and rebellion to capitalism. Mike Brake, for example, says that youth cultures provide 'magical solutions' to the lives of members and they can escape the social problems of being working class whilst being able to express freedom and experiment with ideas or music. He also says this is an illusion. So young people join youth cultures as a response to their class position.

Interactionist suggestions include the idea that the media glamorise certain behaviours and attract young people to them so Cohen argued that the mods and rockers were not particularly significant till over-reporting of the riots brought attention to their behaviour and created a desire among young people to join in. Youth cultures are therefore attractive to young people who join them for fun and excitement as much as for a statement of any kind.

Commentary

This response has focussed on theory so it will gain credit for being sociological. It has avoided the temptation of looking at personal reasons people may have for joining youth cultures such as for reasons of style or a taste for the music. This gives the candidate an opportunity to display knowledge of concepts such as the 'magical solution' and to name some writers and theories. These are always welcomed by the examiners. The real strength of this writing is that each paragraph is related directly to the question.

WJEC/Eduqas AS papers question 3 a(ii)

This number question will only arise on AS papers and does not appear on full A level papers. It takes the form of a small piece of information followed by the command to write about **two** things. This will probably be to explain two reasons why a particular social change has taken place or to describe two features of a social phenomenon. For WJEC, 10 marks are available, (AO1 is 6marks and AO2 is worth 4 marks). For Eduqas, more detail is required because AO1 is worth 10 marks and AO2 is worth 5 marks.

WJEC EDUQAS	Research has shown that young people are very likely to be represented in a negative way in the media. Explain two reasons why young people may be viewed as a problem in contemporary Britain.

In this question, the item tells you about negative views in the media, but the command asks about why young people are seen as a problem. Be careful, because you must follow the command. The item is useful, because it gives one good reason why young people are viewed as a problem.

The example offered below is for WJEC. To meet the needs of Eduqas or to hit higher bands for WJEC, then more detail will be required. You might want to work on this example to see how it could be improved to meet the assessment objectives with as few alterations as possible. Alternatively, write your own response.

Weaker response

Young people are seen as a problem in society because the media has a moral panic and they are presented as criminals and there is gun crime. This means that people are frightened of them and they shouldn't be because there is no need. It's because there are not enough jobs so young people have to commit crime. If there were more jobs young people wouldn't need to commit crime.

There are bad stories in the papers, so that Cohen wrote about the mods and rockers and he found that the fights were exaggerated. There was another moral panic about hoodies and people who wore them were not allowed in shops so young people are seen in a very bad way by people.

Commentary

Only one point is made, which is that young people are presented in a negative view in the media. This would gain few marks in an examination, despite the mention of Cohen. There are some clear examples of moral panics, but these are not particularly useful as the question is about **why** young people are seen as a problem. The examiners will be looking for reasons: they are presented badly in the media, so moral panics develop. Alternatively, they are associated with crime, many do not have jobs, and often their bad behaviour is seen in public. Youth subcultures are associated with drug-related behaviours and gang culture is seen as a youthful activity. Two of those ideas could have been picked out and developed with reference to reasons for their being seen as a problem.

WJEC/Eduqas all papers question 3 extended response essays

In all papers, you will be given a choice of two extended response essays for your option on youth cultures. You will write one essay on this topic. Despite the fact that the essay questions will be very similar in style and level of demand, the number of marks available for the essays and their weightings will vary hugely according to the paper that you will be sitting. See the table below:

Qualification	WJEC AS level	Eduqas AS level	Eduqas A level
Marks available	30	25	35
Weightings AO1, AO2, AO3	14, 4, 12	9, 4, 12	12, 11, 12

The types of command words that you might be given could include the following. Each will require you to do something slightly differently and sometimes they may be combined in one essay.

- **Discuss** – Present key points and raise important issues with them.
- **Evaluate** – Judge from available evidence the strengths and weaknesses of an idea.
- **Explain** – Set out purposes or reasons why something is as it is.
- **Identify** – Name or pick out key features of something.
- **Outline** – Set out main characteristics.
- **Assess** – Weigh up or make balanced judgements as to whether a sociological idea is true or has value.

> Discuss Marxist views of youth cultures.
>
> WJEC
> EDUQAS

The command for the question requires you to describe and explain relevant points and build up a balanced argument for and against Marxist views of youth cultures with supporting detail. You will plan your essay by listing five or six possible points that you might want to make about Marxist views of youth culture and then offer a short assessment of the value of each when you write the essay. It might be useful to focus on some writers in the Marxist tradition of the study of youth culture, so a possible plan could be:

- Marxist views of social class and how it relates to the development of youth cultures as an act of rebellion and resistance.
- Paul Corrigan – aggressive youth styles are a response to boredom.
- Willis – anti-school subcultures are a response to capitalist values of school.
- Phil Cohen – young people respond to the loss of working-class community by mimicking the middle classes, or assuming exaggerated working-class behaviour.
- Hall and Jefferson – youth cultures are symbolic resistance to capitalism.
- Mike Brake – youth culture is a 'magical' response; working-class youth solves the problem of exploitation through the development of a culture.
- Criticisms of the Marxist view as dated and so class-focussed it misses other important issues such as gender and racism.

There are other writers and each might be equally useful to refer to in an essay, but you have a limited amount of time and will therefore need to be selective in what you choose to write about.

Mid-range response

Marxist theories of youth culture are based on the work of Karl Marx and studies of social class, so writers from a Marxist perspective are always looking for signs of working-class resistance to capitalism. This makes it different from functionalism, which just sees youth cultures as a normal transition period from youth to adulthood. Most of the work from a Marxist point of view in Britain was produced by the Birmingham Centre for Contemporary Studies (CCCS) in the 1970s, so it is a bit dated. It tends to look at economics as causing problems for young people.

CCCS writers said that social class differences between working-class and middle-class youth explained why youth cultures developed. They say that there is evidence for this in that lots of youth cultures emerged in working-class areas when there were economic problems. This is not true because the hippies tended to be middle class and also, Teddy boys emerged when there were lots of jobs and people had more money to spend on things like fashions and music.

The CCCS said that strikes, inner city decay, immigration and high unemployment in the 1970s meant that young people developed youth cultures as a response to their problems. It affected their styles, so Teddy boys imitated richer people's styles from the Edwardian era and skinheads wore exaggerated working-class male clothing such as Doc Marten's and braces to show their working-class style. Thus the CCCS approach was not pure Marxism because it looked at style and cultural factors as causing youth cultures.

Lots of studies from the CCCS such as Teddy boys (Jefferson 1976), skinheads (Clarke 1976) hippies (Brake 1980) have all been concerned with issues of class. They say that youth cultures are resistant to capitalism and inequality in society.

Many Marxists would say that youth cultures were created by the media and capitalists because they can choose certain street styles and make them fashionable. Young people have money to spend on fashion and consumerism so capitalists make a lot of profits from selling youth culture to young people. So Thornton said that club culture is more about being cool than class.

Commentary

This response has a great deal of knowledge and understanding but does not really develop any of the points in a lot of detail. It would get credit for the names mentioned and the fact that there is an overview of Marxism that is reasonably accurate and clear. It is near the top mark band but needs development, perhaps with more detail on the studies. The reference to Thornton could have been the basis of a very useful paragraph criticising Marxism, but it should not be in a conclusion, which is a summary of what went before. New ideas should never be introduced in the conclusion and this example reads as an afterthought.

Exam questions: Education

In Eduqas papers, Education as a topic forms part of Component 1 examinations. WJEC papers have Education as part of Unit 2. Nevertheless, the questions for WJEC AS level and for Eduqas AS level will be similar to each other, while the 'A' level question for Eduqas is slightly different.

You will be need to plan your responses to education very carefully whichever specification you are following:

- WJEC expects you to write two restricted response answers and one extended essay chosen from two options.
- Eduqas expects three restricted response answers and one extended essay chosen from two options for AS level.
- For Eduqas A level, there is one restricted response essay and an extended essay chosen from two options.

The restricted response questions will focus on patterns of educational attainment and reasons for those patterns. The WJEC and Eduqas AS papers will offer a graph or a piece of stimulus material and candidates will be expected to describe and explain what they see. This is quite a high-level skill, so in preparation, you might want to collect data and graphs about educational attainment. It is not difficult to do this if you keep an eye out for newspaper and television stories which show what is happening in education. It might even be a good idea to keep a scrapbook of cuttings relating to such information.

All papers will expect you to be able to explain an idea, or a concept or a pattern in children's educational attainment. This is one reason why you should be developing your revision around key words and ideas. Remember that examiners will expect you to know and use the important ideas of sociology, so if your revision of key terms is weak, you may miss easy marks because you do not recognise a term or an idea.

Extended essays will use the same command words as those for the extended essays on family, so be certain that you are familiar with the requirements for each type of answer. You may be required to evaluate a view or a theory, or to assess the significance of something such as gender or class on educational attainment.

Choosing an extended essay to answer is an important examination skill. Read the questions very carefully and map out possible answers. It may be that something that seems difficult is not that complicated once you stop and think about what may be required. Examiners do not set out to trap you, but sometimes you may be put off by unusual wording. Stopping to plan out an answer may help you to understand what is needed. Do not answer a question you do not understand.

Make sure that you have some ideas, evidence, examples of studies, key terms and points you want to make for the question that you have chosen. Often, once you start writing, other ideas will appear and as you relax, you will remember more. There are no rules about which question you must answer first. Some people choose to start with questions that they understand so that they have a good start. Others leave their best questions till last, so that they are relaxed and can think carefully. Whatever you do, make sure that you number your answer correctly and clearly.

WJEC/Eduqas AS level questions on Education, part (a)

There will be an item which will be a piece of stimulus material which could be written, graphical or a table. This item will be drawn from a piece of recent research or from government data and for WJEC, data will be drawn from a Welsh source where information is available. There will be two parts to the question that follows the item. Although the questions are similar for both qualifications, the weightings and marks available will be different depending on the qualification for which you are entered. Slightly more detail will be required in the WJEC response to (a) (ii) as more marks are available.

There are two parts to the question following the stimulus item:

⦿ Part (a) (i) will require the candidate to take findings and to interpret the stimulus.
⦿ Part (a) (ii) will require candidates to explain two reasons for the findings in the stimulus.

Qualification	WJEC AS level	Eduqas AS level
Marks available for part a (i)	10	10
Weightings AO1, AO2	6, 4	4, 6
Marks available for part a (ii)	15	10
Weightings AO1, AO2	10, 5	6, 4

Have a look at the following possible example of an Education, part (a) question:

WJEC EDUQAS

(a) Study the following item and answer all of the questions.

Percentages of pupils achieving 5 GCSEs with A*–C grades in Wales according to ethnic background 2011–13

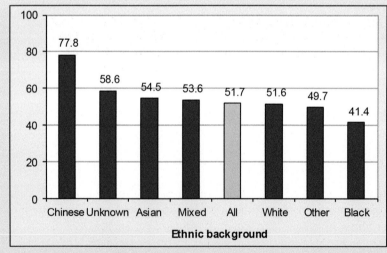

Question a (i) Summarise the content of the table showing the GCSE attainment of different ethnic groups 2011–13.

Question a (ii) Explain **two** sociological reasons for the relationship between ethnicity and educational attainment at GCSE as shown in the item.

The markschemes show that you are expected to pick out a variety of findings, including patterns and trends if applicable. You also need to make points that are supported with evidence from the item.

Stronger response to a (i)

The table shows that in the period 2011–13, children from a Chinese ethnic background performed above the national average at GCSE; 77.8% of children from this ethnic background achieved 5 A*–C grades whereas the average pass rate was 51.7%. This is approximately 25% better performance for children from Chinese ethnic backgrounds.

The lowest attaining groups were from white, other and Black ethnic backgrounds who achieved less than the average. Black children were the lowest achieving group with an average attainment of 41.4% which is 10% lower than the national average. The difference between the highest scoring group (Chinese) and the lowest scoring group (Black) was approximately 35%.

Commentary

Although the focus is on data taken from the bar chart, there is some attempt to process the information and to identify the key findings. There is description, but it is not necessary to offer reasons or explain the information because that is part (ii) of the question.

Stronger response to a (ii)

There are many reasons for the patterns shown in the graph, but the two most significant can be linked to racism and to culture.

Many sociologists have claimed that Black children are the victims of racism in British schools; for example, Wright, Sewell and Modood have all suggested that education in Britain is institutionally racist. This can be as a result of the school system discriminating against Black children in terms of the curriculum and of the racism of individual teachers who find Black children threatening. This means that many Black children reject schools and schooling and this will have an impact on their results.

One explanation for the success of Chinese ethnic background children is that the home culture emphasises success and views education as a route to high achievement. For example, Amy Chua describes the Tiger Mother. Chinese parents are not accepting of educational failure. Children have a high work ethic and parents engage with the children's schools.

Commentary

There is a slight lack of balance so that racism is explored in more detail than cultural factors that lead to success or failure. For example, Indian heritage children succeed in education but the cultural factors that contribute to their success may be linked to their social class background.

Weaker response to a (ii)

There are lots of reasons for the failure of ethnic minority children to do well in school and these can be linked to racism and home culture. British schools are racist and sociologists have found that teachers are prejudiced against Black children so that they fail in school. One sociologist found that Black girls do better because they reject the labels that schools give them.

People from ethnic minorities are often from lower-class backgrounds and do less well in school because they lack resources. Working-class children are labelled as failures and therefore do less well because they are seen as not able and are put into lower sets. Boys tend to do less well than girls as well because they form anti-school subcultures.

Commentary

This starts badly because the bar chart does not show that ethnic minorities fail; the situation is more complex than that. Some ethnic minorities underachieve, but others do rather better than the average. There are many assertions about the education system in Britain, but not much reference to supporting studies or evidence. It's difficult for a marker to pick out the key points in the second paragraph because although some of the points are relevant and could be developed and used, it is all a bit of a jumble of ideas.

Eduqas A level questions on Education, part (a)

The A level part (a) question is worth 15 marks and the weighting is towards AO1 (9 marks) rather than AO2 (6 marks). It is a more straightforward test of your ability to write a clear explanation of an idea or reasons for a particular feature of British society. Examiners will be looking for several points and these should be linked to the question. There will be direct reference to supporting evidence from studies or statistics. This is specified in the question so the command must be met.

EDUQAS

(a) Using sociological evidence and examples explain the influence that material deprivation may have on educational attainment.

Stronger response

Material deprivation refers to a lack of educational or other physical resources, such as good food, which may have an impact on a child's educational attainment. Britain is an increasing unequal country in terms of wealth; so many children are without the necessary resources to do well in school, having poor diets, poor housing, living in areas with underperforming schools and not having access to equipment such as the Internet.

Harrison, in the 1980s found that children in Hackney, a poor area of London, lived in homes with fewer books, lack of play space, fewer holidays and lack of attention from their parents who were working long unsocial hours. They also attended schools with the poorest examination results in London. Harrison claimed that lack of basic necessities made it difficult for children to succeed in school.

Ridge in the 2000s found that poorer families found it difficult to afford lunch, uniforms and trips so their children had less stimulating experiences in and out of school. They were less likely to have been on holiday or have activities such as dance or music lessons. This meant that they took a negative view of school which will affect their performance.

Smith and Noble found that wealthy parents would move to areas where the schools had better examination results and teachers had higher expectations of children and so poorer children attended less successful schools. This means they have less opportunity.

In addition, children from poorer families may be encouraged to leave school early in order to get jobs and help with family income. They are not encouraged to go to university and acquire debts that cannot be paid back.

The evidence shows that material deprivation can have a huge effect on the educational attainment of poorer children who will find it more difficult to succeed in school.

Commentary

The term is clearly defined and explained. It is linked to contemporary Britain and by taking a wider view of how material deprivation affects children by including home circumstances, the candidate has been able to write more. By focussing on three studies, the candidate is showing AO1. By using the findings to explain why material deprivation affects school attainment, then AO2 is demonstrated.

WJEC/Eduqas all papers Education extended response essays

In all papers, you will be given a choice of two extended response essays for your option on education. You will choose one essay on this topic. Despite the fact that the essay questions will be very similar in style and level of demand, the number of marks available for the essays and again, their weightings, will vary according to the paper that you will be sitting. For all of the qualifications, you will see that AO1 carries fewer marks than AO2 and AO3 combined, so your focus should be on essay writing skills rather than knowledge alone.

See the table below:

Qualification	WJEC AS level	Eduqas AS level	Eduqas A level
Marks available	30	25	35
Weightings AO1, AO2, AO3	13, 5, 12	9, 4, 12	12, 11, 12

Possible question – all qualifications

> Assess the usefulness of functionalist views of education to an understanding of education in contemporary UK.

WJEC
EDUQAS

This is a complicated question because not only are you expected to understand the theory, but to consider how useful it is when trying to understand modern British society. You will need to make judgements, and to focus carefully on functionalist viewpoints.

Two possible routes through this question are to:

◉ Focus on functionalism and what functionalists have to say, but looking at modern Britain.
◉ Focus on functionalism, but consider whether other theories are more useful to understanding contemporary UK.

Weaker response to extended essay

There are two basic questions that functionalists attempt to answer. The first is to consider the importance and functions of education for society and the second is to consider the relationship between education and the social system. Durkheim said that the main function of the education system was to transmit social norms and values. He said that education, especially in history, will help children to develop a sense that they are part of a social group. He said that education acted to create social solidarity. He also said that schools teach children to cooperate with people who are not family or friends.

Talcott Parsons, a major sociological writer, said that schools are the second most important agency of socialisation after the family. Education acts as a bridge between the family and wider society. In the home, the child is looked at as an individual, but in wider society, people are judged in terms of standards that apply to everyone. School prepares children for this type of universal standard by measuring them against their ability to do well in examinations and against school rules.

Durkheim and Parsons both said that education provides a trained workforce for society. It ensures that the most important jobs go to the most talented people. The education system is a ladder of opportunity for talented people who will rise to the top and less able people will do the worst jobs. They called this idea meritocracy. This creates a division of labour, where people all do different jobs to make sure society is fair and works well. Davis and Moore suggested that inequality in education and society was a good thing because it made people work harder.

New Right thinkers use functionalist ideas and support them. Marxists, feminists and interactionists criticise these ideas.

Commentary

Superficially, this looks like a very good essay, but it would not do well under examination conditions for two reasons. These are that there is no evaluation or assessment of functionalism and that there is no reference to education in the contemporary UK. You should note that it is possible to reach the very top band for AO1 and score very low marks on AO2 and AO3. It is possible that the candidate ran out of time before writing any assessments or using any UK research for examples, or it may be that the essay was learned off by heart and then not applied to the question. In either case, this candidate has worked extremely hard but cannot gain the highest marks due to poor examination skills. Note, too, that in places the expression is not clear either, for example, who are the 'they' in the third paragraph?

293

Methods of sociological enquiry (Research methods)

In each paper, there is a focus on actual social research by sociologists. You will be offered a stimulus item which can be the basis of a question and which may be useful as a guide to encourage thinking.

- In both Eduqas papers, Research methods as a topic forms a separate component, Component 2.
- WJEC papers have Research methods as part of Unit 2 but candidates are also expected to answer questions on Education at AS level. A further question on Research methods appears on Unit 4, where candidates are expected to design a study.

In this section, WJEC and Eduqas will be discussed separately, but points made may apply to all of the qualifications as there is some overlap of style and content. We suggest you read the advice given for all of the qualifications, but focus very carefully on your own paper.

WJEC Methods of sociological enquiry Unit 2

The item is likely to focus on Wales, and research about Wales, so it may be helpful to familiarise yourself with some recent research that has been published.

WJEC **1** Read the item and answer each part of the following question

The Active Adults Survey Wales

The Sports Council for Wales has been surveying people in Wales since the 1980s in order to track the number of people participating in sporting activity. The findings are used to inform government policy, so representativeness and generalisability are important. Quantitative data are collected.

The study is a large scale **survey** of 13,145 people aged 15 and above living in households in Wales. Households are selected at random and then interviewers select someone from the household to answer the questions. They then visit the household to conduct a face-to-face interview with the selected participant. Interviewing took place over a year and collected demographic information about age and health as well as discovering details about participation levels in various activities.

a) Using material from the item and sociological knowledge, explain the meaning of the term **survey**. (5)

b) Using material from the item and sociological knowledge, explain **two** possible reasons for using a large sample group. (10)

c) With reference to the item and sociological studies, discuss why many researchers choose to use quantitative methods. (20)

Source *http://sport.wales/research--policy/surveys-and-statistics/active-adults-survey.aspx*

WJEC Unit 2	1 a)	1 b)	1 c)
Marks available	5	10	20
Weightings AO1, AO2, AO3	3, 2, 0	6, 4, 0	9, 5, 6

1 a) Using material from the item and sociological knowledge, explain the meaning of the term **survey**. (5)

WJEC

Stronger response to 1 a)

A survey is a method of sociological research that collects statistics about people's behaviour, for example, in the item, data is collected about numbers participating in sports. A well-known survey is the Millenium cohort study which tracks children born in 2000–01. Usually surveys are conducted on large groups of people in order to gather information that can refer to the population as a whole. Questions tend to be structured so that the research is reliable, whether interviews or questionnaires are used.

Commentary

The main points are made clearly and concisely. There is an example which is explained and reference to the item. Key terms are used effectively.

b) Using material from the item and sociological knowledge, explain **two** possible reasons for using a large sample group. (10)

WJEC

Mid-range response to 1 b)

People use large sample groups in social research because it is easy to identify patterns and trends from large groups of people. If a large sample group is used, then there is less likely to be sample bias. This is where findings from one single person will influence the results too much. The research will probably therefore be more representative of the whole social group being studied. For example, in the item, over 13,000 were studied.

Another reason for using a large sample group is to make the research more generalisable. The findings can apply to the whole population. For example, in the item, it is possible to take the results from the sample and discover patterns that probably apply to all of Wales.

Commentary

You may not always be so lucky as to get such a clear hint in the item as this, but if you read it carefully, you will probably get a clue as to what is required. However, the response is a little short and it could have been developed with reference to other studies that use or have used large samples such as the Mass Observation study. There is very little added to this response that could not have been drawn from the item, and the command asks for additional sociological knowledge.

c) With reference to the item and sociological studies, discuss why many researchers choose to use quantitative methods.

(20)

Mid-range response

Quantitative research methods are used to collect scientific data using statistical analysis to interpret the results. They are used to measure how people behave, what they think and feel but in a numerical way. The item shows that data is collected regarding sporting behaviour and also personal details so that there can be correlations between age and activity rates, for example.

Emile Durkheim used quantitative methods in his study on suicide in order to discover whether suicide was a social fact. He used official statistics and analysed patterns and trends. This approach is positivist because it is scientific so it can be used to compare information.

This approach is useful for studying large numbers of people, because it is quicker and easier to collect information using structured interviews and questionnaires than interviewing people. In addition findings can be gathered and processed quickly using statistical programmes on the computer. Some National Census findings are available within a year or so of the study. The research results do not need the same amount of analysis as qualitative research.

Commentary

This answer is a little short for 20 marks. It lacks the necessary depth and detail. There is reference to sociological studies, which is a strength, but specific mention of the advantages for quantitative methods applied to sociological studies is needed for AO3. Quantitative methods could have been compared favourably with qualitative methods for the purpose of data gathering and data comparison. More use of the key terms: ethics, reliability and validity was needed and these can be used as a simple plan for many of these extended response questions.

Eduqas AS level and A level Methods of sociological enquiry Component 2

There are four parts to the question and you have no choice of question to respond to, whichever qualification you are entered for, because all the part-questions are compulsory.

There is some overlap in styles of questions between AS and A level, so look carefully and see what style of questions you should prepare for.

Eduqas AS component 2 1 hour 15 minutes	1a	1b	1c	1d
Marks available	5	10	10	25
Weightings AO1, AO2, AO3	3, 2, 0	6, 4, 0	6, 4, 0	10, 5, 10
Eduqas A level component 2 1 hour 45 minutes	1a	1b	1c	1d
Marks available	5	5	20	30
Weightings AO1, AO2, AO3	3, 2, 0	2, 3, 0	14, 6, 0	8, 10, 12

Student educational and development outcomes at age 16

EDUQAS

A study aimed to describe the links between family background, home and school learning on the academic attainment of pupils aged 16. It looked at how the experience of education differs for particular groups of children including gender, special needs or disadvantage through poverty.

In 1997, 141 preschool educational classes such as nurseries and playgroups were selected from around the country. In each, 20 children under school age were recruited to the study and assessed. This made a cohort of over 2,800 children who formed part of the **sample**. In addition, 300 children who had not had any preschool educational experiences were added to the study when they entered the reception class in school. These children have been tracked as part of a longitudinal study and assessed for educational progress at regular intervals. Approximately 80% of the original group were still part of the sample in 2013 and they took GCSE examinations in that year. Six months after finishing their GCSE courses, the children were contacted and asked to complete a postal questionnaire to find out their GCSE grades and what further education, employment or training they were undertaking.

Source: *https://www.gov.uk/government/uploads/system/uploads/attachment_data/file/351496/RR354_-_Students__educational_and_developmental_outcomes_at_age_16.pdf*

Eduqas AS component 2 – possible questions

EDUQAS

a) Using material from the item and sociological knowledge, explain the meaning of the term **sample**. (5)

b) Using material from the item and sociological knowledge, explain **two** reasons why the researchers decided to use longitudinal methods in their research. (10)

c) Explain **two** strengths of the sampling process in this research. (10)

d) With reference to sociological studies, discuss the strengths and weaknesses of using postal questionnaires in sociological research. (25)

EDUQAS Eduqas A level component 2 – possible questions

1 a) Using material from the item and sociological knowledge, explain the meaning of the
term **sample**. (5)

   b) Using material from the item and sociological knowledge, explain **one** reason why the
researchers decided to use longitudinal methods in their research. (5)

   c) With reference to sociological studies, discuss the strengths and weaknesses of using
postal questionnaires in sociological research. (20)

2 As an A level Sociology student, you have been asked to design a research project to collect data on
attitudes to pre-school education, such as nurseries and playgroups, amongst a sample of mothers
in your area. (30)

   a) Describe each stage of your research design, justifying the reasons for your choices at
each stage.

   b) Discuss problems that may occur and the impact of these problems on the quality of the
data collected.

Question 1 a) Eduqas AS level and A2 level

EDUQAS Using material from the item and sociological knowledge, explain the meaning of the
term **sample**. (5)

Weaker response

A sample is a group of people who are studied in
a sociological study and they can be interviewed
or questioned. In the item, they were given a
questionnaire. Samples can be picked randomly to
make sure that a lot of people can give different kinds
of answers to make the results more representative,
so for example the Census interviews everyone.

Commentary

This is a very disappointing response. It starts fairly
well but much of the information is irrelevant and it is
clear that the candidate does not really understand
the meaning of Census or of random sampling. Some
credit can be given for using technical language if it is
used with understanding. In this case, it is not clear that
representativeness is understood.

Question 1 b) Eduqas AS and A level

Question 1 b) is similar on both AS and A level. The only variation is the number of reasons that need to be offered to gain the marks. See the questions below.

AS level

EDUQAS

Using material from the item and sociological knowledge, explain **two** reasons why the researchers decided to use longitudinal methods in their research.

(10)

A level

EDUQAS

Using material from the item and sociological knowledge, explain **one** reason why the researchers decided to use longitudinal methods in their research.

(5)

Each individual reason in AS level will be marked separately. Twice as much should therefore be written than is necessary for the full A level. Possible reasons for using longitudinal studies include:

- Social change can be tracked.
- Changes in life circumstances can be described.
- The influence of past experiences on current behaviour can be seen.
- Researchers can test how expectations in the past can be linked to present outcomes.

Any of the above can be applied to the question.

Stronger response

One aim of the study described in the item was to discover if there is a link between pre-school education and subsequent performance at GCSE, thus researchers were interested in how the influence of past experiences might affect current behaviour and school performance. By tracking the same cohort of children over a period of time it was possible to discover a variety of influences on their GCSE results. It increases the reliability of the study because the same children were returned to at various stages in their lives. Another important study is the UK British Household Panel Survey which followed the same group of participants and is a measure of social change.

Commentary

This answer may be a little long and wordy for five marks, but the assessment criteria are met. There is a clear link to the question and an example of a study.

Question 1 c) Eduqas AS level only

Explain **two** strengths of the sampling process in this research.

(10)   EDUQAS

Weaker response

Sampling is used to learn about large groups of people, so that the group that is being studied is known as the target population. It is difficult to study every person in a group, so sociologists select a particular group known as a sample. There is a variety of methods of sampling, so, for example, a random sample is when you pick people at random to answer your questionnaire. A strength of this is that you get a variety of opinions. This is an important method in sociology.

A second strength of sampling is that you can get a smaller number of people to fill in your questionnaire and it is easier to handle the results. This makes the research quick and easy to carry out.

Commentary

This answer is worthy of very few marks because it does not address the terms of the question. Despite some use of technical language, and some fair points, there is no reference to the actual research project under discussion and so there are no marks awarded for providing context to the study.

Question 1 d) Eduqas AS level and 1 c) Eduqas A level

Note that the same question is worth 25 marks for AS level and 20 marks for A level.

EDUQAS | With reference to sociological studies, discuss the strengths and weaknesses of using postal questionnaires in sociological research.

Stronger response

A postal questionnaire is when letters containing questionnaires are sent to households. Probably the best known such questionnaire is the Census which is distributed to every household in the UK. The householders complete the questionnaires and return them to the researchers.

There are a variety of strengths and weaknesses to the method. The most obvious strength is its convenience. It takes less time to distribute a questionnaire to a group of people than to interview the same number of people to obtain responses. Sample sizes can be much larger, and assuming that response rates are high, then this increases reliability. The costs of postal questionnaires may be lower than other methods, because all that is required is printing and postage. Increasingly, however, researchers are turning to online surveys such as SurveyMonkey which have the same advantages but no associated costs with printing and distribution. Respondents may have more time to think about their answers and this could increase the validity of their responses. It may even reduce interviewer effects as the presence of a researcher may affect how people complete the surveys. If the topic is embarrassing, a postal survey may be more ethical than an interview as it saves people from embarrassment.

Weaknesses of postal questionnaires are that response rates are generally very low. There are more serious issues of validity which can be affected in a number of ways. With a postal questionnaire, the researcher does not know who filled in the form or whether it was taken seriously at the time. It is possible that the sample who do complete the questionnaire are self-selecting and therefore unrepresentative because those who have no opinions will not complete the survey. It is also possible that questions were misread and because no-one was present to help the respondent, the survey will be incomplete or inaccurate, further affecting validity.

Commentary

The strength of this answer is that it is easy to read. Strengths are dealt with and then weaknesses are addressed. This simple structure makes the marks easier to find. A weakness is that there are few references to studies, but this is because few studies depend on postal questionnaires as their main method. To compensate, the candidate has referred to a more modern method of data collection and this will be credited.

Question 2 A level Eduqas only

As an A level Sociology student, you have been asked to design a research project to collect data on attitudes to pre-school education, such as nurseries and playgroups, amongst a sample of mothers in your area. **EDUQAS**

(30)

(i) Describe each stage of your research design, justifying the reasons for your choices at each stage.

(ii) Discuss problems that may occur and the impact of these problems on the quality of the data collected.

Stronger response

I would probably choose to undertake a qualitative study of mothers in order to understand their feelings and because the brief asks about attitudes. Qualitative methods are more appropriate for finding out about feelings than scientific methods which tend to focus on behaviour. Statistical methods might give me an overview of attitudes but I would not get the same level of understanding of how important mothers feel pre-school education is from quantitative research.

I would operationalise the term pre-school education to any formal organisation such as nursery schools or playgroups where children meet in groups and are taught away from their parents. I would probably look at mothers of young children because mothers of older children would probably know or care less about pre-school education programmes. This means that I may have some problems obtaining a sample, because mothers of children of this age are not listed in any way so I would have to consider sampling processes with care.

I would probably conduct unstructured or semi-structured interviews to collect my data as I am choosing to gather qualitative data on attitudes. This would allow me to choose a number of areas of questioning and to aim to address the key issues in a relaxed and informal manner. I would aim to gather depth of information and probe mothers about their attitudes to pre-school education. This could be difficult because I have not had training as an interviewer, so hopefully this would enable me to develop skills.

There are many ethical issues in any study involving children and such a personal area of life, so I would allow mothers to refuse to take part if they so wished. I would also allow them permission to see the final report if they wanted. I would tell mothers that if my questions were inappropriate, I would not be upset if they refused to answer. The problem with this is that my research may not be quite as valid as it may be the mothers who refuse to participate who have interesting things to say.

I would take my sample from a playgroup or a nursery school. This is a convenience sample. I would ask mothers if they wish to participate, and if they know others who might be willing to help. This is a snowball sample. I would aim to complete between ten and twenty interviews from the group. Unfortunately, my results would be biased because I would not be likely to access mothers who do not send their children to pre-school education.

I would attempt to meet the mothers on neutral territory, perhaps at the playgroup or nursery so that they would feel comfortable. Ethically, I should avoid using my home or theirs because it could place me in danger. I would have a list of ten or twelve areas of questioning and perhaps give this to mothers in advance to increase validity because they could think about the topic in advance. They could also then raise issues if they so wanted or if they felt that my research was asking the wrong questions. This is known as active research as respondents can participate in the research process. I would record the interviews and make notes of what was said so I could check my findings.

I would expect collating the research to be a difficult process. I might pick out key themes in what the mothers said and then go back to my notes for good quotations to add to my report.

Commentary

The strengths of this research design lie in the structure of the report. Each paragraph refers to a stage in the research process and mentions why a decision has been taken and a problem that could arise. Another positive in the answer is the use of key terms such as ethics, reliability and validity. These are listed in the markschemes for the paper, where a rough guide to an essay plan is offered. Clearly the candidate understands the research process and recognises that some weaknesses exist in the design. This shows the ability to be self-critical and recognise that the design of a research project will influence the quality of the results.

Weaker response

I would create a questionnaire and give it out to mothers that I know who have young children. I would target people with children under the age of five which is when the children start school.

The questionnaire would consist of 20 questions and I would ask some open and some closed questions to find out details about the mothers such as where they lived and if they send their children to playgroups or nurseries. It is important to know who they are and where they live so that I can guess what social class they come from. I could then find out if middle-class mothers are more likely to send the children to playgroups than working mothers.

If I could arrange for 30 mothers to fill in my questionnaire that would give me good results as I would get a variety of opinions and it would be easy to draw graphs because I could get percentages. This would make my research more reliable, valid and practical. It would be ethical.

The most important question would be to find out whether mothers can afford to send their children to playgroups or nurseries. This is a problem in my area as lots of people do not have much money so I could use the findings to support the idea that the council should do more to support mothers. I think pre-school education is really important and mothers should be helped to get this for the children if they want it.

Some of the problems that I might have is that mothers might not want to take part and so I could offer a prize of a bottle of wine to get them to hand in the questionnaires like a raffle.

In the questionnaire, I would ask questions about whether mothers work and what they think that playgroups are for. This would make it reliable and I could repeat it in the future. It would be ethical as I would not be asking questions that really upset people and if it is an anonymous questionnaire then people can tell the truth which makes it valid and reliable.

Commentary

One of the key problems with this design is that while there are a lot of very good ideas, the whole response is disorganised and not explained in any logical order. Although technical language is used, it is not used in such a way that the marker can be certain that the term is fully understood. Lack of planning and thought can be seen when sentences are too long and contain far too many ideas. To do well on the research design question, it is important that the planning is made part of the design so that decisions can be made in the light of the aims.

Answers

Acquiring Culture through Socialisation

T1
a) the way of life of a group of people
b) the physical things that people create
c) the ideas that people share
d) this is any idea that is created and given meaning by people
e) emphasise the importance of living as a group
f) emphasise personal freedom and choice
g) people are forced to behave
h) moral codes become part of everyday thinking

T2
a) False
b) False
c) False
d) True
e) True
f) True

T3
a) The process by which humans learn and internalise their culture's norms and values
b) The child learns from the immediate family in the home
c) People are deliberately and consciously manipulated to ensure they follow social rules
d) Any social group or organisation that passes on cultural norms and values to others
e) A social situation in which we feel comfortable and at home
f) Children learn and copy from their parents and others

T4
a) whereby people modify their behaviour in order to fit in with a group
b) the assumptions and beliefs that are taught unintentionally in schools
c) collective conscience as a set of socially accepted and shared norms and values
d) media and it is claimed people model their actions on what they see on the television
e) and is where workers understand the work practices and attitudes of other employees

T5
a) False
b) True
c) False
d) True
e) True
f) True
g) False

Theory

T1
a) Theory
b) Concept
c) Evidence
d) Sociology
e) Debates
f) Social policy

T2
a) Socialisation
b) Organic analogy
c) Consensus
d) Macro-sociology
e) Functionalism
f) Positivism

T3
a) and believed that all social relationships could be explained in terms of who controlled wealth.
b) based on the maximisation of profit for the owners.
c) to belief systems that people have about how society should be run.
d) change is natural to society.
e) are said to have 'false consciousness'.
f) policy because many politicians come from wealthy backgrounds.

T4
a) Patriarchy
b) Feminism
c) Other
d) Gender
e) Sex
f) Sexism

T5
a) Ethnography
b) Micro-sociology
c) Social interaction
d) Social construction
e) Qualitative research
f) Social role
g) Labelling theory

T6
a) it emerged in France in the 1980s.
b) because people value consumption and image over reality.
c) they claim contemporary society is swamped with media ideas.
d) claim to offer the truth as they say everything is relative.
e) are leading meaningless lives because all they care about is image.
f) because they reject the idea that there is anything with meaning.

T7
a) Trickle-down theory
b) Conservative Party
c) New Right
d) Capitalism
e) Welfare state
f) Taxation

Research methods

T1
a) is favoured by positivists
b) refers to the accuracy of data
c) is based on many factors
d) place an emphasis on meanings
e) follow scientific methods
f) are concerned with what is right or wrong
g) consists of words

T2
a) respondents
b) reliable
c) interviewer bias
d) open, closed
e) valid data
f) interview

T5
a) Sampling frame
b) Representative sample
c) Opportunity sample
d) Stratified samples
e) Quota sample
f) Random sample

T6
harm
consent
purpose
deception
sensitive
confidentiality
anonymity

T7
a) operationalisation, time, money, and access.
b) refers to the group that the researcher wishes to generalise her findings to.
c) personal experiences, events in society and political priorities.
d) government, business or research councils.
e) access to target populations and samples.
f) operationalise a concept.

T8
a) Positivism
b) Interpretivism
c) Quantitative
d) Qualitative
e) Realist

Family

T1
a) Functionalism
b) Feminism
c) Postmodernism
d) Interactionism
e) Marxism

Activity
Functionalist sociologists view the **family** as being a specific arrangement of a group of people who are linked by blood or **legal** ties. They tend to claim that the **best** form of family is a **nuclear** family consisting of **heterosexual** parents and their children. More recent theories of family suggest that the actual **structure** of the family is unimportant, what is important is the **quality** of the relationships and the **emotions** in families. They say that many people no longer choose **traditional** family forms because they view emotional **connection** as more important.

T2
a) Single parents by choice
b) Blended or reconstituted family
c) Sandwich generation
d) Beanpole family
e) Unmarried couples with children
f) Gay family
g) Child freedom
h) Living apart together (LAT)
i) Co-parenting (parenting partnerships)

T3

Reason for family change	Explanation of why it has caused family change
Technology	1. Women have fewer children as medical changes mean they can control reproduction, this mean that families are smaller. 2. Families can keep in touch over long distances more easily and this strengthens relationships.
Legal change	1. Laws mean that same-sex marriages are now legal and so there are now gay families. 2. People can divorce more easily, leading to singlehood and lone parenthood.
Economy	1. There are fewer jobs for men available, so single breadwinner families are less common. 2. More women work, so they are not dependent on men for their happiness.
Norms and values	1. People have more choices in their lives, so a variety of family forms is now acceptable. 2. Women need not be ashamed of having children and being unmarried, so many choose to be single parents.

T4

Reasons for singlehood and living alone	Choice factors	Situational factors
Younger people	Leaving parents' home	Removed from parental home
Older people	Money to be able to live alone Job reasons Individuality	Relationship breakdown No one to share home with
	Good health Good social networks	Children leave home Partner dies

T5
a) Social construction
b) Expressive role
c) Child-centred
d) Consumer goods
e) Disappearing childhood
f) Emotional climate
g) Toxic childhood

T6
a) Triple shift
b) Dual burden
c) Segregated conjugal roles
d) Joint conjugal roles
e) Lagged adaptation
f) Dark side of family

T7
a) people are at risk of harm and exploitation from carers.
b) between 40 and 50, though carers can be all ages.
c) full-time employment as well as caring responsibility.
d) because they are less likely to maintain social contacts with friends and family.
e) caring for children and their own parents.
f) the period between retirement and extreme old age when ill health is an issue.

T8
Strengths
The functionalist approach stresses the emotional importance of family life.
The approach shows a link between individuals and the whole of society.
This theory shows how the family supports social structure and society.

Weaknesses
The approach is very positive and overlooks the fact that families are not all good.
By stressing the importance of the nuclear family, it is critical of other types of family.
It does not understand that other social structures can take on family roles.

T9
Marxists believe that family life supports **capitalism**. It does this in a number of ways. Marxists claim that families evolved so that men could pass on wealth and property to their **children** and they could control **women**. Families act as a unit of **consumption**, because they buy the products produced by capitalism. Men control the family, this is known as **patriarchy**. They are able to release the stress and frustration of their paid **work** in their homes.

T10
a) Radical feminism
b) Patriarchy
c) Malestream
d) Liberal feminism
e) Marxist feminism

T11
a) Family of choice
b) Individualism
c) Fragmented society
d) Negotiated family
e) Confluent love
f) Plastic sexuality

T12
a) 1980s
b) Margaret Thatcher
c) Golden age
d) Charles Murray
e) Nuclear family
f) Welfare benefits

Youth cultures

T1

a) A term used to describe a set of norms and values shared by a group of adolescent people
b) A peer group refers to those people who are of the same age and status
c) This term is used to describe the cultural norms and values of the majority of the people in a society
d) The transition period between childhood and adulthood
e) A small group within a culture who have different norms, values and cultural beliefs

T2

a) False
b) False
c) True
d) True
e) True
f) True

T3

a) Crepe shoes, draped jackets in pale colours, thin bootlace ties
b) Being extremely well dressed and smart, threatening use of flick-knives as a fashion accessory
c) Rock and Roll
d) Pony tails for girls and quiffs for boys
e) Many Teds became the rockers of the 1960s, the look was revisited in the 1970s when it became associated with early punk and glam rock style
f) Aggressively racist in the later stages of the culture

T4

a) Functionalism
b) Feminism
c) Postmodernism
d) Marxism
e) Interactionism

T5

Area of life in which young people are controlled	Suggested example
Sexuality	Young people are not allowed to watch sexually explicit films under the age of 18
Work	Young people may not take on paid work under the age of 13
Freedom to live where you choose	You cannot move out of the parental home under the age of 16
Politics	You may not vote under the age of 18
Control over your body	You may not get a tattoo or piercing under the age of 18
Leisure	You may not buy alcohol under the age of 18

T6

a) Girls' subcultures are under-studied and a response to patriarchy
b) Girls are adopting male behaviours and developing masculine attitudes
c) Working-class boys reject schools and form anti-school subcultures as a response to capitalism
d) Boys form anti-school subcultures as an alternative route to status
e) African Caribbean boys form subcultures as a response to racism from teachers
f) A variety of subcultural responses develop in schools among Asian girls in response to social pressures
g) Asian and Black girls develop subcultures that lead to success, not failure, whilst also rejecting much of what they hear in school

T7

1) A deviant act takes place
2) The media create a news story about the action which is sensational
3) The news story catches the public mood and people buy newspapers
4) The media further exaggerate events and write more stories so deviants are seen as folk devils
5) The public become very concerned and politicians and the police are put under pressure to act
6) Deviants begin to live up to their label because of self-fulfilling prophecy
7) Social control is imposed on the deviants, many of whom are seriously punished.
8) New laws may be created
9) Eventually the story is boring and the newspapers and media move on to the next thing

T8

a) Youth cultures are an attempt to find a magical solution to the problems of inequality in society
b) Youth cultures are based on existing friendship networks
c) Youth cultures are about fun and excitement not class boundaries
d) Punk is a form of resistance to capitalism
e) Skinhead style is loosely based on traditional work clothes for men
f) Youth rebellion against the Vietnam war was carried out by those with most to lose by rejecting society
g) Working-class culture has different values from middle-class culture, leading to youth cultures developing
h) Youth culture is an alternative route to success for working-class boys

T9

a) Socially accepted patterns of behaviour for people of different biological sex
b) People maintain social connections in a private space thanks to new technologies
c) The view that boys no longer have a concept of what it is to be masculine
d) People blur the lines between gendered behaviours
e) Hatred and fear of women
f) Males assume exaggerated masculine characteristics and style
g) Girls in the 1970s viewed bedrooms as places of safety
h) Hatred and fear of gay people

T10

a) Traditional Jamaican musical forms
b) A belief in and actions supporting the view that one race (ethnicity) is somehow superior to another
c) A religious and spiritual movement that looks to the symbolic return of those of Black African heritage to Africa and the rejection of materialism
d) People who cannot gain respect through the usual channels turn to alternative methods of gaining respect, such as criminality
e) People reject the dominant mainstream culture and fight against it by forming their own cultural styles
f) Young people form cultures that retain elements of their heritage culture but attach other cultural forms to create a new cultural form
g) A hybrid culture developed from a combination of Asian cultural forms and British and American youth cultural styles

T11

a) True
b) False
c) True
d) True
e) True
f) False
g) True

T12

a) Maffesoli
b) Spectacular youth culture
c) Alix Sharkey
d) Muggleton
e) 1970s feminists
f) Post modernists
g) Hebdige

T13

a) Batchelor
b) Venkatesh
c) Kinsella
d) Parker
e) Centre for Social Justice
f) Shaw and McKay
g) Miller

T14

a) Functionalist
b) Functionalist
c) Feminist
d) Marxist
e) Functionalist
f) Marxist
g) Feminist
h) Postmodernist

T15

a) Sarah Thornton
b) Mike Brake
c) Muggleton
d) Len Barton
e) Corrigan
f) Hall and Jefferson

T16

a) A social system where males hold the power and control society
b) Research that is carried out from the point of view of the male
c) A range of ideologies linked to the idea that women and men should be more equal in society
d) The idea that males no longer know what it is to be a man and feel threatened by the rise of women
e) Women and girls are overlooked and missing from much academic writing despite their presence in society
f) Youth cultures are located in a domestic setting such as the home rather than on the streets

T17

a) There are significant and meaningful style differences between middle-and working-class young people in Britain
b) What neo-tribes have in common is a single-minded pursuit of fun and excitement
c) We can now choose what identity we wish from a supermarket of style
d) People no longer identify with a single culture, but may belong to modern tribes
e) Fusion styles represent an attempt to make something new and original from choices of the present
f) The Internet has resulted in virtual youth cultures developing where ideas from a number of cultures are adapted according to local tastes and ideas

T18

a) False
b) False, it was Chambliss
c) True
d) True
e) True
f) True

Education

T1

a) The education system is a ladder of opportunity for the best people to get to the top.
b) The education system exists to ensure that children learn to accept inequality as normal and acceptable.
c) The education system exists to ensure that male power and dominance over women is maintained.
d) Children are labelled by teachers in schools and learn to act according to those labels.
e) Teachers and pupils work together to construct knowledge.

T2

a) Marxism
b) Feminism
c) Functionalism
d) Functionalism
e) Functionalism

T3

a) Comprehensive school
b) Public school
c) Grammar school
d) Academy
e) Faith school

T4

a) Material deprivation
b) Cultural deprivation
c) Cultural capital
d) Cultural reproduction
e) School organisation theory
f) Labelling theory
g) Subcultural theory

T5

a) Interactionists
b) Feminism
c) New Right
d) Postmodernism
e) Genetics and biology
f) Gender socialisation
g) School organisation theory
h) Hegemonic masculinity
i) Feminism
j) New Right

T6

a) False
b) True
c) False
d) True
e) True
f) True

T7
a) True
b) True
c) False
d) True
e) True
f) True

T8
a) Working-class culture is inferior to middle-class culture.
b) Working-class children are seen as having little or no ambition to improve their situation.
c) Schools are middle class and do not understand the cultural differences between themselves and working-class pupils.
d) Poor people develop a culture that keeps them poor.
e) Forms and patterns of speech that vary between the different social classes.
f) Working-class culture is not valued and the middle class have access to knowledge of social systems and structures that give them advantages.

T9
a) OECD PISA
b) Becker
c) Cicourel and Kitsuse
d) Wright
e) Ball, Keddie, Lacey and Hargreaves
f) Stoll and Fink

T10
a) Functionalist
b) Functionalist
c) Marxist
d) Feminist
e) Functionalist
f) Functionalist

T11
a) Cultural capital
b) Hidden curriculum
c) Ideology
d) Capitalism
e) Counter-school culture
f) Correspondence theory
g) Conflict theory

T12
a) False
b) True
c) True
d) True
e) True
f) False

T13

Support	Reject
Setting processes continue to operate to the disadvantage of working-class students.	Class cultural factors also influence pupils' attitudes to school. Peer pressure among many working-class boys was a significant factor inhibiting their educational achievement
Teachers may also use informal 'ability' groupings within formally mixed ability classes.	When asked: 'If you had a choice what would you choose to learn?' students responded as follows: Jamie: 'Nothing'. George: 'Nothing'. Andy: 'No idea'. Paul: 'Definitely nothing'.
Teachers may label working-class pupils negatively and middle-class pupils often receive preferential treatment.	Some teachers are well informed sociologically and show sympathetic concern for working-class students or feel themselves to be working class
Teachers demonstrated prejudicial views of working-class parents. 'I'm afraid some parents are just pig ignorant'.	Interactional theories do not explain the origin of the labels.

T14
- We have a cultural 'pick and mix', so we choose ideas, products and clothing from a variety of sources.
- Image and impression management are very important to people.
- We interact with highly developed technologies which are changing regularly.
- We take spiritual and cultural ideas from a variety of sources.
- We tend to be individualistic and look after our own and ourselves.
- We are far more concerned with consumerism and labels than with making things.
- We tend to be absorbed in 'virtual worlds' on television and through computer games.
- Society has become more unpredictable.
- We live in information rich societies that gather vast amounts of data about people.

T15
a) Individual failure
b) Cultural deprivation
c) Poverty and material deprivation
d) School factors
e) Structural views

Glossary

Access
Before any information can be collected, the researcher needs access to those under study, i.e. some contact needs to be made. Some groups are more difficult to reach than others and access might be negotiated via a gatekeeper.

Achieved status
Some positions in life do not come automatically, we have to earn them. For most people their job is an example of an achieved status.

Adolescent/adolescence
A term used to describe a teenager, the period between childhood and adulthood.

Agents/agency of socialisation
These are the parts of society that help transmit culture, e.g. the family, mass media and peer group.

Ascribed status
Some positions in life are given automatically; being a child or pupil, for example. These are examples of ascribed status.

Aspirations
Another term for ambitions or aims in life.

Beanpole family
The extended family of several generations (grandparents, parents, children) with few people in each generation.

Bedroom culture
The subculture of young teenage girls who do not have the freedom boys often have to spend leisure time outside the home; it is a contrast to street culture.

Boomerang children
Adult children, returning to their parents' home after a period away living independently.

Causal relationship
One thing brings about or causes another. In the natural sciences it is often possible to identify a causal relationship; e.g. apply heat to water and that causes the water to expand and eventually evaporate. In sociology, identifying direct cause and effect relationships is more difficult as behaviour is subject to many different influences at the same time.

Child-centred
The modern family is said to be child centred in contrast to the 'children should be seen but not heard' attitude of the past.

Closed questions
These are questions that limit the respondent's answers, usually requiring them to select an answer from a list provided by the researcher. They are useful when collecting quantitative data.

Cohabitation
When a couple live together as though they are married, but without having gone through the legal process of marriage.

Collective conscience
Durkheim introduced this term to describe the shared ways of thinking in a society.

Collectivism
This view of society emphasises the group over the individual; in collectivist societies the group shares responsibility for the well-being of all.

Companionate marriage
A marriage in which the partners share activities and also share responsibility for each other's emotional well-being.

Concept
A concept is an idea. Different theories tend to use different concepts or use the same concept in different ways.

Consensus
This is another word for agreement. Functionalists see society as based on an agreement, or consensus, about values.

Content analysis
This is a way of studying the nature of media content. It can be either quantitative, e.g. how much time/space is given to a topic; or it may be qualitative, e.g. is coverage positive or negative?

Correlation
A correlation is a connection between two things. In statistics it implies the extent to which two variables relate to each other. This may be positive or negative.

Correspondence principle
Bowles and Gintis used this term; the education system 'corresponds' to, or matches, the world of work; at school, a young person is prepared for their adult life as a worker.

Counter-culture
A counter-culture is a subculture that rejects the morality of the mainstream culture.

Counter-school culture
A subculture based around challenging the expectations of teachers and the school.

Crisis of masculinity
Social changes such as changing job structures and increased rights, opportunities and independence for women have, say some, resulted in men no longer being clear about their role in society. Old ideas of what it is to be a man, e.g. breadwinner/head of the family, are no longer relevant; however, new ideas have yet to be clearly worked out.

Cult of the individual
In modern societies the focus is on individual rights and responsibilities rather than social groups.

Cultural diversity
Cultures vary across the world and change over time; this is used as evidence for the importance of nurture theories.

Culture
This refers to the shared, learned, way of life in a society.

Culture of resistance
When a group develops its own values that are opposed to those of the culture of the dominant class, Marxists term this a culture of resistance.

Delinquent subculture
These are informal youth groups who break the law.

Demographic/demography
Demography is the study of the population. In addition to counting how many people there are, statistics are also collected about patterns of growth, migration and the age structure. The information is used to inform social policy and planning.

Deterministic
Some theories suggest that people have little or no choice about how to behave, social structures and expectations determine behaviour. The opposite of this is 'free will'. In practice, we can choose how to act but we need to be aware of the possible social consequences of our behaviour.

Deviant
A deviant is someone who breaks social rules.

Discourse
This refers to how we think and discuss ideas about people, society and how it is organised; it includes the relationships within society. What we think about and how we think reflect the society we live in: the language available, the distribution of power and the ideas we are exposed to. Over time, challenges to dominant ideas emerge and new forms of discourse develop.

EAL
This is an abbreviation for 'English as an Additional Language'.

Elective singlehood
This occurs when someone chooses to be single rather than part of a couple.

Ethics/ethical issues
Researchers must follow ethical or moral guidelines when collecting data. Avoiding harm to the participants and the person conducting the study is the most important factor.

Ethnography
This is associated with the interpretive approach to research. Ethnography is the direct observation of a group, and often involves participation to investigate the way the group experiences and interprets the social world.

Ethos
The ethos of a school refers to its spirit or atmosphere: for example, is there an emphasis on rules and conformity or is there a more relaxed approach to school life? Some schools are keen to have a reputation for sport or music while others are noted for their academic success.

Expressive roles
These are those aspects of family life that are based on emotional ties, rather than on practical needs.

Extended family
This refers to relatives beyond the nuclear family such as grandparents, uncles/aunts and cousins.

Fatalistic
Those who are fatalistic tend not to plan for the future because they believe that they have little influence over what happens to them.

Feminism
This is a sociological theory and political view that gender is the most important division in society; the main argument is that in modern society women are often oppressed by men.

Feminist critique
The challenge to traditional views of the family developed by feminists.

Feral children
Some children do not experience the usual process of socialisation, and are known as feral or 'wild' children. They are under- or unsocialised.

Fit thesis
Functionalists have argued that the nuclear family emerged in industrial societies because it was a good fit for the new way that the economy operated.

Focus group
A research method adopted from market research. A guided conversation on a specific topic, between carefully selected respondents.

Folk devils
These are groups of people that have been demonised by the media.

Forced singlehood
When a partnership ends, e.g. through death or divorce, singlehood has been forced on a person.

Formal control
Some social control is done on the basis of clearly laid down written rules and laws, e.g. rules in school or the workplace about punctuality.

Gang
Term often associated with groups who engage in criminal activities; membership often has to be earned by demonstrating loyalty to more senior members of the group.

Gatekeeper
If gaining access to a group is difficult then the support of a gatekeeper might be necessary. This is someone with the trust and respect of the group who can ease the introduction of the researcher.

Genderquake
The effects of campaigning for women's rights have been called a 'genderquake': there has been a fundamental change in attitudes towards women and their role in society.

Generalisability
If research is to go beyond telling us about a particular group or situation being studied, it must be capable of being generalised. This means the findings are applicable to the wider society.

Golden age
Those who believe the family is in decline often refer to an unspecified period past, when families were happy and supportive , and children well behaved. Clearly this is an unrealistic view of the past, and is ironically termed the 'golden age' of the family.

Habitus
This is the social setting we are used to and feel comfortable in, we fit in.

Halo effect
This idea is linked to labelling theory. Those who have been labelled positively tend to be seen positively in the future; this might mean being given the benefit of the doubt, e.g. a 'good' student might be believed that their reason for being late is genuine.

Hawthorn Effect
People behave differently when they know they are being studied. This can affect the validity of the data that is collected.

Hegemonic masculinity
The term hegemonic masculinity aims to explain how and why men are able to maintain their dominance over women; this is done by presenting anything that is 'feminine' as inferior. From defining some tasks as 'women's work' to phrases such as 'big boys don't cry', a view of a particular type of masculinity is presented as the norm for society.

Hidden curriculum
At school we learn a great deal more than the subjects on the timetable: functionalists point out that norms and values are also transmitted. For Marxists, the hidden curriculum reflects the ideology of capitalism; for feminists, patriarchal ideas are reinforced.

Hierarchy
This refers to different levels within an organisation; the higher up the position is, the more power and authority it has. Instructions go down the hierarchy from top to bottom.

Hypothesis
A hypothesis is a testable statement or prediction; different theories make different predictions. If research confirms a hypothesis, then it also supports the theory. Often a scientific hypothesis suggests a relationship between two factors, that the rise in divorce may be caused by changes in the laws governing marriage.

Ideological state apparatus (ISA)
A Marxist term for a social institution that transmits the ideology of the dominant class and thus helps maintain their power. Education, the family and the mass media are important examples.

Ideology
An ideology is a set of ideas that attempts to explain why society is organised the way it is, based on a view of how society should be organised.

Individualism
This contrasts with collectivism: the individual is valued above the group. In an individualist society it is up to everybody to look after themselves.

Informal control
This type of control is not so clearly defined as formal control, but is still important. The expectations of our family, friends or bosses influence our behaviour.

Institutional racism
Racism is discrimination against someone due to their race or ethnicity. Institutional racism occurs when the way an institution is organised and operates results in racial discrimination.

Instrumental roles
This refers to those aspects of family life that are based on practical needs, such as shopping, cooking and cleaning.

Interpretivism
This sociological approach emphasises the importance of finding out what things and behaviour mean to those involved. Interpretivists collect and analyse quantitative data.

Interviewer bias
Sometimes the interviewer influences the answers given by respondents.

Joint conjugal roles
Conjugal roles refers to the roles of men and women in relationships. Joint conjugal roles is when there is little difference in the roles, and activities and interests are shared.

Ladder of opportunity
Those who see the education system as meritocratic believe it offers opportunities for talented and hardworking people to improve their position in society.

Laddishness
This term is used derogatively to describe rowdy, often sexist, behaviour by young men. In the classroom this can mean disruptive behaviour and challenges to the teacher's expectations.

Lagged adaptation
As the roles of women have changed, men have had to change too. This is usually a delayed reaction, as men lag behind women.

LGBT
An abbreviation for 'lesbian, gay, bisexual and transgender'.

Literature review
Before starting on their own research, sociologists will consider what research has already been done on the topic.

Lone parent
An adult with no partner with responsibility for a child/children. Also known as a single parent.

Longitudinal study
If the same sample is studied a number of times, this is a longitudinal study.

Macro-sociology
This another term for the structural approach in sociology which involves looking at society as a whole and how different social institutions combine to make a social structure.

Magical solutions
Mike Brake and others are associated with the idea that working-class youth turn to subcultures to provide solutions to economic and social problems. These solutions are imaginary and therefore 'magical'.

Malestream
Feminists introduced this word to describe the way that much sociology either ignored women or failed to treat them as different from men.

Malestream bias
Before the impact of feminism on sociology, research typically focussed on males; it is a play on the term 'mainstream'.

Market forces
Supporters of the New Right believe that the best way to provide services is through competition between different suppliers, rather than through a state-run monopoly. Competition provides choice for service users and only those suppliers offering a good service will survive.

Material culture
Some aspects of a way of life are physical things, clothing or buildings, for example.

Material deprivation
To be deprived means that you lack something. Material deprivation refers to a lack of money, which in turn results in limited access to other important things such as decent housing, food and a pleasant lifestyle.

Meritocracy/meritocratic
If a system is based on fair competition, where talent and effort decide who succeeds, then it is meritocratic, i.e. based on merit. Functionalists see the education system as meritocratic.

Methodological pluralism
See triangulation.

Micro-sociology
Micro-sociology starts with people and their interaction, before moving on to look at social institutions and society.

Nature–nurture debate
This debate is about influences on social behaviour: are we born knowing how to behave (nature) or do we learn what to do (nurture)?

Negotiated families
As families and relationships are less restricted by tradition and social expectations than in the past, people are able to arrange or negotiate their relationships on more personal terms.

Neo-conventional family
As more women have entered the job market, the new conventional family consists of two employed adults and fewer children than in the past.

Neo-tribe
A loose group of people of similar tastes and interests.

New bedroom culture
Young people who create online friendships and communities.

Non-material culture
This refers to those aspects of culture such as language, laws and attitudes that are based on ideas that people share.

Non-representative sampling
It is not always possible to identify and study a representative sample and so a non-representative group might be studied. It may not be possible to generalise from a non-representative sample to the rest of the population.

Norms
These are the rules or guidelines for expected behaviour.

Nuclear family
A nuclear family consists of two generations: parents and children.

Objectivity
This means being un-biased, or neutral. Positivists believe that research should aim to be objective. Critics argue that objectivity is not possible, your values and beliefs inevitably influence what you study and how you study it.

Observation: covert
Observation can be undertaken without the knowledge of those being studied, this is covert or secret.

Observation: non-participant
Sociologists can collect information about social behaviour by watching behaviour. Non-participant observation involves watching without becoming involved.

Observation: overt
If those being studied know about it, this is termed overt observation.

Observation: participant
Collecting data in this way means the researcher joins in the activities that are being studied, becoming a member of the group concerned.

Official statistics
Sociologists often make use of data collected by governments and other official bodies, especially when studying the effects of social policies. The Census (every 10 years in the UK) and the General Household Survey (annual) provide quantitative information about society and how it is changing. Such material is particularly useful for identifying patterns and trends in society.

Open (or open-ended) questions
These allow the respondent to answer in their own words; usually used to collect qualitative data.

Operationalisation
Before data can be collected, terms must be defined. For example, poverty might be defined and then measured in terms of income.

Opportunity sample
Also known as a convenience sample, the researcher studies whoever is willing and available to take part in the study. Most research by students uses an opportunity sample.

Organic analogy
To help us understand how society develops and works, functionalists compare society to a body. In a body, cells are organised into organs that all have different functions for the body. In society, people are organised into different institutions that perform different tasks for society.

Other
The process of defining yourself as what you are not, so men have an identity as 'not feminine'.

Particularistic values
Sometimes values are associated with a small group such as a family, and often there are different expectations for different individuals.

Patriarchy
Feminists use this term to refer to societies dominated by men and where women have little power.

Peer group
Our peers are those of similar social status, e.g. the same age group or same job.

Pilot study
A small-scale test or practice before the main study. The pilot study can reveal any problems with the method allowing them to be corrected before the main study is underway.

Positivism
The approach in sociology that aims to use scientific methods as far as possible. Positivists collect and analyse quantitative data, focussing on behaviour that can be seen and measured or counted.

Primary data
Data collected by researchers themselves.

Primary socialisation
We first learn about our culture in the family, this is our primary socialisation.

Property
Property is something owned by someone; in patriarchal societies women are treated as though they are owned by men, e.g. their fathers or husbands.

Public schools
In Britain, public schools are the oldest, most exclusive fee-paying schools, such as Eton or Winchester. This is confusing as in most countries public schools are those in the state sector, paid for out of taxation.

Qualitative data
Data that is in words, describing social situations and their meanings, e.g. answers to open-ended questions.

Quantitative data
Numerical or statistical data, e.g. population statistics, examination results.

Questionnaires
A list of questions, prepared by the researcher; all respondents answer the same questions. A questionnaire is completed by the respondent; increasingly the data is collected through online surveys.

Quota sample
This is sometimes used when there is no sampling frame available. Respondents are selected by the researcher on the basis of key characteristics; e.g. a study may need 100 males and 100 females aged under 40; the researcher chooses respondents who match the criteria.

Random sample
A sample is random if every member of the target population has the same chance of being selected. The researcher has no choice over who is selected, for example, a lottery system or names in a hat.

Realism
Realists argue that both interpretivism and positivism and their preferred research methods have strengths and weaknesses. It makes sense to select methods that are the most suitable for the issue that is being studied.

Reflexive
Interpretivists believe that social behaviour is not an automatic response to events or the behaviour of others. Before we act we have to decide what is meant and consider how others will view what we do, we have to reflect on our actions.

Reliability
Research is said to be reliable if it would produce similar results if repeated in similar circumstances. Reliable methods are standardised.

Replicate
This is another term for 'repeat'; when discussing research it means to repeat a method or research project in a way as close to the original as possible.

Representative sample/ representativeness
A representative sample is one which shares the same characteristics as the population under study.

Repressive state apparatus
A Marxist term for social institutions that help maintain the power of the dominant class through the threat of force or coercion. The armed forces and the police are examples.

Resistance theory
A Marxist idea that youth culture is a working-class resistance and reaction to capitalism.

Risk society
A term used by postmodernists; as our social roles are less rigidly defined and we have more choices so we may face more risk as relationships are less certain.

Rites of passage
A ceremony or public event that marks the initiation of a person to the next stage of life.

Role
The part or function we play in a situation, organisation or group.

Role allocation
Functionalists see this as one of the main reasons there is an education system. Through the process of selection, people are directed towards different types of work depending on their interests and abilities.

Role model
Those people who we look up to and copy behaviour from are our role models.

Sampling
It is not possible to study all of the population all of the time. The people who are studied are a sample of the total; the Census aims to collect data from every household, the General Household Survey is based on a sample of up to 10,000 households.

Sampling frame
This is a list of all the people in the target population. In a school the register is a sampling frame.

Sanction
This can either be negative, e.g. a punishment, or positive, e.g. a reward. It is the response we get from others.

Sandwich generation
This occurs when adults have responsibilities not only for their children, but also for the older generation; they are sandwiched between their parents and their children.

Saturated family
The family is no longer is a place of shared experiences and values. Instead it is individuals who are increasingly involved in or saturated by activities, often away from other family members or using technology inside the home.

Scapegoating
Blaming someone for a problem in order to avoid dealing with the real issue.

Secondary data/sources
Information that has been collected by others and is then used in a new piece of research; this might be earlier research studies or data collected by governments or other bodies.

Secondary socialisation
As we grow older, agents of socialisation outside the family begin to have an influence. These include the peer group and the education system.

Secularisation
This refers to the decline in participation in religion and the accompanying decline in the influence religion has in society.

Segregated conjugal roles
This refers to relationships where there are clear differences between the responsibilities of women and men within a family.

Semiology
The study of social symbolism.

Service sector
The economy consists of different sectors: the primary sector is concerned with raw materials, the secondary sector with manufacturing goods. The service, or tertiary, sector is concerned with activities such as education, health care, retail and finance, i.e. providing services rather than goods

Single parent
See lone parent.

Sink schools
This is a pejorative term, used to describe schools, usually in deprived areas, that have poor examination results. This makes it difficult to attract both good teachers and bright pupils, and so results continue to be lower than elsewhere; the school sinks to the bottom of the league tables.

Snowball sample
Another method used when there is no sampling frame available. The researcher makes contact with a suitable respondent who in turn introduces other people. This method is used with 'hard-to-reach groups'.

Social change
Over time societies change: for example, the expected ways of behaving, or the way that social institutions are organised.

Social class
One form of social differentiation is social class. This division is often based on occupation.

Social cohesion
Durkheim thought that to operate smoothly a society needed values that were shared by all of its members. If people identify with their society and are committed to its values, then there is social cohesion.

Social construction
This refers to how people define concepts and social rules. As they are socially constructed they can change over time and vary from place to place. For example, how women are expected to behave is socially constructed: the expectations of the 21st century are very different from those of the 19th.

Social construction of youth
This is a social and not a biological category to which young people in our culture may belong.

Social control
This refers to the written and unwritten rules that we follow. This contributes to social order.

Social power
Power is the ability to influence the behaviour and thinking of others.

Socialisation
This is the life-long process of learning the culture of the society we live in.

Spectacular subcultures
A term coined by Hebdige to describe youth cultures such as punks and mods, groups who were significantly different in values and behaviour from those which had gone before. Very large numbers of young people felt themselves to be part of that group identity.

Glossary

Status
This can refer to our position in society, e.g. student, teacher and so on, or to the amount of respect that we receive.

Stigma
A negative social judgement about someone or something.

Stratified sample
A sampling frame can be sub-divided and then a sample is taken from each sub-group. This should help produce a representative sample; for example, a sample from each year group in a school.

Structured interviews
Structured interviews involve the interviewer reading out a prepared set of questions to the respondent. Answers are recorded by the interviewer and each interview is conducted in the same way.

Subjectivity
The opposite of objectivity; interpretivists are interested in how social actors see the world, their research aims to identify these subjective views.

Survey
A survey is a study of a topic, usually on a large scale. Questionnaires are usually used, to collect quantitative data. Douglas's Home and the School (1964) was a survey of educational attainment based on a longitudinal study.

Symbolic annihilation
When a social group is either absent from the media or mis-represented, it is said to have been symbolically annihilated. Feminists argue that this happens to women; typically there is less coverage of women than men in the media; furthermore, women are portrayed in stereotyped ways, often focussing on their appearance rather than their abilities.

Target population
This refers to the entire group the researcher is interested in.

Territory
The area that 'belongs' to a gang.

Tertiary socialisation
Some sociologists distinguish between secondary and tertiary socialisation; tertiary socialisation occurs in adulthood.

Theory
A theory is a set of ideas that seeks to explain why things are the way they are. Theories consist of a set of related concepts and to be taken seriously should be supported by evidence.

Toxic childhood
As children are increasingly exposed to a wide range of social pressures, they are less able to enjoy a care-free existence, instead their experience is being poisoned.

Transgressive women
If women do not conform to traditional stereotypes and expectations they can be seen as 'transgressing' or going beyond their roles. Transgressive women are often targeted for criticism and/or hostility.

Transition
This is a period of change from one stage of life to the next.

Triangulation and methodological pluralism
Triangulation means using two or more methods to study an issue, e.g. an observation study may be combined with a questionnaire. Combining interpretive and positivist approaches is called methodological pluralism.

Tribe
A term used by Maffesoli to describe small style conscious groups in cities who develop a way of living that becomes the germ of youth culture.

Trickle down theory
This theory suggests that as the rich get richer, in turn the poor will benefit as wealth will trickle down to them.

Triple shift
This is a feminist idea; women have three responsibilities: their paid job, household tasks and providing emotional support to their family.

Under-attainment/ underachievement
A teacher might be concerned at the underachievement of a particular individual who is not fulfilling their potential. Sociologists use this term when discussing the average performance of groups in the education system. A group is said to underachieve (or under-attain, the words are used interchangeably) if it has poorer results than average.

Underclass
This is usually used as a pejorative term; it refers to people who rely on welfare benefits rather than work for their income.

Unit of consumption
This is a Marxist term; in modern societies family members go out to work and earn money which is spent on buying goods and services consumed by the family. In traditional societies families often worked together to produce their own goods.

Universalistic values
These are associated with society as a whole, rather than a group within it. The values are applied equally to everyone.

Unstructured interviews
An unstructured interview is more like a conversation; the interviewer has some questions to be covered, but each interview can proceed in a different way, depending on the answers that are given.

Validity
Data is valid if it is truthful and measures what it claims to measure. For example, church attendance figures tell us how many people go to church, they do not measure how many people are religious.

Values
The basic beliefs that members of a society share; they provide the basis for acceptable behaviour.

Variables
This refers to an identifiable social characteristic that can be isolated in research, for example gender, age, educational qualifications. Positivists often investigate the relationship between variables.

Vocationalism
Vocationalism refers to attempts to better prepare young people for the world of work, and especially the introduction of work-related subjects such as engineering or health and social care.

Welfare system
The support provided to families from the government, either in the form of benefits or services such as education, health and welfare support.

Youth
The period of life between being a child and taking on the responsibility of adulthood.

Youth culture
A set of norms and values shared by young people.

Youth subcultures
These are specific group cultures that are within youth culture.

Index